Learning Mobile App Development

Learning Mobile App Development

A Hands-on Guide to Building Apps with iOS and Android

Jakob Iversen
Michael Eierman

✦ Addison-Wesley

Upper Saddle River, NJ • Boston • Indianapolis • San Francisco
New York • Toronto • Montreal • London • Munich • Paris • Madrid
Cape Town • Sydney • Tokyo • Singapore • Mexico City

Visit us on the Web: informit.com/aw

Library of Congress Control Number: 2013951436

ISBN-13: 978-0-321-94786-4
ISBN-10: 0-321-94786-X

Text printed in the United States on recycled paper at R.R. Donnelley in Crawfordsville, Indiana.

First printing: December 2013

Editor-in-Chief
Mark Taub

Senior Acquisitions Editor
Trina MacDonald

Senior Development Editor
Chris Zahn

Managing Editor
Kristy Hart

Project Editor
Andy Beaster

Copy Editor
Barbara Hacha

Indexer
Heather McNeill

Proofreader
Sara Schumacher

Technical Reviewers
Frank McCown
Aileen Pierce
Ray Rischpater
Valerie Shipbaugh

Editorial Assistant
Olivia Basegio

Media Producer
Dan Scherf

Interior Designer
Gary Adair

Cover Designer
Chuti Prasertsith

Compositor
Nonie Ratcliff

❖

Dedicated to Kim, Katja, Rebecca, and Natasja.

Dedicated to my wife, Theresa, and daughters,
Lindsey and Kyra.

❖

Contents

Preface

Welcome to mobile application development!

Developing apps can be fun and is potentially lucrative, but it is also quickly becoming a core skill in the information technology field. Businesses are increasingly looking to mobile apps to enhance their relationships with their customers and improve their internal processes. They need individuals skilled in developing the mobile apps that support these initiatives.

This book is intended to be an introduction to mobile app development. After you successfully complete the book, you will have the basic skills to develop both Android and iPhone/iPad apps. The book takes you from the creation of an app through the publication of the app to its intended audience on both platforms. We (the authors) have been teaching technology for many years at the collegiate level and directly to professionals and strongly believe that the only way to learn a technology is to use it. That is why the book is structured as a series of tutorials that focus on building a complete app on both platforms.

Although the book is an introduction, it does cover many of the unique features of the mobile platforms that make apps a technology offering new capabilities that businesses may use to enrich or augment their operations. The features covered in the book include using the device's capability to determine its location, using hardware sensors and device components in apps, and mapping.

If you have suggestions, bug fixes, corrections, or anything else you'd like to contribute to a future edition, please contact us at jhiversen@gmail.com or michael.eierman@gmail.com. We appreciate any and all feedback that helps make this a better book.

—Jakob Iversen & Michael Eierman, September 2013

What You'll Need

You can begin learning mobile application development with very little investment. However, you will need a few things. The following list covers the basics of what you need for Android programming:

- **Eclipse and the Android SDK**—You can download the SDK from Google (http://developer.android.com/sdk/index.html) as an Android Development Tools (ADT) bundle that includes the Eclipse Integrated Development Environment (IDE), Android development tools, Android SDK tools, Android platform tools, the latest Android SDK, and an emulator. The ADT bundle is for Windows only. If you are going to develop on the Mac, you will have to download Eclipse separately and use the preceding URL to get the various other tools. If you have an existing Eclipse installation, you can use this location to add the Android tools. Appendix A, "Installing Eclipse and Setup for Android Development," has more details on how to install the tools. If your existing Eclipse installation is earlier than the Helios version, we recommend that you update your installation to be perfectly in sync with this book. If you cannot upgrade, you should still be able to work the tutorials. Some of the menu commands may be slightly different and some of the windows may have minor differences, but you should still be able to complete the tutorials.

- **An Android device**—This is not necessary for purely learning, but if you plan to release your apps to the public, you really should test them on at least one device. The more types of devices, the better—Android on different manufacturers' devices can sometimes behave in different manners.

- **Familiarity with Java**—Android apps are programmed using the Java programming language. You should be able to program in Java. At a minimum you should have programming in some object-based programming language such as C# or C++ so that you can more easily pick up Java.

The following list covers the basics of what you need for iPhone/iPad programming:

- **A Mac running Mac OS X Lion (v 10.8 at a minimum)**—iPhone/iPad programming can be done only on a Mac. That Mac should have a fair amount of disk space available and a significant amount of RAM so you don't have to spend as much time waiting for things to compile and execute.

- **Xcode 5**—Xcode is an IDE provided by Apple available from Apple's iOS Dev Center (http://developer.apple.com/ios). Xcode 5 is free, but you can only run the apps you develop on the simulator provided with Xcode. If you want to distribute your apps, you must sign up as a registered developer ($99/year for individuals, $299/year for corporate developers). If you are a teacher at the university level, your university can sign up for the University Program (http://developer.apple.com/support/iphone/university). This will allow you and your students to test apps on actual devices but does not allow public distribution of the apps you create. If you are a student at a university, check with the computer science or information systems department to see if they have signed up for this program.

- **An iOS device**—As with Android, this is not necessary for learning how to program an iOS app, but it is important for testing apps that you want to release to the public. Additionally, some features of iOS programming cannot be tested on the simulator. Appendix B, "Installing Xcode and Registering Physical Devices" has more details both on installing Xcode and the work needed to be able to test your apps on a physical iOS device.

- **Knowledge of Objective-C 2.0**—iOS apps are programmed in Objective-C. Objective-C is a language that extends the C programming language and is organized like the SmallTalk object-oriented programming language. If you have previous experience with Java or C++ it will ease your transition to Objective-C. Appendix C, "Introduction to Objective-C," contains an introduction to Objective-C that will help you with that transition.

What if I Can't Upgrade My Lab Computers?

Xcode 5 requires OSX 10.8. If your existing Macs cannot be upgraded to 10.8 you should still be able to use this book to learn iOS development. In that case use Xcode 4.6. The sample code provided with this book will not work, but you should be able to develop your own working code by working through the tutorials. Some of the menus and windows will be different, but the tutorial will still work.

Your Roadmap to Android/iOS Development

This book is intended as an introduction to mobile development for both Android and iOS. Although the book provides everything you need to know to begin creating apps on both platforms, it is not intended to be a comprehensive work on the subject. The book assumes programming knowledge. At a minimum you should have taken at least one college-level course in the Java or C programming languages. Mobile development introduces issues and concerns not associated with traditional development, but at its core requires the ability to program. Experience with an IDE is a plus. This book will help you learn the Eclipse and Xcode IDEs but if you have some understanding and experience prior to working through this book, it will ease your learning curve.

As a beginner's book, that should be enough to successfully work through the tutorials. However, to truly master Android and iOS development there is no substitute for designing and implementing your own app. For this you will likely need some reference books. Following is a list of books we have found helpful in our app development efforts. Of course, if all else fails—Google it! And then you'll likely end up with the good folks at StackOverflow.com, which has quickly become a trusted source for answers to programming questions.

- *iOS Programming: The Big Nerd Ranch Guide,* by Joe Conway & Aaron Hillegass (Big Nerd Ranch, 2012)

- *Programming iOS 6,* by Matt Neuburg (O'Reilly, 2013)

- *iPad Enterprise Application Development BluePrints: Design and Build Your Own Enterprise Applications for the iPad,* by Steven F. Daniel (Packt Publishing, 2012)

- *Android Wireless Application Development,* by Lauren Darcy & Shane Conder (Addison-Wesley, 2011)

- *Android Wireless Application Development Volume II: Advanced Topics,* by Lauren Darcy & Shane Conder (Addison-Wesley, 2012)

How This Book Is Organized

This book guides you through the development of mobile applications on both Android and iOS. The book focuses on building a single, complete app on both platforms from beginning to publication. The book is meant for the beginner but goes into enough depth that you could move into developing your own apps upon completion of the book. The philosophy embedded in the book's approach is that the best way to learn to develop is to develop! Although the book begins with Android development, you could choose to begin with iOS without any problem or setback in understanding. However, we do suggest that you read Chapter 2, "App Design Issues and Considerations," before beginning either platform. After that, you can choose either Chapters 3–8 on Android or Chapters 9–14 on iOS. You could even switch back and forth between the platforms, reading first the introduction to Android in Chapter 3, then the introduction to iOS in Chapter 9, and then continue switching back and forth between the platforms.

Here's a brief look at the book's contents:

- **Part I, "Overview of Mobile App Development"**

  - **Chapter 1, "Why Mobile Apps?"**—Mobile apps are a potentially disruptive technology—technology that changes the way business works. This chapter explores the potential impact of mobile technology and discusses how apps can and do change the way organizations do business.

  - **Chapter 2, "App Design Issues and Considerations"**—Mobile technology has different capabilities and limitations than more traditional computing platforms. This chapter discusses many of the design issues associated with app development.

- **Part II, "Developing the Android App"**

  - **Chapter 3, "Using Eclipse for Android Development"**—Eclipse is an open source development environment commonly used for Android development. Chapter 3 shows how to use Eclipse to build a simple "Hello World" app. The chapter is your first hands-on look at app development.

  - **Chapter 4, "Android Navigation and Interface Design"**—The limited amount of "real estate" on a mobile device typically requires multiple screens to build a complete app. This chapter introduces how you program movement between screens in Android. The chapter explores in depth on how a user interface is coded in Android where the number of screen sizes that your app has to accommodate is relatively large.

  - **Chapter 5, "Persistent Data in Android"**—Business runs on data. An app has to be able to make sure important data is preserved. This chapter explores two types of data persistence methods in Android: the persistence of large and complex data in a relational database using SQLite and simple data persistence through SharedPreferences.

  - **Chapter 6, "Lists in Android: Navigation and Information Display"**—Chapter 6 introduces a structure ubiquitous in mobile computing—the list. Lists display data in a scrollable table format and can be used to "drill down" for more information or to open new screens. This chapter explains how to implement a list in an Android app.

- **Chapter 7, "Maps and Location in Android"**—Displaying information on a map can be a very effective way to communicate information to an app user. This chapter examines implementing Google Maps in an app and also demonstrates how to capture the device's current location.

- **Chapter 8, "Access to Hardware and Sensors in Android"**—Mobile devices come equipped with a number of hardware features that can enhance an app's functionality. The code required to access and use these features is discussed in this chapter.

- **Part III, "Developing the iOS App"**

  - **Chapter 9, "Using Xcode for iOS Development"**—Chapter 9 begins the book's discussion of iOS. Xcode is the development environment used to develop iPhone and iPad apps. Xcode and iOS development is introduced by guiding you through the implementation of a simple "Hello World" app.

  - **Chapter 10, "iOS Navigation and Interface Design"**—Just as in Android, interface design and navigation between screens are important concepts to master in mobile development. This chapter guides you through the development of a Storyboard for app navigation and demonstrates how to use Xcode's Interface Builder to implement a user interface.

  - **Chapter 11, "Persistent Data in iOS"**—Many of the same data persistence features available in Android are also present in iOS. One primary difference is that the database feature of iOS is implemented through a wrapper kit called Core Data. Core Data enables the updating and querying of an underlying SQLite database.

  - **Chapter 12, "Tables in iOS: Navigation and Information Display"**—Tables in iOS provide the same type of information presentation format as Lists in Android. Tables display data in a scrollable table format and can be used to "drill down" for more information or to open new screens. Chapter 12 describes how to implement this very important mobile computing concept.

  - **Chapter 13, "Maps and Location in iOS"**—Chapter 13 covers the implementation of maps and capturing device location information on an iOS device. It is analogous to the Android chapter on maps and location.

  - **Chapter 14, "Access to Hardware and Sensors in iOS"**—This chapter demonstrates the techniques used to access hardware features of the device. It covers many of the same sensors and hardware features covered in the Android chapters on the topic.

- **Part IV, "Business Issues"**

  - **Chapter 15, "Monetizing Apps"**—One of the reasons many people consider getting into mobile application development is to make money. Both Android and Apple provide a marketplace for apps that has a wide reach. This chapter discusses various approaches to making money from your apps and briefly discusses organization of your app development business.

- **Chapter 16, "Publishing Apps"**—After you have developed an app, you'll likely want to make that app available to its intended audience. This chapter discusses publishing apps on Google Play and the App Store, as well as distribution of corporate apps that are not intended for the public at large.

- **Appendixes**

  - **Appendix A, "Installing Eclipse and Setup for Android Development"**—This appendix provides instruction on installing the Eclipse development environment and how to set up Eclipse specifically for Android development.

  - **Appendix B, "Installing Xcode and Registering Physical Devices"**—This appendix provides instruction on installing iOS development environment, Xcode, and describes how to register iOS devices so that they can be used to test your apps.

  - **Appendix C, "Introduction to Objective-C"**—This appendix provides a brief tutorial on the Objective-C language.

About the Sample Code

The sample code for this book is organized by chapter. Chapters 3 and 9 contain a single "Hello World" app in Android and iOS, respectively. Chapters 4 through 8 build a complete Android contact list app, and Chapters 10 through 14 build the same contact list app in iOS. Each chapter folder contains the code for the completed app up to that point. For example, at the end of Chapter 7 the code includes the code developed for chapters 4, 5, 6, and 7. The exception to this single completed app per folder model is in chapters 7 and 13. These chapters demonstrate several approaches to getting location information on the mobile device. Each technique has a folder with the complete app that demonstrates the technique. If a book chapter requires any image resources, you will find those images in the respective chapter.

Getting the Sample Code

You'll find the source code for this book at https://github.com/LearningMobile/BookApps on the open-source GitHub hosting site. There you find a chapter-by-chapter collection of source code that provides working examples of the material covered in this book.

You can download this book's source code using the git version control system. The Github site includes git clients for both Mac and Windows, as well as for Eclipse. Xcode already includes git support.

Contacting the Authors

If you have any comments or questions about this book, please drop us an e-mail message at jhiversen@gmail.com or michael.eierman@gmail.com.

Acknowledgments

Acknowledgments from Jakob Iversen

Thank you goes out to Mindie Boynton at the Business Success Center in Oshkosh for organizing the training seminars that formed the first basis for the tutorials at the core of the book. Thank you also to all the students taking those seminars for keeping the idea alive and providing feedback and catching mistakes in early versions.

Thanks go as well to everyone who worked with us at Pearson: Trina MacDonald, Chris Zahn, and Olivia Basegio, all of whom worked hard to answer our questions and keep us in line. Thank you also to the technical editors, Valerie Shipbaugh for making sure the material was accessible to the target audience and Aileen Pierce for detailed insights in getting the original material updated for iOS 7.

Thank you to my family and friends for providing support and encouragement during long hours of programming and writing. Especially to my wife, Kim, and daughters, Katja, Rebecca, and Natasja, for picking up the slack around the house.

Acknowledgments from Michael Eierman

A big thank you is owed to my friend and business partner George Sorrells. After I showed him an app that I was fooling around with he said, "We should sell that!" That led to a level of work in Android and iOS that gave me the depth of knowledge required to write this book. I'd also like to thank Mindie Boynton at the Business Success Center in Oshkosh for organizing the training seminars that helped us develop the tutorials that are the basis for this book.

Thanks go as well to the good people at Pearson, Trina MacDonald, Chris Zahn, and Olivia Basegio, who worked so hard to get this book in shape. Thank you also to the technical editors, Valerie Shipbaugh, Ray Rischpater, and Frank McCown, for their help in getting many of the inevitable technical errors and oversights eliminated from the text. I would especially like to single out Frank McCown for in-depth reviews that greatly improved the final product.

Finally, thank you to my friends and family. They supported me by providing feedback on the apps I was developing and encouraged me to continue the effort even when things were most frustrating. My wife, Theresa, and daughters, Lindsey and Kyra, deserve extra special thanks for putting up with my constant work on app development and writing this book.

About the Authors

Jakob Iversen, Ph.D. is Associate Professor of Information Systems, Chair of the Interactive Web Management Program, and Director of Information Technology Services at the University of Wisconsin Oshkosh College of Business. His current research interests include software process improvement, agile software development, e-collaboration, and mobile development. Dr. Iversen teaches and consults on web development, mobile development, technology innovation, information systems management, strategy, and software development processes.

Michael Eierman, Ph.D is a Professor of Information Systems and Chair of the Information Systems Department at the University of Wisconsin Oshkosh College of Business. Dr. Eierman has worked in the information systems field for nearly 30 years as a programmer, analyst, and consultant, but primarily as a teacher. From the very first class taken in college at the suggestion of an advisor, information systems have been his passion. His research has taken many directions over his years as a professor but is currently focused on the impact of collaborative and mobile technology. Dr. Eierman is also co-owner and manager of Ei-Sor Development, LLC—a provider of Android and iOS apps designed for the outdoorsman.

Part I

Overview of Mobile App Development

Why Mobile Apps?

Mobile, Mobile, Mobile! Mobile technology is certainly receiving a lot of attention in the IT world as well as the general business world right now. It seems everyone is executing a mobile strategy, designing a mobile app, or worrying about managing mobile devices. But why all the buzz? What makes mobile so special that it garners this much attention? In this chapter you explore some of the key reasons behind the hype. It really is not "much ado about nothing!"

Transformative Devices

For all the hype, there must be something that makes these devices important. There is! Mobile devices add a host of new possibilities for business and personal software because they are truly the first mobile computing platforms. Although laptops and netbooks are moveable, their size significantly impacts how easily they are transported. Very few people carry a laptop during their every waking hour to every location they visit! However, if this were their only advantage, mobile devices would not be causing such a stir. There is much more.

One key feature of a mobile device is the capability to be made aware of its current environment through built-in sensors. Mobile devices have sensors designed to capture where they are, where they're going, and the environment around them. Sensors can identify their present location to within a few meters and capture their current heading, orientation, and acceleration. Additionally, they can recognize how close they are to another object through a proximity sensor. These devices also have the capability to capture information about the ambient environment, including light levels, temperature, pressure, and magnetic field.

Another important feature of a mobile device is the capability to communicate with other computing devices through a variety of mechanisms. A laptop can communicate using Wi-Fi and Bluetooth. However, mobile devices also have these communication capabilities; they can communicate via cellular signals and using Near Field Communication (NFC). Wi-Fi is not available in all situations, and its range is measured in yards, whereas cellular's range is measured in miles. Bluetooth may be too short range to be useful in many situations, but too long in other situations. The range of communication using Bluetooth is measured in feet, whereas the range of NFC is measured in inches. If a device wants to communicate with another device based on its proximity, broadcasting in inches may be preferable to broadcasting and listening in feet.

In addition to these capabilities not present in other computing platforms, mobile devices have most of the same features, such as being able to display and manipulate data. Some of these features have enhanced usability because they are on a device that is easily moved. One example of this is the camera. Although many laptops and desktops have cameras built in, their usefulness is limited because they cannot easily be moved. Data input is also similar because a user can use either a keyboard or speech to enter data or instruct the device to perform some operation. Again, these features may be more useful because data can be entered at its source, when it is produced, rather than after the fact when human memory errors can impact the integrity of the data. Another similarity is that mobile devices also have the capability to store data in a number of formats, including in relational databases. Finally, mobile devices are also computers.

Taken together, the added capabilities of mobile devices compared to traditional computing platforms means that the smartphone and tablet are the most dramatic change in technological capability since the introduction of the PC. Dramatic change in technological capability enables the reexamination of the assumptions that business processes and products are based on! Organizations base the design of what they do and how they do it on available technology. If technology changes, the assumptions about what can be done are no longer valid. This invalidation of previous assumptions is disruptive, and if existing organizations don't re-examine their products and processes, it is likely that their competitors and start-ups will.

Reaching Customers

Smartphone users almost always have their device within reach. Organizations want to be ready when a potential customer is interested in a product or service. If customers have to wait until they get home to their computers, or worse yet, go to an actual store to get information about or purchase their product, it may be too late. Individuals may forget about what they wanted, or worse yet, a competitor's product may be available and the sale is permanently lost. Additionally, smartphone adoption rate and sales have greatly outpaced PC sales in recent years. In many homes, they may be the only way to access the Internet. Furthermore, tablet sales are expected to surpass PC sales in the near future, and many consumers are choosing tablets instead of a PC, rather than in addition to a PC. Companies that provide their service over the Internet may be left behind in these situations if they do not have a mobile strategy.

In many cases a website designed to be mobile friendly may be enough to hold or attract the customer. However, to truly tie your organization to the customer, an app is required. Many organizations are pursuing both approaches. Apps can provide a stronger link to your organization because static data and the basic interface is always available on the device, reducing the amount of data that needs to be transferred and providing quicker access than having to always download this information. An app also can provide some functionality even when the device cannot connect to the Internet. In these situations, customers could make a purchase when they get the urge, and the transaction could be uploaded when the device gets a data connection. Having the app always available on the device may lead to your organization being one of the first choices when the consumer is in the buying mood. Additionally, the app's consistent interface may help the individual learn it so that working with your organization becomes quicker and easier than working with others.

Having a mobile app can also support brand loyalty and awareness. Some organizations have developed apps that allow customers to interact with their brands in positive ways. For example, Starbucks lets customers define favorite drinks and collect rewards within their app. Axe has developed several games where the player has to collect Axe cans to earn points. Nestlé has an app that promotes fitness, and Zyrtec gives asthma patients tools to keep track of symptoms and current pollen levels. Finally, Kimberly-Clark helps parents with potty training their toddlers in the Pull-Ups Big Kid App (Figure 1.1). Although these apps could also be available on a traditional computing platform, having them on a mobile app allows the customer to access them quickly when they happen to think of it, even if they are standing in line or sitting on a bus. This allows the company to have a positive interaction with a customer in more situations than only when the customer is sitting at a computer.

Figure 1.1   Screen shot of Pull-Ups app from Kimberly-Clark Inc.

The Good Old Days

Ever hear the phrase "Banker's Hours"? Many years ago, banks had very limited customer service times, and getting to the bank to perform your business required going at hours not particularly friendly to many people's schedules. The technology of that time required that the bank have time to complete transactions after the customer left. To have enough time in the day to complete the work, they had to limit the amount of time they were available to the customer. This phrase became pejorative because people thought that the customer service hours were the only time that bankers worked and because the limited access frustrated customers.

However, with the advent of better technology, banks were able to expand their customer service hours, and the Internet made interacting with your bank something you could do anytime, anywhere. These days, a bank would not have much of a customer base if it did not provide online access. Mobile devices expand this problem. With many customers using a smartphone as their only Internet access, banks that don't provide mobile-friendly access will begin to lose customers to those that do—or never have a chance to gain that customer.

One area where mobile devices enable a strong potential for disruption of the assumptions made about a business process is the payment industry, where a lot of companies are innovating to provide consumers and businesses the capability to make and receive payments. For instance, Square provides small retailers a simple solution to accept credit cards via a mobile device and even use an iPad as a cash register, complete with inventory and listing of all products in the store. Although customers may not be able to easily get a printed receipt, the capability to easily email receipts may be even better. PayPal also allows for sending money easily to individuals. Although PayPal has this capability on a traditional computing platform, the capability to do it on a mobile device enables the customer to get money quickly to someone, wherever they may be.

The final, and potentially most important, advantage of an app is that it can take full advantage of the device's hardware and software capabilities to provide the customer with capabilities that make your products an easy option for them. The device's location could be used to guide potential customers to a nearby store or even find a product within a store. The device camera could be used to present your products that are similar to the product image capture. Captured UPC codes could be used to provide product information and prices. NFC or Bluetooth could be used to alert customers that they are near your product in the store. The potential is there. An app provides the capability to realize that potential. For example, Amazon has an app that the consumer can use to scan UPC codes to compare a competitor's product to theirs.

Changing Business Process

One of the most exciting possibilities associated with mobile technology is the potential it has to impact business processes. Processes are designed within the parameters of the available technology. When technology drastically changes, new forms are enabled. When that technology is cheap, change is enabled in areas that may have previously seen limited impact of the technology. Businesses are paying significant attention to mobile because these qualities suggest that the technology may have implications for strategic and tactical advantage, or, as demonstrated with the banking app, become competitive necessities.

Several years ago, business process reengineering (BPR) received significant attention in the business and academic worlds. The idea of reengineering was important because of what was termed the "productivity paradox." For years, organizations were investing a significant amount of money in information technology without realizing corresponding significant increases in productivity. Investigation found that a major contributor to this problem was that organizations were using the new technology simply to automate existing processes. Information technology was applied to portions of the existing process to make it faster or increase accuracy. This approach produced improvements, but they were incremental rather than revolutionary. As businesses became more adept with the technology and the technology became more capable, it was recognized that the full potential of the technology was not being realized, and companies began rethinking entire processes to take advantage of the technology. Noteworthy improvements in process measures were realized, and BPR was born.

Mobile technology is likely to follow a similar path in application to business processes. However, that path could be traversed much more quickly because of the past experience of applying technology to business processes. The excitement over mobile technology is evidence that a more aggressive approach to reengineering processes may be truer than a simple automation approach.

Still, there is room for automation, especially in smaller businesses that may have found that the cost, complexity, and nonmobile nature of traditional computing platforms made technological solutions to their business process infeasible. Bossy (Figure 1.2) is an example of this. The app is designed for the dairy farmer. As the farmer attends his cows, with Bossy he has at his fingertips a complete display of the actions that need to be taken on different animals in his herd. This automates the process of tracking the animals on paper or on a desktop computer with written notes used while attending the herd.

Fence Builder Pro (Figure 1.3) is an app designed to support the fence-building industry. Although some big fence-building organizations exist, the majority of fence-building companies are much smaller, family owned businesses in which technology plays a very limited role. Fence Builder Pro is designed to manage job scheduling and communication. Jobs performed by these smaller organizations typically last on the order of hours, rather than days or weeks, precluding the need for more traditional project management software. Additionally, a need exists to quickly rearrange the schedule because of outside influences such as the weather, material delivery errors, and interaction with external agencies. Because these externalities can change quickly, and because of the short nature of jobs, there is a need to quickly communicate the new schedule to the field crew. Fence Builder Pro is innovative for the industry because the schedule is also loaded on the crew foreman's device. When the company's owner changes the schedule, it is automatically communicated to the foreman.

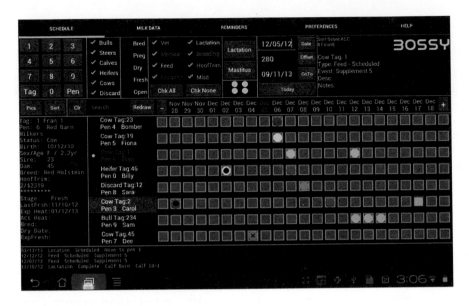

Figure 1.2   Bossy—an app for the dairy farmer.

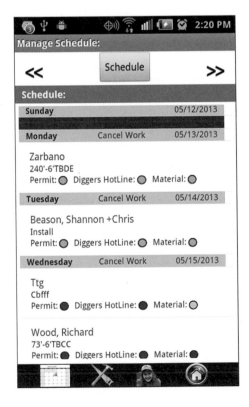

Figure 1.3   Fence Builder Pro—an app for the small job shop.

These two apps represent innovation in business processes that could not have been done without a mobile device. In contrast to consumer apps, these apps sell for much more money. They represent a significant investment by the developer in analysis and design and are focused on a much smaller market.

Large organizations can also benefit from process redesign based on mobile technology, and many are creating mobile development teams to explore, design, and implement process solutions. The focus for these companies is on internal processes, and they are large enough to absorb the cost of creating apps to support their processes. These apps are generally not available to other companies via an app market, although some apps available to consumers hint at the internal process changes. One such example is the insurance company apps that allow customers to provide insurance claims.

Although this provides an added convenience to the consumer, the benefit is much larger to the insurance company, because claims are reported electronically and with no people at the insurance company involved in receiving and recording the claim. Claims can also potentially contain much more accurate, rich, and timely information. For example, State Farm's Pocket Agent app lets their customers report an auto incident; they can include pictures taken with the device camera, tag the report with GPS coordinates, and draw a sketch of the scene. It's not hard to imagine that State Farm also has mobile apps for insurance agents and claims adjusters that use the data entered into Pocket Agent, so the entire process can be changed to take the mobile devices into account.

Making Money

A final reason that mobile is all the rage is that many enterprising individuals see the potential to start businesses and make money. The Google Play Store and the Apple App Store provide the app developer access to the market of app purchasers. The developer does not have to worry about product distribution, returns, or payment collection. The store does all this and conveniently deposits the proceeds into the developer's bank account. Additionally, smartphone users automatically go to these stores to get new apps or browse for apps that might interest them. One final and very big reason for the strong focus on app development is that Google and Apple either support or provide the development environments needed to create apps for their stores. Taken together, this creates significant potential for individuals or small businesses to make money in the app market.

Apps make money for their producer through several approaches. Apps can be sold for a one-time fee, like other products. Consumers buy the app through the appropriate store and it is theirs for use whenever they like. The more apps the developers sell, the more money they make. Ad supported apps make money by including an advertisement on a small portion of the screen. Anytime a user clicks an ad, the developer makes money. Both Google and Apple provide developers access to the code to display ads and a service to provide the ads and track the clicks. In contrast to a paid app, the only time the developer gets paid is if an ad is clicked (Apple's ad service also pays per view of the ad, but the amount is significantly less than a click). The amount of money generated by a single click is very small, so to make much money it is important to get a lot of users of the app. A third approach to making money is to provide for in-app purchases. With this model, the user gets the app for free but needs to make a purchase to get additional features. For example, a developer might provide a game for free but require a purchase for more advanced levels of the game. Another approach is subscription based. The app provides functionality that requires access to the developer's data or other services. To use the service, users buy a monthly or annual subscription.

The combination of device capabilities, an accessible market, and a diverse and large number of developers makes the app market exciting and innovative. Because the market for consumer apps puts a significant focus on free or low-cost apps, the challenge for a developer is to create a product that appeals to a lot of people. Fortunately, the capabilities of the mobile computing platform enable the implementation of apps that can do things in a variety of domains that could never be done before. Chapter 15, "Monetizing Apps," has a more in-depth discussion of how to make money from the apps you have created.

Innovation Using Device Capabilities

Figure 1.4 shows an app that takes advantage of device capabilities to provide a product not previously available. This is a paid app called GoFishing! It uses the device's capability to capture its location, connect to the Internet, and store data to allow fishermen to record their fish the moment they catch them, including where they were, what the weather conditions were like, and how the fish was caught. The app provides search and mapping capability so that the fisherman can locate previously successful locations, methods, and conditions to use in future efforts. This functionality is not possible without the mobile device's sensors and Internet access.

Summary

Mobile technology is receiving significant attention in the business and IT worlds. The technology represents a dramatic change in technological capacity that has enabled potential economic advantage for those able to take advantage of it. Mobile technology is the basis of innovations in reaching customers, and in redesigning business processes and software products that lead to the creation of many small businesses.

Exercises

1. Find an app that uses device capabilities to provide a product that previously couldn't exist. Explain what makes this app important or innovative.

2. Find an app designed to support a business process. What is the business process? How does the app propose to improve it?

3. Identify and explain a specific business process. How might this process be automated with mobile technology? How might it be completely redesigned?

Figure 1.4   An app that innovates based on device capabilities.

2

App Design Issues and Considerations

App development for mobile devices is, in many ways, similar to development for other platforms. However, in other ways, development requires attention to items that are not even present in traditional development. Mobile devices have operating systems that run apps differently than traditional programs do, have access to environmental sensors that are not available in laptop and desktop computers, have a limited power supply, and have a much smaller screen. This chapter provides an overview of the design issues associated with these differences. The chapter also discusses differences between iOS and Android devices that impact design. The chapter concludes with an introduction to the app that will be developed to illustrate design and development for both platforms.

App Design

Designing for the specific device your app will run on is extremely important! Applications that work well on a traditional computer may be complete disasters if ported to a mobile platform without redesigning the logic to fit the device's capabilities. Additionally, the capabilities of the device enable you to design an application that can do different things than an application on a traditional computer. Apps are cheap and easy to obtain. If yours doesn't work well, there is likely to be an acceptable alternative. A well-designed app can be a delight to use. A poorly designed app will not be used for long, if at all. The operating system, device size, and mobility all impact design and must be accounted for.

Operating System Design Issues

The primary technical difference between mobile device operating systems and operating systems used on laptop and desktop computers is that the mobile operating system is not a true multitasking system. On mobile devices, only one app can be active at a time. When another app is started, or the app is interrupted by another app (for example, a phone call), the app that was running gets put in the background. It remains in the background until the user specifi-cally accesses it again. If it remains in the background too long, or if available memory gets too low, the operating system may kill it. This back-and-forth between different states is called the app's life cycle. Both Android and iOS apps have a life cycle. The life cycle is based on the user's interaction with the app and the operating system's need for memory and processing resources. As users interact with the device, they may switch between apps or different views within a single app. When this happens the app goes through different states, requiring the developer to handle this switch so that users don't lose data or get unnecessarily interrupted in the task they were performing. This makes understanding, and designing for, the app life cycle extremely important to the successful app developer.

Android Life Cycle

To understand the Android life cycle it is useful to first understand the states that an Android app user experiences. When users touch an app's icon, the app is started and becomes visible to the users. While the app is visible, the users can interact with it. This is considered the *Resumed* or running state. As the users interact with the app, they may be interrupted with a pop-up window, or they may be distracted and not touch the screen for a period of time. If the users stop interacting for a period of time, the app will fade but still be partially visible. In either of these two cases the app enters the *Paused* state. If the users close the pop-up or touch the screen, the app becomes fully visible again, and the app again enters the *Resumed* state. If users don't touch the screen for a longer period of time and the screen goes black, or the user starts another app so that the original app is no longer visible, the app enters the *Stopped* state. If users turn on the screen or use the Back button to get back to the app, the app again enters the *Resumed* state. An app can remain in the *Stopped* state for quite some time. However, if the device is rebooted or a user runs a number of other apps before coming back to the original app, that app can be *Destroyed* by the operating system to free up resources for other apps that the user is actually interacting with. To design an app that functions well given this pattern of use, developers must understand what happens as the app enters and leaves these states, as well as what they should design the app to do in those instances. This requires understanding the Android life cycle.

The Android life cycle (see Figure 2.1) begins when a user touches an app's icon. This action causes the onCreate method in the app's initial activity to execute. This method includes code to load the screen (called a *layout*) associated with the initial activity to load. The developer needs to place code in this method that initializes variables and layout objects to the settings required for the user to begin interacting with the app. After the activity has been created, the onStart method is executed. This method does not have to be implemented but is useful if the app requires certain settings to be the same for every time the app starts, whether it is an initial start after the activity is created or restarted after the activity is brought back from a stopped (but not destroyed) state. After the activity has started, the onResume method is executed. This method also does not have to be implemented but is very useful to return the app to the running state that the app was in before it paused. This includes turning on system services used by the app (for example the GPS or the camera), restarting animations, and any other settings needed to allow users to pick up where they left off.

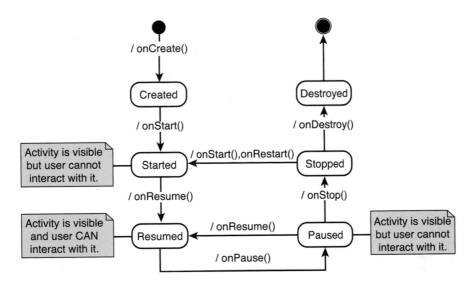

Figure 2.1   Android life cycle.

When a user stops directly interacting with the app, the path to destruction begins. None of the methods executed on the path to destruction have to be implemented. However, they often serve a useful purpose and should be considered. The first method executed is onPause. This method should be used to stop services that the app is using, to stop animations, or to store important state information so that users can start using the app exactly as they left it. If the app is about to become invisible, the onStop method will be executed. This method should make sure important data is permanently stored so that as system resources are consumed by other apps, they are not lost. Finally, if not restarted, the onDestroy method will be executed just before the operating system takes away all the app's resources. This is your last chance to capture important data before all is lost.

iOS Life Cycle

The life cycle for iOS is similar to Android's. However, iOS uses both an app life cycle and a screen (called *view*) life cycle to accomplish essentially the same things. As with Android, the life cycle (see Figure 2.2) begins when the user taps an app's icon. The application: didFinishLaunchingWithOptions: method is similar to an activity's onCreate method. However, in iOS this method is used to set up the operating environment for the complete app, not just a single activity.

The applicationWillResignActive: method is executed when the app is interrupted, similar to when the onPause method is executed in Android. Finally, when the app is no longer visible, the applicationDidEnterBackground: method is executed. As with Android, code in these methods should be used to turn off services and save important data for the user before it's potentially lost.

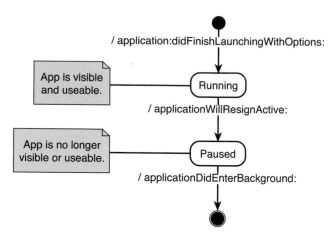

Figure 2.2   iOS App life cycle.

Unlike Android, iOS has a separate life cycle for displayed screens (called ViewControllers). The view life cycle (see Figure 2.3) begins after the application has finished loading or the user goes to a different page in the app. After the view is loaded into memory, the viewDidLoad: method executes. This method is executed only once if the view stays in memory. You should write code in this method to set the initial state of the view. After the view has loaded into memory, just before the view is visible to the user, the viewWillAppear: method is executed. Code in this method should be used to load any data into the views that will be visible to the user and turn on services that the user needs to interact with the app. This method executes every time the view reappears on the device.

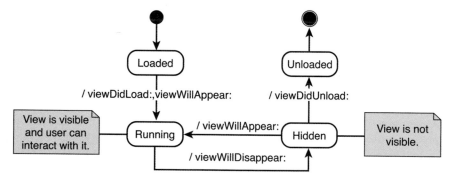

Figure 2.3   iOS View life cycle.

Just like in Android, if an app is interrupted, or the user doesn't interact with the device for a period of time, or the user moves to another view in the app, the view is pushed into the background. Just before this happens, the viewWillDisappear: method is executed. Code in this method should turn off services and take steps to save the user's data. If the user doesn't interact with the view for a period of time while it is in the background, iOS may reclaim its resources. Just before the view is released from memory, the viewDidUnload: method is executed. This is the developer's last chance to preserve important data used in the view.

Understanding and properly coding the app to take advantage of the methods associated with the life cycle are important to ensuring a good user experience with your app. Take the time to understand these life cycles, and your app development experience will be significantly less frustrating!

Screen Size and Orientation Issues

The most obvious difference between mobile and traditional application design is the amount of real estate you have to work with. The mobile device has significantly less area to design the interaction that your users can experience with your app. Poor interface design is the easiest way to get bad reviews for your app. Mobile devices are also used in different situations than traditional computing devices are. App users are often multitasking (walking, talking with friends, and so on). The app design must allow users to switch to your app and do what they want to do right away, before they are distracted again. If users can't easily figure out how to use the app, no amount of help will satisfy them. This is no different from traditional development. However, the very limited screen real estate makes it a significant challenge. In addition, the focus among app developers has been on very good user interface design, so the competition is fierce for apps that work really well.

In response to the limited screen size, both iOS and Android have the capability to scroll to interface elements not on the screen. Scrolling can be both horizontal and vertical. However, both scrolling capabilities should be used judiciously, especially horizontal scrolling. Scrolling down a list has become a natural action on both traditional computers and mobile devices. However, horizontal scrolling has not. Horizontal scrolling should be reserved for use for elements that start on the main screen and extend off the screen. Users won't naturally think to horizontally scroll to look for items they can't find on the main screen. Even vertical scrolling should be limited. Lists are obvious choices for vertical scrolling, but other types of interface elements should be limited. Additionally, when scrolling, you must also fix certain elements so that the user can perform needed operations without scrolling back through the entire contents of the screen.

The obvious answer to the limited screen size is to carefully plan the user's interaction with your app. Screens should focus on one, or a very limited and coherent, set of tasks that the user can or would want to do. Navigation should be planned and designed so that it is obvious to the user how to proceed to the next task. If a task requires multiple steps, those steps should be designed as distinct screens, and the user should be guided through the screens needed to complete the whole task.

Although screen size is a nontrivial design issue, the fact that by default, a screen's orientation can change as the user turns the device also presents design issues. When the user turns the device from vertical to horizontal orientation, the layout or view reorganizes to that orientation. This significantly changes the amount of vertical and horizontal real estate for your interface. Interface elements that were obvious to the user in the vertical orientation may become inaccessible in the horizontal orientation. Again, this can be a very frustrating experience for your user, unless you carefully plan for the layout in both orientations, and thoroughly test it as well. Scrolling can be implemented to alleviate some of the problems associated with orientation change. However, simply adding scrolling may not solve the user experience issues. If you cannot make it work in an alternative orientation, as a last resort you can code the app to work in only one orientation.

The solutions to these screen size and orientation issues are planning and design. What does the user want to do with your app? What can your user do with your app? What are the logical steps needed to accomplish those tasks given the device limitations? These are the types of questions you must answer to design a successful app.

Connectivity Issues

One of the most important aspects of mobile devices is that they are able to communicate with other devices and the Internet. This enables the capability to create very powerful and useful apps. However, this also poses design problems. The device's capability to connect can be lost, or the connection speed may be very slow. Additionally, these problems can arise if the device moves even a few feet. Compounding the problem is that users may not recognize or even understand that there is a connectivity problem while they are using your app. Apple requires that all apps submitted to the app store include a user warning when the network connection is lost, but this doesn't address slow speeds, and is not required by Android at all.

Again, design and planning are your solutions.

The primary issue that the app developer has to be concerned with is blocking the user from working with your app. When the app gets or sends data, it can take a significant amount of time. Users are unlikely to be happy waiting for this action to complete before doing other tasks. This means you have to plan for uploading and downloading data asynchronously, which means you have to make it run outside the main thread of the app. It also means that the rest of the app should be designed to provide other things users can do unless the data is absolutely necessary for the task. If a user tries to do something that requires the data, provide a warning. The warning should provide enough information to help users decide what they should do next. If there is no connection or if there is a weak signal, tell them and give them options.

> ### Users Can't Wait!
>
> In my first app, I (Michael) made this mistake. The app retrieved weather information as part of its functionality. I included it on the main thread of the application. Everything worked fine in testing because I was in an area with good connectivity. But the first time I used it in the field where there were connectivity problems, I couldn't use the app at all! I could see the screen, but nothing worked because it was waiting for the weather. The screen eventually timed out, and I retried starting the cycle again. This was very frustrating. If I had purchased the app, I would have immediately demanded a refund.

Uploading important data is also a concern. As with a download, uploads should be performed asynchronously. You need to check that the upload was completed fully so that if a connection is lost during the upload, the user's data is not corrupted. This means that the data should be cached locally until it is successfully uploaded. Finally, you may need to provide functionality to upload the data when a good connection becomes available.

Communication problems external to the app can impact your app's performance. You must plan for this possibility to provide the best user experience possible.

Battery Issues

Mobile devices are just that—mobile. This means that they are not always connected to a power source. They rely on batteries for their power, and batteries can be drained. Your job as a developer is to not drain those batteries unnecessarily. This is not just a courtesy issue. If every time your app is used the user's device quickly becomes a brick, it will be noticed. An app that quickly drains power will not get used, will get bad reviews, and eventually will not get downloaded at all.

The primary power draw for devices is the display. You cannot do much about that except to make sure that your code is efficient and doesn't take an unnecessary amount of time to complete the work that the user wants to do. Also, you should make sure that users can pick up where they left off if the app is interrupted so the screen doesn't need to be on so long.

After the screen, the primary power drains are the sensors. Global Positioning System (GPS), camera, communication, and other sensors are all big power draws. Fortunately, it is within your power to control these things. You control access to device hardware within your app and should turn on these capabilities only just before the user needs them. You should also turn them off as soon as the user completes the task that requires these items.

The app's life cycle plays an important role here. If the app is interrupted, all device access or use should be suspended immediately. When the app is about to become active, turn on as late as possible only those device capabilities needed. For example, in the previously mentioned app that uses weather data, the weather retrieval is started as one app activity becomes active. If the weather data is successfully retrieved, it is time stamped. The next time the activity becomes active, the weather data will be retrieved only if it is outdated, thus saving battery power.

Some battery issues are beyond your control. You cannot make an app that extends battery power. However, you can definitely make an app that significantly reduces battery life. Be sure to plan for battery use when designing your app.

Hardware Issues

A very cool aspect of mobile computing is the set of hardware components available on the device. Many devices have the capability to locate the device within a few meters using the GPS, have sensors that can capture device orientation, have lights that can be turned on and off, have cameras, and have other hardware components that allow the device to interact with the environment. Access to these components can make fun and useful apps. However, employing them within your app is not without potential problems. The battery issue was discussed in the previous section, and this is always a concern when using hardware devices. However, each component has its own set of issues that, when used poorly, can make an app less desirable.

The first issue to be aware of is availability of the component. Different manufacturers make Android devices, and some include devices that others do not. iOS devices are generally more homogeneous, but differences still exist. Because of this, it is very important to consider how important the component is to the primary functionality of your app. If it is only tangential, you may want to consider not using it because using it will often prevent the app from be loaded onto the device. At best, the absence of the hardware component on the user's phone or tablet will cause frustration with your app. Another concern is situational availability. For example, for a device to get a GPS signal, the device has to have the capability to get the satellite signal required for operation. If the user is indoors, the GPS may not work.

It's My Fault!

Early on in my app development efforts, I (Michael) created an app that uses GPS data to map certain points. This app was made available in the Android Play Store, but to try to expand the availability of the app, I submitted it to the Amazon App Store. Unlike Android, Amazon reviews the apps submitted to them before they make them available. They rejected it because it didn't work! I couldn't believe it. It always worked for me. However, they were testing it indoors where it never got a GPS reading, and therefore nothing worked. My design didn't account for this possibility, and the entire functionality was dependent on getting a GPS reading. Realizing that much of the app's functionality did not require the GPS, I redesigned it to handle the situation, and Amazon eventually accepted it. However, if this happened to a user, you may not get a second chance—or worse, the user might write a scathing review of your app.

A second issue to be aware of is time delays. To access a hardware component you must use the component's Application Program Interface (API). The component may take some time to turn on and respond with the information you need. If this delay is significant, it may impact the user experience in such a way that your app is viewed negatively. For example, the GPS system takes time to acquire enough satellite signals to accurately locate your device. This could take more than a minute. Stopping app function until this happens should be avoided if possible. If the user is left waiting for the device to respond, the screen may time out. This issue may be encountered even if you did everything properly and turned off the services when the app is about to be sent to the background, and then turned them on again when the user re-opens the app. However, if the activation of the device takes time, your app will end up hanging every time it returns from the background. This vicious circle will not please the user. The proper solution to this particular problem is to use a separate execution thread to do the initialization, thus allowing the user to interact with other parts of your app while the services are being activated.

A final important issue with the use of hardware devices is accuracy. There are several aspects of this issue. First, the accuracy of the component can differ among manufacturers. Consider what the minimal level of accuracy is needed for effective use of your app, and design for that.

Be sure to give the user options if the required level of accuracy is not available. Second, accuracy often takes time. For example, to find the location of the device within a few hundred meters is often very quick. However, accuracy of a few feet often takes much more time. What is the required level of accuracy for your app's functionality? What can the user do if the device cannot achieve this? How quick does the acquisition of location need to be? All are important considerations when you are designing the app. A very good design strategy when you need better accuracy is to keep the user informed of progress. The Google Maps app provides an example of this. When finding your location on the map, the app first shows a big blue circle that gets progressively smaller as the accuracy improves. Finally, how the device returns data to the app may impact the level of accuracy your app can access. Again, using GPS as an example, the number of digits reported for the latitude and longitude coordinates dictate the level of accuracy of those coordinates. In some cases, the number of digits reported can differ. This is primarily an issue for the Android platform because it can differ among versions of the Android OS.

Device Differences

Android devices (phones and tablets) and iOS phones and tablets each have a unique set of hardware and software capabilities that make the way the user interacts with the device different for each. Again, to fully capture the device's capabilities and not degrade the user experience, you must design for those unique characteristics. Remember, users can and will do things you are not expecting. Even if it makes no sense to you, they will do it! If the app crashes or loses important data because of something they did, it does not matter: IT IS YOUR FAULT! Plan accordingly.

It's Your Fault!

I (Michael) have an app that uses GPS data to map certain points. Against my better judgment, I was asked to allow the manual entry of GPS coordinates for the app. One user contacted me about why his app was always crashing when he tried to display the map. We went back and forth on potential fixes. (He really liked the app and wanted to use it. Most users would just delete your app). I could not figure it out, so I finally asked him to send me his data. He wasn't entering GPS coordinates! He just entered information about the location. I assumed that my users would know to enter the exact GPS coordinates, not just the location name without exact coordinates. I had to add an error message to the manual location entry to handle the situation. You never know what a user is going to do!

Android

Android devices originally used four hardware buttons (see Figure 2.4) to support the user's use of the device. These buttons were the Home button, the Menu button, the Search button, and the Back button. The user could press any of these buttons at any time during use of your app, which would impact the functioning of your app. The Home and Back buttons worked independently of your code, whereas the Menu and Search buttons provided functionality only if your app was specifically coded to use these buttons.

Figure 2.4   Android hardware buttons.

However, more recent Android devices (running Android 3.0, API 11 and greater) have replaced these buttons with virtual buttons at the bottom of the screen and an action bar at the top of the screen (Figures 2.5 and 2.6, respectively). The Back and Home virtual buttons remain the same in both form and function. However, the Menu and Search buttons were eliminated, and a Recents virtual button was added. The Recents button shows the user's recently used apps. The action bar displays the app's icon and title and the menu. Menu items will be displayed with an icon (if defined). If there are too many menu items to be displayed with an icon, the extra menu items are accessible through the three vertical dots on the right side of the menu bar. If an app is targeting older versions of Android as well as newer, the action bar presents only the three dots at the far right. When pressed, these dots perform the same function as the Menu button.

Figure 2.5   Android virtual buttons.

Figure 2.6   Android action bar.

The Home button immediately moves your app to the Stopped state. This causes the onPause and onStop methods to execute. It will not destroy the app unless it needs the system resources. This means you must pay attention to these events even though you may not be anticipating this behavior when your app is in use.

The Back button immediately goes back one action or activity. This can have several implications for your code. For example, if the user is looking at an activity and presses the Back button, the visible activity will be immediately moved to the Stopped state (causing the onPause and onStop methods to execute). It will move the previous activity into the Running state. This will cause the `onStart` and `onResume` methods to execute for that activity. If your activity has displayed a pop-up, the activity is currently in the Paused state (because it is partially visible). Pressing the Back button will hide the pop-up and cause the `onResume` method to execute, and your activity will be placed in the running state. If the soft keyboard is displayed, your app is also in the Paused state. Pressing the Back button will hide the keyboard and again put your activity in the Running state.

If the user presses the Menu button, your app will not do anything unless you have specifically programmed it to have a menu. Menus can be useful ways to provide the user with access to functionality that is not used as the normal course of events in using your app; thus, you don't want to waste valuable screen real estate to provide access to that functionality.

Finally, the Search button also does nothing unless you code it. You can use this button to allow the user to search for information within your app.

The hardware/virtual buttons provided by Android devices either have an impact on your app or can be used to extend the functionality of your app. In either case it is important to plan for the impact of these buttons when designing your app.

iOS

The primary hardware button of concern on iOS devices is the Home button. This button immediately moves any app presently running to the background. The `viewWillDisappear:`, `applicationWillResignActive:`, and `applicationDidEnterBackground:` methods will all be called. Plan your app so that this action will not cause problems.

Both Android and iOS have a button that puts the device to sleep or reboots it. This action also must be handled. Fortunately, the same methods that put the app in the background for other actions are executed so, typically, no additional programming is required to prepare for this.

Introducing Your First App

To learn both Android and iOS design and development, you will build the same app on each platform. Building the same app on both platforms is useful for understanding differences and similarities between the platforms. The app you will build is called *MyContactList*. Building a contact list app is a good way to learn mobile development for two reasons. First, its purpose and function is generally understood, so a significant part of any application development effort (understanding the functional requirements) does not need to be explained. Second, a contact list app requires utilizing many basic and advanced features of mobile development; therefore, it is very useful in providing a context for learning these concepts.

The MyContactList app consists of four different screens. Each screen is used to illustrate basic app development concepts you will use in almost any subsequent app you develop. Additionally, you'll learn how to navigate between screens in an app.

Contact Screen

The contact screen shown in Figure 2.7 is used to enter, edit, and save information about people in your contact list. While developing this screen, you learn some of the fundamental concepts of mobile user interface design and data entry. Later on, you use this screen as a way to learn how to create and store data in a database on a mobile platform. Finally, the contact screen shows you how to integrate hardware capabilities into an application by using the device's camera to capture a contact's picture and to make a phone call by tapping the contact's phone number.

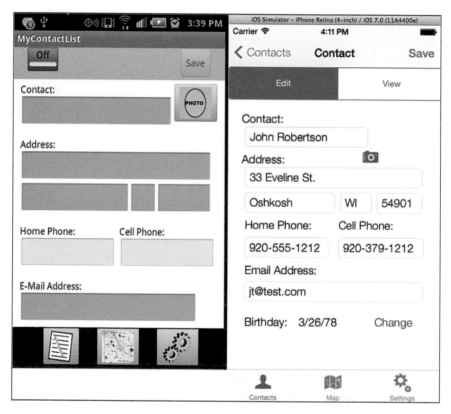

Figure 2.7   The Contact screen.

Contact List Screen

The contact list (see Figure 2.8) is used to search for basic contact information and allow selection of a contact for further action (for example, editing and deleting). Lists are very important components of many apps on both Android and iOS. Developing this screen teaches you how to integrate them into any future app. This screen also demonstrates how to access information provided by hardware components of the device.

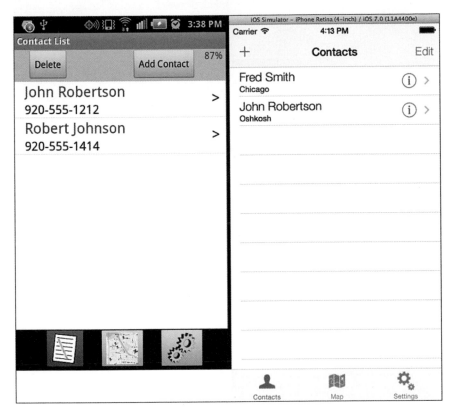

Figure 2.8   The Contact List screen.

Map Screen

The map screen (see Figure 2.9) is used to display the recorded location of a single contact or all your contacts on a map with a pin. The screen also demonstrates how to display the device's present location on the map and how to switch between different map views. The usefulness and importance of maps on mobile devices needs no further explanation. Through the development of this screen you learn how to integrate mapping into your apps. Additionally, the screen will be used to demonstrate another approach to accessing sensor information.

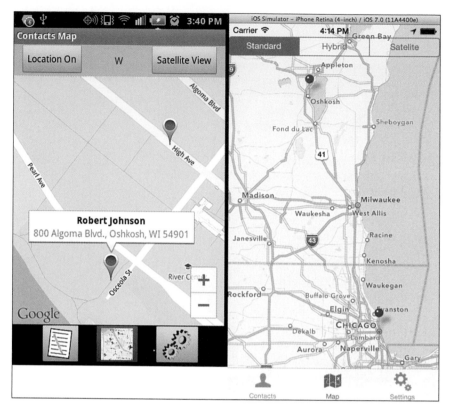

Figure 2.9   The Map screen.

Settings Screen

The Settings screen (see Figure 2.10) is used to set the sort order for the contacts in the Contact List. In developing this screen, you learn to use a method of data persistence designed for capturing and storing individual pieces of data. This type of data persistence is often used to capture user preferences for an app. You also learn to use a different type of display widget (view).

Summary

App development is different from traditional software development. You must design to take advantage of, and be aware of, the impact of the mobile operating system and the hardware that the app is running on. If you do not design your app to account for these differences in the device, you will ensure that your app does not get much use. Android and iOS devices have many similarities and differences that require planning when you are developing an app that will run on both device families. To learn both platforms and learn the differences between them, you will develop the same app for both platforms in the next two sections of the book.

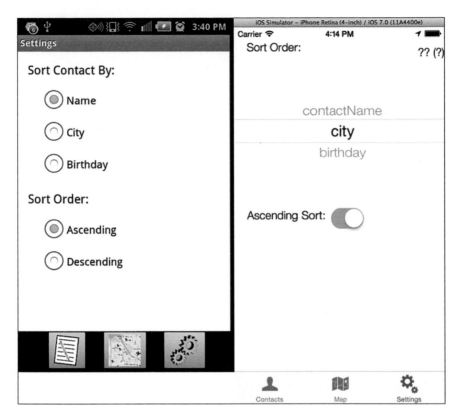

Figure 2.10   The Settings screen.

Exercises

1. Find an app that runs on both platforms. Download and run it. Identify the similarities and differences between the platforms.

2. Find out what uses the most battery power on the mobile device. On Android find the battery usage information. This can be in different places on different Android devices but is typically in the Settings app. Scroll through the list of power draws. What requires the most? What requires the least? Note: This feature is not available on iOS.

3. Open an app that uses the GPS (for example, Google Maps). Look at the status bar at the top of the device. What icons are there? What are they doing? Watch until the device goes to black and then turn it on again. What changes occurred in the status icons? Now switch to the home screen. What happened to the status icons?

Part II

Developing the Android App

3

Using Eclipse for Android Development

This chapter is an introduction to building a complete Android app. The chapter includes creating a new app project, exploring the components of an Android app, setting up the emulator to run and test apps, and building a variation of the traditional Hello World app. This and the following chapters in this part assume that you have access to Eclipse and that it is set up for Android development. If this is not the case, refer to Appendix A, "Installing Eclipse and Setup for Android Development" before continuing.

Starting a New Project

Eclipse is a powerful, open source, integrated development environment (IDE) that facilitates the creation of desktop, mobile, and web applications. Eclipse is a highly versatile and adaptable tool. Many types of applications and programming languages can be used by adding different "plug-ins." For example, plug-ins are available for a very large number of programming languages as diverse as COBOL, PHP, Java, Ruby, and C++, to name a few. Additionally, plug-ins provide the capability to develop for different platforms, such as Android, Blackberry, and Windows. Many of the tools in the Eclipse IDE will be explained through the act of developing an Android app.

Android is a mobile operating system designed for smartphones and tablets. The operating system is very powerful, enabling access to a diverse set of hardware resources on a smartphone or tablet. Android is provided by Google and is continually updated, improved, and extended. This makes the development of apps for Android smartphones and tablets both exciting and challenging. As with Eclipse, the many features of the Android environment are best explained through the act of developing an app.

Setting Up the Workspace

Eclipse uses the concept of a workspace for organizing projects. Because Eclipse can be used to develop many types of applications, this is very useful. A workspace, in reality, is just a folder on some drive on your computer. The folder contains the application's code and resources, code libraries used by the application (or references to them), and metadata that is used to keep track of environment information for the workspace.

To begin, run Eclipse. The Workspace Launcher dialog window opens, asking which workspace you want to use. The default workspace (or last used) is displayed in the dialog window's text box. Most IDEs are designed with the idea that developers are going to be working on the same machine each time they work on a project. This can cause problems in the education environment where students do not have the ability to work on the same machine and/or store their work on the machine they are currently working on. If you are using your own machine, you can skip to the next section; your workspace was created when you installed Eclipse and is ready to go. However, if you are working in an environment where you cannot use the same machine each time, you need to set up a workspace on either a flash drive or on a network drive. Determine which of these options is best for your situation and perform the following steps:

1. Create a folder in your selected location named **workspace**.

2. Go back to the Workspace Launcher and browse to your new folder. Click OK.

   Often in a situation where you change the workspace to a location not on the machine that Eclipse is installed on, Eclipse will not be able to find the Android SDK. If it cannot find the SDK, a dialog window opens. If this happens, you will have to tell Eclipse where the files are located by performing the next steps.

3. Click Open Preferences on the dialog window and browse to the sdk folder. This is usually located in the .android folder. Click Apply.

   The available Android versions should be displayed in the window.

4. Click OK to close the dialog window. Your workspace is now ready to begin Android development.

Creating the Project

The traditional beginning tutorial for many different languages and development platforms is "Hello World." Your first Android app will be a slightly modified "Hello World" app. In Eclipse, all Android apps are created within a project. To create your first app, you will have to create your first project. Creating a new project requires stepping through a series of windows and making choices to configure your app. To get started, from Eclipse's main menu choose File > New > Android Application Project. You should see the New Android Application dialog window, as shown in Figure 3.1.

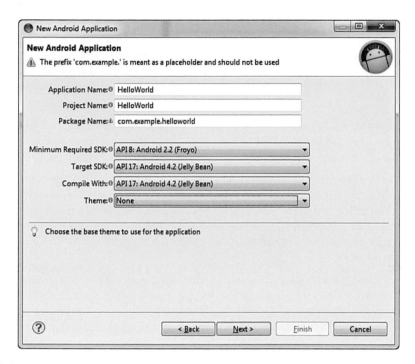

Figure 3.1   Initial new Android application window configured for "Hello World."

Fill out the screen as shown. The application name is displayed on the phone's screen as the name of the app. You can use spaces if you want. As you type the name, the project name and package name will be completed. There are no spaces allowed in these items. The wizard will remove them as you type. Don't put them back in either of these fields. The package name is important. For this initial project you don't need to change the default. However, if you are building an app for sale, in place of "example" you should put your company name. This identifier will be used in the Play Store to link your apps to the services they use and connect all your apps.

Next, click the Minimum Required SDK drop-down. A list of potential Android SDKs are listed. SDK stands for Software Development Kit, and it is a set of tools and code libraries used to write software for a specific platform. Each release of the Android OS is associated with an SDK so that programmers can write code for that platform. An application programming interface (API) is a set of routines that allow a program (app) to access the resources of the operating system to provide functionality to the user. The minimum required SDK determines what phones and other Android devices will be able to install your app. (Phones and tablets using Android operating systems earlier than this selection will not even see your app in the Play Store.) This selection will also determine the features you can program into your app. The recommended minimum is the default: *Froyo API 8.* An app that has this minimum will be accessible to more than 90% of the devices "in the wild."

The Target SDK should usually be set to the latest version of the Android operating system. At the writing of this book, that version is the Jelly Bean (API 17). After you release an app, you should periodically update these values and recompile your app as new versions of Android are released. At times, new versions of the operating system can affect the performance of your app, so it is best to keep the app up to date. The Compile With target should also be the latest SDK.

Themes are a useful way to ensure a consistent look for your app. However, because this is an introduction you will not be using them in this book. Click the drop-down and select None as your theme.

After you have verified that your selections match those in Figure 3.1, click the Next button and the Configure Project window will be displayed. You should accept the defaults on this screen. After you learn the app creation process, you may want to modify the default settings to better match your requirements. However, by using the defaults, some work is done for you that can easily be changed later as needed. Click the Next button to display the Configure Launcher Icon window.

The Configure Launcher Icon window allows you to associate an icon with your app that will be displayed on the phone's screen along with the app name. Notice the different sizes of the icons. If you are providing an icon for your app, you will have to supply several sizes of the same picture. This is because Android apps can run on any Android device that meets the app's SDK requirements. However, these devices can have different screen resolutions and different screen sizes. By supplying different icon sizes, the app will pick the one that best matches the device it is running on. This helps ensure that your app will show up as you design it, regardless of the characteristics of the device it is running on. Suggested sizes for app icons are 32×32, 48×48, 72×72, 96×96, and 144×144 pixels for low to extra high density screens. Accept the default icon for this app by clicking the Next button.

The Create Activity window is the next step in configuring your project. An Activity is a core component of any Android application. Activities are typically associated with a visible screen. Most of the core functionality of an app is provided by an activity and its associated screen (called a *layout*). Click among the different activity options. Notice that when you have selected some of them, the Next button is disabled. The choices are limited by your choice of minimum and target SDK. Eclipse won't let you use features that will not work on the devices you targeted. In this case, because you selected API 8 as the minimum SDK that your app would be allowed to run on, some activity types are not available, even though they are available in the target SDK you selected.

From the list of possible activities, choose Blank Activity and click the Next button. The Blank Activity window is displayed (Figure 3.2). This allows us to configure the first Activity in our app. With this screen we can change the name of the activities we create. In the Activity Name text box, delete MainActivity and type HelloWorldActivity. Notice below Activity Name is Layout Name. As you typed in the activity name, the text in this box changed to reflect the text you entered. A layout is an XML file that provides the user interface for the activity. Layouts are discussed in detail later. For now, just remember that every activity has an associated layout file.

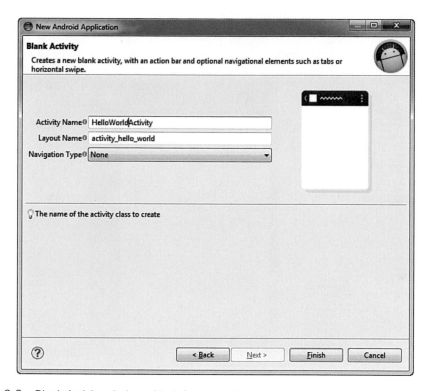

Figure 3.2   Blank Activity window with default selections.

The final item on this page is Navigation Type. Select it and click among the options. Notice that just like the Create Activity window, you are not allowed to use some navigation types. Again this is based on the SDK choices you made earlier. Select None as your Navigation Type and click Finish. Your app project is created! Depending on the capability of your computer, it may take some time to create the project. When Eclipse has finished creating your project, your Eclipse environment should look like Figure 3.3.

Components of the IDE

Many of the items in the IDE will be explained as needed. For now you will examine just a few. The top center section is the *Editor*. Much of the development work is done here, including the UI design and writing code. It should currently be displaying the layout for the HelloWorldActivity in Graphical Layout mode. You can switch between graphical layout and the XML code that generates the layout with the tabs below the layout. One tab will always say Graphical Layout. The other will be the filename of the layout. In this case it is activity_hello-world.xml.

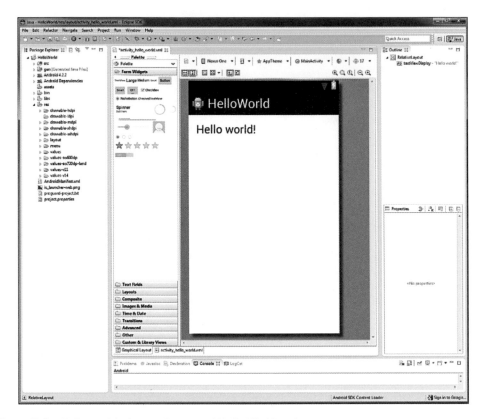

Figure 3.3   Eclipse with the newly created Hello World project.

The left side of the IDE shows the Package Explorer. The Package Explorer displays the structure of the Android app and is used to move between different components of the app. Many of these items will be generated for you, and many others you will work with as you create your app. The src folder will contain all the Java code files for the app. Each file typically represents one class. Double-click the folder and its subfolders until you see HelloWorldActivity.java. This is where the code to create the activity's functionality is written. Double-click the HelloWorld.java file. The file contents are displayed in the editor with some Java code listed. This code is explained later.

Next, look for the res folder in the Package Explorer. This folder contains a number of folders that all contain a different kind of resource file needed for your Android app. One very important note about resource files: There are no capital letters allowed in the file names! Double-click through the drawable-xxx folders. The drawable folders are for images. Android uses Portable Network Graphics (PNG) files for its images. Notice the ic_launcher.png file is in all the drawable folders except the drawable-lhdp folder. Each one of these files is the launcher icon in a different size to match the size recommendations for different screen resolutions.

The lhdp folder does not contain an icon because no Android devices with low resolution are available with an API 8 or higher. When your app is installed on a device, Android automatically uses the one appropriate for the device it is installed in by selecting it from the correct folder.

Next is the layout folder. This folder holds all the layouts for the user interface of your app. The menu folder holds the menu items to be displayed in your app when a user clicks the device's menu button. Menu functionality is not required for an app, and this book will not work with them.

The final set of folders is that of the values folders. Double-click the values folder. Three XML files will be displayed: dimens.xml, strings.xml, and styles.xml. The values files hold configuration data for an Android app. Android uses this information to limit the hard-coding of potentially changeable data. For example, the dimens.xml file could hold a value for screen title size that could be reused on each layout in the app. If you later decide that you want the screen title size to be different, you only have to change the value in the dimens.xml file and it automatically applies the new size to all titles that use that dimension. The values folders with a dash and number or other information are for values to be used for specific versions of the Android operating system. This enables the developer to take advantage of different OS capabilities within the same app. Some common values files are described below:

- dimens.xml—Values for the display size of items in a layout.
- color.xml—Values for the displayed color of item in a layout.
- strings.xml—Values for text.
- array.xml—Defines string arrays and the values in those arrays.
- ids.xml—IDs that cannot be reused by items in layouts.

The Android Manifest

The final and very important item in the Package Explorer that we will examine is the AndroidManifest.xml file. The manifest file is not in a folder but is listed as one of the folder independent files following all the folders in the project. Double-click this file. The Manifest editor will be displayed in the editor. The manifest is used to configure the whole app and tell the device it is installed on what it can and should be able to do. There are multiple tabs (at the bottom of the editor) associated with the manifest. These are used to configure different aspects of your app. The Manifest tab (which is the initial tab open) includes several important elements. First, note the Version Code and Version Name elements. Version code is an integer value. It is used to indicate that there is a new version of the app available. Increasing the value enables the Play Store to notify users of the app that a new version is available. It also controls the install of the upgrade so that no user data is lost during an upgrade. The Version Name is the displayed version of your app. Beyond that it is nonfunctioning. However, it is good practice to have a consistent approach to changing this so that you know what version of the app is at issue when communicating with users about their problems with the app. Click Uses Sdk. The current selections for minimum and target SDK are displayed. These can be modified here. Next click the Application tab at the bottom of the editor. This tab provides the capability to configure specific operational and display elements of the app. Finally, click the AndroidManifest.xml tab. The selections made in the editors generate code that is displayed here.

Interpreting the XML

Although the tabs in the Manifest editor can be used to create a basic configuration of the manifest, the ability to read and manipulate XML is a critical skill for the Android app developer. Modifying a manifest to allow your app to do more advanced behaviors is common, and most online help on doing so, either from the Android Developer site or developer forums, is provided in XML. To get started, take a look at the manifest components in the AndroidManifest.xml file (Listing 3.1).

Listing 3.1   **Manifest XML**

```
<?xml version="1.0" encoding="utf-8"?>
                                                              //1
<manifest xmlns:android="http://schemas.android.com/apk/res/android"
    package="com.example.helloworld"
    android:versionCode="1"
    android:versionName="1.0" >
                                                              //2
    <uses-sdk
        android:minSdkVersion="8"
        android:targetSdkVersion="17" />
                                                              //3
    <application
        android:allowBackup="true"
        android:icon="@drawable/ic_launcher"
        android:label="@string/app_name"
        android:theme="@style/AppTheme" >
                                                              //4
        <activity
            android:name="com.example.helloworld.HelloWorldActivity"
            android:label="@string/app_name" >
                                                              //5
            <intent-filter>
                                                              //6
                <action android:name="android.intent.action.MAIN" />
                                                              //7
                <category android:name="android.intent.category.LAUNCHER" />
            </intent-filter>
        </activity>
    </application>

</manifest>
```

The manifest contains a number of XML elements. Those elements and their attributes define basic operational aspects of your app. Refer to the numbers in Listing 3.1 to see the complete code associated with each element explanation below.

1. The `<manifest>` component is the root element. The attributes associated with this element define the application package, version code, and version name (as well as others).

2. The `<uses-sdk>` element and its attributes define the minimum and target SDKs for the app.

3. The `<application>` element has both attributes and child elements that configure how the app works. Application attributes in this manifest define the app icon, theme, and name. Each activity in an app must have an entry in the `<application>` element. In our manifest there is one activity: the one created when we created the project. Its attributes identify the Java class file for the activity and the display name of the activity. Currently, that name is the same as the app's name.

4. The `<activity>` element tells the operating system that an activity has permission to run in your application. All activities used in an app must be defined in the manifest. If they are not, the app will crash when the user navigates to that activity. In this element the Java source file for the activity and the activity's title are identified.

5. A child element of the `<activity>` element, the `<intent-filter>` element, defines what the Android OS should do with this activity. Not all activities will have an intent-filter. Specifically, activities that you want users to launch when they are using the app do not need intent-filters. However, for this app you want this activity to be displayed when the user runs it.

6. Therefore, the `<action>` tag identifies the activity as the main or first activity to run.

7. The `<category>` tag tells the OS to use the app launcher to start this activity.

Configuring the Emulator

Now that you have some understanding of the development environment, you are almost ready to start creating the app. Don't worry. Future projects will take less time to set up. You could start coding at this point, but until you tell Eclipse how to execute the app, you will not be able to see your results. Therefore, the next step will be to set up the test environment.

Android apps may be tested on either the emulator provided by the Eclipse IDE or on an Android device. The emulator is a program that simulates an Android device. If you choose to test on the emulator, you should also test on several varieties of real devices before you publish your app. Real devices often perform differently than the emulator. If you do not test on a real device, you will likely have many unhappy users.

To set up the emulator, we first must set up an Android Virtual Device (AVD). An AVD is a software replication of one or more types of Android devices. Multiple AVDs with different characteristics may be set up for testing. To set up an AVD we use the AVD Manager. From the main menu select Window > Android Device Manager to display the Android Virtual Device Manager (Figure 3.4).

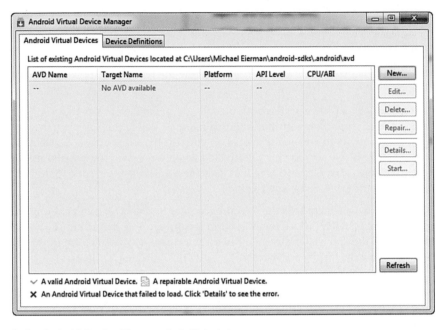

Figure 3.4   Android Device Manager in initial state.

The manager opens with the Virtual Devices tab displayed. Click the Device Definitions tab. This displays all the device configurations your system knows about. Scroll through these to see how many devices your app could run on. Press the Device Definitions tab and then click the New button. The Create New Android Virtual Device (AVD) window is displayed. Complete the device definition as follows, changing only these options:

AVD Name: MyTestDevice

Device: 3.2 QVGA (ADP2) (320 x 480: mdpi)

Target: Android 4 2.2 – API Level 17

SD Card: Size 1024 MiB

When you click the Device drop-down, a large number of devices are available. Scroll down the list to find the device: 3.2 QVGA (ADP2) (320 x 480: mdpi) and select it. After you've selected the device, choose ARM from the CPU/ABI drop-down. Most devices have an SD card. However, if you want to test your app for those that do not, don't change anything for the SD Card option. Click OK. The new AVD will be displayed in the Android Virtual Devices tab. Click the new AVD named MyTestDevice that now shows in the existing AVD list, and the buttons on the right of the AVD Manager will be enabled. Click the Start button and the Launch Options window will be displayed. Leave all the defaults. Checking the Scale Display to Real Size box will show the virtual device at the size of the real device. However, this can be hard to use during initial development. Checking the Wipe User Data box will wipe out any data created in a previous session. It is useful to leave the data intact so that you will not have to reenter data every time you want to test some aspect of the app.

> ### Note
> I like to start my development with one of the smaller devices because I find it easier to scale up when developing the user interface than to scale down. Also, I like to pick a lower API for the device for similar reasons. Later, you can create different AVDs to test different device configurations.

Click Launch. The Start Android Emulator window will display and start loading the AVD. When it is done, the virtual device displays (Figure 3.5) and begins further loading. The speed at which the device loads depends greatly on your computer. At times it can be quite slow. If I am testing with the emulator, my first task when beginning any development session is to start the virtual device so that it is ready when I am. After the AVD is displayed, you can close the Start Android Emulator and AVD Manager windows. The AVD will remain running.

Figure 3.5   Android Emulator at initial launch.

Setting Up Run Configurations

The final step in setting up the test environment is to tell our app to use this newly created AVD. To do this you need to set up a Run Configurations.

1. From the main menu select Run > Run Configurations. The Run Configurations window is displayed.

2. Click Android Application in the left side of the screen. Then click the New button, which is the leftmost button above the text box that says Type Filter Text. The window changes, showing configuration options. Change the name to HelloWorldRunConfig.

3. Use the Browse button to select your HelloWorld project. Click the Launch Default Activity option button.

4. Click the Target tab. Click the box next to MyTestDevice. When you start testing on a real device, you will need to click the option button next to Always Prompt to Pick Device. This displays a device selection window where you can pick the device you want to test on.

5. Click the Apply button and then the Close button. You are ready to begin coding your app!

Coding the Interface

As mentioned earlier, the interface for any Android app is created through the use of a layout file. A layout file is an XML file that contains the XML used to create the objects and controls that the user can interact with. The first step in coding the HelloWorld app is to modify the layout so that it has some controls that the user can interact with. Your modifications will be simple. You will make the app take a name entered by the user and display Hello [entered name] after a button click.

Double-click the activity_hello_world.xml file in the layout folder of the Package Explorer to begin work coding the interface. If it is already open in the editor, click the activity_hello_world.xml tab at the top of the editor (Figure 3.6, #1). If the Graphical Layout is displayed, click the activity_hello_world.xml tab at the bottom of the editor (Figure 3.6, #2). The XML code that creates the user interface is displayed with two *elements* in it. The root element is a RelativeLayout. Because Android devices have so many screen sizes and resolutions, it is often best to design the UI components as relative to one another rather than designing them as a fixed position. Because the RelativeLayout is the root, it encompasses the whole screen. You must have only one layout root in an Android layout file. All other items are children of this root element.

Examine the attributes of the RelativeLayout element (Listing 3.2). A closer look at the attributes reveals a certain structure. Attributes have the format *library:attribute name = "attribute value"*. First, all the attributes in the listing start with android: This indicates that the attribute is associated with Android SDK library and that is where the compiler should look for information on what to do. Other libraries are available from third parties. Adding other libraries will be covered later in this text. The attribute name and values differ based on the element to which they are applied.

Figure 3.6 Editor and layout tabs.

Listing 3.2 **Layout XML**

```
<RelativeLayout xmlns:android="http://schemas.android.com/apk/res/android"
    xmlns:tools="http://schemas.android.com/tools"
                                                                        //1
    android:layout_width="match_parent"
    android:layout_height="match_parent"
                                                                        //2
    android:paddingBottom="@dimen/activity_vertical_margin"
    android:paddingLeft="@dimen/activity_horizontal_margin"
    android:paddingRight="@dimen/activity_horizontal_margin"
    android:paddingTop="@dimen/activity_vertical_margin"
    tools:context=".MainActivity" >
                                                                        //3
    <TextView
        android:layout_width="wrap_content"
        android:layout_height="wrap_content"
        android:text="@string/hello_world"/>

</RelativeLayout>
```

1. The first attributes of interest in the RelativeLayout are `android:layout_` `width="match_parent"` and `android:layout_height="match_parent"`. These attributes define the size of the element. In this case the value `"match_parent"` indicates that the layout should be the height and width of the device screen. If a child element of RelativeLayout has this value for either `layout_height` or `layout_width`, it will fill up as much of the RelativeLayout as it can.

2. The next few attributes: `paddingRight`, `paddingLeft`, `paddingBottom`, and `paddingTop`, all tell Android that it should not fill the entire screen with the RelativeLayout. Instead, there should be blank space between the edge of the screen and the edge of the layout. The amount of space is dictated by the value. The values in these attributes are your first introduction to the use of the XML files in the values folder. To refer to values from these XML files, Android also has a specific structure. That structure is *"@xml_file_name/value_name"*. All values are enclosed in quotation marks. The value for the attribute `android:paddingBottom` is `"@dimen/activity_vertical_` `margin"`. This tells Android it should use the value named `activity_vertical_margin` from the dimens.xml file. Double-click the dimens.xml file in the values folder in the Package Explorer. The file will open to the Resources tab. Click the dimens.xml tab at the bottom of the editor. This displays the XML used to define the dimensions. The `<dimen>` tag is used to define each dimension. Each dimension has a name attribute, a value, and then a closing tag that looks like this: `</dimen>`. The value between the beginning tag and the closing tag is the value that Android uses as the size of the padding.

   Valid dimensions for Android include `px` (pixels), `in` (inches), `mm` (millimeters), `pt` (points), `dp/dip` (density-independent pixels), and `sp` (scale-independent pixels). It is generally recommended that `dp` be used for most dimensions and `sp` be used for specifying font sizes. These two units of measure are relative to screen density. They help keep your UI consistent among different devices. The reason that the `sp` unit is recommended for fonts is because it also scales to the user's preference in font size.

3. The only child element of the RelativeLayout, and thus the only item on the screen, is a TextView. TextView is Android's version of a label. It is primarily used to display text. This element currently has only three attributes. The two size attributes differ from the RelativeLayout in that they have the value `"wrap_content"`. This tells Android to size the TextView to the size of the text displayed in it. The only other attribute tells Android what text to display. In this case it gets the text from the strings.xml file in the values folder. Open the strings.xml file and examine the XML to find the "hello_world" item. Note that its value is "Hello World!", exactly what is displayed in the running app and on the Graphical Layout view of the activity_hello_world.xml file. The TextView does not have any attributes describing its positioning, so Android puts it in the first available position, which is the very top-left position in the RelativeLayout.

Switch back to the Graphical Layout view of the activity_hello_world.xml file. At the left of the layout is a panel titled Palette. Palette contains a set of folders with different components (called widgets) that can be used to design a user interface. If it is not open, click on the Form Widgets folder in the Palette. Form Widgets contains a set of widgets for designing the user interaction with your app. Hover your mouse over each of the icons to see what type of control the widget implements. Notice that some controls have multiple versions that enable you to pick the size that you want for your interface.

A TextView that displays "Hello World" is already on the layout. This is used to display your app's message. However, the size of the text needs to be bigger. To the right of the editor should be a panel with a tab with the label Outline (Figure 3.7). If this is not present, click Window > Show View > Outline to display it. The top of the tab should show the structure of the layout. It should have RelativeLayout as its root and textView1 indented below it. The TextView should be displaying "Hello World" after it. As widgets are added to the layout, they are displayed in the structure. This is very useful because sometimes controls are added to the layout that get lost (not visible) in the Graphical Layout. However, if they are in the layout they will be displayed in the structure.

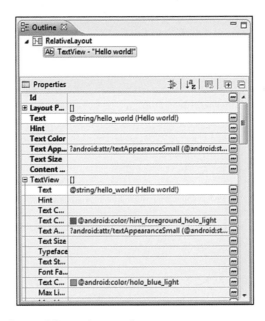

Figure 3.7   Layout Outline and Properties panels.

Below the structure is the Properties window. If you haven't clicked anything in the Graphical Layout, that window will be displaying <No Properties>. Click "Hello World" in the Graphical Layout. The Properties window should populate with all the attributes that can be set for a TextView widget. Locate and click the ... button next to the bold attribute Text Size. The Resource Chooser window is displayed. Two dimensions created when the project was created are listed (the padding margins). Click the New Dimension button at the bottom of the Resource Chooser. In the window that opens, enter **message_text_size** as the dimension name and **24sp** as the value. Click OK until you have closed these two windows. The size of Hello World! should be increased. Open the dimen.xml file and switch to the XML view to see the dimension you created. Close this file and click back to the activity_hello_world.xml tab. Switch from Graphical Layout to the XML view and examine the XML changes to the TextView element. Switch back to the Graphical Layout.

> **Note**
>
> The values files are used to hold values that are going to be reused in your app. Unfortunately, the only way to know what values are available is to open the file and inspect its contents for the value you'd like to use. We recommend that when you add values, you name them very clearly and limit the number of values you use to keep it somewhat manageable. Naming clearly is very important because Eclipse's code completion capability will list the value names but not their actual value.

Locate the Small TextView widget just below the Form Widgets folder label. Click and drag it to the layout, position it as in Figure 3.8, and drop it. Notice the green arrows pointing to the left side of the layout and to the Hello World! TextView. These arrows show what object the widget is relative to for positioning purposes. Click the XML view (Listing 3.3). A number of changes have been made to the XML.

Listing 3.3   **Layout XML with TextView Added**

```
<RelativeLayout xmlns:android="http://schemas.android.com/apk/res/android"
    xmlns:tools="http://schemas.android.com/tools"
    android:layout_width="match_parent"
    android:layout_height="match_parent"
    android:paddingBottom="@dimen/activity_vertical_margin"
    android:paddingLeft="@dimen/activity_horizontal_margin"
    android:paddingRight="@dimen/activity_horizontal_margin"
    android:paddingTop="@dimen/activity_vertical_margin"
    tools:context=".HelloWorldActivity" >

    <TextView
                                                                    //1
        android:id="@+id/textView2"
        android:layout_width="wrap_content"
        android:layout_height="wrap_content"
        android:text="@string/hello_world"
        android:textSize="@dimen/message_text_size" />

    <TextView
        android:id="@+id/textView1"                                 //2
        android:layout_width="wrap_content"
        android:layout_height="wrap_content"
        android:layout_alignLeft="@+id/textView2"                   //3
        android:layout_below="@+id/textView2"
```

```
    android:layout_marginLeft="19dp"                                            //4
    android:layout_marginTop="36dp"
    android:text="Name:"                                                        //5
    android:textAppearance="?android:attr/textAppearanceSmall" />               //6

</RelativeLayout>
```

1. The Hello World! TextView now has an attribute `android:id="@+id/textView2"`. To correctly relatively position the new TextView, Android needed a way to reference it so it added the ID. The `+id` tells Android to create the ID for the widget. IDs can be defined in the ids.xml values file. However, to use these IDs for widgets, you need to define them prior to use, and they cannot be reused. Using `+id` enables you to tell Android to create an ID for the widget as you need it. `textView2` is not a very useful ID. It does not describe what the TextView is used for, so change the ID to `textViewDisplay`.

2. The new TextView also has a `+id`. However, it is different from the first one. `+ids` may be reused in different layouts but cannot be reused within the same layout! Next come the widget size attributes. All items in a layout must contain these attributes.

3. As the arrows on the Graphical Layout showed, this widget is positioned relative to the Hello World! TextView. The layout attributes are the XML used to do the relative positioning. `alignLeft` tells Android to align this widget's left edge with the referenced widget's left edge. `alignBelow` tells Android to position the widget below the referenced widget.

4. The margin attributes `layout_marginLeft` and `layout_marginTop` tell Android how much space to put between the widget and the referenced widget. Change the left margin to 20dp and the top margin to 55dp. You will often have to tweak these values to get the layout to look exactly the way you want it to.

5. The `android:text` attribute indicates what text should be displayed. This attribute is underlined with a yellow triangle on the left edge. This is a warning. Hover over or click the yellow triangle. The warning is displayed. The value `"Small Text"` is a hard-coded value. Android wants all values to be referenced from a value's XML file. This is for ease of maintenance. You can change a string value used multiple times just once in the strings.xml file, and the changes will be made throughout your app. Also, by substituting a different string's.xml file, you can adapt your app to different languages more easily. To simplify this example, leave the string hard-coded but change it to meet your needs. Delete `"Small Text"` and replace it with `"Name:"`.

6. The final attribute in the new TextView is `textAppearance`. The value for this attribute references the Android attr.xml file and is used in place of the `textSize` attribute. The attr.xml file is a file supplied by the Android SDK. Switch back to the Graphical Layout view. The TextView you added should now be displaying Name:.

UI Design—Android Versus iOS

UI design in Android is done through relative positioning of the controls that make up the interface. However, in iPhone and iPad, absolute positioning is used. Absolute position holds the control to a fixed position on the screen. The use of absolute position makes the design of the UI easier. Unlike in Android, when you move a control it has no effect on other controls in the UI. Often in Android, moving one control changes the whole design. This can be frustrating! When moving or deleting a control in an Android layout, especially if you do this in the XML, be sure to check the impact of the change in the Graphical Layout.

Interface design is not without its challenges in iOS. Devices that run iOS have a fixed screen size, which is controlled by Apple. This enables the use of absolute positioning because all device screen sizes are known by the developer. However, this means that the UI has to be created multiple times for each device that you want your app to run on. These different screens all run on the same code, so during design, the developer must be sure to be perfectly consistent among the different screens needed.

Figure 3.8   A Small TextView positioned properly on a Graphical Layout.

Locate and click the Text Fields folder in the Palette. A number of widgets for entering information are displayed. The widget for entering data in Android is called an `EditText`. Each of
the EditText widgets listed is configured for the entry of a different type of data. The different
configurations dictate what soft keyboard is displayed when the widget is clicked and, in some
cases, how the text is formatted as it is entered. For example, the EditText with the number 42
in it will display a keyboard with only numbers on it, whereas the EditText with `Firstname`
`Lastname` in it will display an alpha character keyboard and it will capitalize each word
entered. Drag the Firstname Lastname EditText to the right of the `Name:` `TextView`. As you are
dragging it, pay attention to the green arrows. You want this relative to the Name: TextView,
so there should be only one arrow, and it should point at the TextView. A dotted green line
should go from the bottom of the TextView through the EditText. This aligns the EditText with
the bottom of the TextView.

Click the Form Widgets folder and drag a Small Button below the EditText. In this case you
want the green arrow pointing to the EditText and the dotted green line going through the
middle of the bottom, from the top of the screen to the bottom, to center it horizontally in the
RelativeLayout.

> **Note**
>
> Although Eclipse is a very powerful and useful tool in Android development, the need to make
> all items in the UI relative makes designing a layout difficult. We recommend that you use the
> Graphical Layout to get the UI approximately correct and then fine-tune in the XML.

Switch to the XML view for the layout. Locate the `EditText` element. Change the default
id to `"@+id/editTextName"` so that we have some understanding what data that widget is
handling. Change the `marginLeft` attribute to `"5dp"`. There are two new attributes. The first
is `android:ems`. This attribute sets the displayed size of the layout to 10 ems. Ems is a size
measurement equal to the number of capital Ms that would fit into the control. The second
new attribute is `android:inputType`. This attribute tells Android how you want text handled
as it's entered and the type of keyboard to display when the user is entering data.

Locate the `Button` element. Change the default id to `"@+id/buttonDisplay"`. There is also a
new attribute in this element: `layout_centerHorizontal`. This attribute is set to true to tell
Android to center the widget in the parent. Finally, change the text attribute to `"Display"`.
Change the value in the `layout_below` attribute to `@+id/editTextName` to match the change
you made in the `EditText` element. Switch to the Graphical Layout to see the changes.

Run the app in the emulator using Run > Run Configurations > HelloWorldRunConfig and
click the Run button to see the layout as it would appear running (Figure 3.9). The first time
you run the emulator, you will have to slide the lock to unlock the device (like a real phone).
Note that the emulator might be behind Eclipse, so you will have to minimize windows or in
some other way bring it to the foreground. The button clicks but does not do anything. For this
you need to write code.

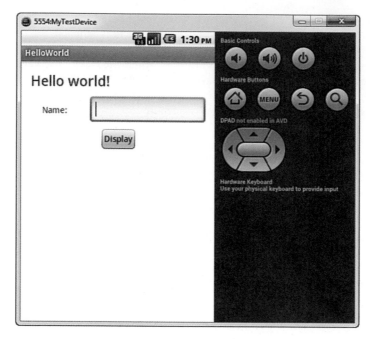

Figure 3.9   Initial run of Hello World.

> **Note**
>
> Either close the activity_hello_world.xml file or switch to the XML view after you are done editing it. The reason is that if you close Eclipse with the layout file open in Graphical mode, Eclipse will take a long time opening the project the next time you want to work on it.

Coding App Behavior

Code to give behavior to the layout is written and stored in the Java class file associated with the layout. Open the HelloWorldActivity.java file by double-clicking it. If it is already open, click its tab in the editor. You should see the basic code structure (Listing 3.4).

Listing 3.4   **Initial Activity Code**

```
                                                           //1
package com.example.helloworld;

                                                           //2
import android.os.Bundle;
import android.app.Activity;
import android.view.Menu;

                                                           //3
```

```
public class HelloWorldActivity extends Activity {

    @Override
                                                                    //4
    protected void onCreate(Bundle savedInstanceState) {
        super.onCreate(savedInstanceState);
        setContentView(R.layout.activity_hello_world);
    }


    @Override
                                                                    //5
    public boolean onCreateOptionsMenu(Menu menu) {
        // Inflate the menu; this adds items to the action bar if it is present.
        getMenuInflater().inflate(R.menu.main, menu);
        return true;
    }
}
```

This code was generated by Eclipse when you created the activity at the start of the HelloWorld project. It is important to understand what this code does to properly code an activity.

1. At the top of the file is the keyword "package" followed by `com.example.helloworld`. This identifies this class as belonging to the Hello World package. All source Java files (in src folder) will have this entry as the first code in the file.

2. After the package line and before any other code are the imports. Click the plus (+) sign in front of the `import android.os.Bundle;` line of code. You should now see three import lines. This code is used to get the source code needed for your activity. The Activity class provides the functionality required for any class that uses or interacts with other Activities used in this class. The Menu class provides the functionality for the menu that is displayed when the user presses the device's Menu button. The Bundle import requires a bit more explanation.

    A `Bundle` is an object for passing data between activities. In this way we can have an application that can perform some activity based on what another activity has done or the data it has used. You will use this functionality later in the book. However, Bundle also performs another very important function. It passes data back to the activity itself. When the user rotates the device, the displayed activity is destroyed and re-created in the new orientation. So that the user doesn't have to start over if this happens, the activity stores its current state just before it is destroyed in a bundle and passes that data to itself when it re-creates the activity in the new orientation.

3. The `public class` line of code begins the Activity class and declares that this class is referred to as `HelloWorldActivity` and that it is a subclass of the SDK-provided Activity class. Within the class are two methods, `onCreate` and `onCreateOptionsMenu`.

Before each method declaration is @Overide. This annotation tells the compiler that the following method is to be used in place of the super class's method of the same name.

4. The onCreate method is the first method executed by the Activity when it is started. The method has a parameter that is of type Bundle named savedInstanceState. This is the object that contains information on the state of the Activity if it was destroyed in an orientation change as explained earlier. The next line super.onCreate calls the super class's onCreate method. Because this method is overriding the Activity class's inherited onCreate method, it must call that method explicitly to use that functionality to create the Activity. It is passed the savedInstanceState bundle. The final line of code is setContentView(R.layout.*activity_hello_world*). This code tells the activity to use the activity_hello_world.xml file as the layout to be displayed when the activity is running. It is very important to understand the parameter R.layout.*activity_hello_ world*. The R parameter tells the compiler that we want to use a resource from the layout folder named *activity_hello_world*. Whenever we want to access or manipulate a resource, it has to be referred to in this manner. However, this does not refer directly to the res folders; instead it refers to a file generated by the compiler that is named R.java. To see this file, double-click into the gen folder in the Package Explorer until you see it. You should not edit this file because it is automatically generated by the compiler. The onCreate method will be modified with our code to add further functionality to the activity.

5. The onCreateOptionsMenu(Menu menu) method is called when the user clicks the device's Menu button. It returns a Boolean (true or false) value indicating whether the menu was successfully created. The first line of code (getMenuInflator()) gets an object that can create a menu from the running activity. It then tells it to inflate (create) a visual representation of the menu based on the main.xml file in the menu resource folder and refer to it with the name "menu".

Adding Code

Our app has only one function, to display the name entered into the EditText when the Display button is pressed. Enter the code in Listing 3.5 before the last curly bracket in the activity Java file:

Listing 3.5   **Display Button Code**

```
                                                                            //1
private void initDisplayButton() {
    Button displayButton = (Button) findViewById(R.id.buttonDisplay);       //2
    displayButton.setOnClickListener(new OnClickListener () {               //3

        @Override
        public void onClick(View arg0) {
```

```
        EditText editName = (EditText) findViewById(R.id.editTextName);      //4
        TextView textDisplay = (TextView) findViewById(R.id.textViewDisplay); //5
        String nameToDisplay = editName.getText().toString();                //6
        textDisplay.setText("Hello " + nameToDisplay);                       //7
      }
    });
  }
```

This code does the work and illustrates a number of important concepts in Android development.

1. This line declares a new method in the HelloWorldActivity class. The method is only useable by this class (private) and does not return any value (void). The method signature is initDisplayButton(). The signature, or name, of the method is completely up to you. However, you should name it to give some idea what it does.

2. Associate the code with the button on the layout. This line of code declares a variable of type Button that can hold a reference to a button and then gets the button reference using the command findViewById. All widgets on a layout are subclasses of the View class. The method findViewById is used to get a reference to a widget on a layout so it can be used by the code. The method can return any View object, so you have to use (Button) before it to cast the returned View to a Button type before it can be used as a Button by the code. Button is underlined in red after you type it in. This is because the code for the button class is not automatically available in the class. You have to import it. Fortunately, this is easy. Hover your cursor over the underlined word and a menu will pop up. Select Import Button... Do this for any other items underlined in red.

3. Set the button's listener. There are a number of different listeners for widgets, which gives great flexibility when coding app behavior. For this button we use an onClickListener. The code creates a new instance of the listener and then adds a method (public void onClick(View arg0)) to be executed when the button is clicked.

4-5. The code for when the button is clicked gets references to the EditText where the name was entered and the TextView where the message will be displayed.

6. The name entered by the user is retrieved from the EditText and stored in a String variable named nameToDisplay.

7. The text attribute of the TextView is changed to the value of the String variable.

Notice that initDisplayButton() is underlined in yellow. This is because the method is never called by the code. To call it and get the behavior associated with the button to execute, you have to call the method in the onCreate method. After the setContentView line of code enter

initDisplayButton();

The yellow underline goes away and your code is done! Run the app in the emulator using Run > Run Configurations, and click the Run button to test your first app. You could also run your app using Run > Run or by pressing Ctrl+F11.

Connecting Code to UI—Android Versus iOS

In both Android and iOS (iPhone and iPad), the user interface (UI) and the code that makes the UI work are stored in different files. This means that both types of app coding require that the code has to be linked to the UI in some way. The chapters in this book that cover iOS explain the process of "wiring up" an interface using the features of the Xcode IDE. However, in Android, connecting the UI to the code is done entirely in the code itself.

Whenever some code needs to use a widget on a layout, it has to get a reference to it using the `findViewById` command. This requires extra coding but provides great flexibility. Forgetting to connect the code to the UI widget needed in both operating systems will result in a runtime error.

Summary

Congratulations! You have built your first app. You created an Android project, designed and coded a user interface, and, finally, made the app do something. Along the way you learned the process of Android App development, the Eclipse development environment, and the components of an Android app.

Exercises

1. Change the Hello World app to allow the entering of a first and a last name and display "Hello *firstname lastname!*" when the button is clicked. Be sure to label the `EditTexts` to reflect the new data that is to be input.

2. Add a Clear button. The Clear button should remove any data in the `EditText`(s) and change the display back to "Hello world!"

3. Create a new Android Virtual Device that uses a bigger device to test your app on a different screen size. Run the app using the new AVD.

4

Android Navigation and Interface Design

App development for mobile devices is, as discussed in Chapter 2, "App Design Issues and Consider-ations," both similar to and different from development for other platforms. Navigation within an app follows this pattern. Different functionality is provided on different screens (windows in a traditional environment), and the app designer has to both provide the capacity to switch between those screens and make it easy and relatively obvious for users to do so when they want or need to access the func-tionality provided by them. Likewise, screen design is both similar to and different from the traditional user interface design. In a traditional environment, a window design is made up of a set of visible objects that give the user the ability to accomplish some component of the overall task. This is the same in the mobile environment. However, the objects available for design differ in both form and function, the amount of screen real estate available is much more limited, and often the amount of real estate available changes among devices that can use your app. This chapter introduces you to many of the principles and components of interface design and navigation in the Android platform. To learn these things, the chapter guides you through the development of MyContactList navigation and the develop-ment of the Contact interface.

Activities, Layouts, and Intents

The primary structural components for an Android app are `Activities` and `Layouts`. These objects work together to present a display that the user can interact with. `Intents` are objects that are used to switch between activities in an app. All three objects are used as the basis for the structure of your app. Understanding the role and responsibilities of these objects is very important to effective development of an Android app.

The `Activity` Class

The `Activity` class is designed to handle a single task that the user can perform. Activities almost always have a visible component that allows the user to interact with the activity to perform the task. The `Activity` class is not directly instantiated in an Android app. Rather, it is subclassed for every activity that the user needs to perform in the app. These subclasses are stored as `.java` files in the app project's `src` folder. This allows developers to inherit all the functionality of the `Activity` class and add their own unique functionality through Java code. One of the most important inherited functions of the `Activity` class is the capability to respond to life cycle events such as `onCreate` and `onPause` (refer to Chapter 2 for a discussion of the Android life cycle).

The `Activity` class has a number of important subclasses. Only two of these subclasses are used in this book. The first of these is `FragmentActivity`. Fragments were a new addition to the Android OS in the `HoneyComb` version (SDK 11). Fragments allow the developer to include multiple tasks or panes within a single activity. If you are targeting only versions of Android later than SDK 11, you're not likely to use the `FragmentActivity` subclass because this class is used to make an app backward compatible to OS versions earlier than 11. Because this book's focus is to build apps that may be run on as many devices as possible, SDK 8 is used as the minimum rather than 11. Therefore, in addition to the `Activity` class, at times you will need to use the `FragmentActivity` class. Map objects require the use of the `FragmentActivity` subclass. You will use this class in Chapter 7, "Maps and Location in Android," when you implement the map functionality of your app.

The second `Activity` subclass you will use is `ListActivity`. `ListActivity` is designed to specifically support the development of a list interface. A list is a very useful way to present a large amount of data in a manner that makes it easy for users to navigate through to find the data they are interested in. The `ListFragment` class is used in Chapter 6, "Lists in Android: Navigation and Information Display," when you implement the contact list functionality of your app.

Layout

A layout is the visual component of a user interface in Android. The layout is not a class but rather an XML file that is used to tell the operating system what visual objects are to be displayed, how those objects are configured, and where those objects should be displayed on the screen. The XML in the file does use objects. The objects that make up an Android interface are referred to as *widgets*. Widgets are subclasses of the `View` class. Android widgets include widgets to define where other widgets are displayed (for example, `RelativeLayout`), to directly interact with the user (for example, `RadioButton`), and to provide some type of navigation within the interfaces (for example, `ScrollView`). Developing an understanding of the layout XML is a critically important task for the new Android developer.

Layouts can also be defined at runtime by instantiating the widgets that make up an interface and configuring them as needed. This can be very useful in some cases. However, designing the interface is more difficult because you cannot see the layout until you run the app. You will be designing your interface with XML in this book rather than at runtime.

Intents

An `Intent` is a class that is used to describe an operation to be performed. `Intents` are the primary way in which the developer starts new activities within the app. This is how you will use them in the app you develop for this book. However, `Intents` can also be used to communicate between activities. An `Intent` is essentially a message that defines an action to be taken and the data that the action is to be performed on. `Intents` can be used to start activities or broadcast both within and outside the app to provide instructions and data to other activities.

Activities, layouts, and intents are important components of an Android app. You will use all of them in almost every app you develop.

Creating the Interface

The MyContactList app requires four activities and four layouts to provide the functionality described in Chapter 2. The app will use `Intents` to switch between activities and pass data between these activities. Your first task in creating the MyContactsList app is to make sure you have access to the image resources provided with this book. You will need four image files. One image is the app icon (appicon.png) and the other three are used in the app for navigation (contactlisticon.png, settingsicon.png, mapicon.png). Every app needs a project, and MyContactList is not different. Your second task is to create a new project.

Importing a Project

The completed project for each chapter is available in the online resources for this book (https://github.com/LearningMobile/BookApps). You can import the project by following these steps:

1. Unzip the chapter code.
2. Create a new project by selecting File > New > Android > Android Project from Existing Code. Click Next.
3. Use the Browse button to navigate to the unzipped code folder. Select MyContactList, check Copy Projects into Workspace, and click Finish.

The project will be created in your workspace. You will have to set up a Run Configuration to execute the app. If you don't want to import the whole project, you can inspect the different files by navigating through the MyContactList folder.

Sometimes when importing a project, Eclipse has problems. If your imported project will not run, do the following:

1. Right-click the project name and select Properties > Java Build Path.
2. Click the Order and Export tab.
3. Check Android Private Libraries. Click OK.
4. Clean the project (Project > Clean).

Create the Project

Create a new Android project by selecting File > New > Android Application project.

1. Use the following values for the first window presented by the project creation wizard:

    Application Name: MyContactList

    Project Name: MyContactList

    Package Name: com.example.mycontactlist

    Minimum Required SDK: API 8

    Target SDK: API 17

    Compile with: API 17

    Theme: None

2. Click Next. Accept the defaults on this screen by clicking Next again.

3. On the Configure Launcher Icon window, use the Browse button to select appicon.png from the location where you placed the resource files (available online). Click Next.

4. On the Create Activity window, verify that Blank Activity is selected, and click Next.

5. Change the name of the activity to ContactActivity in the Blank Activity window. Make sure the navigation type is set to none. The navigation is coded by you later in the chapter. Click Finish.

To code the navigation, you need more than one activity. Create three more blank activities using the following process. Expand your MyContactList project in the Package Explorer. Expand the src folder. Expand the com.example.mycontactlist folder so that you can see ContactActivity.java. Right-click com.example.mycontactlist (Figure 4.1).

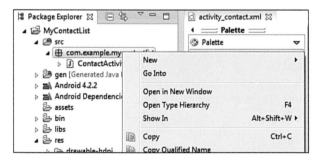

Figure 4.1   Adding a new activity.

1. Select New > Other. The Select a Wizard window displays. Expand the Android section and double-click on Android Activity.

2. Select Blank Activity and click Next. Enter ContactListActivity for the name of the activity and Contact List as the title (Figure 4.2). Click Finish.

Figure 4.2   New Activity properly configured.

3. A new file, ContactListActivity.java, is entered in the Package Explorer right below ContactActivity.java. If it is somewhere else, right-click the file and click Delete. Start over. The file must be in the source code folder for your package, or the app will not run correctly.

Repeat this process to add another two activities to your project. Give the activities the names ContactMapActivity and ContactSettingsActivity. Set their titles to Contacts Map and Settings, respectively. Find the res folder in the Package Explorer and expand the layouts folder. You should have four layout XML files, one for each activity.

Create the Navigation Bar

The navigation bar for the MyContactList app sits at the bottom of the screen and allows the user to quickly move between different functions in the app by tapping one of the images on the bar (Figure 4.3). The navigation bar is made up of three ImageButtons contained within a RelativeLayout. The RelativeLayout is set to be just big enough to hold the three buttons and placed within the root RelativeLayout that was placed in the layout file by the wizard when you created the activity. The navigation layout is anchored to the bottom of that layout so that it always appears at the bottom of the screen.

Figure 4.3   Complete navigation bar layout.

ImageButtons can only use image files that are within the project. To add the images to the project:

1. Right-click on the drawable-hdpi folder in the res folder and select Import from the pop-up menu.

2. In the Import window that opens, expand the General folder and select File System. Click Next.

3. Click the Browse button in the File System window and navigate to the location where you placed the contactlisticon.png, settingsicon.png, and mapicon.png files.

4. Click the check box next to each image you want to import and click Finish. Expand the drawable-hdpi folder to verify the import.

5. Open the activity_contact.xml file if it is not already open by double-clicking it in the Package Explorer. Make sure that it is open in the Graphical Layout in the Editor window.

6. Click the Hello World! TextView and delete it.

7. Open the Layouts folder in the Palette to the left of the Graphical Layout. Locate the RelativeLayout and drag it onto the MyContactList layout. Position the layout anywhere on the screen. The exact location is set by you in the XML later in this chapter. The size of the layout is very small because the default layout_height and layout_ width attributes are initially set to "wrap_content." Initially, the layout has no widgets in it so it sizes very small. This makes it difficult to place widgets within it. Fortunately there are approaches to working around this issue. Open the Images and Media folder in the Palette and make sure that the Outline display is visible on the right side of the editor (Figure 4.4).

8. Click and drag an ImageButton from the Palette across the editor to the outline. Position the cursor on the indented RelativeLayout below the root RelativeLayout and release. A window opens that allows the selection of the image.

9. Select contactlisticon and click OK. The outline should look like the right side of Figure 4.4, and the button with the icon is displayed in the Graphical Layout.

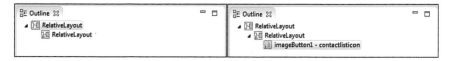

Figure 4.4   Outline before and after ImageButton drag and drop.

Now that the `RelativeLayout` has some content, it is easier to work with.

1. Switch to the activity_contact.xml view in the editor. Locate `relativeLayout1`'s `layout_width` attribute and change its value from `"wrap_content"` to `"fill_parent"`.

2. Switch back to Graphical Layout. Click relativeLayout1 in the Outline. A much bigger layout should be highlighted. Drag another image button to the right of the first one and select the mapicon image.

3. Repeat step 2 for the last button. Use the settingsicon image and make sure it is positioned to the right of the mapicon button.

The layout may look a little strange, but that's okay for now; final configuration will be done with XML. However, before you do that, you have to create a color resource to give the layout the proper background color.

To create a color resource, navigate to the `values` folder in the `res` folder and right-click it. Select New > Other from the pop-up menu and complete the following steps:

1. Expand the Android folder in the Select a Wizard window and select Android XML Values File. Click Next.

2. Type "color" into the File: text box. Click Finish.

3. The Android Resource editor opens in the editor window. Click the Add button. Select @ Color in the window that opens and click OK.

4. Type "navbar_background" for the Name and "#1a1a48" for the value. Switch to the XML view by clicking the color.xml tab at the bottom of the editor. Your XML should look like that in Listing 4.1.

Listing 4.1   **Resource XML**

```xml
<?xml version="1.0" encoding="utf-8"?>
<resources>
    <color name="navbar_background">#1a1a48</color>
</resources>
```

Close the color resource file by clicking the x to the right of the color.xml name tab at the top of the editor. Be sure to click Yes to save the changes. Switch to activity_contact.xml. The rest of the navigation bar will be configured in XML.

Several changes need to be made to the XML to give the navigation bar the correct look. First, you will change the default layout of the whole screen. Second, the navigation bar `RelativeLayout` is modified to position it at the bottom of the screen and have the blue background color. Finally, the layout of the `ImageButtons` are modified to center the middle button and position the other two buttons around it. Refer to Listing 4.2 to complete the navigation bar.

Listing 4.2   **Activity_Contact.xml**

```
                                                                                    //1
<RelativeLayout xmlns:android="http://schemas.android.com/apk/res/android"
    xmlns:tools="http://schemas.android.com/tools"
    android:layout_width="match_parent"
    android:layout_height="match_parent"
    tools:context=".ContactActivity" >

                                                                                    //2
    <RelativeLayout
        android:id="@+id/navbar"
        android:background="@color/navbar_background"
        android:layout_width="fill_parent"
        android:layout_height="wrap_content"
        android:layout_alignParentBottom="true" >

                                                                                    //3
        <ImageButton
            android:id="@+id/imageButtonList"
            android:layout_width="wrap_content"
            android:layout_height="wrap_content"
            android:layout_centerVertical="true"
            android:layout_toLeftOf="@+id/imageButtonMap"
            android:layout_marginRight="20dp"
            android:src="@drawable/contactlisticon" />

                                                                                    //4
        <ImageButton
            android:id="@+id/imageButtonMap"
            android:layout_width="wrap_content"
            android:layout_height="wrap_content"
            android:layout_centerVertical="true"
            android:layout_centerHorizontal="true"
            android:src="@drawable/mapicon" />

                                                                                    //5
        <ImageButton
            android:id="@+id/imageButtonSettings"
            android:layout_width="wrap_content"
            android:layout_height="wrap_content"
```

```
        android:layout_centerVertical="true"
        android:layout_marginLeft="20dp"
        android:layout_toRightOf="@+id/imageButtonMap"
        android:src="@drawable/settingsicon" />

    </RelativeLayout>
</RelativeLayout>
```

Very specific changes need to be made to the XML to get the desired look. The following explains the changes to each widget in the activity_contact.xml.

1. The first change is to the default layout attributes of the whole screen. By default, the Blank Activity Wizard puts padding around the layout. To use the whole screen, these attributes have to be removed. Locate the `paddingBottom`, `paddingTop`, `paddingLeft`, and `paddingRight` attributes in the root `RelativeLayout` and delete them.

2. The `RelativeLayout` that contains the `ImageButton` is changed to a position at the bottom of the layout and is given a dark blue background and a meaningful ID.

   a. Add an `id` attribute using this code: `android:id=@+id/navbar`.

   b. Add the `background` attribute and set its value to `"@color/navbar_background."` This refers to the color resource file previously created.

   c. Add the `layout_alignParentBottom` attribute and set its value to "true." This tells Android to always position the layout at the bottom of the screen regardless of any other widgets in the layout.

   d. Finally, remove all other attributes not shown in the listing. These are left over from the random positioning of the layout when it was first dragged to the layout.

3. The two image buttons on either end of the navigation bar are positioned relative to the middle button, which is centered in the layout. All buttons are given meaningful IDs.

   a. Change the id of the first button to `"@+id/imageButtonList."`

   b. Add the attribute `layout_toLeftOf` and set its value to `"@+id/imageButtonMap."`

   c. Add the attribute `layout_marginRight` and set its value to `"20dp"` to position it to the right of the centered Map button.

   d. Add the attribute `centerVertical` and set its value to `"true."`

   e. Remove all other attributes not shown in the listing. Note the `src` attribute and its value. This is where the image file is associated with the `ImageButton`. The image can be changed by changing its value.

4.-5. Modify the remaining buttons in a similar way to match the XML in the listing.

> **Note**
>
> You may get two warnings after you have completed the preceding changes. The first warns that the `RelativeLayout` may be useless. This is because you have a `RelativeLayout` within a `RelativeLayout` that has no other objects in it. After you add other objects later in this chapter, this warning will go away. The second warning is "Missing contentDescription attribute on image." The `contentDescription` value is used by alternative access modes, such as a screen reader that describes what is on the screen. You can safely ignore this warning. If you want your app to be accessible in a nonvisual manner, include the following in your `ImageButton` XML: `android:contentDescription="your description of the image"`.

Switch to the Graphical Layout view. The navigation bar should be dark blue, positioned at the bottom of the screen, and the map button should be positioned in the center. If this is not the case, review the XML to make sure it matches Listing 4.2.

When the navigation bar is properly configured, you can copy it into each of the other three layouts. Switch to activity_contact.xml, and then highlight and copy all the XML that defines the navigation bar. Be sure to include the start `<RelativeLayout` and end `</RelativeLayout>` tags. Open the activity_contact_list.xml file in the layouts folder by double-clicking it. Switch to the XML and delete all the XML associated with the "Hello World" `TextView` that was automatically generated when you created the `Activity`. Paste the copied code just before the last `</RelativeLayout>` tag in the file. Delete the padding attributes in the root `RelativeLayout`. Switch to Graphical Layout to verify that the navigation bar is properly displayed. Close the file and repeat the process to add the navigation bar to activity_contact_map.xml and activity_contact_settings.xml.

Create the Contact Layout

The contact activity provides functionality associated with adding and modifying information about individual contacts. Although it is the most complicated layout in the MyContactsList app, it also demonstrates the use and configuration of a significant number of interface elements available in the Android platform. The relative nature of Android layouts makes development challenging; however, the concepts discussed in this chapter should help make the creation of a layout routine.

There are three major sections in this layout. The navigation bar completed in the previous section is one of these. One of the other two is another `RelativeLayout` at the top of the screen to display the buttons that allow the user to access overall functionality for the screen—in other words, a layout that will function as a toolbar. The other is a `ScrollView` that holds all the widgets that allow the user to enter information about a contact. A `ScrollView` is used to ensure that users can access all the data entry widgets regardless of the size of their device.

Create the Toolbar

The toolbar consists of a `RelativeLayout` positioned at the top of the root layout, a `ToggleButton` to switch between editing and viewing modes, and a `Button` to allow the user to save changes to the contact's information. Open activity_contact.xml if it is not already open. Switch to Graphical Layout and drag a `RelativeLayout` to the screen. Don't worry about its position, but do not put it on the navigation bar. Again the `RelativeLayout` is very small, so you'll have to use the Outline to load the first widget. Open the Form Widgets folder in Palette and locate the `ToggleButton` widget (the one that says Off). Drag the `ToggleButton` to the new `RelativeLayout` in the Outline.

Switch to the XML view and change the `RelativeLayout`'s `layout_width` attribute's value to `"match_parent"`. Switch back to Graphical Layout and drag a `Button` to the right of the `ToggleButton`. The last thing to do before switching to XML to configure the toolbar is to create another color resource for the toolbar's background. Double-click the color.xml file. If the file opens to XML, click the Resource tab at the bottom of the editor and click the Add button. Add the color resource with the name "toolbar_background" and value "#bebebe". Save and close the color resource file.

Switch to XML view and refer to Listing 4.3 to modify the XML so that the toolbar appears at the top of the screen with the proper size and widget spacing.

Listing 4.3   **Toolbar XML**

```
                                                                    //1
<RelativeLayout
    android:id= "@+id/toolbar"
    android:background= "@color/toolbar_background"
    android:layout_width= "match_parent"
    android:layout_height= "wrap_content"
    android:layout_alignParentLeft= "true"
    android:layout_alignParentTop= "true" >
                                                                    //2
    <ToggleButton
        android:id= "@+id/toggleButtonEdit"
        android:layout_width= "wrap_content"
        android:layout_height= "wrap_content"
        android:layout_alignParentLeft= "true"
        android:layout_marginLeft= "20dp"
        android:text= "ToggleButton" />
                                                                    //3
    <Button
        android:id= "@+id/buttonSave"
        android:layout_width= "wrap_content"
        android:layout_height= "wrap_content"
        android:layout_alignParentRight= "true"
        android:layout_marginRight= "20dp"
        android:text= "Save" />

</RelativeLayout>
```

There are only a limited number of new attributes to discuss in the XML. Make sure your toolbar XML matches the listing.

1. The `layout_alignParentTop` attribute locks the relative layout to always appear at the top of the devices screen. The `layout_alignParentLeft` locks the `RelativeLayout` to lock its left edge to the left edge of the screen. Technically, the `alignParent` attributes do not lock to the screen but refer to the containing layout. Since the root `RelativeLayout` is the containing layout it has the effect of locking to the screen edges.

2-3. The `layout_alignParentLeft` and `layout_alignParentRight` attributes used in the `ToggleButton` and the `Button` refer to the toolbar `RelativeLayout` as the parent. With these attributes set to true it does not matter where the layout is placed. They will always remain fixed to those positions within the layout.

Switch to Graphical Layout. The toolbar should appear at the top of the screen with a gray background (see Figure 4.5).

Figure 4.5   Complete toolbar layout.

Create the Data Entry Form

The data entry portion of the ContactActivity allows users to enter information on their contacts. The data entry form primarily relies on the `EditText` and `TextView` widgets that were introduced in the Hello World! app. New concepts introduced include configuring the `EditTexts` to limit and format the input, movement (tabbing) through the data entry widgets, using a custom pop-up window to enter the birthday with a `DatePicker` widget, and using a `ScrollView` to expand the "real estate" available. The Birthday button and its functionality shown on the screen in Chapter 2 are added in Chapter 8, "Access to Hardware and Sensors in Android."

Open the activity_contact.xml file (if it is not open) and switch to Graphical Layout. Open the Composite folder in the Palette. Drag a `ScrollView` to anyplace between the toolbar and the navigation bar. Notice that just like the `RelativeLayout`, the `ScrollView` is too small to be useful. Switch to activity_contact.xml to edit the XML so that it is usable. Refer to Listing 4.4 to properly configure the `ScrollView`.

Listing 4.4   **ScrollView XML**

```
                                                                    //1
<ScrollView
    android:id="@+id/scrollView1"
    android:layout_width="match_parent"
```

```
    android:layout_height="wrap_content"
    android:layout_alignParentLeft="true"
    android:layout_below="@+id/toolbar"
    android:layout_above="@+id/navbar"   >
```
                                                                        //2
```
    <RelativeLayout
        android:layout_width="match_parent"
        android:layout_height="match_parent" >

    </RelativeLayout>
</ScrollView>
```

Examine the XML on your screen. Notice that it is somewhat different from Listing 4.4. These differences are explained below. Change your XML to match Listing 4.4.

1. The `layout_width` attribute is changed to `"match_parent"` to use the full screen. The height is left as `"wrap_content"` to allow the ScrollView to expand or contract based on its contents and the device size. The margin attributes are eliminated to allow the use of the full screen. Finally, the `layout_above` attribute is added to prevent the ScrollView from overwriting the navigation bar.

2. By default, the `ScrollView` has a `LinearLayout` as its only contents. `ScrollViews` can have only one widget as their contents. However, if that widget is some type of layout, more widgets can be added as long as they are within that layout. `LinearLayouts` allow a simple display of widgets one right after the other either vertically or horizontally. To get a more complex display, the `LinearLayout` is replaced with a `RelativeLayout`. You could do this by deleting the `LinearLayout` and then dragging a `RelativeLayout` onto the `ScrollView`. However, it is far easier just to change the XML. Change your XML to match that in the listing.

After making the changes to the XML, switch back to Graphical Layout. The basic structure of the data input screen is complete. The next step is to add the widgets that the user can interact with to save contact information.

Open the Form Widgets folder in the Palette and drag a Small `TextView` (Small Text) onto the `ScrollView`. You might have trouble with this. The `ScrollView` is set to be the area between the toolbar and the navigation bar. However, you cannot place a widget in the `ScrollView` because it already has its one widget, the `RelativeLayout`. Although the `RelativeLayout` is set to match the parent `ScrollView`'s height and width, the lack of content is making it wrap its content to a very small area. If you are having problems, drag the `TextView` to the `RelativeLayout` in the `ScrollView` in the Outline area instead. Then switch to XML view and modify the `TextViews` attributes so that its ID is `textContact`, is aligned to the top and left of its parent, and it has a left margin of `10dp`, a top margin of `5dp`, and displays `Contact:` as its text.

Add an `EditText` for the user to enter the contact name. Open the Text Fields folder in the Palette and drag an `abc EditText` to underneath the `TextView`. Switch to the XML and refer to Listing 4.5 to configure the `EditText`.

Listing 4.5   **Contact Name EditText XML**

```
<EditText
    android:id="@+id/editName"
    android:layout_width="wrap_content"
    android:layout_height="wrap_content"
    android:layout_alignParentLeft="true"
    android:layout_marginLeft="10dp"
    android:layout_below="@+id/textContact"
android:ems="14"                                              //1
android:imeOptions="actionNext"                               //2
android:inputType="textCapWords" >                            //3

<requestFocus />                                              //4
</EditText>
```

Modify the XML as shown. You have worked with many of the attributes already. However, a few require additional explanation:

1. The `ems` attribute tells Android how big the `EditText` should be. The unit `ems` is the number of capital M's that could fit into the widget. It often takes some experimentation with the number to get the widget to size the way you'd like it.

2. The `imeOptions="actionNext"` attribute/value pair tells Android to show a Next button on the soft keyboard. When the user presses that button, focus will move to the next `EditText`. This is how tabbing is implemented in Android apps.

3. The `inputType` attribute tells Android what type of keyboard to display and how to format the data as its entered. The value `textCapWords` tells Android to display an alpha keyboard and to capitalize each word as it's entered.

4. The final item in the XML `<requestFocus />` is not an attribute. It is a tag to tell Android to put the cursor in this widget when the layout is displayed. You should have only one of these in a single layout file.

Switch back to Graphical Layout to review the impact of the changes. Switch back to the XML. The next widget will be added completely through XML. Locate the TextView XML and copy all of it from the <TextView initial tag and including the /> closing tag. Paste it after the EditText XML. Modify the XML to match Listing 4.6.

Listing 4.6   **Address TextView XML**

```
<TextView
    android:id="@+id/textAddress"
    android:layout_width="wrap_content"
    android:layout_height="wrap_content"
    android:layout_alignParentLeft="true"
    android:layout_below="@+id/editName"
    android:layout_marginLeft="10dp"
    android:layout_marginTop="15dp"
    android:text="Address:"
    android:textAppearance="?android:attr/textAppearanceSmall" />
```

Next, copy all the `EditText` XML and paste it after the `TextView` XML. Be sure to include the `</EditText>` closing tag. Delete the `<requestFocus />` tag. Refer to Listing 4.7 to configure the XML.

Listing 4.7   **Address EditText XML**

```
<EditText
    android:id="@+id/editAddress"
    android:layout_width="wrap_content"
    android:layout_height="wrap_content"
    android:layout_alignParentLeft="true"
    android:layout_marginLeft="10dp"
    android:layout_below="@+id/textAddress"
    android:ems="14"
    android:imeOptions="actionNext"
    android:inputType="textCapWords" >

</EditText>
```

Switch to Graphical Layout. Your layout should look like Figure 4.6. If it does not, return to the XML and verify your settings.

The next step is to add the three `EditTexts` required to enter the city, state and zip code of the contact. Drag and drop or copy XML to add these widgets to your layout. Refer to Table 4.1 for parameter values for each `EditText`. Attributes that have a value "---" in the table should not be included for that particular widget. The table introduces three new attributes. The `layout_toRightOf` attribute is used in place of the `layout_below` attribute to position a widget next to another widget. The `layout_alignBottom` attribute tells Android to lay out the widgets so that their bottom edges match, regardless of height or width of the widget. Some input has a limited number of characters that should be entered. The `maxLength` attribute is how the developer limits the number of characters that can be entered into an `EditText`. Finally, the `nextFocusDown` attribute is used when it is difficult for Android to figure out which of the `EditTexts` should get focus next. This attribute is used to specifically identify which widget should get focus after the current one.

Figure 4.6   Contact layout.

Table 4.1   **Attribute Values of City, State, and Zip Code `EditTexts`**

Widget	City	State	Zip Code
Attribute			
+id	editCity	editState	editZipcode
layout_width	wrap_content	wrap_content	wrap_content
layout_height	wrap_content	wrap_content	wrap_content
layout_alignParentLeft	true	—	—
layout_marginLeft	10dp	—	—
layout_below	@+id/editAddress	—	—
layout_toRightOf	—	@+id/editCity	@+id/editState
layout_alignBottom	—	@+id/editCity	@+id/editState
ems	8	2	4

Widget	City	State	Zip Code
maxLength	—	2	5
imeOptions	actionNext	actionNext	actionNext
nextFocusDown	@+id/editState	@+id/editZipcode	@+id/editHome
inputType	textCapWords	textCapCharacters	numberSigned

Verify with Graphical Layout that the interface looks like Figure 4.7. If everything looks correct, the next step is to add the phone number fields. You will need to add two TextViews and two EditTexts to the layout for the phone information. Configure the widgets using the information in Table 4.2

Table 4.2   **Attribute Values of Phone Widgets**

Widget	Home Text	Home Edit	Cell Text	Cell Edit
Attribute				
+id	textHome	editHome	textCell	editCell
text	Home Phone:	—	Cell Phone:	—
layout_width	wrap_content	wrap_content	wrap_content	wrap_content
layout_height	wrap_content	wrap_content	wrap_content	wrap_content
layout_alignParentLeft	true	true	—	—
layout_marginLeft	10dp	10dp	—	—
layout_marginTop	15dp	—	—	—
layout_below	@+id/editCity	@+id/textHome	—	—
layout_toRightOf	—	—	—	@+id/editHome
layout_alignBottom	—	—	@+id/textHome	@+id/editHome
layout_alignLeft	—	—	@+id/editCell	—
ems	—	7	—	7
maxLength	—	14	—	14
imeOptions	—	actionNext	—	actionNext
nextFocusDown	—	@+id/editCell	—	@+id/editEMail
inputType	—	phone	—	phone

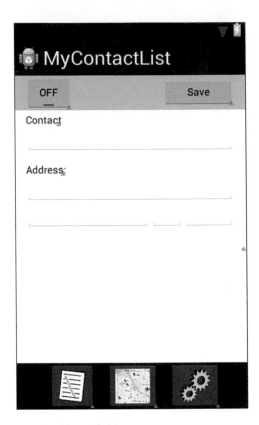

Figure 4.7   Contact layout with address fields.

The phone number labels (TextViews) are above the EditTexts used for input of those phone numbers. This layout poses challenges because the size of the EditText inputs can and will change based on the device the user runs the app on. Given that, you cannot set the labels at a fixed position because the inputs below them will change and no longer align with their labels. This makes the interface look sloppy.

The solution implemented in XML provided earlier is to align the cell phone label with the bottom of the home phone label, but rather than position it to the right of the home phone label, you align it with the left edge of the cell phone input. That way, as the EditTexts change size, the Cell Phone: label will always be directly above the cell phone input. A new attribute value/pair, layout_alignLeft="@+id/editCell, is used to implement this solution. One other item of note in these widgets is the maxLength attribute of the EditTexts. Note that they are set at 14 rather than 10, which is the number of digits in a U.S. phone number. The maxLength of input is the total length, including formatting and spaces. When formatting is added to the phone number, the input length becomes greater than 10. For example, a phone number formatted as (111) 222-4444 would be 14 characters long. When completed, your layout should look like Figure 4.8.

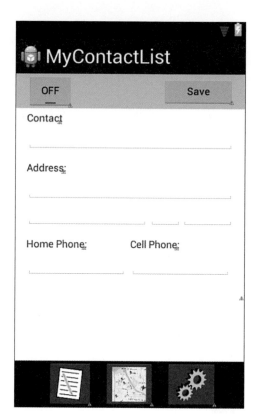

Figure 4.8   Contact layout with phone fields.

The final elements of the contact activity layout are the email and birthdate inputs. You need a TextView and an EditText for the email input and two TextViews and a Button for the birthday input. One of the birthday TextViews will be used to display the birth date and the Button will be used to open a pop-up window. Configure these widgets as identified in Table 4.3 and Table 4.4.

Table 4.3   **Attribute Values of Email Widgets**

Widget	Email Text	Email Edit
Attribute		
+id	textEMail	editEMail
Text	E-Mail Address:	—
layout_width	wrap_content	wrap_content
layout_height	wrap_content	wrap_content

Widget	Email Text	Email Edit
layout_alignParentLeft	true	true
layout_marginLeft	10dp	10dp
layout_marginTop	15dp	—
layout_below	@+id/editHome	@+id/textEMail
ems	—	13
inputType	—	textEmailAddress

Table 4.4   **Attribute Values of Birthday Widgets**

Widget	Birthday Text	Date Text	Button
Attribute			
+id	textBday	textBirthday	btnBirthday
text	Birthday:	01/01/1970	Change
layout_width	wrap_content	wrap_content	wrap_content
layout_height	wrap_content	wrap_content	wrap_content
layout_alignParentLeft	true	—	—
layout_alignParentRight	—	—	true
layout_marginLeft	10dp	10dp	—
layout_marginRight	—	—	10dp
layout_marginTop	15dp	—	—
layout_below	@+id/editEMail	—	—
layout_toRightOf	—	@+id/textBday	—
layout_alignBottom	—	@+id/textBday	—
layout_alignBaseline	—	—	@+id/textBirthday
paddingBottom	25dp	25dp	—

The Change Birthday button uses several new attributes. The button should be anchored to the right side of the screen so that its position doesn't change as the birthday value changes. To do this, you use the `layout_alignParentRight="true"` attribute/value pair, and to make it have a margin from the screen, you use the `layout_marginRight="10dp"` attribute/value pair. The birthday widgets are all on one line. To make this work, the `layout_toRightOf` and `layout_alignBottom` attributes are used with the birthday date display `TextView`. However, the button is aligned to the right of the screen with the attribute previously discussed. To make it line up with other widgets, a new attribute, `layout_alignBaseline`, is used. This aligns the center of the button with the bottom of the widget it refers to. Because a button is bigger than the other widgets, aligning it bottom to bottom would make it tall enough on the screen to cover a portion of the email `EditText`. Finally, the `paddingBottom="25dp"` attribute/value pair provides whitespace in the `ScrollView` after the last widget. Without this, the birthday widgets would be appear right above the navigation bar and the button would be partially hidden by it. Test this yourself by executing the app on the emulator before you add the padding attribute. To test on the emulator, you have to create a new Run Configuration like you did for the Hello World app, except this one would use the MyContactList as the project. If you are using the same workspace as you did for Chapter 3, "Using Eclipse for Android Development," you do not have to create a new virtual device. You can select the same device as you did in that chapter. Remember that you also need to start the emulator. When the layout is displayed on the emulator, click and hold on any whitespace in the layout and drag to the top of the emulator screen. Try it again after you add the padding.

When the layout is complete, verify that it looks like Figure 4.9. Examine the bottom of the figure closely. The `ScrollView` was selected (surrounded by a thin blue line) before the screenshot was taken. Notice that the bottom blue line runs through the navigation bar. This is where the bottom of the Change button would be if the `paddingBottom` attribute had not been added. In other words, it would have been partially obscured by the navigation bar.

Congratulations! You have completed your first real layout in Android. However, there is one more layout task to complete before writing code to make the layout do something—that is to create a layout for the birthday selection dialog box.

Create the Dialog Layout

Although Android provides a `DatePickerDialog` class that provides the functionality needed, you are going to create the dialog from scratch to learn how to create and use custom dialogs in an app. The birthday selection date dialog is relatively simple. It displays a `DatePicker` widget, which allows the user to select a specific date, and Cancel and OK buttons. Development of this pop-up introduces the use of two new layouts, `LinearLayout` and `TableLayout`.

Begin by adding a new XML layout file to the project.

1. Right-click the layouts folder in the Package Explorer and select New > Other from the pop-up menu.

2. Expand the Android folder in the window that opens, and double-click Android XML Layout file. Enter dateselect as the name of this new layout.

3. Click Finish, and the new layout will open in the editor and dateselect.xml will be displayed in the layout folder of the Package Explorer.

The wizard creates the layout file with a `LinearLayout` with a vertical orientation as its root layout. This means that all widgets added will be stacked on top of the other. To see this, drag a `DatePicker` object from the Time & Date folder in the Palette and then two small buttons. Notice that whatever you do, they always end up one on top of another. This is not the best design for OK and Cancel buttons! This problem will be fixed by using a `TableLayout`. Leave the `DatePicker`, but delete the two buttons. Then open the Layouts folder in the Palette and drag a `TableLayout` to the editor, making sure it is positioned after the `DatePicker`. The layout is empty, but you can see where it is because it is highlighted with a thin blue rectangle.

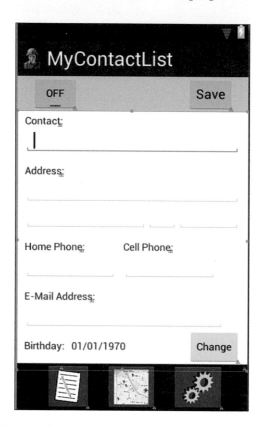

Figure 4.9   Completed contact layout.

> **Note**
>
> Adding the `DatePicker` to the layout may cause an error screen to show up at the bottom of the editor. You can ignore this. Although it says it can't find the `DatePicker` class, it will at runtime. This is a bug in some versions of Eclipse.

Examine the Outline. Notice that the `TableLayout` also contains some `TableRows`. If there is more than one row, delete the extras by right-clicking them in the Outline and selecting Delete from the pop-up menu. Drag two buttons to the remaining `TableRow` either on the editor or in the Outline. Verify that they are in the proper position by looking at the Outline (Figure 4.10). Switch to dateselect.xml to configure the widgets.

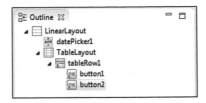

Figure 4.10   Outline after adding buttons.

The modifications to this XML are relatively simple as compared to the data entry form.

1. Add an `id` attribute to the `LinearLayout` with the value `@+id/dateSelectLayout`. An ID is needed for this layout to be able to tell the pop-up window what layout to display.

2. Change the ID of the `DatePicker` widget to `@+id/birthdayPicker`.

3. Add the following attribute to the `DatePicker` just after the `id` attribute: `android:calendarViewShown="false"`. Some versions of the Android OS will automatically show a picker and a calendar if this line is not included.

4. Change the id's and text attribute values for the first and second buttons to `@+id/btnCancel`, `Cancel` and `@+id/btnOk`, `Ok`, respectively.

5. Switch to Graphical Layout to view the results. Notice that the two buttons have different sizes. This is a problem for usability. It makes the interface look asymmetrical and one button more difficult to select than the other.

6. Switch back to the XML and change the `layout_width` attribute of both buttons from `wrap_content` to `120dp`.

7. Switch back to Graphical Layout. If the buttons are the same size, your pop-up layout is complete (Figure 4.11)!

Figure 4.11   Completed pop-up layout.

The DatePicker widget will display only at runtime. However, you don't write the code to open the dialog until later in this chapter, so you will have to wait to test it. When you do run the app you should see something like Figure 4.12 when you change the contact's birthday.

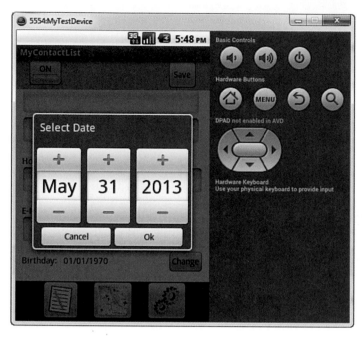

Figure 4.12   DatePicker displayed in running app.

Activating the Interface

The primary function of the Contact activity is to save information about the user's contacts. The saving of data is beyond the scope of this chapter but is addressed in the next chapter. However, other functions can be implemented at this time. This section demonstrates the coding of the navigation bar, coding the toggle button to switch between editing and viewing modes, coding the Change Birthday button to display the dialog window, and coding the dialog.

Code the Navigation Bar

Movement and data transfer between activities is done with Intents as discussed earlier in this chapter. The use of Intents makes coding navigation relatively simple. The Intent does most of the work. Open the ContactActivity.java file in the src folder by double-clicking it.

Begin by coding the List `ImageButton`. Enter the code in Listing 4.8 before the last } in the ContactActivity.java file.

Listing 4.8   **List Button Code**

```
private void initListButton() {                                                //1
    ImageButton list = (ImageButton) findViewById(R.id.imageButtonList);       //2
    list.setOnClickListener(new View.OnClickListener() {
        public void onClick(View v) {
            Intent intent = new Intent(ContactActivity.this,                    //3
                    ⮕ContactListActivity.class);
            intent.setFlags(Intent.FLAG_ACTIVITY_CLEAR_TOP);                    //4
            startActivity(intent);
        }
    });
}
```

When you enter the code, some of the objects may be underlined in red. This indicates that the compiler doesn't know what that object is. To fix this, rest your pointer on the underlined object and select the Import statement from the list of hints that appear. If there is no Import option, it is likely that you misspelled the object name. This code is used to associate the `ImageButton` named `imageButtonList` on the `activity_contact` layout with the code that is executed when it is pressed.

1. A variable to hold an `ImageButton` is declared and `findViewById` gets the widget named `imageButtonList`. FindViewById returns the widget as a generic object, so it must be cast `(ImageButton)` to an `ImageButton` before it can be assigned to the variable.

2. A listener is added to the `ImageButton`. A listener makes a widget able to respond to different events. In this case, the listener makes the `ImageButton` able to respond to the user pressing it.

3. An `Intent` variable is declared and a new `Intent` is created and assigned to it. The intent constructor requires a reference to its current activity (`ContactActivity.this`) and to know what activity it should start (`ContactListActivity.class`).

4. An intent flag is set to tell the operating system to not make multiple copies of the same activity.

The completed method name `initListButton()` is underlined in yellow. This indicates that the method is never used. To use it, enter `initListButton();` after the `setContent` `(R.layout.activity_contact)` line of code in the `onCreate` method at the beginning of the file. This code calls the button initiation code at creation of the activity so that it is ready for use when the user sees the layout. The yellow line should disappear. Complete the navigation bar code by copying the preceding code for each of the two remaining `ImageButtons`, and make the following changes for the first new method:

初始化列表按钮

initListButton() to initMapButton()

R.id.imageButtonList to R.id.imageButtonMap

ContactListActivity.class to ContactMapActivity.class

Similar changes should be made to the second new method:

initListButton() to initSettingsButton()

R.id.imageButtonList to R.id.imageButtonSettings

ContactListActivity.class to ContactSettingsActivity.class

Be sure to call the new methods in the onCreate method. The navigation bar is now ready for testing. Run the app on the emulator and test that each button opens the correct activity. Because the navigation bar is not currently coded for these activities, you will have to use the Back button to return to the ContactActivity.

Code the Toggle Button

Coding the toggle button is relatively easy, if not somewhat tedious. It is easy because you need only to enable or disable the interface. It is tedious because each widget that the user could interact with must be enabled or disabled separately. The ToggleButton's functionality requires the creation of three methods. One method will initialize the button to respond to the user. A second method will enable all the data entry widgets, and the third will disable all the widgets. First enter the code in Listing 4.9 after the navigation bar button code to initialize the ToggleButton. Remember to import any items underlined in red.

Listing 4.9   **ToggleButton Initialization Method**

```
private void initToggleButton() {
    final ToggleButton editToggle = (ToggleButton)
            ➡findViewById(R.id.toggleButtonEdit);                         //1
    editToggle.setOnClickListener(new OnClickListener() {

        @Override
        public void onClick(View arg0) {
            setForEditing(editToggle.isChecked());                        //2
        }
    });
}
```

The code is very similar to the navigation button initialization methods. A reference to the widget is grabbed and an onClickListener is added to the button. There are a few differences that need some explanation.

1. The final keyword is added to the statement that gets the reference to the ToggleButton to prevent the variable assignment from changing. This is required because it is being used in the button click code. It ensures that the widget referred to cannot change, so the code is always working on the same thing.

2. The onClick method calls the setForEditing method, passing it true if the button is toggled for editing and false if it is not.

The next step is to code the methods to do the enabling and disabling of the form. Enter the code in Listing 4.10 to create the setToEditing() method.

Listing 4.10   **Code to Enable the Data Entry Form**

```
private void setForEditing(boolean enabled) {
    EditText editName = (EditText) findViewById(R.id.editName);
    EditText editAddress = (EditText) findViewById(R.id.editAddress);
    EditText editCity = (EditText) findViewById(R.id.editCity);
    EditText editState = (EditText) findViewById(R.id.editState);
    EditText editZipCode = (EditText) findViewById(R.id.editZipcode);
    EditText editPhone = (EditText) findViewById(R.id.editHome);
    EditText editCell = (EditText) findViewById(R.id.editCell);
    EditText editEmail = (EditText) findViewById(R.id.editEMail);
    Button buttonChange = (Button) findViewById(R.id.btnBirthday);
    Button buttonSave = (Button) findViewById(R.id.buttonSave);

    editName.setEnabled(enabled);
    editAddress.setEnabled(enabled);
    editCity.setEnabled(enabled);
    editState.setEnabled(enabled);
    editZipCode.setEnabled(enabled);
    editPhone.setEnabled(enabled);
    editCell.setEnabled(enabled);
    editEmail.setEnabled(enabled);
    buttonChange.setEnabled(enabled);
    buttonSave.setEnabled(enabled);

    if (enabled) {
        editName.requestFocus();
    }

}
```

Add the following two lines of code to the onCreate method to initialize the ToggleButton and set the screen so that it is not in editing mode when it opens:

```
initToggleButton();
setForEditing(false);
```

Run the app to test the button. You may find one "error." The Contact name field looks disabled when the app opens, but it has focus and will allow data to be entered. Earlier versions of the Android OS always want to put focus on an `EditText` and will do so on the first `EditText` it finds in a layout. This is a relatively well-known bug/feature. There are a number of hacks to get around it. For demonstration purposes, one such hack is included in the sidebar. However, not every approach works or is reasonable for all circumstances. If you want to stop the autofocus from occurring, you should do it on a case-by-case basis.

Hacking Autofocus of EditText

One approach to stopping the autofocus places a dummy layout in the root layout to grab the focus. It is set to be focusable but has no size so it is not visible. This approach also clears the focus from all widgets in the `setForViewing()` method allowing the `LinearLayout` to grab the focus. Enter the following XML as the first element after the root `RelativeLayout` in the activity_contact.xml file.

```
<LinearLayout
    android:focusable="true"
    android:focusableInTouchMode="true"
    android:layout_width="0px"
    android:layout_height="0px" />
```

Next, modify the if statement at the end of the `setForView()` method in the ContactActivity.java file so that it looks like the following:

```
if (enabled) {
    editName.requestFocus();
}
else {
    ScrollView s = (ScrollView) findViewById(R.id.scrollView1);
    s.clearFocus();
}
```

After you disable all the widgets, this code clears the focus from all of them so that the dummy `LinearLayout` can grab it. If you enter this code, your app will now properly switch between editing and viewing modes.

Code the `DatePicker` Dialog

The `DatePicker` dialog is a window that opens when the user presses the Change button. A custom dialog requires both a layout, which you have already created, and a class that contains the code that gives the dialog its behavior. Using a custom dialog in an activity also requires changes to the activity code. The following describes how to code the `DatePickerDialog` class and make changes to the ContactActivity to display and use the dialog.

The first task is to create a new class to hold the custom dialog code. Right-click com.example.mycontactlist in the src folder and select New > Class from the pop-up menu. Enter

DatePickerDialog for the Name and click Finish. The new class opens with a limited amount of code. Replace all that code except the first line (package com.example.mycontactlist) with the code in Listing 4.11.

Listing 4.11 **DatePickerDialog Code**

```
import android.os.Bundle;
import android.support.v4.app.DialogFragment;
import android.text.format.Time;
import android.view.LayoutInflater;
import android.view.View;
import android.view.ViewGroup;
import android.view.View.OnClickListener;
import android.widget.Button;
import android.widget.DatePicker;

public class DatePickerDialog extends DialogFragment {                    //1

    public interface SaveDateListener {                                   //2
        void didFinishDatePickerDialog(Time selectedTime);
    }

    public DatePickerDialog() {                                           //3
    // Empty constructor required for DialogFragment
    }

    @Override
    public View onCreateView(LayoutInflater inflater, ViewGroup container,
        ➥Bundle savedInstanceState) {                                    //4
        final View view = inflater.inflate(R.layout.dateselect, container);

        getDialog().setTitle("Select Date");

        final DatePicker dp = (DatePicker)
          ➥view.findViewById(R.id.birthdayPicker);

        Button saveButton = (Button) view.findViewById(R.id.btnOk);
        saveButton.setOnClickListener(new OnClickListener() {
            @Override
            public void onClick(View arg0) {
                Time selectedTime = new Time();                          //5
                selectedTime.set(dp.getDayOfMonth(), dp.getMonth(), dp.getYear());
                saveItem(selectedTime);
            }
        });
        Button cancelButton = (Button) view.findViewById(R.id.btnCancel);
        cancelButton.setOnClickListener(new OnClickListener() {
```

```
            @Override
            public void onClick(View v) {
                  getDialog().dismiss();
            }
      });
      return view;
}

private void saveItem(Time selectedTime) {                                    //6
   SaveDateListener activity = (SaveDateListener) getActivity();
   activity.didFinishDatePickerDialog(selectedTime);
   getDialog().dismiss();
   }
}
```

A significant number of important concepts for Android app development are introduced in this code. Fortunately, dialog coding follows the same pattern, so after you understand the components, you can apply them whenever you need your app to show a dialog window.

1. The declaration of the class includes the keywords extends DialogFragment. This makes the DatePickerDialog class a subclass of the DialogFragment, which in turn is a subclass of the Fragment class discussed earlier in this chapter. All custom dialogs in an Android app should be created in this way.

2. A listener must be created with the DialogFragment. This is how the dialog communicates the user's actions on the dialog back to the activity that displayed the dialog. The listener must have a method to report the results of the dialog. The activity will have to implement the listener to handle the user actions.

3. A constructor for the class is required. It almost always is empty.

4. This method is the workhorse of the class. It creates the View from the resources in the layout file associated with it by the line inflater.inflate(...). The method also gets references to the widgets on the layout and sets up listeners for the widgets in the layout so that they can respond to user action.

5. Time objects are used to hold dates and times. This object stores a time/date as a number of milliseconds (millis) from Jan. 1, 1970. A new time object is created, and when the user clicks the OK button, it grabs the user selections on the DatePicker and sets the time object to that time. Finally, it calls the saveItem method to report the selection to the main activity.

6. The saveItem method gets a reference to the listener and calls its method to report the results of the dialog.

Save the DatePickerDialog class. This pattern is always used with custom dialogs. Each dialog needs a listener interface and associated method, a constructor, an onCreateView method, and a call to the listener method. The call to the listener method does not necessarily have to be in its own method as it is here. Finally, the dialog must be dismissed at the end of every code path in the `DialogFragment`.

Before the dialog can be tested, it must be implemented in the activity that uses it. In this case it is the ContactActivity. Switch to or open the `ContactActivity.java` class. The following steps must be done in the exact order listed here, or potential problems may occur.

1. Locate the class declaration: `public class ContactActivity extends Activity` and change `Activity` to `FragmentActivity`. This makes your `ContactActivity` a subclass of the `FragmentActivity` discussed earlier in the chapter. This is required to use `DialogFragments`.

2. `FragmentActivity` will be underlined in red and a whole bunch of errors will show up in the code. Hover your cursor over `FragmentActivity` and select Import FragmentActivity (android.support.v4.app). The `FragmentActivity` class is in the android.support.v4.app library, which is a set of code that provides objects to make some features in newer Android operating systems work in older versions.

3. Add the words `implements SaveDateListener` after `FragmentActivity` so that the class declaration is `public class ContactActivity extends FragmentActivity implements SaveDateListener {`. After making the change, `SaveDateListener` will be highlighted in red. Hover over it to get the pop-up menu and select Import.

4. `ContactActivity` becomes highlighted in red. Hover your cursor over it and select Add Unimplemented Methods from the pop-up menu. When an activity implements a listener, it must implement the methods associated with the listener so that the results may be used in the activity.

5. Scroll down to the bottom of the ContactActivity.java file. You should find the following code. If not, delete your changes and repeat the preceding steps.

```
@Override
public void didFinishDatePickerDialog(Time selectedTime) {
    // TODO Auto-generated method stub
}
```

The `didFinishDatePickerDialog` method is the code that will handle the date that the user selected. Enter the following two lines of code in place of the TODO line:

```
TextView birthDay = (TextView) findViewById(R.id.textBirthday);
birthDay.setText(DateFormat.format("MM/dd/yyyy", selectedTime.toMillis(false)).
toString());
```

Some of the code may be highlighted in red, indicating that it needs to be imported. In the case of `DateFormat` you will see two import options. Choose android.text.format. This code gets a reference to the `TextView` that will display the date and set its text attribute to a string produced by the `DateFormat.format` method.

You are almost ready to test your dialog. The last thing to do is to code the Change button to make it display the dialog. Add the code in Listing 4.12 to the ContactActivity.

Listing 4.12   **Change Birthday Button**

```
private void initChangeDateButton() {
    Button changeDate = (Button) findViewById(R.id.btnBirthday);
    changeDate.setOnClickListener(new OnClickListener() {

        @Override
        public void onClick(View v) {
            FragmentManager fm = getSupportFragmentManager();          //1
            DatePickerDialog datePickerDialog = new DatePickerDialog(); //2
            datePickerDialog.show(fm, "DatePick");                      //3
        }
    });
}
```

Most of the code is standard initialization of a button to respond to the user pressing the button. The code to be executed when the click occurs displays the dialog.

1. A `FragmentManager` is a required object to manage any and all fragments displayed in an activity. It needs to be imported. There will be two choices; again, choose the one from the Android support library (android.support.v4.app).

2. A new instance of the `DatePickerDialog` class is created.

3. The `DatePickerDialog`'s show method (inherited from `DialogFragment`) displays the dialog. The method requires an instance of a `FragmentManager` and a name, which the `FragmentManager` uses to keep track of the dialog.

Be sure to call the `initChangeDateButton()` method in the `onCreate` method of ContactActivity. The app interface is ready to be tested! Run it to be sure that the dialog is displayed and the correct date is placed in the `TextView`.

Summary

Creating layouts is a lot of work! In this chapter you learned how to use Eclipse to create an Android layout file that is the user interface for an app activity. Development of a layout requires use of both the graphical editor and modification of the associated XML to get the exact design you want. Experimentation is often the key to getting the layout to look the way you want it to.

`Intents` are used to switch between `Activities` and sometimes pass data to those `Activities`. You learned how to use `Intents` to implement a navigation bar that allows the user to move between different `Activities` in your app.

Finally, you learned how to use `Fragments` to implement a custom dialog window. You also learned how to display the custom dialog and to communicate the results of the user interaction with the dialog back to activity so that it could act on those actions.

Exercises

1. Create a new color resource to be used as the background for the data entry part of the ContactActivity. Search on the Web for the color and associated Android color code (color codes always start with a # symbol) and add it to the color.xml file. Set the background of the data entry part of the layout to that color resource.

2. Make the navigation work for all activities in the app. Copy the navigation bar XML code to the layout associated with each activity. Copy the Java code that makes the buttons work to the Java file associated with each activity. You will have to modify that code to reference the activity it is in rather than ContactActivity. Add code to disable the ImageButton associated with the activity that is displayed.

3. Modify the DatePickerDialog layout so that the Cancel/OK buttons are centered. Hint: You'll have to use the gravity attribute in the TableRow.

4. Add the hack to your code to stop the autofocus of the EditTexts.

Persistent Data in Android

The capability to have data that the app uses or relies on to continue to be available regardless of changes to the app's state as it moves through the app life cycle is vital to the user experience with the app—and for the app itself to be a useful tool. For this to occur, the data needs to persist through these life cycle changes. Android provides several ways in which the developer can make data persist. This chapter introduces you to three of these data persistence approaches. A significant amount of time will be spent on understanding and using the SQLite database system incorporated with Android, but the chapter also discusses storing data in files and demonstrates how to store individual pieces of data in an object that persists across an app's life cycle.

Preferences, Files, and Database

The three approaches to data persistence discussed in this chapter are `SharedPreferences`, standard flat file input/output, and the SQLite database system. Each of these approaches provides capabilities that are relevant for different tasks in an app. `SharedPreferences` are often used for a limited set of data that represent user choices about the way they want the app configured. They may also be used for other data that needs to persist across life cycle changes. Flat files are useful for backing up data and transmitting to other users. Finally, databases are the workhorses for data manipulation, storage, and retrieval. Developing an understanding of where, when, and how to use these data persistence approaches is very important to effective development of an Android app.

Preferences

Preferences are implemented through use of the `SharedPreferences` class. A `SharedPreferences` object can be used to store primitive data (for example, integers and strings) in a key/value pair. Each value has its own key for storage and retrieval of that data. `SharedPreferences` are stored in memory private to the app and will persist as long as the app remains installed on the device. App upgrades will not impact the values stored with `SharedPreferences`.

There are two main modes for accessing `SharedPreferences`: `getSharedPreferences` (`"String preference name"`, `integer mode`) and `getPreferences(integer mode)`. The `getSharedPreferences` mode is used when you want to have more than one set of preferences for an app, or you want the preferences available to any `Activity` in the app. Each set is given a name that is used as the key to access that particular set of preferences. If you need a set of preferences only for a single `Activity`, then you can use the `getPreferences` method. With each of these methods you need to set an access mode. Using 0 (zero) makes the preferences private to the app. Preferences may also be given a mode that makes them readable or writeable from outside the app. However, this is discouraged because it opens potential security holes. Data is stored by using a method appropriate to the value being saved (for example, `putBoolean` or `putInt`) and supplying a string that will be the key for future access to that value. Likewise, data is retrieved from the object using the string key with the appropriate get method (for example, `getBoolean` or `getInt`). Specific implementation of the `SharedPreferences` method of data persistence will be explained later in this chapter.

Files

Files are written and read as a stream of bytes. This means that to the Android system, a file is one thing. It does not have parts, such as different objects, within it. The advantage to this is that the system stores the data efficiently and does not have to worry about what data is stored within the stream. Thus, many kinds of data can be stored in a file. The disadvantage is that it is up to the developer to code the reading and writing of the file so that the data can be used appropriately when it is needed. For example, the developer can embed XML in the stream to identify the different types of data. Another approach is to embed commas in the file to distinguish different pieces of data. However, in either case, the user of that file must know its structure to use it correctly.

Files can be written to either internal or external storage. Files written to internal storage are private to the app. They will persist as long as the app is installed on the device. Files written to external storage (such as an SD card) are not private to the app. Other apps can access them and if the device is connected to a computer, they are accessible (including being able to modify and delete) to the user of the computer. Files are written and read from storage using the `FileOutputStream` and `FileInputStream` objects in a similar fashion to any regular Java program. Although files can be very useful persistence tools, they will not be discussed further in this book.

Database

Android supports the use of SQLite databases. SQLite is a fully functional relational database management system (RDBMS) that can integrate into any host application. It does not require an independent server process to execute. A relational database system allows the developer to give meaning to the data stored within it by separating the data into tables (for example, a customer table and an order table. Each table will hold data pertinent for each instance of whatever is stored in the table (for example, data for each customer). SQLite also provides capabilities for retrieval and manipulation of the stored data through the use of queries written in Structured Query Language (SQL). Almost any type of data can be stored and manipulated using a SQLite database, although some data types have more limited support than other RDBMSs.

Data stored in a SQLite database is private to the app and will persist as long as the app is installed on the device. An app may create and use multiple databases, and each database can have many tables, making data storage via SQLite both extensive and flexible. Databases are the workhorse data storage of many apps and are discussed extensively in this chapter.

> ### Android Versus iOS: Data Persistence
>
> Android and iOS offer essentially the same three types of data persistence mechanisms discussed in this chapter. The functionality provided by `SharedPreferences` in Android is provided by the `NSUserDefaults` object in iOS. File input and output is also provided in iOS. Finally, iOS also implements SQLite databases in a very similar manner to Android. iOS does offer a storage solution called Core Data that offers an object-oriented approach to storing data, but this is usually added on top of a SQLite database. Although in all cases the code has different commands because the programming languages are different, the functionality is the same, so porting data persistence between platforms requires work. However, the concepts are easily replicated.

Creating the Database

The MyContactList app uses a simple, one table database to provide the data storage and manipulation functionality described in Chapter 2, "App Design Issues and Considerations." Two new classes will be created to provide the database functionality. One class is used to create, modify, and delete the tables included in the database. The other class is used for data access. It provides methods to open and close the database and the queries used to store, access, and manipulate the data in the tables. The focus in this chapter is to make the `ContactActivity` able to store a contact's data. Retrieval and manipulation of that data is introduced in later chapters.

Create the Database Helper Class

The recommended approach to using SQLite in an Android app is to create a Database Helper class whose only function is to provide for the creation, modification, and deletion of tables in the database. The new class is defined as a subclass of the `SQLiteOpenHelper` class. Much of the required functionality for working with databases is inherited from the `SQLiteOpenHelper` class although some of its methods will be overridden to implement the functionality required for this app.

1. Right-click com.example.mycontactlist in the src folder of the Package Explorer.

2. Select New > Class and enter ContactDBHelper as the name of the new class.

3. Type the code in Listing 5.1 into the new class. You will have to import many of the objects after you have entered the code.

Listing 5.1   **Code for the Database Helper Class**

```
import android.content.Context;
import android.database.sqlite.SQLiteDatabase;
import android.database.sqlite.SQLiteOpenHelper;
import android.util.Log;

public class ContactDBHelper extends SQLiteOpenHelper {                  //1

    private static final String DATABASE_NAME = "mycontacts.db";        //2
    private static final int DATABASE_VERSION = 1;                      //3

    // Database creation sql statement
    private static final String CREATE_TABLE_CONTACT = "create table contact (_id
➥integer primary key autoincrement, "                                  //4
                    + "contactname text not null, streetaddress text, "
                    + "city text, state text, zipcode text, "
                    + "phonenumber text, cellnumber text, "
                    + "email text, birthday text);";

    public ContactDBHelper(Context context) {                           //5
        super(context, DATABASE_NAME, null, DATABASE_VERSION);
    }

    @Override
    public void onCreate(SQLiteDatabase database) {                     //6
        database.execSQL(CREATE_TABLE_CONTACT);
    }

    @Override
    public void onUpgrade(SQLiteDatabase db, int oldVersion, int newVersion) {  //7
➥Log.w(ContactDBHelper.class.getName(),
            "Upgrading database from version " + oldVersion + " to "
                + newVersion + ", which will destroy all old data");
        db.execSQL("DROP TABLE IF EXISTS contact");
        onCreate(db);
    }
}
```

The previous code is relatively standard and all that is needed to create the SQLite database and the one table required for the MyContactList app. The code can be copied and modified for other apps. The code and its potential modifications are described next:

1. The class `ContactDBHelper` is declared as a subclass of `SQLiteOpenHelper`. Most of its functionality is inherited from this class.

2. A static variable is declared to name the database. A database name is required. Use the `.db` extension.

3. A static variable to hold the database version number is declared and initialized to 1. This variable is important. Every time the database is accessed, the existing database version is compared to the one here. If the number is higher, the `onUpgrade` method is executed.

4. A string variable is declared and assigned to a SQL command that creates the table. It is good practice to define the table definitions in this manner so that when a change to a table needs to be made, all you have to do is change the definition in one place and increment the version number. Declare a similar variable for each table needed in your database.

5. The constructor method calls the super class's constructor method. Nothing else needs to be done in this method. The constructor creates a new instance of `ContactDBHelper`.

6. The `onCreate` method is called the first time the database is opened. If the database named in the `DATABASE_NAME` variable does not exist, this method is executed. The method executes the SQL assigned to the `CREATE_TABLE_CONTACT` variable.

7. The `onUpgrade` method is executed when the database is opened and the current version number in the code is higher than the version number of the current database. This method first deletes the contact table and then executes the `onCreate` method to create a new version of the table. Carefully planning the data needed by your app is important so that you don't have to use this method much. What happens in this method is entirely up to the developer. Care must be taken because if a table is dropped, all the user data currently in the table is lost. If you need to add columns to the table, consider executing an `ALTER TABLE` SQL command rather than a drop, and re-create the table. The `Log` command writes a message to the LogCat, which is a system for collecting and viewing system debug information. You can view LogCat by selecting Window > Show View > Other... > LogCat. This command may be eliminated if you want.

A database helper class is recommended practice in Android. The primary function of the class is to determine what must be done on creation of the database and what must be done when the database is upgraded. The next step is to create a class that does the opening and closing of the database and contains the queries used to store and retrieve data from the database.

Create the Data Source Class

Create a new class named `ContactDataSource`. Enter the code in Listing 5.2, being sure to import any objects underlined in red.

Listing 5.2   **ContactDataSource Required Code**

```
public class ContactDataSource {

    private SQLiteDatabase database;                              //1
    private ContactDBHelper dbHelper;

    public ContactDataSource(Context context) {                  //2
        dbHelper = new ContactDBHelper(context);
    }

    public void open() throws SQLException {                     //3
        database = dbHelper.getWritableDatabase();
    }

    public void close() {                                        //4
        dbHelper.close();
    }
}
```

The required methods are quite limited and fairly self-explanatory.

1. Variables are declared to hold instances of the SQLite database and the helper class. You will get a warning on the SQLiteDatabase line because you don't use it yet.

2. The helper class is instantiated when the data source class is instantiated.

3-4. Open and close methods are used to access and end access to the database.

The rest of the code in this class is dependent on the needs of the app. In the case of the MyContactsList app, the ContactActivity needs to be able to insert new contacts and update data for existing contacts. This is done by creating a method for each operation. The data for insertion or updating a contact is passed to these methods with a Contact object.

The Contact class does not exist, so the first task is to create that class. Create another new class in the src folder named Contact. Enter the code in Listing 5.3 to create the Contact object. The ContactActivity uses this object to store data entered by the user and pass it to the data source class. Enter the code in Listing 5.3 to create the Contact class. Import any needed classes. Note that two time classes are listed when you rest your pointer on the underlined Time. Use the android.text.format Time class.

Listing 5.3   **The Contact Class**

```
import android.text.format.Time;

public class Contact {
        private int contactID;
        private String contactName;
```

```java
private String streetAddress;
private String city;
private String state;
private String zipCode;
private String phoneNumber;
private String cellNumber;
private String eMail;
private Time birthday;

public Contact() {
       contactID = -1;
       Time t = new Time();
       t.setToNow();
       birthday = t;
}

public int getContactID() {
       return contactID;
}
public void setContactID(int i) {
       contactID = i;
}
public String getContactName() {
       return contactName;
}
public void setContactName(String s) {
       contactName = s;
}
public Time getBirthday() {
       return birthday;
}
public void setBirthday(Time t) {
       birthday = t;
}
public String getStreetAddress() {
       return streetAddress;
}
public void setStreetAddress(String s) {
       streetAddress = s;
}
public String getCity() {
       return city;
}
public void setCity(String s) {
       city = s;
```

```
        }
        public String getState() {
                return state;
        }
        public void setSLate(String s) {
                state = s;
        }
        public String getZipCode() {
                return zipCode;
        }
        public void setZipCode(String s) {
                zipCode = s;
        }
        public void setPhoneNumber(String s) {
                phoneNumber = s;
        }
        public String getPhoneNumber() {
                return phoneNumber;
        }
        public void setCellNumber(String s) {
                cellNumber = s;
        }
        public String getCellNumber() {
                return cellNumber;
        }
        public void setEMail(String s) {
                eMail = s;
        }
        public String getEMail() {
                return eMail;
        }
}
```

The Contact class is a very simple class. It declares variables for each piece of data needed for a contact and declares a method to set the value of the variable and a method to get the value of the variable (getters and setter). The only really important code is in the class constructor method. Notice that in this method the contact's ID is set to -1. This is used by the app to determine if the contact is new and needs to be inserted or the contact already exists and needs to be updated. The birthday variable is also initialized to the current date. This allows the app to assume that there will always be a Time value in the birthday variable.

After the Contact class has been created, you can now code the insert and update methods in the ContactDataSource class. Enter the code in Listing 5.4 to create these methods. Enter the code after the close() method.

Listing 5.4 **Insert and Update Contact Methods**

```
public boolean insertContact(Contact c) {
    boolean didSucceed = false;                                        //1
    try {
        ContentValues initialValues = new ContentValues();             //2

        initialValues.put("contactname", c.getContactName());          //3
        initialValues.put("streetaddress", c.getStreetAddress());
        initialValues.put("city", c.getCity());
        initialValues.put("state", c.getState());
        initialValues.put("zipcode", c.getZipCode());
        initialValues.put("phonenumber", c.getPhoneNumber());
        initialValues.put("cellnumber", c.getCellNumber());
        initialValues.put("email", c.getEMail());
        initialValues.put("birthday",
           ➥String.valueOf(c.getBirthday().toMillis(false)));

        didSucceed = database.insert("contact", null, initialValues) > 0;   //4
    }
    catch (Exception e) {
        //Do nothing -will return false if there is an exception        //5
    }
    return didSucceed;
}

public boolean updateContact(Contact c) {
    boolean didSucceed = false;
    try {
        Long rowId = Long.valueOf(c.getContactID());                   //6
        ContentValues updateValues = new ContentValues();

        updateValues.put("contactname", c.getContactName());
        updateValues.put("streetaddress", c.getStreetAddress());
        updateValues.put("city", c.getCity());
        updateValues.put("state", c.getState());
        updateValues.put("zipcode", c.getZipCode());
        updateValues.put("phonenumber", c.getPhoneNumber());
        updateValues.put("cellnumber", c.getCellNumber());
        updateValues.put("email", c.getEMail());
        updateValues.put("birthday",
           ➥String.valueOf(c.getBirthday().toMillis(false)));

        didSucceed = database.update("contact", updateValues, "_id=" + rowId,
           ➥null) > 0;                                                 //7
    }
```

```
      catch (Exception e) {
         //Do nothing -will return false if there is an exception
      }
      return didSucceed;
   }
}
```

The two methods are very similar. The primary difference is that the `updateContact` method uses the Contact ID to overwrite values in the Contact table, whereas the `insertContact` method just inserts contact data and the database inserts the ID because the `_id` field was declared as an autoincrement field.

1. A Boolean variable is declared and assigned the value false. Both the update and insert methods return a Boolean to tell the calling code if the operation succeeded. The value is initially set to false and then changed to true only if the operation succeeds.

2. The `ContentValues` object is used to store a set of key/value pairs that are used to assign contact data to the correct field in the table.

3. The values for the table are retrieved from the `Contact` object, associated with the correct field, and inserted into the `ContentValues` object. Note that the date is stored as `millis`, because SQLite doesn't support storing data as dates directly.

4. The database's insert method is called and passed the name of the table and values to insert. The method returns the number of records (rows) successfully inserted. The value is compared to zero. If it is greater than zero, then the operation succeeded and the return value is set to true.

5. If the method throws an exception, the return value is already set to false, so we don't have to do anything.

6. The update procedure needs the contact's ID to correctly update the table. This value is retrieved from the `Contact` object and assigned to the variable `rowId`.

7. The database's update method is called to place the changes in the database. Just like the insert method, if the operation is a success, the method returns the number of records affected. If this number is greater than zero, the operation was successful.

The SQLite database is ready for use. An object to create and upgrade the database has been implemented. Another object to open, close, and access the database has also been created. You are now ready to save contact data!

Using the Database

The three classes, `Contact`, `ContactDBHelper`, and `ContactDataSource`, are used in the `ContactActivity` class to implement the saving of contact data to the database. This will require implementing several new methods and modifying some existing methods. Because the methods to retrieve contacts have not been implemented yet, the update functionality will be only partially implemented at this time.

The first step is to provide an association between the `ContactActivity` class and a `Contact` object. This is implemented by declaring a private variable in the `ContactActivity` class. Enter the following code after the class declaration and before the `onCreate` method:

```
private Contact currentContact;
```

Next associate the `currentContact` variable with a new `Contact` object by entering the following code as the last line in the `onCreate` method:

```
currentContact = new Contact();
```

Notice that while you are using a new object (`Contact`) in the `ContactActivity` class, you do not have to import it. That's because you created the `Contact` class as a part of the com. example.mycontactlist package. Android already knows about this class, so it does not have to be imported.

The final step in modifying existing code is to add a line of code in the `didFinishDatePickerDialog` method to store the selected birthday in the `Contact` object. Add the following line of code as the last line of code in that method:

```
currentContact.setBirthday(selectedTime);
```

This code uses the `Contact` class's `setBirthday` method to assign the date selected in the custom dialog to the `currentContact` object.

Capture User-Entered Data

The first new method needed is used to capture the user data as it's typed and store it in the `currentContact` object. The method itself does not capture the data. Rather, it sets up listeners on all the `EditTexts` where data can be entered. If the text changes, the listener then executes the code to set the attribute that holds the code in the `currentContact` object. The method is called in the `onCreate` method of the `ContactActivity` so that the listeners are ready to go when the `ContactActivity` is ready for input. To start, enter the following line of code after all the other init methods in the `onCreate` method:

```
initTextChangedEvents();
```

Next, create a new method in the `ContactActivity` class called `initTextChangedEvents()`. Place this method after the other init methods currently in the class. Enter the code in Listing 5.5.

Listing 5.5   **TextChanged Event Code**

```
private void initTextChangedEvents(){
    final EditText contactName = (EditText) findViewById(R.id.editName);         //1
    contactName.addTextChangedListener(new TextWatcher() {                        //2

        public void afterTextChanged(Editable s) {                               //3
            currentContact.setContactName(contactName.getText().toString());     //4
```

```
        }
        public void beforeTextChanged(CharSequence arg0, int arg1,
                              ➥int arg2, int arg3) {                          //5
            //  Auto-generated method stub
        }
        public void onTextChanged(CharSequence s, int start, int before,
                              ➥int count) {                                   //6
            //  Auto-generated method stub
        }
    });

    final EditText streetAddress = (EditText) findViewById(R.id.editAddress);   //7
    streetAddress.addTextChangedListener(new TextWatcher() {
        public void afterTextChanged(Editable s) {
          currentContact.setStreetAddress(streetAddress.getText().toString());   //8
        }
        public void beforeTextChanged(CharSequence arg0, int arg1,
                              ➥int arg2, int arg3) {
            //  Auto-generated method stub
        }
        public void onTextChanged(CharSequence s, int start, int before,
                              ➥int count) {
            //  Auto-generated method stub
        }
    });
}
```

Listing 5.5 is not the complete method. A listener has to be added for all the other EditTexts
in the layout. However, the code is essentially the same for each EditText. Take time to understand this code before adding the rest.

1. A reference to the Contact Name EditText is assigned to the variable contactName. The
   variable is declared as final because it is used inside the event code.

2. A TextChangedListener is added to the EditText by creating a new TextWatcher
   object. The TextWatcher object requires that three methods (lines 3, 5, and 6) are
   implemented, even though you will use only one of these events.

3. The afterTextChanged method is a required method for the TextWatch object. It is
   called after the user completes editing the data and leaves the EditText. This is the
   event that this app uses to capture the data the user entered.

4. This code is executed when the user ends editing of the EditText. It gets the text
   in the EditText, converts it to a string, and sets the contactName attribute of the
   currentContact object to that value.

5. The beforeTextChanged method is a required TextWatcher method. This method is
   executed when the user presses down on a key to enter it into an EditText but before
   the value in the EditText is actually changed.

6. The `onTextChanged` method is also a required `TextWatcher` method. The method is executed after each and every character change in an `EditText`.

7. The pattern repeats for another `EditText` in the layout, except that value is assigned to a different attribute of the `currentContact` object.

8. This code gets the value entered into the `editAddress` `EditText`, converts it to a string, and sets the `streetAddress` attribute of the `currentContact` object to that value. It is essentially the same as the code in number 4, except that it gets the value from a different widget and assigns it to a different attribute.

This code needs to be repeated for the remaining `EditText`s in the activity_contact.xml file. This includes the remaining address `EditText`s, the phone and cell number `EditText`s, and the email `EditText`. You can copy and paste the code you already entered or type it. In either case, but especially with the copy/paste approach, make sure you get a reference to the correct widget (`R.id.widget+id`) and assign the value to the correct Contact attribute.

The next step in coding the `initTextChangedEvents` method is to set the phone number `EditText`s to autoformat the number as it's typed. Enter the following code as the last code in that method:

```
homephonevariable.addTextChangedListener(new PhoneNumberFormattingTextWatcher());
cellphonevariable.addTextChangedListener(new PhoneNumberFormattingTextWatcher());
```

This code adds a listener to the phone number `EditText`s that calls the `PhoneNumberFormattingTextWatcher` object, which in turn adds the appropriate formatting as the user types.

The final step is to add `initTextChangedEvents();` to the `onCreate` method to set up the listeners when the activity is opened.

Save User-Entered Data

The `intTextChangedEvents` method you just created sets the stage for saving the contact's data. It sets the `EditText`s to update the `ContactActivity`'s contact object with any changes users make as they make them. All that is left is to pass that object to the insert or update method in the `ContactDataSource` class so that the changes can be stored in the database. This requires the addition of a method that initializes the Save button and executes the code that will do the save operation when the button is pressed.

The initialization of the Save button is similar to the initialization of all the other buttons you have coded so far. The only difference is what happens when the button is pressed. Enter the code in Listing 5.6 before the `initTextChangedEvents` method you just created. Don't forget to call the method in the `onCreate` method where the rest of the button initialization methods are called.

Listing 5.6   **Save Button Code**

```
private void initSaveButton() {
    Button saveButton = (Button) findViewById(R.id.buttonSave);
    saveButton.setOnClickListener(new View.OnClickListener() {

        @Override
        public void onClick(View v) {
            ContactDataSource ds = new ContactDataSource(ContactActivity.this);    //1
            ds.open();                                                              //2

            boolean wasSuccessful = false;                                          //3
            if (currentContact.getContactID()==-1) {                                //4
                wasSuccessful = ds.insertContact(currentContact);
            }
            else {
                wasSuccessful = ds.updateContact(currentContact);
            }
            ds.close();                                                             //5

            if (wasSuccessful) {                                                    //6
                ToggleButton editToggle = (ToggleButton)
                                ➥findViewById(R.id.toggleButtonEdit);
                editToggle.toggle();
                setForViewing();
            }
        }
    });
}
```

The only new code in this method is the code associated with the save operation. The basic save operation opens the database, checks if this is a new contact to be inserted or if it should be updated, and if the save was successful, to change the screen back to view rather than editing mode.

1. A new `ContactDataSource` object is instantiated.

2. The database is opened. It is good practice to open the database just prior to using it and close it as soon as you are done.

3. A Boolean variable is declared and set to false. This variable captures the return value of the `ContactDataSource` methods and is used to determine the operations that should be performed upon success or failure of the method.

4. The currentContact's id is compared to -1. Only new contacts will have a -1 value. If it is a new contact, the `insertContact` method is called and passed the `currentContact` object. Otherwise, the `updateContact` method is called to save the new data.

5. The database is closed as soon as possible. Do not forget to close the database! If you do not close it, strange errors can show up during execution.

6. The return value is checked. If the save operation was successful, the `ToggleButton` is toggled to viewing mode, and the screen is set for viewing. If it was not successful, the activity remains in editing mode.

Test the code on the emulator. You may notice one discrepancy. When you push the Save button and the screen changes to viewing rather than editing mode, the keyboard remains displayed if you didn't dismiss it with the Back button. If you don't have this happen, edit your Android Virtual Device. Look for Hardware Keyboard Present and uncheck it. Stop and restart the emulator. Many Android devices do not have a hardware keyboard, and if your app keeps the soft keyboard displayed when the user is clearly done, it will make the user think that the app doesn't work properly.

Correct this by adding a method that dismisses the keyboard that is called when the Save button is pressed. The code in Listing 5.7 is a partial method to do this. Place this method before the `didFinishDatePickerDialog` method.

Listing 5.7   **Partial hideKeyboard() Method**

```
private void hideKeyboard() {
    InputMethodManager imm =
        ➡ (InputMethodManager)getSystemService(Context.INPUT_METHOD_SERVICE);
    EditText editName = (EditText) findViewById(R.id.editName);
    imm.hideSoftInputFromWindow(editName.getWindowToken(), 0);
    EditText editAddress = (EditText) findViewById(R.id.editAddress);
    imm.hideSoftInputFromWindow(editAddress.getWindowToken(), 0);
}
```

Repeat the last two lines of code in Listing 5.7 for each `EditText` in the layout (changing variable names and `EditText`s). The first line gets a system service that manages user input. The second line gets a reference to an `EditText`, and the third line closes the keyboard. Every `EditText` must receive this treatment because there is no way of knowing which `EditText` users were working with when they pressed the Save button. Add a call to this method in the `initSaveButton` method just before the `ContactDataSource` is instantiated.

Test the modification in the emulator. Another discrepancy is exposed (again, only if you have the hardware keyboard disabled in the AVD). The keyboard hides, but the screen remains focused on the last `EditText` used. When the user saves the data and the screen displays in view mode, it should be focused at the top of the screen. It does not do this. Fortunately, there is an easy fix. Tell the `ScrollView` to focus on the top of the screen. Change the block of code that requests focus for the contact name `EditText` in the `setForEditing` method to the following to change the `ScrollView`'s focus to the top of the screen when switching to viewing mode:

```
if (enabled) {
    editName.requestFocus();
}
else {
    ScrollView s = (ScrollView) findViewById(R.id.scrollView1);
    s.fullScroll(ScrollView.FOCUS_UP);
}
```

If you added the hack of the autofocus discussed in Chapter 4, "Android Navigation and Interface Design," you can add the second line of code just before the s.clearFocus() line. The focus up must be before the clear focus. Otherwise it will override the clear, and autofocus will again occur. Test the app again. Everything should work as expected.

One last problem exists with the ContactActivity. If the user adds a new contact, presses the Save button, and then edits the data and presses Save again, another contact will be added rather than updating the contact just entered. This is because the currentContact object still has an ID of -1. There are a number of approaches to fixing this problem. You could clear the screen and make users get the contact from the contact list (not yet implemented) if they want to edit it. You could retrieve the newly inserted contact and reload the screen with all the newly entered data and the id that was created by the auto increment of the ID when the contact was inserted into the database. Or you could get the new ID and set the currentContact ContactID attribute to that value. That is the approach used here. Open the ContactDataSource and create a new method using the code in Listing 5.8.

Listing 5.8   **Retrieve the New Contact ID**

```
public int getLastContactId() {
    int lastId = -1;
    try {
        String query = "Select MAX(_id) from contact";          //1
        Cursor cursor = database.rawQuery(query, null);          //2

        cursor.moveToFirst();                                    //3
        lastId = cursor.getInt(0);                               //4
        cursor.close();                                          //5
    }
    catch (Exception e) {
        lastId = -1;
    }
    return lastId;
}
```

Notice that the structure of this method is similar to the other insert and update methods. A try and catch is used to handle an error if it occurs, and a value, set to failure initially, is returned. However, because this is a method to retrieve data from the database rather than save it to the database, there are some significant differences.

1. An SQL query is written to get the maximum value for the _id field in the contact table. The last contact entered will have the maximum value because the _id field is set to autoincrement.

2. A cursor is declared and assigned to hold the results of the execution of the query. A cursor is an object that is used to hold and move through the results of a query.

3. The cursor is told to move to the first record in the returned data.

4. The maximum ID is retrieved from the recordset. Fields in the recordset are indexed starting at 0.

5. The cursor is closed. Just like with closing the database, it is best to close the cursor as soon as you are done using it. Forgetting to do so can lead to errors during execution.

Save the ContactDataSource.java file and open the ContactActivity code. Navigate to the initSaveButton method. Enter the following code after the line of code that inserts a new contact (not the update):

```
int newId = ds.getLastContactId();
currentContact.setContactID(newId);
```

The first line uses the newly created retrieval method to get the newly inserted contact's ID. The second line sets the currentContact object's ID to the retrieved value.

Use the Debugger

The ContactActivity is finished for now. However, it is difficult to test the recently added functionality because currently it does not retrieve contact data. Therefore, to test that the functionality you just added is working properly you have to watch it run. This is done using the debugger.

The first step in using the debugger is to set a breakpoint. A breakpoint tells the debugger to halt execution at that line of code. This gives you the capability to inspect the values in the variables and step through the code line by line. There are two ways to set a breakpoint. The first is to double-click the light gray vertical bar to the left of the code. This will put a blue dot that represents the breakpoint in the bar (Figure 5.1). This method is quick but can cause problems because if you are not completely on the vertical bar, it will collapse the method that the line of code is in. This isn't really a problem because you can just expand it again, but it can be frustrating. The second method is to right-click the vertical bar and select Toggle Breakpoint from the pop-up menu. If you are in the wrong location you will not get that menu option.

To check whether the currentContact is getting a new ID, set a breakpoint in the initSaveButton method on the hideKeyboard() line (Figure 5.1). When you run the program, execution will halt at this line. After the breakpoint is set, run the app using the emulator and the Debug Configuration you set up for the app. Fill in some values and press the Save button. The Confirm Perspective Switch window opens, telling you that you need to open the Debug Perspective. Click Yes. In the bottom left of the Debug Perspective, you will see the app code with the hideKeyboard() line highlighted. The app has halted on that line and is waiting for your command. To control execution during debugging, use the Debug toolbar buttons at the top of the perspective (See Figure 5.2). Different versions of Eclipse have these buttons in different locations and order at the top of the perspective, so you'll have to look for them.

```java
private void initSaveButton() {
    Button saveButton = (Button) findViewById(R.id.buttonSave);
    saveButton.setOnClickListener(new View.OnClickListener() {

        @Override
        public void onClick(View v) {
            hideKeyboard();
            ContactDataSource ds = new ContactDataSource(ContactActivity.this);
            ds.open();

            boolean wasSuccessful = false;
            if (currentContact.getContactID()==-1) {
                wasSuccessful = ds.insertContact(currentContact);
                int newId = ds.getLastContactId();
                currentContact.setContactID(newId);
            }
            else {
                wasSuccessful = ds.updateContact(currentContact);
            }
            ds.close();

            if (wasSuccessful) {
                ToggleButton editToggle = (ToggleButton) findViewById(R.id.toggleButtonEdit);
                editToggle.toggle();
                setForViewing();
            }
        }
    });
}
```

Figure 5.1   Code with breakpoint set.

Figure 5.2   Debug control buttons.

Hover over each of these to find the one that says Step Over. This advances the execution by one line. Click this button and watch the code step line by line until you reach the `currentContact.setContactID(newId)` line. Note that if your code doesn't follow this path, you've done something wrong and need to examine the code to see that it matches the code in the previous listings. On the upper right of the perspective is a pane with two tabs: Variables and Breakpoints (see Figure 5.3). Click the Variables tab if it is not already selected.

Figure 5.3   Variable inspection tab.

In the Variables tab, find the `newId` variable and verify that its value is greater than -1. This number may be significantly higher than -1 if you have run the app several times already. If it is not greater than -1, review your code. Now step the code one more line and inspect the `currentContact` variable. You may have to expand `currentContact` to see its attributes. If you cannot find `currentContact` in the variables list, expand the variable named `this`, which represents the whole activity, so it will have all the activity variables in it. Expand it until you find `currentContact`. Check to see that the contact ID attribute is the same as the `newId` value. If it is, you have successfully created an activity that can save data to a database!

The debugger can be stopped in several ways. The first would be to click the Terminate button in the toolbar. The Terminate button is the one with the red square as an icon. The second is to locate your debug configuration in the debug tab (typically in the top left of the perspective). Right-click the configuration name and select Terminate from the menu.

An alternative to stepping through the code with the debugger is to use logging. With this approach you place `Log` statements in your code in places where you'd like to know the value of variables or that the method was executed. When your code executes, these statements will be written to LogCat (see the discussion of Log statement and LogCat in the "Create the Database Helper Class" section earlier in this chapter). This is a useful approach if you have to run through a significant amount of code to get to the code you are interested in.

Using Preferences

`SharedPreferences` are an easy way to store bits of information that need to persist over the life cycle of an app. In the MyContactList app, preferences are set in the `ContactSettingsActivity`. This activity is developed so that you can learn how to use `SharedPreferences`. To do so, the layout is first coded and then the Java file is edited.

Create the Settings Layout

Open the activity_contact_settings.xml file. If you have not already done so, add the navigation buttons to the layout. Do this by opening the activity_contact.xml file and copying the `RelativeLayout` xml with the +id set to `navbar` to the activity_contact_settings.xml. Be sure to include the end `</RelativeLayout>` tag. While in the XML view, delete the `TextView` XML and delete the padding attributes in the root `RelativeLayout`. Switch to Graphical Layout to verify that the navigation bar is visible and in the correct position. There should be no whitespace around the navigation bar.

In Graphical Layout, drag two medium `TextViews` and two `RadioGroup` widgets from the Form Widgets folder in the Palette to the layout. The `RadioGroup` widget looks like three circles in a row. Positioning of these widgets should be similar to Figure 5.4.

Switch to `activity_contact_settings.xml` and modify the XML to match Listing 5.9. Only attributes that need to be added or modified are shown for each widget in the listing. Do not change or modify any other attributes.

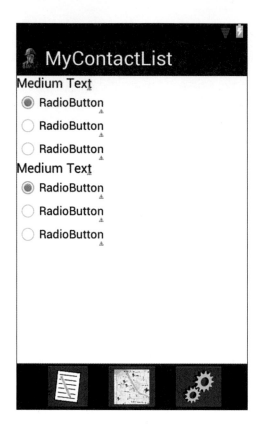

Figure 5.4   ContactSettings layout loading widgets.

Listing 5.9   **RadioButton and TextView XML**

```
<TextView
    android:layout_marginLeft="15dp"
    android:layout_marginTop="15dp"
    android:text="Sort Contact By:"

<RadioGroup
    android:layout_alignParentLeft="true"
    android:layout_marginLeft="35dp"
    android:layout_marginTop="10dp"
```

```
    <RadioButton
        android:id="@+id/radioName"
        android:text="Name" />

    <RadioButton
        android:id="@+id/radioCity"
        android:text="City" />

    <RadioButton
        android:id="@+id/radioBirthday"
        android:text="Birthday" />
</RadioGroup>

<TextView
    android:id="@+id/textView2"
    android:layout_marginLeft="15dp"
    android:layout_marginTop="15dp"
    android:text="Sort Order:"

<RadioGroup
    android:layout_marginLeft="35dp"
    android:layout_marginTop="10dp"

    <RadioButton
        android:id="@+id/radioAscending"
        android:text="Ascending" />

    <RadioButton
        android:id="@+id/radioDescending"
        android:text="Descending" />

</RadioGroup>
```

After the modifications have been made, switch to Graphical Layout and verify that the layout looks like Figure 5.5.

Code the Page's Behavior

The settings activity's function is relatively simple. When a user presses one of the choices, that value is stored as a key/value pair in SharedPreferences. When the page is accessed, the activity reads the stored preferences and sets the RadioButtons to the stored value. The value stored in a SharedPreferences is used in ContactListActivity to sort the list of saved contacts.

Figure 5.5   Completed ContactSettings layout.

Open the ContactSettingsActivity.java file and complete the following steps:

1. Copy the ImageButton initialization methods from the ContactActivity.java to the ContactSettingsActivity.java file so that the navigation bar will work. These methods are initMapButton(), initListButton(), and initSettingsButton(). Paste this code before the last } in the ContactSettingsActivity.java file.

2. When the code is pasted into the ContactSettingActivity class, it will produce errors. That is because the current activity in the Intent code is referencing the ContactActivity. Change this for each to be the ContactSettingActivity (some versions of Eclipse may do this for you).

3. Change the code in the initSettingsButton() method so that the button is disabled. Use the following code:

```
private void initSettingsButton() {
    ImageButton settings = (ImageButton) findViewById(R.
id.imageButtonSettings);
    list.setEnabled(false);
}
```

4. Call the three methods in the onCreate method.

After you have completed coding the navigation bar, you have to code the activity so that it displays the current preference. Create a method called initSettings and refer to the code in Listing 5.10 to get it to properly configure the activity at startup.

Listing 5.10 **Code to Initialize the Activity**

```
private void initSettings() {
    String sortBy = getSharedPreferences("MyContactListPreferences",
        ➥Context.MODE_PRIVATE).getString("sortfield","contactname");        //1
    String sortOrder = getSharedPreferences("MyContactListPreferences",
        ➥Context.MODE_PRIVATE).getString("sortorder","ASC");

    RadioButton rbName = (RadioButton) findViewById(R.id.radioName);          //2
    RadioButton rbCity = (RadioButton) findViewById(R.id.radioCity);
    RadioButton rbBirthDay = (RadioButton) findViewById(R.id.radioBirthday);
    if (sortBy.equalsIgnoreCase("contactname")) {                            //3
        rbName.setChecked(true);
    }
    else if (sortBy.equalsIgnoreCase("city")) {
        rbCity.setChecked(true);
    }
    else {
        rbBirthDay.setChecked(true);
    }

    RadioButton rbAscending = (RadioButton) findViewById(R.id.radioAscending);   //4
    RadioButton rbDescending = (RadioButton) findViewById(R.id.radioDescending);
    if (sortOrder.equalsIgnoreCase("ASC")) {
        rbAscending.setChecked(true);
    }
    else {
        rbDescending.setChecked(true);
    }
}
```

The initSettings method gets the values stored in *SharedPreferences* to set the RadioButtons to the value that the user checks.

1. A string variable is declared, and the value for the field to sort contacts by is retrieved from SharedPreferences. The getPreferences method is used to get the SharedPreferences object because there is no need to have multiple SharedPreferences objects in this app. The SharedPreference file is opened as a private object. The getString method is called on the SharedPreference object to retrieve the string value associated with the sortfield key. If there is no value stored for that key, the default value of contactname is assigned to the variable. The next line does the same thing for the preferred sort order.

2. A reference to each radio button in the sort field `RadioGroup` is assigned to a variable.

3. The value retrieved for the preferred sort field is evaluated to determine which `RadioButton` should be set as checked.

4. The same operations are performed to set the sort order to the order preferred by the user.

The next step is to create a method to store the selected user preference for each option. Two methods are required, one for each RadioGroup. When the user presses a RadioButton in one of the groups, which RadioButton pressed is determined and then the value associated with that RadioButton is saved in SharedPreferences. Refer to Listing 5.11 for the code for these methods.

Listing 5.11   RadioButton Click Code

```
private void initSortByClick() {
    RadioGroup rgSortBy = (RadioGroup) findViewById(R.id.radioGroup1);
    rgSortBy.setOnCheckedChangeListener(new OnCheckedChangeListener() {

        @Override
        public void onCheckedChanged(RadioGroup arg0, int arg1) {
            RadioButton rbName = (RadioButton) findViewById(R.id.radioName);
            RadioButton rbCity = (RadioButton) findViewById(R.id.radioCity);
            if (rbName.isChecked()) {
                getSharedPreferences("MyContactListPreferences",
                    ➥.MODE_PRIVATE).edit()
                    ➥.putString("sortfield", "contactname").commit();
            }
            else if (rbCity.isChecked()) {
                getSharedPreferences("MyContactListPreferences",
                    ➥.MODE_PRIVATE).edit()
                    ➥.putString("sortfield", "city").commit();
            }
            else {
                getSharedPreferences("MyContactListPreferences",
                    ➥.MODE_PRIVATE).edit()
                    ➥.putString("sortfield", "birthday").commit();
            }
        }
    });
}

private void initSortOrderClick() {
    RadioGroup rgSortOrder = (RadioGroup) findViewById(R.id.radioGroup2);
    rgSortOrder.setOnCheckedChangeListener(new OnCheckedChangeListener() {

        @Override
        public void onCheckedChanged(RadioGroup arg0, int arg1) {
```

```
            RadioButton rbAscending = (RadioButton)
                                ➥findViewById(R.id.radioAscending);
     if (rbAscending.isChecked()) {
              getSharedPreferences("MyContactListPreferences",
                   ➥.MODE_PRIVATE).edit()
                   ➥.putString("sortorder", "ASC").commit();
          }
          else {
              getSharedPreferences("MyContactListPreferences",
                   ➥.MODE_PRIVATE).edit()
                   ➥.putString("sortorder", "DESC").commit();
          }
       }
    });
}
```

Much of the code in these two methods has already been discussed. The only new code is the code used to save the selected preference. Examine the listing to find the `getPreferences` method. This method gets a reference to the `SharedPreferences` object using private mode. It then sends the message `edit()` to the `SharedPreferences` object to open it for editing. Next, the message `putString` is sent to the editable `SharedPreferences` object to save the value. The first parameter in the `putString` method is the key and the second is the value to be saved. Finally, the message `commit()` is sent to the changed `SharedPreferences` object to make the changes persist.

Add calls to these methods in the `onCreate` method and then run and test the Settings activity. You should select a sort field value and a sort order value. Navigate to another activity and then navigate back to the Settings activity. If the values remain as you selected them, the activity is completed! These values stored in the `SharedPreferences` object are used in Chapter 6, "Lists in Android: Navigation and Information Display," to present a sorted list of contacts to the user.

Summary

Data that exists beyond the execution of the app is said to persist. In this chapter you learned several methods to make data persist in your app. You also learned how to get that persistent data for use in the app. A SQLite database is used to store complex data. You created a class (`ContactDBHelper`) to create and update the database and its contents. You created a class (`ContactDataSource`) to access the database. Finally, you created a class (`Contact`) to pass a contact's data from and to the database methods.

The second method you learned to persist data was through the `SharedPreferences` object. The `SharedPreferences` object is used to store primitive bits of data, such as strings and integers. You learned how to put data into a `SharedPreferences` object to save user choices on contact sort order, and you learned how to get those choices from the object to display the user's past choices.

Exercises

1. Add the choice of a background color to the settings activity. Create a couple of new color resources in color.xml. Add these choices as a RadioGroup to the settings screen. You will have to modify the layout to place all the RadioGroups in a ScrollView so that you can see them all. Make the choice persist in a `SharedPreferences` object. Use the following command in the `onCreate` method of the settings activity to set the chosen background color:

   ```
   scrollviewobject.setBackgroundResource(R.color.colorresourcename);
   ```

2. Create a method in `ContactDataSource` that will only update the Contact's Address. Create a `ContactAddress` object to pass data to the method.

3. Modify the `Contact` table to include a field BFF that is an integer data type. Modify the onUpgrade method of `ContactDBHelper` to insert this new field without losing the data that is currently in the table.

Lists in Android: Navigation and Information Display

Lists are very useful tools and have become ubiquitous in mobile computing. So much so that my daughter asked, after seeing my brother-in-law with a cast needed because of carpal tunnel syndrome from computer use, if she was going to get a similar disease because she does this so often. With that she moved her index finger in the list swipe gesture. Lists are so common because they are a very useful way to organize, display, and access large amounts of data on a very small screen. This chapter explores the implementation of lists in Android. It covers simple lists that exploit the built-in list capabilities of the Android SDK and then examines the development of more complex lists, tailored specifically to the task at hand. Finally, the chapter concludes by introducing passing data between activities, using user preferences to sort a list, and changing the app's launch activity to complete the `ContactListActivity`.

Lists and Adapters

Two components are required for any list implementation in Android: a `ListView` widget and an adapter. The `ListView` widget is an object that can display a vertical list of items that can be scrolled through. An `Adapter` is dynamically associated with the `ListView`. The adapter provides access to the underlying data source for the list. In the case of a simple list, after an adapter is associated with the widget, insertion of data as a list item is handled automatically. In the case of a complex list, the developer must create a subclass of an `Adapter` object and code the display and behavior of the list in the new subclass.

Lists

An `AdapterView` is the super class of all views that are bound to an underlying data source. A `View` is the base class for all user interface components, such as the widgets used in creating layouts. The `AdapterView` has several subclasses, including `GridView`, `ListView`, and

Spinner widgets. The visible component of a list is implemented with a ListView widget in an XML layout file. The widget has attributes that allow the user to configure some aspects of the display. In many ways, a ListView is a standard widget. However, if given the special ID of @id/android:list and a special subclass of Activity, many of the tasks of list implementation are easier because the developer can take advantage of many built-in features of the SDK. To take advantage of these features, the Activity associated with the layout containing the ListView must be a subclass of ListActivity rather than Activity. You don't have to use the ListActivity subclass, but that requires more coding, so only the ListActivity approach is used in this chapter.

Adapters

Adapters act as a link between the view and the underlying data source for the list. Lists require the use of an adapter. The adapter provides access to the data items and is responsible for creating a View for each item. A view determines how each list item is displayed. In most cases, this display is uniform for each data item. The display does not have to be uniform, but in that case, developers must implement their own adapters to create the different views.

The super class for all adapters is BaseAdapter, which is an abstract class. The BaseAdapter class has three subclasses, ArrayAdapter, CursorAdapter, and SimpleAdapter. The ArrayAdapter is used to bind an Array or ArrayList to a view. An ArrayAdapter is always parameterized. That means it must be told what kind of data it is going to bind to a view. This data can be simple, such as String, or more complex, such as the Contact object created in the previous chapter. CursorAdapter is an abstract class that binds data from a database cursor to a view. It has a concrete subclass, SimpleCursorAdapter, that is used to map a row layout to fields in a cursor. The SimpleAdapter class is used to bind static data to a view.

The ArrayAdapter is commonly used in list implementation. A solid understanding of how to use this class can be easily extended to other adapter types where appropriate. In this chapter the ArrayAdapter class is used to implement both a simple list and a complex list.

Simple Lists

The simple list implementation displays only the contact name of each contact in the user's contact database. For now, the user will be able to scroll through this list and click the list to open the ContactActivity, but little else.

Create the Data Source Method

The first step to implementing the simple list is to have data. For this, you need to add a method to the ContactDataSource class that will retrieve each contact's name. Open ContactDataSource.java and add the code in Listing 6.1 to create a method for getting this data from the database.

Listing 6.1   **getContactName** Code

```
public ArrayList<String> getContactName() {
    ArrayList<String> contactNames = new ArrayList<String>();          //1
    try {
        String query = "Select contactname from contact";              //2
        Cursor cursor = database.rawQuery(query, null);

        cursor.moveToFirst();                                          //3
        while (!cursor.isAfterLast()) {
            contactNames.add(cursor.getString(0));
            cursor.moveToNext();
        }
        cursor.close();
    }
    catch (Exception e) {
        contactNames = new ArrayList<String>();                        //4
    }
    return contactNames;
}
```

Much of this method is similar to the method you wrote in the previous chapter to retrieve the last contact's ID number. The primary difference is that the query can return more than one record to the cursor, so you have to implement a loop to retrieve all the records.

1. The return value for this method is an ArrayList. An ArrayList is an object that acts like an array in that the data it holds can be accessed through an index. In contrast to an array, the ArrayList is not a fixed size. It can grow as data is added to it. An ArrayList is parameterized. That is the <String> portion of the code. This says that the values in the ArrayList are all of the String data type. Parameters for an ArrayList can be more complex objects. Later, you will parameterize an ArrayList to hold the Contact objects.

2. The SQL query is set up to return the contactname field for all records in the contact table.

3. A loop is set up to go through all the records in the cursor. The loop is initialized by moving to the first record in the cursor. Next, the while loop is set up to test if the end of the cursor's record set has been reached. Within the loop, the contact name is added to the ArrayList, and the cursor is advanced to the next record. Forgetting the moveToNext() command will leave your method in an infinite loop because it will never reach the end of the recordset.

4. The ArrayList is set to a new empty ArrayList in case the routine crashes partially through its filling. This way, the calling Activity can test for an empty list to determine if the retrieve was successful.

Create the Layout

Now that you have a way to get contact data, the next step is to modify the activity_contact_list.xml file to include a `ListView` widget. Open this file and delete the HelloWorld TextView if you have not already done so (see creating the layout in the "Using Preferences" section of Chapter 5, "Persistent Data in Android"). Also add the navigation bar if you haven't done that. Be sure to delete the `paddingLeft`, attributes, and the like in the root `RelativeLayout`. In Graphical Layout, from the Composite folder in the Palette, drag a `ListView` to anywhere on the layout. Switch to activity_contact_list.xml and modify the XML for the `ListView` widget to match Listing 6.2.

Listing 6.2   **ListView XML**

```
<ListView
    android:id="@id/android:list"
    android:layout_width="match_parent"
    android:layout_height="wrap_content"
    android:layout_alignParentLeft="true"
    android:layout_alignParentTop="true"
    android:layout_above="@+id/navbar" >
</ListView>
```

This XML does not include any new attributes. However, it does include a new value. Examine the `android:id` attribute. Notice that the id value is not a `+id`. It is `@id/android:list`. This identifies this widget as using an Android-supplied ID. You use this to get access to the built-in behaviors in `ListActivity`. After you've made the XML modifications, your layout should look like Figure 6.1.

Code the Activity

After the layout is complete, open ContactListActivity.java. Add code to make the navigation buttons work. Be sure to disable the List button (see "Code the Page's Behavior" in Chapter 5). Next, change the class declaration line of code so that it extends `ListActivity` rather than `Activity`, as shown next:

public class ContactListActivity **extends** ListActivity {

You will have to import `ListActivity`. Next, enter the code in Listing 6.3 in the `onCreate` method after the calls to the button initialization methods.

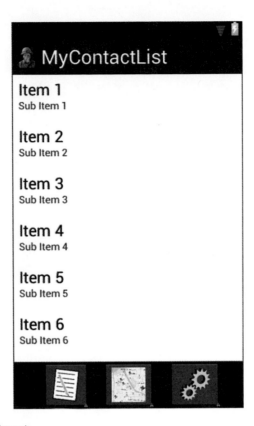

Figure 6.1   Initial list layout.

Listing 6.3   **Simple List Activation Code**

```
ContactDataSource ds = new ContactDataSource(this);
ds.open();
ArrayList<String> names = ds.getContactName();
ds.close();

setListAdapter(new ArrayAdapter<String>(this,
    android.R.layout.simple_list_item_1, names));
```

Most of the code in Listing 6.3 should be familiar. The first four lines create a new
ContactDataSource object, open the database, retrieve the contact names using the method
you created, and close the database. The last line is new. Its purpose is to associate the
ListView widget with the Adapter that has the data to be displayed. To do so, it instantiates

a new `ArrayAdapter` that is parameterized to hold `String` data, providing it its context (this), the layout to use for a list item (`android.R.layout.simple_list_item_1`), and an `ArrayList` with the data to be displayed (names). The layout is provided by the Android SDK, which is why the reference to the layout begins with `android` rather than `R`. Notice that you did not have to get a reference to the `ListView` widget like you have done every other time you accessed a widget in a layout. This is because of the use of `android:list` ID and the `ListActivity`. All that work is built in to the `Activity`. Run the app on the emulator and tap the List button in the navigation bar. Your display should look like Figure 6.2. If you have no data entered, the screen will be blank. Hit the Back button and enter a contact. Then tap the List button again. It is more likely that you have a bunch of junk contacts leftover from testing the app up to this point.

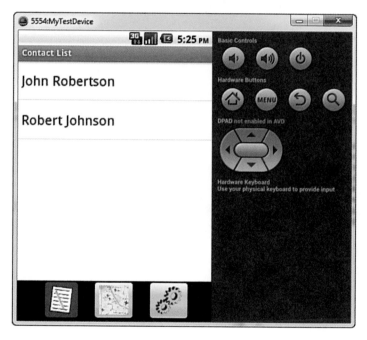

Figure 6.2   Initial list running in emulator.

A list of data is much more useful if it allows the user to do something with the data. In time, you will make the tap of a contact in the list open the `ContactActivity` with that user's data displayed. After the following code is entered, the tap of a contact just opens the `ContactActivity`. Place the code in Listing 6.4 in the `ContactListActivity`'s `onCreate` method after the code that sets the list adapter, and fix the imports.

Listing 6.4   **Code to Respond to an Item Click**

```
ListView listView = getListView();
listView.setOnItemClickListener(new AdapterView.OnItemClickListener()
{

    @Override
    public void onItemClick(AdapterView<?> arg0, View arg1, int arg2,
                            ➥long arg3) {
        Intent intent = new Intent(ContactListActivity.this,
                            ➥ContactActivity.class);

        startActivity(intent);
    }
});
```

The pattern in this code should be starting to get familiar. A reference to the layout widget is grabbed. In this case, you used the `ListActivity`'s `getListView()` method rather than `findViewById`. Next, a listener for the behavior you are interested in responding to is added to the widget. Finally, the app's response to the user's behavior is coded. Run the app on the emulator. Click any one of the contacts in the list and the `ContactActivity` should open.

That's all you need to code a simple list. Simple lists are useful for basic information display. To make a more interesting list that works exactly as you need for your app, you must code your own adapter and list item layout.

Complex Lists

The `ContactListActivity` needs to have more functionality than can be coded in a simple list. In this activity, the list displays the contact's name in a large blue font and the contact's phone number in a smaller black font below the name. The list item also displays an arrow indicating that tapping the contact leads to some other activity. In this case, the `ContactActivity` will open and the contact's data is displayed. The list also allows the deletion of one or more contacts. To get this functionality, you need to create data source methods, create your own list item layout, and create your own adapter.

Create the Data Source Method

The complex list displays and uses several bits of data about a contact. To function properly, it needs all the data for a contact. This requires a method to retrieve contact data for all contacts from the database. Open or switch to ContactDataSource.java to create a new method that returns that data as `Contact` objects in an `ArrayList`. Use the code in Listing 6.5.

Listing 6.5   **getContacts Method**

```java
public ArrayList<Contact> getContacts() {
    ArrayList<Contact> contacts = new ArrayList<Contact>();
    try {
        String query = "SELECT * FROM contact";
        Cursor cursor = database.rawQuery(query, null);

        Contact newContact;
        cursor.moveToFirst();
        while (!cursor.isAfterLast()) {
            newContact = new Contact();                            //1
            newContact.setContactID(cursor.getInt(0));
            newContact.setContactName(cursor.getString(1));
            newContact.setStreetAddress(cursor.getString(2));
            newContact.setCity(cursor.getString(3));
            newContact.setState(cursor.getString(4));
            newContact.setZipCode(cursor.getString(5));
            newContact.setPhoneNumber(cursor.getString(6));
            newContact.setCellNumber(cursor.getString(7));
            newContact.setEMail(cursor.getString(8));
            Time t = new Time();                                  //2
            t.set(Long.valueOf(cursor.getString(9)));
            newContact.setBirthday(t);

            contacts.add(newContact);
            cursor.moveToNext();
        }
        cursor.close();
    }
    catch (Exception e) {
        contacts = new ArrayList<Contact>();
    }
    return contacts;
}
```

This code is very similar to the method used to retrieve the contact name. The primary difference is that it retrieves all the data for each contact and places that data in a Contact object before it adds it to the ArrayList (which is now parameterized to hold Contact objects). There are some notable differences:

1. A new Contact object is instantiated for each record in the cursor. All the values in the record are added to the appropriate attribute in the new object. Care must be taken to get the proper field. You need to know the structure of your table for this. The first field in the table creation SQL statement is index 0 in the cursor, the second field is index 1, and so on.

2. A new `Time` object is created to hold the contact's birthday. Dates are stored in millis, so the time object is set to the proper date using the `set(long millis)` method. After the birthday object is created, it is inserted into the `Contact` object.

Create the Layout

A complex list relies on the `ListView` widget, but also requires a custom list item layout. The list item layout is a layout like any other layout. However, it is organized so that it displays important information from one of the items in the underlying data source. It typically contains significantly fewer widgets than an activity's layout and is organized in a rowlike manner. There are several steps you need to take to create the list item layout for this chapter.

1. Add some colors to the color.xml value file. Use `#ff0000` as the value for the color named system_red, `#ffffff` as the value for the color named system_white and `#0000ff` for the color named system_blue. Save the file.

2. Create a new XML layout file by right-clicking the layout folder in the Package Explorer and selecting New > Other > Android XML Layout File. Give the file the name list_item.

3. Switch to list_item.xml after the file opens in the editor, and change the root layout from `LinearLayout` to `RelativeLayout`. Remember to make this change also in the closing tag.

4. Return to Graphical Layout and drag two large `TextView`s, one medium `TextView`, and one small `Button` to anywhere on the layout.

5. Switch to list_item.xml and configure the XML as identified in Listing 6.6.

Listing 6.6   **List Item Layout XML**

```
<RelativeLayout xmlns:android="http://schemas.android.com/apk/res/android"
    android:layout_width="match_parent"
    android:layout_height="match_parent" >
                                                                            //1
    <TextView
        android:id="@+id/textContactName"
        android:layout_width="wrap_content"
        android:layout_height="wrap_content"
        android:layout_alignParentLeft="true"
        android:layout_alignParentTop="true"
        android:layout_marginLeft="15sp"
        android:textColor="@color/system_red"
        android:text="Contact Name"
        android:textAppearance="?android:attr/textAppearanceLarge" />
                                                                            //2
```

```
    <TextView
        android:id="@+id/textPhoneNumber"
        android:layout_width="wrap_content"
        android:layout_height="wrap_content"
        android:layout_alignParentLeft="true"
        android:layout_marginLeft="15sp"
        android:layout_below="@+id/textContactName"
        android:text="Phone Number"
        android:textAppearance="?android:attr/textAppearanceMedium" />
                                                                        //3
    <Button
        android:id="@+id/buttonDeleteContact"
        style="?android:attr/buttonStyleSmall"
        android:layout_width="wrap_content"
        android:layout_height="wrap_content"
        android:layout_alignParentTop="true"
        android:layout_marginTop="10dp"
        android:layout_alignParentRight="true"
        android:layout_marginRight="10dp"
        android:layout_toLeftOf="@+id/textContinue"
        android:textColor="@color/system_red"
        android:background="@color/system_white"
        android:visibility="invisible"
        android:focusable="false"
        android:focusableInTouchMode="false"
        android:text="Delete" />

</RelativeLayout>
```

All the heights and widths of the widgets are set to wrap_content so that they adapt to the data that is displayed within them. Much of the XML should be familiar to you. However, a few items need to be explained.

1. The contact name TextView is set to position itself at the top left of the list item. It is set to have a large style, and the textColor attribute is set to the system resource for the blue color.

2. The phone number TextView is positioned below the contact name TextView. It uses the default color so the textColor attribute is not used.

3. The button widget introduces many new attributes. The first of these are the attributes that give the appearance desired. The attribute textColor sets the button text to the red color rather than the default. The background attribute sets the button's background color to white, which matches the background of the list item. This gives the appearance that there is no button, just text to click. The visibility attribute is used to hide the button until the user chooses to delete some contacts.

The focusable and focusableInTouchMode attributes are new, and both are set to false. This is important to the behavior of the list. By default, if a list has a widget that responds to some user event, that widget controls all clicks on the list item. In other words, if the user selected the list item, but not the widget, instead of opening the ContactActivity, the widget's method would execute and delete the contact. Setting these two attributes to false corrects that behavior.

Change the button's visibility attribute value to visible so you can see it in the layout, and switch to Graphical Layout. Your layout should look like Figure 6.3. If it does, switch back to list_item.xml and change the visibility attribute back to invisible.

Figure 6.3   List item layout.

Create the Custom Adapter

A custom list item is of little use without a custom adapter. Custom adapters are always created as subclasses of another type of adapter that is the closest fit for the behavior needed. Create a new class called ContactAdapter in the com.example.mycontactlist source folder. Modify the class by adding the code in Listing 6.7.

Listing 6.7   **ContactAdapter Code**

```
                                                                    //1
public class ContactAdapter extends ArrayAdapter<Contact> {
                                                                    //2
    private ArrayList<Contact> items;
    private Context adapterContext;
                                                                    //3
    public ContactAdapter(Context context, ArrayList<Contact> items) {
            super(context, R.layout.list_item, items);
            c = context;
            this.items = items;
    }
                                                                    //4
```

```
@Override
public View getView(int position, View convertView, ViewGroup parent) {
    View v = convertView;
    try {
        Contact contact = items.get(position);


                                                                        //5

        if (v == null) {
            LayoutInflater vi = (LayoutInflater)
            ➥adapterContext.getSystemService(Context.LAYOUT_INFLATER_SERVICE);
            v = vi.inflate(R.layout.list_item, null);
        }

                                                                        //6

        TextView contactName = (TextView)
        ➥v.findViewById(R.id.textContactName);
        TextView contactNumber = (TextView)
        ➥v.findViewById(R.id.textPhoneNumber);
        Button b = (Button) v.findViewById(R.id.buttonDeleteContact);
        contactName.setText(contact.getContactName());
        contactNumber.setText(contact.getPhoneNumber());
        b.setVisibility(View.INVISIBLE);
    }
    catch (Exception e) {
        e.printStackTrace();
        e.getCause();
    }
    return v;
    }
}
```

A custom adapter is relatively easy to construct. However, it is important to understand the components so that it works properly.

1. The ContactAdapter class is declared as a subclass of ArrayAdapter that has been parameterized to hold only Contact objects.

2. Two variables are declared for the class. The items variable holds the ArrayList of Contact objects that have been retrieved from the database. The adapterContext variable holds a reference to the context, in this case the ContactListActivity, where the list is being displayed.

3. The constructor method for the ContactAdapter class is passed the context and the ArrayList of contacts. It calls its super class constructor method (ArrayAdapter), passing it the context, contacts, and the layout file used for the items. It then assigns the contacts and context that were passed in to the items and c variables, respectively.

4. The getView method is the workhorse of this class. This method is called for every item in the underlying data source up to the number of list items that can be displayed in the ListView. As the user scrolls through the list, this method is called to display contacts in

the `ArrayList` as they are scrolled into view. The `ListView` passes the index of the item to be displayed and the `View`, which is the list item layout if it exists, null if it does not. This is done so that list item views can be reused as they scroll off the screen rather than re-creating a new view. This saves system resources.

5. If there isn't an existing view to be reused, the `LayoutInflater` service is called to instantiate the `list_item` layout you previously created. You can use this to inflate multiple views and use them as needed based on the underlying data.

6. References to the widgets on the `list_item` layout are acquired and used to set the widget to the proper settings for the contact it displays.

Code the Activity

You are almost ready to test your custom adapter. But first you need to change the `ContactListActivity` code to retrieve contact objects rather than contact names, set the `ListView` to use the custom adapter, and code the `onItemClick` method to pass the selected contact's ID to `ContactActivity`. The first two changes require changing only one line of code each. Switch to the ContactListActivity.java. Code the activity to retrieve `Contact` objects rather than names by changing the

```
ArrayList<String> names = ds.getContactName();
```

line of code to

```
final ArrayList<Contact> contacts = ds.getContacts();
```

The `final` keyword needs to be added because you will now use the `ArrayList` inside the `onItemClick` method.

Code the activity to use the new adapter by changing the

```
setListAdapter(new ArrayAdapter<String>(this,
    ➥android.R.layout.simple_list_item_1, names));
```

line to

```
setListAdapter(new ContactAdapter(this, contacts));
```

Finally, modify the `onItemClick` method to pass the contact ID. Find the `onItemClick` method in the `onCreate` method of the `Activity`. Modify the code to match Listing 6.8.

Listing 6.8   Selected Item Click

```
@Override
                                                                          //1
public void onItemClick(AdapterView<?> parent, View itemClicked, int position,
                        ➥long id) {
  Contact selectedContact = contacts.get(position);                      //2
    Intent intent = new Intent(ContactListActivity.this, ContactActivity.class);
```

```
intent.putExtra("contactid", selectedContact.getContactID());                    //3
    startActivity(intent);
}
```

Very little needs to be done to the method. All this method has to do is get the selected contact from the contacts `ArrayList`, get the required data from it, and pass the data to the `ContactActivity`.

1. The method declaration is functionally the same. However, change the name of the method parameters from the generic `arg` so that it is easier to understand what each parameter is.

2. Create a variable named `selectedContact` and retrieve the contact from the `ArrayList` using the position value. The position value is the index of the item tapped in the list, and it matches the index of the contact in the `ArrayList` that is displayed in that list item.

3. Place the contact ID in the bundle that is passed to the `ContactActivity`. The method `putExtra(key, value)` is used to put primitive data types in the `Intent` so that they are accessible by the activity receiving the intent.

Save all your changes and test the adapter on the emulator. If you have properly coded these objects, your `ContactListActivity` in the emulator should look similar to Figure 6.4.

Add Delete Functionality

The final job associated with making the list work properly is to code the capability to delete a contact from the list (and the database). This functionality is primarily implemented in the custom adapter. However, because you don't want the user to accidently delete a contact, the app provides a button to turn the delete functionality on and off. Four tasks need to be completed to implement the delete function:

1. Add a button to the `activity contact_list` layout.

2. Code a method to delete a contact from the database in `ContactDataSource`.

3. Code the custom adapter to delete a contact from the list and database.

4. Code the `ContactListActivity` to use the delete function of the adapter.

First, add the button to the layout and, as long as you're at it, add a button to add a new contact to the layout. The code to implement the new contact button is addressed later in this section. The two buttons are located at the top of the layout in a toolbar just like in the `ContactActivity`. In fact, the easiest way to implement the buttons is to copy the toolbar XML and paste it into the `ContactList` layout file. Whether you copy the XML or type it directly, it should look like Listing 6.9 when completed.

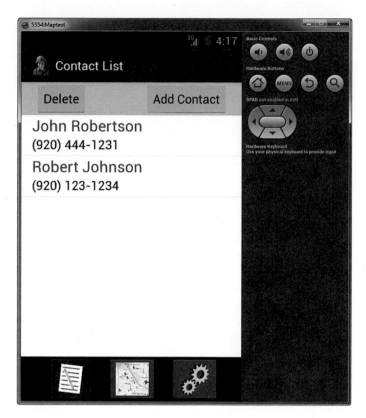

Figure 6.4   List with custom adapter running in emulator.

Listing 6.9   **Toolbar XML for `ContactListActivity`**

```
<RelativeLayout
    android:id="@+id/toolbar"
    android:layout_width="match_parent"
    android:layout_height="wrap_content"
    android:layout_alignParentLeft="true"
    android:layout_alignParentTop="true"
    android:background="@color/toolbar_background" >

    <Button
        android:id="@+id/buttonDelete"
        android:layout_width="wrap_content"
        android:layout_height="wrap_content"
        android:layout_alignParentLeft="true"
        android:layout_marginLeft="20dp"
        android:text="Delete" />
```

```
    <Button
        android:id="@+id/buttonAdd"
        android:layout_width="wrap_content"
        android:layout_height="wrap_content"
        android:layout_alignParentRight="true"
        android:layout_marginRight="20dp"
        android:text="Add Contact" />
</RelativeLayout>
```

If you copied the XML, make sure you change the `ToggleButton` to a `Button`. The XML for the list widget also needs to be modified. In the `ListView`'s attributes, delete the line that aligns the `ListView` with the top of the parent, and add the following line in its place:

```
android:layout_below="@+id/toolbar"
```

This line positions the `ListView` below the toolbar. When complete, switch to Graphical Layout and verify that the layout looks like that in Figure 6.5.

Figure 6.5   Modified ContactListActivity layout.

After you have the layout correct, open ContactDataSource to add a method to delete a contact. This method will be passed the ID number of the contact to delete. Refer to Listing 6.10 to code the method.

Listing 6.10   **deleteContact Method**

```
public boolean deleteContact(int contactId) {
    boolean didDelete = false;
    try {
        didDelete = database.delete("contact", "_id=" + contactId, null) > 0;
    }
    catch (Exception e) {
        //Do nothing -return value already set to false
    }
    return didDelete;
}
```

The deleteContact method is easy to understand. The method is passed the ID as the parameter contacted. A return value to indicate success or failure is set up, and the database's delete method is called. There are three parameters for the delete method. The first is the name of the table to delete from. The second is the Where clause to use to determine which records to delete. The final parameter is a string array of criteria for deletion. Only one of the last two parameters is needed. The other can be null.

Now turn your attention to the custom adapter (ContactAdapter.java) you created earlier. You need to add three methods to this class. The first method is used to display the Delete button in the list_item layout for a selected list item, and it sets a listener for the button click event. The method executed when the user clicks the Delete button removes the contact from the ArrayList, calls a method to hide the Delete button, and calls a method to delete the contact from the database. The second method deletes the contact from the database by calling ContactDataSource, and the third method hides the Delete button. The code for these methods is in Listing 6.11.

Listing 6.11   **Code to Delete from List**

```
public void showDelete(final int position, final View convertView,     //1
                       ➥final Context context, final Contact contact) {
    View v = convertView;
    final Button b = (Button) v.findViewById(R.id.buttonDeleteContact);
                                                                          //2
    if (b.getVisibility()==View.INVISIBLE) {
        b.setVisibility(View.VISIBLE);
        b.setOnClickListener(new OnClickListener() {
            @Override
            public void onClick(View v) {
                hideDelete(position, convertView, context);
```

```
                    items.remove(contact);
                    deleteOption(contact.getContactID(), context);
                }
            });
        }
        else {
            hideDelete(position, convertView, context);
        }
    }
```
//3
```
    private void deleteOption(int contactToDelete, Context context) {
        ContactDataSource db = new ContactDataSource(context);
        db.open();
        db.deleteContact(contactToDelete);
        db.close();
        this.notifyDataSetChanged();
    }
```
//4
```
    public void hideDelete(int position, View convertView, Context context) {
                            ➥View v = convertView;
        final Button b = (Button) v.findViewById(R.id.buttonDeleteContact);
        b.setVisibility(View.INVISIBLE);
        b.setOnClickListener(null);
    }
```

The user enables deleting by tapping the Delete button in the toolbar. This tells the list to respond to a list item selection by showing the Delete button for that list item and enabling the button's capability to respond to a click event. If the user taps a list item that is showing the Delete button but not on the button itself, the button is hidden. If the user taps the Delete button itself, the button's response to a tap event is executed, and the contact is deleted from the database and the list. This functions as essentially a two-phase commit for deleting. The user first has to choose a contact to delete and then choose to delete it. Because of this, there is no need for a warning message on the delete.

1. The showDelete method is the only public method of the three methods coded for the delete functionality of the custom adapter. It is called the ContactListActivity when the user selects a list time with deleting enabled. It is passed the position of the selection in the list, the list item layout with the contact's data in it, the context where the method call originated, and the Contact object associated with the selected list item.

2. The showDelete method checks if the Delete button is visible on the list item layout passed to it. If it is, it calls the hideDelete method. If it is not, it displays the button and enables the button click event. The click event uses Contact object passed to the showDelete method to remove the contact from the ArrayList and remove it from the database.

3. The deleteOption method is code standard for calling a method to access the database. The only new item in this method is notifyDataSetChanged(). This method tells

the adapter that the underlying data source has changed so that the list display will be changed to reflect the deletion.

4. The `hideDelete` method changes the button from visible to invisible and disables the button's `onClick` event.

The final step in coding the delete functionality is to modify ContactListActivity. Open this file and insert a new method to initiate the Delete button using the code in Listing 6.12. The `adapter` variable added below will produce a syntax error until you enter the code in Listing 6.13.

Listing 6.12   **`initDeleteButton()` Code**

```
private void initDeleteButton() {
    final Button deleteButton = (Button) findViewById(R.id.buttonDelete);
    deleteButton.setOnClickListener(new OnClickListener() {
        public void onClick(View v) {
            if (isDeleting) {
                deleteButton.setText("Delete");
                isDeleting = false;
                                                                        //1
                adapter.notifyDataSetChanged();
            }
            else {
                deleteButton.setText("Done Deleting");
                isDeleting = true;
            }
        }
    });
}
```

The code is relatively simple. It sets an `onClickListener` for the button, and when the button is clicked, it checks if the user has deleting enabled. If it is enabled, it is disabled by setting the `isDeleting` variable to false and changing the button display text to Delete. If it is not enabled, the code enables deleting by setting the `isDeleting` variable to true and changing the text of the button to Done Deleting.

This requires adding the `isDeleting` variable. Just after the `ContactListActivity` class declaration add the line

```
boolean isDeleting = false;
```

The one new bit of code in this method is at //1. This code tells the adapter to update itself. This is used to set the list back to the not deleting mode. If the user has selected a list item and the Delete button is visible and the user then clicks Done Deleting, this code removes the display of those buttons. Basically, the code tells the activity to update the UI when the adapter receives the message `notifyDataSetChanged()`. Be sure to call the `initDeleteButton()` method from the `onCreate` method.

The next step is to modify the `onItemClick` method (declared in the `onCreate` method) to handle deleting. Modify this method to match Listing 6.13.

Listing 6.13   **Modified `onItemClick` Method**

```
@Override
public void onItemClick(AdapterView<?> parent, View itemClicked, int position,
                                  ↪long id) {
    Contact selectedContact = contacts.get(position);
    if (isDeleting) {
        adapter.showDelete(position, itemClicked, ContactListActivity.this,
                            ↪selectedContact);
    }
    else {
        Intent intent = new Intent(ContactListActivity.this,
                                ↪ContactActivity.class);
        intent.putExtra("contactid", selectedContact.getContactID());
        startActivity(intent);
    }
}
```

Just as in the `initDeleteButton` method, a variable is used that is not declared. Add the declaration to hold the adapter after the declaration of the `isDeleting` variable. Use this code:

```
ContactAdapter adapter;
```

You will also have to assign the `ContactAdapter` to this variable. In the `onCreate` method, delete this line:

```
setListAdapter(new ContactAdapter(this, contacts));
```

Add this code in its place:

```
adapter = new ContactAdapter(this, contacts);
setListAdapter(adapter);
```

Test your app. If you have properly entered this code, when you tap the Delete button and then tap one of the items in the list, you will see something similar to Figure 6.6. If you then tap the Delete button, the contact should be deleted from the list.

Android Versus iOS: Creating Complex Lists

Creating a list like the one shown in this chapter is much simpler in iOS because a lot of the functionality is available in ready-made controls. In iOS, the list is called a table, and the default delete behavior is as it's described here, where the user taps a button to initiate delete mode and then is able to delete rows until the delete mode is cancelled.

Although the iOS controls provide a lot of functionality and can be customized, you do have less freedom than what is available in Android.

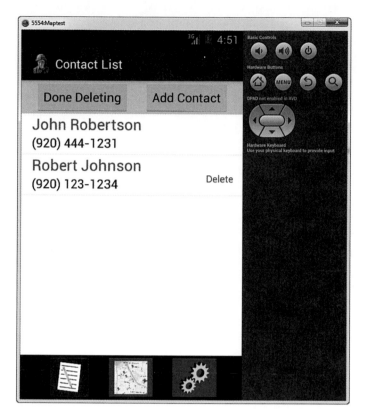

Figure 6.6   Deleting a contact.

You've completed the development of a custom list! The code is relatively involved, but the pattern is the basis for any future complex lists you might want to create. Complex lists are really not that difficult. Through the use of a custom adapter and layout, you can create list items with a significant amount of diverse information, including images if desired.

Completing the `ContactList` Activity

There are a few things left to complete the ContactList Activity. These things include modifying ContactActivity to use the contact ID passed to it, adding an Add Contact button, sorting the list using user preferences, and making the app open to the list rather than a blank contact.

Populating the `ContactActivity` Screen

You've learned how to get a list to respond to the selection of a contact in the list by opening the ContactActivity and passing a contact's ID value to it. The next step is to get the ContactActivity to use that ID to retrieve the contact's data and display it.

Open the ContactDataSource.java file and add a method to retrieve a specific contact based on the contact's ID. Use the code in Listing 6.14 to create the method. This code is essentially the same as the `getContacts` method, except that it returns a single contact rather than an `ArrayList` of all the contacts.

Listing 6.14   **GetSpecificContact Method**

```
public Contact getSpecificContact(int contactId) {                           //1
    Contact contact = new Contact();
    String query = "SELECT  * FROM contact WHERE _id =" + contactId;          //2
        Cursor cursor = database.rawQuery(query, null);

    if (cursor.moveToFirst()) {                                              //3
        contact.setContactID(cursor.getInt(0));
        contact.setContactName(cursor.getString(1));
        contact.setStreetAddress(cursor.getString(2));
        contact.setCity(cursor.getString(3));
        contact.setState(cursor.getString(4));
        contact.setZipCode(cursor.getString(5));
        contact.setPhoneNumber(cursor.getString(6));
        contact.setCellNumber(cursor.getString(7));
        contact.setEMail(cursor.getString(8));
        Time t = new Time();
        t.set(Long.valueOf(cursor.getString(9)));
        contact.setBirthday(t);

        cursor.close();
    }
    return contact;
}
```

The pattern should look very familiar. In this method, there is no loop because only one contact is returned. Also, a `Contact` object is the return value rather than an `ArrayList`. There are three other notable differences:

1. The method has a parameter in its signature. The parameter is an integer that holds the ID of the contact to be retrieved.

2. The SQL query has a `WHERE` clause that is passed the value of the parameter so that only the contact with that `ID` value is returned to the `cursor`.

3. Move to the first record returned. If a contact is found, populate the `contact` object.

Next, a new method needs to be added to `ContactActivity` and its `onCreate` method must be modified. The new method, called `initContact`, is used to retrieve the contact and populate the layout with the values of the retrieved contact. The `onCreate` method is modified to get the passed ID and call the method to retrieve and display the contact. Use the code in Listing 6.15 to create the new method.

Listing 6.15   Method to Load a Contact

```
private void initContact(int id) {
                                                                        //1
    ContactDataSource ds = new ContactDataSource(ContactActivity.this);
    ds.open();
    currentContact = ds.getSpecificContact(id);
    ds.close();
                                                                        //2
    EditText editName = (EditText) findViewById(R.id.editName);
    EditText editAddress = (EditText) findViewById(R.id.editAddress);
    EditText editCity = (EditText) findViewById(R.id.editCity);
    EditText editState = (EditText) findViewById(R.id.editState);
    EditText editZipCode = (EditText) findViewById(R.id.editZipcode);
    EditText editPhone = (EditText) findViewById(R.id.editHome);
    EditText editCell = (EditText) findViewById(R.id.editCell);
    EditText editEmail = (EditText) findViewById(R.id.editEMail);
    TextView birthDay = (TextView) findViewById(R.id.textBirthday);
                                                                        //3
    editName.setText(currentContact.getContactName());
    editAddress.setText(currentContact.getStreetAddress());
    editCity.setText(currentContact.getCity());
    editState.setText(currentContact.getState());
    editZipCode.setText(currentContact.getZipCode());
    editPhone.setText(currentContact.getPhoneNumber());
    editCell.setText(currentContact.getCellNumber());
    editEmail.setText(currentContact.getEMail());
                                                                        //4
    birthDay.setText(DateFormat.format("MM/dd/yyyy",
        ➥currentContact.getBirthday().toMillis(false)).toString());
}
```

Again, this code should be familiar by now. It is similar to the methods used to set the ContactActivity for editing or viewing.

1. The contact is retrieved and assigned to the Activity's currentContact variable.

2. A reference to all the widgets in the layout needed to display the contact's data is to a variable.

3. The widgets are set to display the values in the retrieved contact.

4. The display of the contact's birthday requires a little more work. The time value retrieved for the birthday is converted to millis and then converted to a string value. The DateFormat object's format method uses this value to create a string representation of the date in the given format ("MM/dd/yyyy").

Now you'll code the activity to get the id passed to it and call the initContact method to display the contact. Scroll to the onCreate method and delete the currentContact = new Contact() line. Before the setForViewing() line, add the code in Listing 6.16.

Listing 6.16   **onCreate Code to Get and Use Passed ID**

```
Bundle extras = getIntent().getExtras();
if(extras != null) {
    initContact(extras.getInt("contactid"));
}
else {
    currentContact = new Contact();
}
```

This code checks the intent for extras. If it finds an extra, it gets the contact ID, retrieves the contact from the database, and displays the data in the layout. If there is no extra, it assigns a new contact object to currentContact, effectively setting the currentContact ID to -1. This takes care of coding for the click of the Add Contact button in the ContactListActivity (see "Coding the Add Button" section that follows). The Add Contact button does not pass an extra to the ContactActivity, so the activity is ready to add a new contact's data.

Run your app. If you've done everything correctly, when you tap a name in the contact list, the ContactActivity will open with all the contact's data displayed. Congratulations! You have successfully learned to get data from an item selected in a list and pass that data to another activity.

The ContactListActivity is almost complete. You've got four tasks left:

1. Code the Add Contact button.

2. Modify the list to sort the data according to user preferences.

3. Modify the app to open this activity as the first activity.

4. Modify the onCreate method of this activity to check if there are any contacts saved. If there are no contacts, it will open the ContactActivity instead of the list.

Coding the Add Button

Coding the Add button is just reusing code that you used before (Listing 6.17).

Listing 6.17   **initAddContactButton() Method**

```
private void initAddContactButton() {
    Button newContact = (Button) findViewById(R.id.buttonAdd);
    newContact.setOnClickListener(new OnClickListener() {
        public void onClick(View v) {
            Intent intent = new Intent(ContactListActivity.this,
```

```
➥ContactActivity.class);
          startActivity(intent);
      }
   });
}
```

Remember to call the `initAddContactButton()` method in the `onCreate` method.

Sort the Contacts List

The next task is to code the `ContactListActivity` to sort the contact list according to the preferences set by the user. The first step is to modify the `getContacts` method in `ContactDataSource`. The method needs to be modified to accept the sort field and sort order as parameters and use these parameters in the SQL to perform the actual sort. Switch to ContactDataSource.java and locate the `getContacts` method. Change the message signature from

```
public ArrayList<Contact> getContacts() {
```

to

```
public ArrayList<Contact> getContacts(String sortField, String sortOrder) {
```

Next, change the SQL statement from

```
String query = "SELECT * FROM contact";
```

to

```
String query = "SELECT * FROM contact ORDER BY " + sortField + " " + sortOrder;
```

The next step is to modify the `ContactListActivity` to retrieve the user sorting preferences and pass them to this modified method. Switch to `ContactListActivity`. If you saved your last changes, there will be an error in the code because the method `getContacts()` no longer exists. To fix the error, you must first retrieve the stored user preferences. Enter the following two lines before the line that creates a new `ContactDataSource` object:

```
String sortBy = getSharedPreferences("MyContactListPreferences",
    ➥Context.MODE_PRIVATE).getString("sortfield", contactname");
String sortOrder = getSharedPreferences("MyContactListPreferences",
    ➥Context.MODE_PRIVATE).getString("sortorder", "ASC");
```

Now modify the call to the `getContacts` method to use these values:

```
final ArrayList<Contact> contacts = ds.getContacts(sortBy, sortOrder);
```

Run the app. Change the sort preferences using the Settings screen. You should see the order of the contacts on the list change as you change your preferences. Try changing the sort settings and returning to the list using the list `ImageButton`. Now try changing the sort order and returning to the ContactListActivity using the Back button. You should notice that the list is not re-sorted when you use the Back button, but it is when you use the `ImageButton`. When you use the `ImageButton`, the flag you set causes the old ContactActivityList activity to be destroyed and a new one is created so the `onCreate` method is executed. When you use the Back button, the Activity still exists, so the `onCreate` method is not executed and the sort order is thus never changed.

The solution to this is to place the code that populates the list in the `onResume()` method. As you saw in Chapter 2, "App Design Issues and Considerations," the `onResume` method is executed just before the `Activity` becomes visible. This method will be executed everytime the user navigates to the activity. This is where you need to move some of the code from the `onCreate` method to the `onResume()` method. Use the following steps:

1. After the `onCreate` method, create the `onResume` method.

2. Cut the code from the `onCreate` method that gets the preferences, retrieves the contacts, and sets up the list, and paste it into the `onResume` method.

When complete, your code should look like Listing 6.18.

Listing 6.18   **The onResume Method**

```
@Override
public void onResume() {
    super.onResume();
    String sortBy = getSharedPreferences("MyContactListPreferences",
        ➥Context.MODE_PRIVATE).getString("sortfield", "contactname");
    String sortOrder = getSharedPreferences("MyContactListPreferences",
        ➥Context.MODE_PRIVATE).getString("sortorder", "ASC");

    ContactDataSource ds = new ContactDataSource(this);
    ds.open();
    final ArrayList<Contact> contacts = ds.getContacts(sortBy, sortOrder);
    ds.close();

    adapter = new ContactAdapter(this, contacts);
    setListAdapter(adapter);
    ListView listView = getListView();
    listView.setOnItemClickListener(new AdapterView.OnItemClickListener() {

        @Override
        public void onItemClick(AdapterView<?> parent, View itemClicked,
                ➥int position, long id) {
            Contact selectedContact = contacts.get(position);
            if (isDeleting) {
                adapter.showDelete(position, itemClicked,
                    ➥ContactListActivity.this, selectedContact);
```

```
        }
        else {
            Intent intent = new Intent(ContactListActivity.this,
                ➡ContactActivity.class);
            intent.putExtra("contactid", selectedContact.getContactID());
            startActivity(intent);
        }
    }
  });
}
```

Most of the code has been explained as you wrote it. The one new thing is the creation of the `onResume` method itself. The method overrides the `onResume` method built in to the Activity so the first line in the methods calls that method, and so that all the things that need to happen when activity resumes still happen. Then your code is executed. The code you pasted into the `onResume` method should no longer be in the `onCreate` method.

Set `ContactListActivity` as the Default Activity

The third task is to modify the AndroidManifest.xml file to open the `ContactListActivity` instead of the `ContactActivity` as the initial app activity. Open AndroidManifest.xml by double-clicking it in the Package Explorer. Switch to the XML view if it is not already open. Find the code that matches Listing 6.18 and switch the name and label attributes so that the activity with the intent filter is `ContactListActivity` and its label, and the other activity has the name `ContactActivity` and its label. To do this, delete the strikeout lines (these are the original lines) in Listing 6.19 and add the new lines.

Listing 6.19   **Changing the Launch Activity**

```
<activity
    android:name="com.example.mycontactlist.ContactActivity"
    android:label="@string/app_name" >
    android:name="com.example.mycontactlist.ContactListActivity"
    android:label="@string/title_activity_contact_list" >
    <intent-filter>
        <action android:name="android.intent.action.MAIN" />
        <category android:name="android.intent.category.LAUNCHER" />
    </intent-filter>
 </activity>
<activity
    android:name="com.example.mycontactlist.ContactListActivity"
    android:label="@string/title_activity_contact_list" >
    android:name="com.example.mycontactlist.ContactActivity"
    android:label="@string/app_name" >
</activity>
```

Test the app. If the app does not start with the `ContactListActivity`, try cleaning the project to reload the manifest file. Select Project > Clean. Verify that the `MyContactList` project is selected or Clean All Projects is selected, and click OK. Run the app again. If the list still does not show as the first activity, you will have to modify your debug configuration. Select Run > Debug Configurations. In the window that opens, select your debug configuration if it is not already selected, and then select Launch Default Activity. Run the app again.

Set `ContactActivity` as Default Activity with no Contacts in Database

The final task is to modify the `onResume` method of the `ContactListActivity` to check if there are any contacts in the database. If there are not, the app should open the `ContactActivity`. Refer to Listing 6.20 to make these changes.

Listing 6.20   **Modify the `onResume` Method to Check for Contacts**

```
if (contacts.size() > 0) {                                           //1

    adapter = new ContactAdapter(this, contacts);
    setListAdapter(adapter);
    ListView listView = getListView();
    listView.setOnItemClickListener(new AdapterView.OnItemClickListener() {

        @Override
        public void onItemClick(AdapterView<?> parent, View itemClicked, int
                                    ➥position, long id) {
            Contact selectedContact = contacts.get(position);
            if (isDeleting) {
                adapter.showDelete(position, itemClicked,
                                ➥ContactListActivity.this, selectedContact);
            }
            else {
                Intent intent = new Intent(ContactListActivity.this,
                                            ➥ContactActivity.class);
                intent.putExtra("contactid", selectedContact.getContactID());
                startActivity(intent);
            }
        }
    });
}                                                                    //2
else {
    Intent intent = new Intent(ContactListActivity.this, ContactActivity.class);
    startActivity(intent);
}
```

You are really just adding a few lines of code around an existing body of code. Add the `if` statement before the line that sets the adapter variable to check if there are any contacts retrieved from the database (//1). Close the `if` statement body after the setting of the `onItemClickListener` body of code (//2). Then add the `else` block of code to open the `ContactActivity` if there are no contacts.

Test the app. Delete all the contacts. Rerun the app to see if it opens to the `ContactActivity`. If it does, you have successfully completed this chapter. Congratulations!

Summary

Lists are an important part of almost every app. Lists can be very simple displays of relatively static data, or they can be quite complex, displaying a variety of data and having a diverse set of behaviors. Simple lists can be implemented using components provided with the Android SDK. More complex lists require the development of custom list layouts and adapters.

The `ContactListActivity` is finished! The activity not only displays a list of contacts, but also sorts that list according to user preferences and passes data to the `ContactActivity` to display a selected contact.

Exercises

1. Add the contact's cell phone number to the complex list. The list should display the contact name on the first line and `Home:the number Cell:the number` on the second line.

2. Add another line to the list so that the list displays

   Contact Name

   Street Address, City, State, ZIP,

   Phone number

3. Modify the custom adapter to alternately display the contact name in red and blue. For example, the first name in the list will be red, the second will be blue, the third is red, and so on.

7

Maps and Location in Android

Smartphones and tablets are mobile computing devices. Both parts of that description are why location and maps are important components of many apps. Useful computation can be performed based on the device location. That location can change much faster than the location of a traditional computing device. This enables the app to very quickly change its behavior as it moves to different locations. Knowing how to capture and display location information can help you build powerful apps. This chapter describes how to take advantage of location information within your app. Location sensors can be accessed and used directly through the Android SDK. However maps require more work. This chapter also teaches you how to set up your Eclipse environment to work with maps.

Location Sensors, Maps, and Fragments

This section begins with an overview of sensors, maps, and fragments. Sensors are hardware built in to the mobile device to allow an app to capture environmental data. Maps are used to display data that can be enhanced by a visual representation of its location. Finally, fragments are a newer approach to coding Android Activities.

Location Sensors

Android devices typically have two location sensors. One sensor (network sensor) is based on the cell towers and/or the Wi-Fi access points your device is connected to. This sensor provides the approximate location of the device. The other sensor is based on a built-in Global Positioning System (GPS) receiver. This sensor can provide position information accurate to within a few meters, depending on conditions. However, the GPS sensor is much slower in acquiring its position information than the network sensor. Additionally, not all devices have a GPS sensor.

Location information is accessed within an app through the use of the LocationManager object. A LocationManager is not directly instantiated. It exists as an Android system service, and is accessed through the method getSystemService. The LocationManager object can request updates from either or both sensors. To get the updates, an app has to instantiate a LocationListener. A LocationListener implements the method onLocationChanged. Whenever the sensor reports a location change, that change is captured by the LocationListener, which is passed a Location object, and the onLocationChanged method is executed. A Location object contains information on the new location, including GPS coordinates and altitude, which sensor provided the location, a measure of the accuracy of the coordinate estimate (usually in meters), as well as other information. The onLocationChanged method uses this object to perform operations based on the code the developer provided in the method. To begin receiving location information from the sensors, the LocationManager requests the updates from a specific provider and tells it what LocationListener to use to handle the updates. When the LocationManager requests updates from the GPS, the GPS is activated. However, the GPS must also be enabled by the user to be activated. If it has not been enabled, the code cannot turn it on. It is recommended that the developer test whether the GPS is enabled and inform the user if it is not.

Maps

Maps are implemented using the GoogleMap object in the source code file and a MapFragment in the layout file. These objects are not a part of the standard Android SDK but rather the Google Play Services SDK. This SDK must be installed on your development machine to implement maps in your app. Using Google Maps requires an API key. This key associates your app with an attempt to access the GoogleMap API. This is how you, and Google, can track how often your users access the map portion of your app. The API key is free. Maps are implemented as a MapFragment widget in a layout. The Activity that implements the code to provide the map's behavior must be a FragmentActivity.

Fragments

Fragments were discussed in Chapter 4, "Android Navigation and Interface Design." The FragmentActivity is a subclass of the Activity class. An Activity that needs to implement a map must extend the FragmentActivity class rather than the Activity class. This is required because maps are encapsulated in a MapFragment. This allows a map to be a part of a layout rather than the only thing in a layout.

Setting Up for Maps

There are a few things that need to be done before you can successfully add maps to your app. The first is to load the Google Play Services SDK into your workspace. Select Window > Android SDK Manager. The SDK Manager window opens and shows a list of available SDKs. Scroll through this list until you find the Extras folder. Within this folder, find and check the box next to Google Play Services (Figure 7.1). Click the Install X Packages button. There may be more than just the one package you selected. Some packages have dependencies on other packages, and the SDK manager will want to install any package updates.

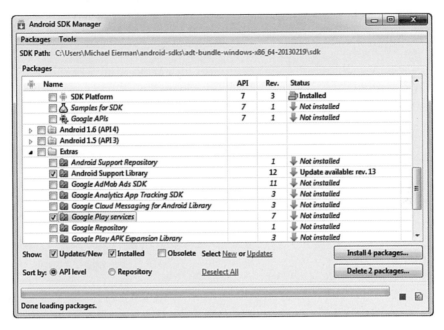

Figure 7.1   Android SDK Manager window.

The Choose Packages to Install window will be displayed. Click the Accept License option button at the bottom right of the window and then click Install (Figure 7.2). Downloading and installation will begin. This may take a significant amount of time. Plan to have something to do while you are waiting. After the SDKs have downloaded, you may have to restart Eclipse.

> **Note**
>
> The process of updating or adding SDKs to Eclipse is known to be "buggy." After executing the previous steps to set up maps, you may have errors throughout your project. If this happens, don't panic! It may take some time, but you'll get it resolved. The first thing to try is a simple clean (Project > Clean). If that does not work, check for updates (this may have been suggested by Eclipse). Select Help > Check for Updates. After all the updates have been installed, restart Eclipse and clean the project after it restarts. If this doesn't work, open the SDK manager again (Window > Android SDK manager). Find the Tools folder and make sure that Android SDK Tools, Android SDK Platform-tools, and Android SDK Build-tools are all updated and installed to the latest version. If not, check them and click Install Packages. Restart Eclipse and clean again.

If you still have errors, the task is much more difficult. One option is to open a source folder that has an error in it (identified by a red x next to the filename). Find the error in the code and hover your cursor over it. Open a browser and execute this search: android *exact error*. Hopefully you will find a solution. A more drastic option is to copy your project to a safe location and reinstall Eclipse.

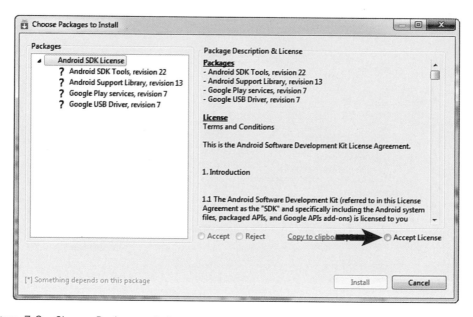

Figure 7.2   Choose Packages window.

Now that the Google Play Services SDK is downloaded, it must be added to your project. To do this, complete the following steps:

1. Select File > Import > Android > Existing Android Code into Workspace, and press Next.

2. Click the Browse button on the window that opens and navigate to the folder <android-sdk>/extras/google/google_play_services/libproject/google-play-services_lib/. You may want to search your computer for this prior to performing this operation because although the folder path is accurate, where the android-sdk folder is on your machine can vary, depending on the installation. Click OK with the google-play-services_lib selected.

3. Check the box next to the project that is displayed in the Project to Import list. Check the box below the list of projects to Copy Projects into Workspace. Click Finish. A new project called google-play-services_lib should show up in the Package Explorer.

4. Right-click the name of your app (MyContactList) in the Package Explorer and select Properties from the pop-up menu.

5. Select Android in the left-side list (Figure 7.3). On the bottom right, click the Add button, select the google-play-service_lib from the window that opens, and click OK. The Google Services Library should show up in the bottom window. Click OK to close the Properties window, and you are ready to go!

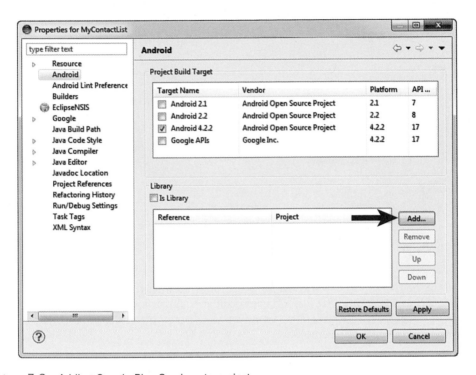

Figure 7.3   Adding Google Play Services to project.

Well, almost ready. To use Google Maps in an app, Google requires that the app contain an API key. There are two types of keys: debug and release. The debug key can work only in debug mode and is associated with your development machine. An app compiled for release with a debug key will not run the maps portion of the app. To release the app, you need to follow a slightly different procedure to register with Google to get a release key. The API key allows you (and Google) to track how often the users of your app access the map functionality. For now, you need only a debug key.

There are several steps to getting a debug key for a maps application:

1. Get the SHA1 fingerprint for your installation. To get the SHA1 fingerprint, select Window > Preferences > Android > Build. Find the SHA1 fingerprint below the Default debug keystore location (Figure 7.4). Highlight and copy it. On a Mac, the command sequence is Eclipse > Preferences > Android > Build.

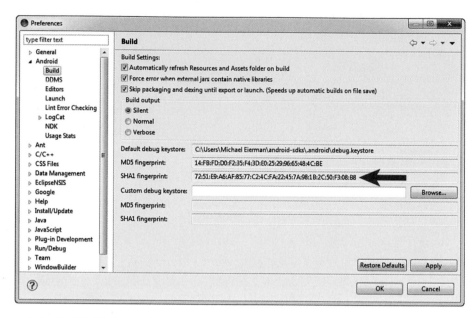

Figure 7.4   Get SHA1 fingerprint.

2. Go to the Google API Console and enter the fingerprint to get the API key. Open a
   browser and type this URL: https://code.google.com/apis/console/. If you are not logged
   in to Google or do not have an account, you will be prompted to get one. The first thing
   you have to do is create a project.

   a. Click Create Project.

   b. Click Services. Scroll through the list until you find Google Maps Android API v2
      and turn it on. You will be presented with a Terms of Service agreement that you
      must agree to if you want to use the maps API.

   c. Click API Access. Click Create New Android Key at the bottom of the screen. A
      window will pop up. Paste your SHA1 fingerprint into the box, followed by a
      semicolon and the package name. For example:

      72:27:E9:A6:AF:85:77:C2:4C:F2:22:45:72:98:1B:2C:50:F3:08:B8;com.example.
      mycontactlist

   d. Click Update or Generate Key. The API key is displayed. Highlight and copy it.

3. Copy the API key into your app manifest file. Return to Eclipse and open the
   AndroidManifest.xml file. Just before the </application> tag at the bottom of the file
   enter the following:

   ```
   <meta-data
       android:name="com.google.android.maps.v2.API_KEY"
       android:value="YourKeyGoesHere" />
   ```

The process of getting a production map key so that you can release the app to other individuals is essentially the same. However, you have to create a new keystore and get the SHA1 fingerprint from that keystore. (see http://developer.android.com/tools/publishing/app-signing.html).

Android Versus iOS: Maps

Setting up your app project and development environment for using maps is significantly more difficult in Android than it is in Xcode. In Xcode, in contrast to what you've seen in this chapter, all you need to do is include the MapKit Framework in the project and you are ready to go.

However, after setup, using maps in either Android or iOS has its own unique challenges. Some things are easier in Android, such as zooming the map or adding annotations to the markers put on a map. Other things are easier in Xcode, such as interacting with the map with the code.

Passing Data Between Controllers

To use maps in your app, you have to give the app permission to use certain device features. These permissions are used to alert the user during installation or upgrade what the app is allowed to access on the device. The user permits that app to use those devices, services, or data by choosing to install the app after reviewing the permissions. Permissions are set in the Android manifest file. If a permission is required by what you are trying to do but is not in the manifest, the app will crash.

Open the AndroidManifest.xml file and enter the permissions in Listing 7.1. Put these permissions after the version number and before the `uses-sdk` tags.

Listing 7.1   **Required Map Permissions**

```
<permission
    android:name="com.example.mycontactlist.permission.MAPS_RECEIVE"
    android:protectionLevel="signature" />

<uses-permission
    android:name="com.example.mycontactlist.permission.MAPS_RECEIVE" />
<uses-permission android:name="android.permission.INTERNET" />
    <uses-permission android:name="android.permission.ACCESS_NETWORK_STATE" />
<uses-permission android:name="android.permission.WRITE_EXTERNAL_STORAGE" />
<uses-permission android:name="android.permission.ACCESS_COARSE_LOCATION" />
<uses-permission android:name="android.permission.ACCESS_FINE_LOCATION" />
<uses-permission
    android:name="com.google.android.providers.gsf.permission.READ_GSERVICES" />

  <uses-feature
      android:glEsVersion="0x00020000"
      android:required="true" />
```

The permissions themselves are pretty self-explanatory, with the possible exception of the Coarse and Fine location permissions. These give permission to use the network and GPS listeners, respectively. When you want to use a new device or service in your app, you will need to look up the required permissions.

> **Note**
>
> Google Maps v2 does not play well with the emulator. You must set up a new AVD that uses Google APIs as its target and check Use Host GPU in the Emulation options section. However, you may still get a blank screen. There are a number of workarounds to be found on the Internet, but we have not gotten any of these to solve the problem. If you get a blank screen with the emulator, you will have to test some of this chapter's code on a real device. The instructions for running on a real device are located later in this chapter (see "Get Coordinates from the GPS Sensor").

Finding Your Location

Finding a location can be performed in two ways. The first involves using the device network and/or GPS sensors to locate the device in real-time. The second uses a known location (for example, an address) and looks up the GPS coordinates via the Internet. Both approaches will be demonstrated. When working with maps, you can use the map's `getMyLocation()` method to get the device's current GPS coordinates. If you need to get location without using a map, there is more work involved. In this section, you build and test several versions of `ContactMapActivity` to learn different approaches to getting location before building the final one used for the app.

Geocoding: Get Coordinates from an Address

In this first approach to getting location, the `ContactMapActivity` will take an entered address and look up and display the GPS coordinates of the address. This process is called *geocoding*. The first step is to create the layout in activity_contact_map.xml. For now, this layout will not use a map object. Refer to Figure 7.5 to code this layout. The exact layout is up to you—you've done all this before. However, to match to the code, use the following IDs for the widgets:

Get Coordinates `Button-@+id/buttonGetLocation`

Latitude output `TextView-@+id/textLatitude`

Longitude output `TextView-@+id/textLongitude`

Accuracy output `TextView-@+id/textAccuracy`

Obviously, the easiest way to code the address portion of the layout is to copy the relevant XML from activity_contact.xml. Some minor changes need to be made to get the Address `TextView` to appear at the top left of the layout. The code for this section uses the same widget IDs for the address `EditTexts` as was used in activity_contact.xml.

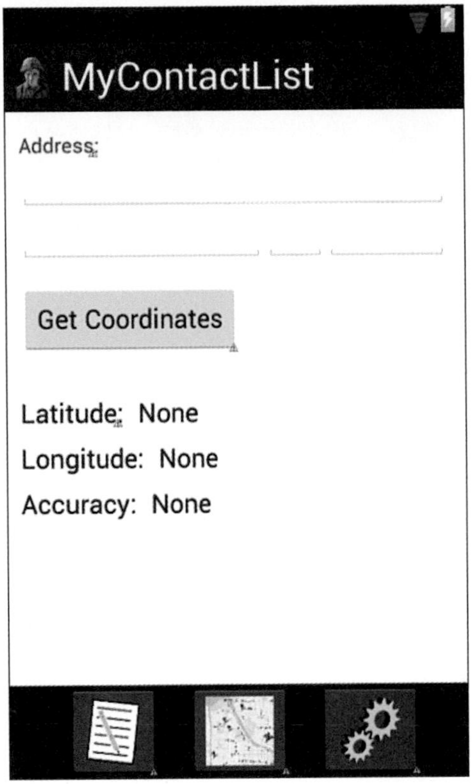

Figure 7.5   Initial Layout for getting location.

After the layout has been created, open the ContactMapActivity.java file to write the code that provides the behavior for the Get Location button. The button will respond to a user tap by retrieving the data entered into the EditTexts and format them into the form required by address look-up service. It will then be sent to the service and the resulting location will be displayed onscreen. Refer to Listing 7.2 to write this code.

Listing 7.2   **Code to Look Up Address Coordinates**

```java
private void initGetLocationButton() {
    Button locationButton = (Button) findViewById(R.id.buttonGetLocation);
    locationButton.setOnClickListener(new View.OnClickListener() {

        @Override
        public void onClick(View v) {
            EditText editAddress = (EditText) findViewById(R.id.editAddress);
            EditText editCity = (EditText) findViewById(R.id.editCity);
            EditText editState = (EditText) findViewById(R.id.editState);
```

```
    EditText editZipCode = (EditText) findViewById(R.id.editZipcode);
                                                                            //1
    String address = editAddress.getText().toString() + ", " +
                        editCity.getText().toString() + ", " +
                        editState.getText().toString() + " " +
                        editZipCode.getText().toString();

    List<Address> addresses = null;                                        //2
    Geocoder geo = new Geocoder(ContactMapActivity.this);                  //3
    try {                                                                  //4
        addresses = geo.getFromLocationName(address, 1);
    }
    catch (IOException e) {
        e.printStackTrace();
    }


    TextView txtLatitude = (TextView) findViewById(R.id.textLatitude);
    TextView txtLongitude = (TextView) findViewById(R.id.textLongitude);
                                                                            //5
    txtLatitude.setText(String.valueOf(
            ➥addresses.get(0).getLatitude()));
    txtLongitude.setText(String.valueOf(
            ➥addresses.get(0).getLongitude()));
        }
    });
}
```

Remember to code the call to the initialization method in the onCreate method! This code introduces a few new items.

1. The proper format for a call to the Geocoding service is the street address with the elements of the address separated by commas.

2. A List object variable parameterized to hold an Address object is declared. The Geo Coding service will return the result with this type of object.

3. A Geocode variable is declared and assigned a new Geocoder object. The Geocoder object has all the information required to contact the host service (Google) via the Internet.

4. The method getFromLocationName method is passed the address to look up as a parameter. The parameter 1 tells the service that you want one response. If you are unsure of the address, you can request more responses. If the service cannot find the exact location, it will return several locations with the best guess as the first entry. Because this method calls a service outside your app, it requires a try and catch to protect the app from errors produced by the service.

5. The latitude and longitude of the first address in the returned list are displayed in the appropriate TextView widgets.

Test your code on the emulator. If the emulator has been set up as suggested in the preceding note, the app will run on the emulator. Click the Maps button in the navigation bar to get to the `ContactMapsActivity`, enter an address, and click the Get Location button. The GPS coordinates should be displayed in the `TextViews`. Try entering a valid and an invalid address to see what happens. Using Geocoding is a good way to find GPS coordinates of address information available to the app. However, it is not very useful in locating the device in real-time. For that, you need to use the sensors.

Get Coordinates from the GPS Sensor

The network sensor uses cell towers and Wi-Fi access points to determine the device's location. It is not as accurate as the GPS sensor, but it is faster. Additionally, it is available on all devices, whereas a GPS sensor is not. For this reason, it might make sense to begin the discussion of getting location from sensors with the network sensor. However, the network sensor cannot be tested on the emulator, whereas the GPS sensor can. Also, the code required to use both sensors is almost identical. For these reasons, the GPS sensor is discussed first.

To use the GPS sensor, you replace the Geocoding code in the Get Location button with GPS listener code. You also add a method to turn off the location sensing when the app enters the Paused life cycle state. First, go to `ContactMapsActivity` and add the following variable declarations just after the class declaration:

```
LocationManager locationManager;
LocationListener gpsListener;
```

You will have to import these classes. Use the `android.location` option, not the `com.google.android.gms` one. Next, go to the `initGetLocationButton` method and replace all the code in the `onClick` method with the code in Listing 7.3. You will also have to import some objects after entering the code.

Listing 7.3 **Code to Get Coordinates with the GPS Sensor**

```
try {
    locationManager = (LocationManager)
        ➥getBaseContext().getSystemService(Context.LOCATION_SERVICE);          //1
    gpsListener = new LocationListener() {                                      //2
        public void onLocationChanged(Location location) {
            TextView txtLatitude = (TextView) findViewById(R.id.textLatitude);
            TextView txtLongitude = (TextView) findViewById(R.id.textLongitude);
            TextView txtAccuracy = (TextView) findViewById(R.id.textAccuracy);
            txtLatitude.setText(String.valueOf(location.getLatitude()));
            txtLongitude.setText(String.valueOf(location.getLongitude()));
            txtAccuracy.setText(String.valueOf(location.getAccuracy()));
        }

        public void onStatusChanged(String provider, int status, Bundle extras) {}
        public void onProviderEnabled(String provider) {}
```

```
        public void onProviderDisabled(String provider) {}
    };

    locationManager.requestLocationUpdates(                              //3
            ➡LocationManager.GPS_PROVIDER,0, 0, gpsListener);
}
catch (Exception e) {
    Toast.makeText(getBaseContext(), "Error, Location not available",
                        ➡Toast.LENGTH_LONG).show();                      //4
}
```

When the user presses the button, the button gets a reference to the system's location manager and instantiates a location listener to get the GPS coordinates and accuracy from a location object each time the sensor detects a location change. Note: location can change even if the device does not move. The sensor will provide a location as soon as it can and then as it zeroes in on the exact location. Everytime accuracy gets better, or worse, new GPS coordinates are produced, and this is reported as a location change.

1. A reference to the `LocationManager` object is assigned to the `locationManager` variable. The `getSystemService` method is sent to the activity's context with a parameter that tells the context that you want the location service manager. In Android, the context of any code is the parent object or method it is placed in. The current context of the code entered in this listing is an `onClickListener`. The method `getBaseContext` is used to get the root context—in this case, an `Activity`—because an `Activity` context is required to get the system service.

2. A new `LocationListener` is instantiated and assigned to the `gpsListener` variable. A `LocationListener` requires the implementation of four methods. However, only the `onLocationChanged` method is needed for the purpose of reporting location. When a location change is detected, it is reported to this method as a location object. The text of the `TextViews` is set by getting the appropriate value from the location object. Note the use of the `String.valueOf` method to convert these values into strings. They are reported as double or float data types, which are not compatible with the `setText` method of the `TextView`.

3. The `LocationManager` is sent the message `requestLocationUpdates` to begin listening for location changes. The parameters in this message tell the `LocationManager` to listen to the GPS sensor with no minimum time between updates, no minimum distance between locations, and to report those changes to the `LocationListener` assigned to the `gpsListener` variable.

   The minimum time and distance parameters are set to zero for demonstration purposes. These values should be set based on how much you expect the device to move during the app's use. Setting values higher than zero can help conserve the battery. This is especially true of the time value. The minimum time is set in milliseconds (2*60*1000 = 120000, or 2 minutes). Minimum distance is set in meters.

4. A `Toast` is displayed if there is an error. A `Toast` is an object that displays a short message for a limited period of time on the user's display. The `Toast` method, `makeText`, requires a context, a message, and a period of time to display the message (`LENGTH_SHORT` and `LENGTH_LONG` are the only options). The `show` method displays the message.

After the changes to the `initGetLocationButton` have been made, you need to add a method to stop the sensors if the Activity's life cycle state changes. To do this, you need to override the Activity's `onPause` method. Create a new method using the code in Listing 7.4 to do this.

Listing 7.4   **onPause Method**

```
@Override
public void onPause() {
    try {
        locationManager.removeUpdates(gpsListener);
    }
    catch (Exception e) {
        e.printStackTrace();
    }
    super.onPause();
}
```

The code is straightforward. The `LocationManager` object is sent the message `removeUpdates` to end listening to the `gpsListener`. This code is within a `try` and `catch` block because it is possible that the activity could pause before the user presses the Get Location button. In that case, neither the `locationManager` nor the `gpsListener` variables would have values, and the code would crash the app. You don't want this to happen. The final code calls the overridden method to execute the standard `onPause` routine for the activity.

Run the code on the emulator and press the Get Coordinates button. Nothing will happen. The button starts the location listener but until the location of the device changes, the `TextViews` will not change. To change the location of the emulator, use the following steps:

1. Change to the Debug Perspective (Window > Open Perspective > Other > Debug.

2. Add the Emulator Controls view. Eclipse provides this view so that the developer can simulate external events (such as location change) on the emulator.

3. Select Window > Show View > Other > Emulator Control. A tab will be added to the Consoles section of the perspective (usually in the lower-right pane).

4. Click the tab and scroll down to the Location Controls, and then click the Manual tab (Figure 7.6).

5. Enter a new latitude and/or longitude value and click the Send button. These values should show up on your app.

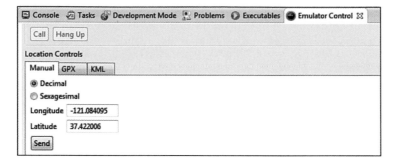

Figure 7.6   Emulator location control.

To test the code on a device that has a GPS, terminate the app running on the emulator (Run > Terminate) and plug an Android device into the computer.

1. Open Debug Configurations (Run > Debug Configurations). Select your debug configuration and then click the Target tab.

2. Select Always Prompt to Pick Device. Press the Apply button and then the Debug button. The Android Device Chooser Window is displayed (Figure 7.7).

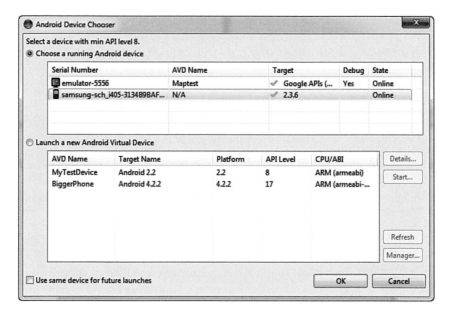

Figure 7.7   Device Chooser window.

3. Your device must be set up to Allow USB Debugging before you can test the app. The location where you can turn this on varies widely among devices. It is usually in the Settings app under USB Settings or Developer Options. This will usually also require the device to be in developer mode, which is also done differently on different devices.

4. Make sure the device is connected to the computer and is unlocked. Select Choose a Running Android Device and then select your device. Click OK. The app will be loaded like on the emulator and begin running when finished. Note: If your device goes to sleep during this process, the app will be terminated.

After the app is running on your device, you can unplug it so that you can walk around and see the location change. If you are indoors, it may take some time to get a GPS reading. In some buildings it will not work at all, so you will have to go outside.

Get Coordinates from Network Sensor

After you've gotten the GPS sensor working, changing or adding a network sensor is very easy. Add the following declaration after the `gpsListener` declaration:

```
LocationListener networkListener;
```

Copy the code that begins with `gpsListener` = and ends just before the `locationManager.requestLocationUpdates` line, and paste it back into the method just before the `location-Manager.requestLocationUpdates` line. You should now have two duplicate `gpsListeners`. Change all the `gpsListener` variables in the code you just pasted to `networkListener` and then add another `requestUpdates` message after the one that is used to request GPS updates.

```
locationManager.requestLocationUpdates(
    ➥LocationManager.NETWORK_PROVIDER,0, 0, networkListener);
```

In the `onPause` method, add the following line to turn off the network listener.

```
locationManager.removeUpdates(networkListener);
```

That's all there is to it! The only real change you made was to request updates from the network sensor rather than the GPS sensor.

To test this, you must run it on a device. The emulator will not detect network sensor changes. This code will work indoors if you can get a Wi-Fi or cell signal on your device.

Often it is desirable to use both sensors because at times one or the other is not available. Although the network sensor is not as accurate as the GPS, for some applications this may be good enough. However, if you are getting location updates from both sensors, you need some way of determining which to use. The way to do this is to write a method to take the current location and compare it to a new location to determine if it is better. To do this, add another variable to hold a location object to your set of declarations at the beginning of the `ContactMapsActivity` class using this code:

```
Location currentBestLocation;
```

Now create a new method called `isBetterLocation` using the code in Listing 7.5.

Listing 7.5 **isBetterLocation Method**

```
private boolean isBetterLocation(Location location) {
    boolean isBetter = false;
    if (currentBestLocation == null) {                                    //1
        isBetter = true;
    }
    else if (location.getAccuracy() <= currentBestLocation.getAccuracy()) {    //2
        isBetter = true;
    }
    else if (location.getTime() - currentBestLocation.getTime() > 5*60*1000) {    //3
        isBetter = true;
    }
    return isBetter;
}
```

This method is an example of the types of checks that can be done to determine if a new location is better than another location.

1. The first check determines if there is an existing location. If not, the new location is considered better.

2. The second check determines if the new location has better accuracy than the existing location. If so, it is considered better.

3. The last check determines how much newer the new location is. Each Location object gets a time stamp when it is created. In this check, if the new location is newer than the old location by more than five minutes, it is considered better, even though it may not be as accurate. This type of check is especially important if you design the app to be used when the device is in motion.

This new method should be called in the onLocationChanged method of both sensor listeners to determine whether you want to use the new location. For example, you could add the following code:

```
if (isBetterLocation(location)) {
    currentBestLocation = location;
    //display in location in TextViews.
}
//no else block...if not better, just ignore.
```

Android Versus iOS: Location Sensors

Working with location data on iOS is similar to Android. However, although iOS devices also have both GPS and network sensors, iOS developers don't have access to the specific sensors. Instead, the developer specifies a desired accuracy of the location data, and the system chooses the appropriate sensor to provide the data. This allows the system to optimize the sensor usage for battery and performance of the device.

Get Coordinates from the Map

The final way to get the GPS coordinates of your device's location is through the map object. The map has built-in methods that access the sensors without writing any code to access the sensors. This makes things easier because all sensor management is handled by the map. The drawback is that you must display a map in the layout to use these features.

Return to activity_contact_maps.xml and delete all the widgets you put in the layout except the navbar. Be sure to leave the root `RelativeLayout`. Next, add the `MapFragment`. The `MapFragment` is not available in the Palette, so it must be added through XML. Refer to Listing 7.6 to do this.

Listing 7.6 **MapFragment XML**

```xml
<fragment
    android:id="@+id/map"
    android:layout_width="match_parent"
    android:layout_height="match_parent"
    android:layout_alignParentTop="true"
    android:layout_above="@+id/navbar"
    class="com.google.android.gms.maps.SupportMapFragment"/>
```

The map object is not coded as a standard widget. Rather, a fragment is added to the layout with the standard set of attributes for size and positioning. The fragment has to be told what type of object it is. That is the reason for the class attribute. In this case, you use the `SupportMapFragment` to make the map object compatible with the earlier versions of Android targeted in this app.

The map doesn't display in Graphical Layout, just the positioning of the fragment. To see a map, you have to write code. Open ContactMapActivity.java. Delete all the code you entered for the sensors and add the code from Listing 7.7.

Listing 7.7 **Code to get Location from Map Object**

```java
                                                                          //1
public class ContactMapActivity extends FragmentActivity {

    GoogleMap googleMap;

    @Override
    public void onCreate(Bundle savedInstanceState) {
        super.onCreate(savedInstanceState);
        setContentView(R.layout.activity_contact_map);
                                                                          //2
        googleMap = ((SupportMapFragment)
            getSupportFragmentManager().findFragmentById(R.id.map)).getMap();
        googleMap.setMapType(GoogleMap.MAP_TYPE_NORMAL);
                                                                          //3
```

```
        googleMap.setMyLocationEnabled(true);
                                                                                  //4

        googleMap.setOnMyLocationChangeListener(new
                              ➥OnMyLocationChangeListener() {

            @Override
            public void onMyLocationChange(Location location) {
                LatLng point = new LatLng(location.getLatitude(),
                                       ➥location.getLongitude());               //5
                googleMap.animateCamera(CameraUpdateFactory.
                                       ➥newLatLngZoom(point, 11));              //6
                Toast.makeText(getBaseContext(), "Lat: "+location.getLatitude()+
                    ➥"Long: "+location.getLongitude()+" Accuracy:   "+
                    ➥location.getAccuracy(), Toast.LENGTH_LONG).show();        //7
            }
        });
    }
```

This code uses a `GoogleMap` object, which is displayed in the fragment on the layout. The `GoogleMap` class provides all the functionality needed to get the GPS coordinates of a location in real-time.

1. The `GoogleMap` object is held within a fragment. To use a fragment, the super class of `ContactMapActivity` must be changed to `FragmentActivity`.

2. An instance of a `GoogleMap` is assigned to the `googleMap` variable. Note the use of `SupportMapFragment`. Again, this is used to make the map compatible with earlier versions of the Android Operating System.

   The `SupportMapFragment` class has to be imported. Normally, this is routine—just hover over the underlined class and select import from the pop-up menu. However, the menu may not find this class. In this case, the import statement must be added manually. To do this, expand the import section above the class declaration and type in this statement:

   ```
   import com.google.android.gms.maps.SupportMapFragment;
   ```

   The map type of normal is a standard highway map. Other valid types include `MAP_TYPE_SATELLITE` for satellite pictures and `MAP_TYPE_TERRAIN` for a map of the terrain features.

3. This enables the map to find the device location. This enables the display of the small blue triangle on the map, which represents the device's location and turns on sensor listeners so that updates to location can be captured and displayed.

4. An `onMyLocationChanged` listener is added to the map with a method, `onMyLocationChanged`, which is executed when a location change is detected.

5. The location object received by `onMyLocationChanged` is used to create a point on the map.

6. The map is zoomed to the location received by the onMyLocationChanged method. The integer 11 represents the zoom level. Zoom levels range from 2 (zoomed out) to 21 (zoomed in).

7. A Toast is used to display the GPS coordinates and accuracy to the user.

To use a map in an Android app, Google requires that some specific code is included in the activity. Listing 7.8 has this code. Enter it after the onCreate method but before the last } in the file.

Listing 7.8   Required Google Code

```java
public void onPause() {
    super.onPause();
}

@Override
public void onResume() {
    super.onResume();
    final String TAG_ERROR_DIALOG_FRAGMENT="errorDialog";

    int status=GooglePlayServicesUtil.isGooglePlayServicesAvailable(this);

    if (status == ConnectionResult.SUCCESS) {
                //no problems just work
    }
    else if (GooglePlayServicesUtil.isUserRecoverableError(status)) {
        ErrorDialogFragment.newInstance(status).show(getSupportFragmentManager(),
                                ➥TAG_ERROR_DIALOG_FRAGMENT);
    }
    else {
        Toast.makeText(this, "Google Maps V2 is not available!",
                            ➥Toast.LENGTH_LONG).show();
        finish();
    }
}

public static class ErrorDialogFragment extends DialogFragment {
    static final String ARG_STATUS="status";

    static ErrorDialogFragment newInstance(int status) {
        Bundle args=new Bundle();
        args.putInt(ARG_STATUS, status);
        ErrorDialogFragment result=new ErrorDialogFragment();
        result.setArguments(args);
        return(result);
    }
```

```
    @Override
    public Dialog onCreateDialog(Bundle savedInstanceState) {
        Bundle args=getArguments();
        return GooglePlayServicesUtil.getErrorDialog(args.getInt(ARG_STATUS),
                                                ➥getActivity(), 0);
    }

    @Override
    public void onDismiss(DialogInterface dlg) {
        if (getActivity() != null) {
            getActivity().finish();
        }
    }
}
```

This code is required and should be entered as written. To test this code, you must run it on a device. Running it on the emulator will cause a "Force Close." Before you run it, make sure that you have entered all the required permissions in the manifest (earlier in the chapter) and entered your API key into the appropriate place in the manifest. When this is done, clean the project (Project > Clean) and then run in Debug mode.

Displaying Your Contacts' Locations

Now that you can find your device's location and display the real-time location on the map, it's time to show your contacts' locations on the map. The map can be accessed from any of the three other activities through the navigation bar. If the user accesses the map from either the contact list or the settings activities, the map should display all the contacts in the database on the map. If the user accesses the map from the contact activity, the map should display only that contact. Implementing the second display type requires coding the ContactActivity to pass the current contact's ID to the map.

Open ContactActivity.java and locate the initMapButton method. This method is modified to pass the contact's ID with the intent. Modify the code in the onClick method to match Listing 7.9.

Listing 7.9　**initMapButton** Modified

```
Intent intent = new Intent(ContactActivity.this, ContactMapActivity.class);
if (currentContact.getContactID() == -1) {
    Toast.makeText(getBaseContext(), "Contact must be saved before it can be
            ➥mapped", Toast.LENGTH_LONG).show();
}
```

```
else {
    intent.putExtra("contactid", currentContact.getContactID());
}
intent.setFlags(Intent.FLAG_ACTIVITY_CLEAR_TOP);
startActivity(intent);
```

There is no new code here. The method checks whether the contact has an ID. If not, a message is posted for the user. If there is an ID, that ID is passed to the ContactMapActivity. Switch to ContactMapActivity.java. Delete the code in the onCreate method associated with enabling the device's location and the location changed listener. The first step is to get the data for mapping. This is done by checking for any extras. If there are no extras, all the contacts are retrieved. If there is an extra, just the information for one contact is retrieved. Enter the code in Listing 7.10 after the setMapType command.

Listing 7.10   **Getting Data for the Map**

```
ArrayList<Contact> contacts = new ArrayList<Contact>();
Contact currentContact = null;
Bundle extras = getIntent().getExtras();
if(extras !=null){
    ContactDataSource ds = new ContactDataSource(ContactMapActivity.this);
    ds.open();
    currentContact = ds.getSpecificContact(extras.getInt("contactid"));
    ds.close();
}
else {
    ContactDataSource ds = new ContactDataSource(ContactMapActivity.this);
    ds.open();
    contacts = ds.getContacts("contactname", "ASC");
    ds.close();
}
```

The next step is to place markers on the map in the location of each contact. Markers can be standard pins or custom icons. Add the following code (Listing 7.11) after the code you just typed in.

Listing 7.11   **Code to Put Markers on a Map**

```
int measuredWidth = 0;
int measuredHeight = 0;
Point size = new Point();
WindowManager w = getWindowManager();
                                                                    //1
if (Build.VERSION.SDK_INT >= Build.VERSION_CODES.HONEYCOMB){
    w.getDefaultDisplay().getSize(size);
```

```
        measuredWidth = size.x;
        measuredHeight = size.y;
    }
    else {
        Display d = w.getDefaultDisplay();
        measuredWidth = d.getWidth();
        measuredHeight = d.getHeight()-180;
    }


    if (contacts.size()>0) {
        LatLngBounds.Builder builder = new LatLngBounds.Builder();          //2
        for (int i=0; i<contacts.size(); i++) {                             //3
            currentContact = contacts.get(i);

            Geocoder geo = new Geocoder(this);
            List<Address> addresses = null;

            String address = currentContact.getStreetAddress() + ", " +
                            currentContact.getCity() + ", " +
                            currentContact.getState() + " " +
                            currentContact.getZipCode();

            try {
                addresses = geo.getFromLocationName(address, 1);
            }
            catch (IOException e) {
                e.printStackTrace();
            }
            LatLng point = new LatLng(addresses.get(0).getLatitude(),
                        ➥addresses.get(0).getLongitude());                   //4
            builder.include(point);

            googleMap.addMarker(new MarkerOptions().position(point).
                    ➥title(currentContact.getContactName()).snippet(address));  //5
        }
        googleMap.animateCamera(CameraUpdateFactory.newLatLngBounds(builder.build(),
                            ➥measuredWidth, measuredHeight, 100));            //6
    }
    else {
        if (currentContact != null) {                                        //7
            Geocoder geo = new Geocoder(this);
            List<Address> addresses = null;

            String address = currentContact.getStreetAddress() + ", " +
                            currentContact.getCity() + ", " +
                            currentContact.getState() + " " +
                            currentContact.getZipCode();
```

```
    try {
        addresses = geo.getFromLocationName(address, 1);
    }
    catch (IOException e) {
        e.printStackTrace();
    }
    LatLng point = new LatLng(addresses.get(0).getLatitude(), addresses.get(0).
➥getLongitude());

    googleMap.addMarker(new MarkerOptions().position(point). title(currentContact.
➥getContactName()).snippet(address));
    googleMap.animateCamera(CameraUpdateFactory. newLatLngZoom(point, 16));     //8
    }
    else {
        AlertDialog alertDialog = new AlertDialog.Builder(
➥ContactMapActivity.this).create();                                            //9
        alertDialog.setTitle("No Data");
        alertDialog.setMessage("No data is available for  the mapping function.");
        alertDialog.setButton(AlertDialog.BUTTON_POSITIVE, "OK", new
➥DialogInterface.OnClickListener() {
        public void onClick(DialogInterface dialog, int which) {
        finish();
        } });
        alertDialog.show();
    }
}
```

The code to put markers on the map uses a number of classes unique to the mapping application. These classes and their methods make up the bulk of the new code.

1. To properly bound a group of points, the app needs to know the size of the display. This code asks the device for the dimensions of the display. Note the methods with a strikeout in them. This indicates that these methods are deprecated and no longer used in new versions of Android. This requires you to test the OS that the device is running and then use the newer methods for the newer OS and the old methods for the old OS. If the getSize method produces an error, add this code before the @Override line just before the onCreate method:

   @TargetApi(Build.VERSION_CODES.HONEYCOMB_MR2)

2. A LatLngBounds.Builder is used to construct the geographic boundaries of a set of GPS coordinates. This line instantiates the builder for use when the app is going to display all contacts in the database.

3. If the contacts ArrayList contains Contact objects, the Activity loops through them, adding each one to the map.

4. A LatLng object is instantiated with the GPS coordinates returned from the Geocoding service. The LatLng object is a point on a map. This point is then included in the LatLngBounds.Builder where it is considered in creating the map boundaries.

5. A `Marker` is added to the map. The marker is a standard marker in the form of a pin. The `addMarker` method is a `MarkerOptions` object. The `MarkerOptions` object is used to set the `LatLng` object as the position on the map for the marker, the title of the marker that is displayed when the marker is clicked by the user, and a snippet, which is displayed under the title when the marker is clicked. A custom image can be added instead of the standard marker by setting the icon attribute of the `MarkerObject` using this form:
`.icon(BitmapDescriptorFactory.fromResource(R.drawable.`*imagename*`)`

6. After all the contact markers have been added, the message `animateCamera` is sent to the map to tell it to zoom in to the location of the markers. A `CameraUpdateFactory` is the object used to set the zoom level. It is passed the boundaries of the zoom through the `LatLngBounds.Builder`, the measured sized of the device display, and the amount of padding to put around the bounds. If the padding is set too small, some of the contact markers will be placed so close to the edge of the screen that the user may not see all the markers.

7. If the contacts `ArrayList` does not contain any objects, the code checks whether there is a single `Contact` object to map. If there is, the address is retrieved, and a `LatLng` object is instantiated for the contact's coordinates; the `LatLng` object is used to add a marker to the map.

8. The zoom level of the map is set differently with one point than with several. To zoom to a single point, the `CameraUpdateFactory` is sent the message `newLatLngZoom`. This message has the `LatLng` object and zoom level as parameters. The marker will be centered in the map and zoomed to level 16.

9. If no contacts are available either in the `ArrayList` or the `Contact` object, the app displays an error message. In this case, an object called an `AlertDialog` is used. An `AlertDialog` displays the commonly used dialog with a title, message, and a button to acknowledge that the user saw the message. This is used rather than a toast because the user is expecting to see contacts on the map. The user may miss the toast and figure the app is not working.

Test the app on a device. Make sure you have entered valid addresses for contacts prior to testing the mapping function.

The map is almost complete. The final touch is to add a toolbar that allows the user to select the type of map to display and to show the user's present location. Switch to activity_contact_map.xml and add a toolbar. You can do this by copying the toolbar previously created in other layouts and modifying the XML. Refer to Listing 7.12 for the modifications.

Listing 7.12   **Map Toolbar XML**

```
<RelativeLayout
    android:id="@+id/toolbar"
    android:layout_width="match_parent"
    android:layout_height="wrap_content"
    android:layout_alignParentLeft="true"
```

```
        android:layout_alignParentTop="true"
        android:background="@color/toolbar_background" >

    <Button
        android:id="@+id/buttonShowMe"
        android:layout_width="wrap_content"
        android:layout_height="wrap_content"
        android:layout_alignParentLeft="true"
        android:layout_marginLeft="20dp"
        android:text="Location On" />

    <Button
        android:id="@+id/buttonMapType"
        android:layout_width="wrap_content"
        android:layout_height="wrap_content"
        android:layout_alignParentRight="true"
        android:layout_marginRight="20dp"
        android:text="Satellite View" />
</RelativeLayout>
```

You also have to modify the fragment position so it lays out below the toolbar you just added. Next, switch to ContactMapActivity.java to add the code for the buttons. Use the code in Listing 7.13.

Listing 7.13   **Toolbar Button Code**

```java
private void initLocationButton() {
    final Button locationbtn = (Button) findViewById(R.id.buttonShowMe);
    locationbtn.setOnClickListener(new View.OnClickListener() {
        public void onClick(View v) {
            String currentSetting = locationbtn.getText().toString();
            if (currentSetting.equalsIgnoreCase("Location On")) {
                locationbtn.setText("Location Off");
                googleMap.setMyLocationEnabled(true);
            }
            else {
                locationbtn.setText("Location On");
                googleMap.setMyLocationEnabled(false);
            }
        }
    });
}

private void initMapTypeButton() {
    final Button satelitebtn = (Button) findViewById(R.id.buttonMapType);
    satelitebtn.setOnClickListener(new View.OnClickListener() {
```

```
    public void onClick(View v) {
        String currentSetting = satelitebtn.getText().toString();
        if (currentSetting.equalsIgnoreCase("Satellite View")) {
            googleMap.setMapType(GoogleMap.MAP_TYPE_SATELLITE);
            satelitebtn.setText("Normal View");
        }
        else {
            googleMap.setMapType(GoogleMap.MAP_TYPE_NORMAL);
            satelitebtn.setText("Satellite View");
        }
    }
});
}
```

Remember to call these methods in the onCreate method. The code is very simple. You are implementing these buttons essentially as toggle buttons. When the user taps the Location button, the code tests to see what the text for the button is. If it is Location On, myLocation is enabled and the button's text is changed to Location Off. If the text is Location Off, myLocation is disabled and the button text is set to Location On. The Map Type button operates in essentially the same manner, except that it changes the map type from normal to satellite and back again.

Finish the code by making the navigation buttons work. Copy the code like you did for the Settings and List Activities. Be sure to disable the Maps button and call the initialization methods in the onCreate method. Test the code. While running the code on a device, you should see a display similar to Figure 7.8. If you test the Location button, be aware that the screen may be zoomed to an area away from where you are currently located. You may have to zoom out the display to see your location.

Summary

Location and maps can be very useful in some apps. A device's location is acquired by listening to either the network or the GPS sensor. You can code the capability to acquire the device's location whether you use maps or not. However, if you use maps, the code for determining your location is much simpler.

Icons can be placed on a map based on their GPS coordinates. The map object has a large number of classes that facilitate the manipulation of maps. Icons on a map are called markers. Markers can use the standard pin icon or a custom item supplied by the developer. Icons can also be made to display information about the location through the use of a title and snippets.

Using Google Maps in an Android requires significantly more setup than other code you have explored in this book. However, after you have set it up, you do not have to redo it for other apps you want to develop.

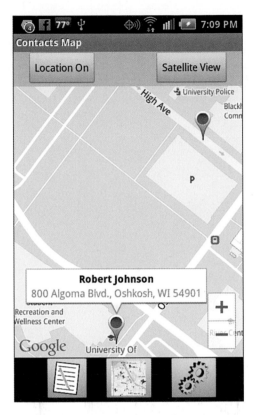

Figure 7.8   Map of Contacts with marker information displayed.

Exercises

1. Create a layout that displays the latitude, longitude, and accuracy for the network sensor and for the GPS sensor. Add a listener for each and have it display its reported location in the appropriate onscreen widget. Run it on a device. Walk around with the app open to this screen and observe the differences.

2. Modify the layout in Exercise 1 to have a third set of latitude, longitude, and accuracy labeled best location. Code a method to test for the best location and put the values in these widgets. Run the app and again observe the results.

3. Modify the markers on the map to use a custom icon. You can download and use an open source graphics program such as Gimp to create your icon. You may have to work with the icon size to get it to display in a reasonable manner on the screen.

4. Add an onMyLocationChanged listener to the completed ContactMapActivity. Have the onMyLocationChanged method add the location to the LatLngBounds.Builder and use the animateCamera method to display your current location along with your contacts on the map.

Access to Hardware and Sensors in Android

Mobile computing devices have hardware features that significantly distinguish them from their more stationary counterparts. Hardware features allow the device to both sense and interact with its environment. These features enable the reexamination of assumptions many developers make when developing a piece of software. The ability to sense and interact with the environment allows the developer to rethink business processes encapsulated in software. Innovative and powerful approaches to solving problems are possible. This suggests that the app developer needs to have a working knowledge of how to integrate the device's hardware features into an app. This chapter describes how to integrate several different hardware features into an app. The chapter covers both sensors that can provide information about the device's internal and external environment and hardware features, such as the camera and phone, provided by the Android platform that can be used independently or integrated into an app. Determining the presence of a sensor on any specific device is also addressed.

Sensors, Managers, and Other Hardware

This section covers more sensors and managers used to access sensor data. The section also covers other hardware on some devices that can be used to augment an app's functionality.

Sensors

Android devices may have any number of sensors. Two of these, the network and GPS sensors, were discussed in the previous chapter. However, other sensors may also be used in apps. In all, the Android platform supports about 12 sensors. However, there is no requirement that a manufacturer of an Android device include all of them. For this reason, it is good practice to always check for the presence of a sensor before attempting to use it. Sensors supported range from sensors that measure the devices' ambient environment, including temperature, relative humidity, atmospheric pressure, magnetic field, and light level, to sensors that detect how the device is moving or rotating.

The `Sensor` class represents all types of sensors. Sensors are instantiated as a system service by the operating system and thus are not instantiated by the apps that use them. Sensors are accessed through the `SensorManager` class. The `SensorManager` is also a system service and not instantiated by an app. In both cases, access is through a reference created by calling the `getSystemService` method within an app.

Two other items are needed to work with sensors, `SensorEvent` and `SensorEventListener`. A `SensorEvent` is an object that is created by a `Sensor` when it has something to report. This object holds information about the event, including a timestamp for when the object was created, the sensor that produced the event, and data that represents the sensor's measurements at the time of the event. A `SensorEventListener` is an interface that is implemented by any app that wants to use sensor information encapsulated in a `SensorEvent`.

Managers

Android devices are computing devices. As such, they have hardware for processing, memory, long-term storage, and to provide power. The Android OS provides objects to facilitate the monitoring of the status of this hardware. For example, the Android OS has a `BatteryManager` that can be used to monitor the battery's status, a `StorageManager` that can be used to monitor the status of long-term storage, and a `PowerManager` that can be used to monitor power consumption.

The objects used to monitor the internal environment of the device are instantiated as system services like the `SensorManager`. Just like with `SensorManager`, you do not instantiate these objects. To use them in an app, you get a reference to the appropriate system service.

Other Hardware

Android devices also have other hardware features, such as a phone and a camera. These devices have an app associated with them to provide access to their functionality. In contrast to accessing the sensors and monitors, these hardware items are accessed by making calls to their Application Program Interface (API). These apps can be opened from within an app to give the user access to their functionality. In this case, the user leaves the app to interact with the device and returns to the app after completing the task. The functionality of the hardware can also be accessed by integrating the features within the app by calling the associated app's API. In this manner, the app developer can provide users with exactly the functionality they need from the device. This is how the popular flashlight apps work. They access and control only the camera's flash from within an app to create entirely new functionality from existing hardware.

Monitoring the Battery

Typically, all versions of the Android OS have some sort of battery-level monitoring display so that the user knows when to recharge the device. However, just because the battery level is displayed to the user doesn't mean that the user will pay attention and plug in the phone or tablet when needed. To avoid complications from the device shutting down during app execution, you may need to monitor the battery within the app so that the app can take necessary precautions if the level gets too low. You may also require the user to have the device plugged in to external power to carry out certain operations that might require a significant power drain.

Monitoring the battery is not crucial to the MyContactList app. However, learning how to do so is useful for understanding one approach used in Android to interact with device hardware. The Android OS has an object that monitors important measures of battery health. Some of these measures include battery temperature, voltage, charge level, and many others. To examine all available measures, review the `BatteryManager` class on the Android Developer site (search for "android batterymanager"). The `BatteryManager` produces a broadcast every few seconds that includes the current reading on these measures. To monitor the battery, the app has to listen for these broadcasts and respond to the measures that are important to the app.

To demonstrate monitoring the battery, you will put a small `TextView` in the toolbar on the `ContactListActivity` to display the current battery level as a percentage. Begin by adding the `TextView` to the activity_contact_list.xml layout file. Use the code in Listing 8.1.

Listing 8.1   XML to Add a `TextView` to `ContactListActivity` Toolbar

```
<TextView
    android:id="@+id/textBatteryLevel"
    android:layout_width="wrap_content"
    android:layout_height="wrap_content"
    android:layout_alignParentRight="true"
    android:layout_marginRight="5dp"
    android:text="100%"
    android:textAppearance="?android:attr/textAppearanceSmall" />
```

Be sure to place this widget within the toolbar `RelativeLayout`. Change the `layout_margin-Right` value of the `buttonAdd` widget from 20dp to 45dp. When complete, your toolbar should look like Figure 8.1.

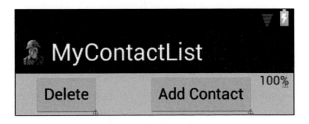

Figure 8.1   Toolbar with battery level TextView.

The next step is to add code to listen for, and respond to, the battery manager's broadcasts. To do so, you have to instantiate a `BroadcastReceiver` object that will capture and respond to the broadcast. A `BroadcastReceiver` is an object that can receive `Intents` sent by other `Activities` both within and outside the app. Generally, you set up a `BroadcastReceiver` to respond only to specific types of broadcasts. The code in the `BroadcastReceiver` typically uses the data from the broadcast `Intent` to perform some action. The final step is to tell the activity to listen for broadcasts from the `BatteryManager` using the broadcast receiver you defined. Enter the code in Listing 8.2 in the `onCreate` method of the `ContactListActivity`.

Listing 8.2 **Monitoring the Battery**

```
BroadcastReceiver batteryReceiver = new BroadcastReceiver() {          //1
    @Override
    public void onReceive(Context context, Intent intent) {
        double batteryLevel= intent.getIntExtra(BatteryManager.EXTRA_LEVEL,0);   //2
        double levelScale= intent.getIntExtra(BatteryManager.EXTRA_SCALE,0);     //3
        int batteryPercent = (int) Math.floor(batteryLevel/levelScale*100);      //4
        TextView textBatteryState=(TextView)findViewById(R.id.textBatteryLevel);
        textBatteryState.setText(batteryPercent+"%");
    }
};

IntentFilter filter = new IntentFilter(Intent.ACTION_BATTERY_CHANGED);   //5
registerReceiver(batteryReceiver, filter);                               //6
```

Not much code is needed to implement battery monitoring because the objects provided with the Android SDK do much of the work. However, much of the code is new and needs some explanation.

1. A `BroadcastReceiver` variable is declared and instantiated with a new `BroadcastReceiver`. This object receives `Intents` and has the code used to respond to the `Intent`. An `Intent` is broadcast from other apps or objects executing on the device.

2. The `Intent` concerning battery status sent by the OS contains information about the battery as `Extras`. This line gets the extra associated with the battery's current charge level. Although the value is retrieved as an integer, it is assigned to a double variable so that it can be used as a double later.

3. The extra associated with the scale used for measuring the charge is retrieved and assigned to a double variable. Capturing the scale is important because different devices may use different scales for measuring charge.

4. The percentage of battery charge left is calculated by dividing the level by the scale. If these two variables were not defined as doubles, this calculation would produce incorrect results because a divide operation needs to produce double value. The result of the calculation is a number between 0 and 1, which is multiplied by 100 to get a percentage. The floor function is applied to take on the integer value of the result.

5. A new `IntentFilter` variable is declared and assigned a new `IntentFilter`. An `IntentFilter` listens for `Intents` that have been broadcast by the system and only lets through the ones the developer is looking for. In this case, the filter looks for Battery Status changed intent. This is required because a `BroadcastReceiver` can respond to any intent. However, you want it to respond only to `Intents` sent by the battery.

6. The `BroadcastReceiver` is registered, which means that the app is told to listen for battery status intents and handle them with the `BroadcastReceiver` defined in the activity.

Run the app. Using the emulator will always produce the same result, and in some cases will not produce any result. However, if you test it on an actual device, you will see different percentages as the battery charges or discharges.

Using Sensors to Create a Compass

The Android OS supports a number of types of sensors. Generally, the sensors are either motion, environmental, or position sensors. Motion sensors detect how the device is moving, environmental sensors capture various measures of the device's ambient environment (for example, the light level), and position sensors capture information that can be used to determine the physical position of the device. Not all devices have all the sensors that the OS supports. This fact has implications for how you code access to the sensors.

Accessing sensor information is not particularly important for the MyContactList app. However, understanding how these are accessed could be important for future apps you develop. In the case of the MyContactList app, you will use sensors to create a simple compass to show users what direction they are headed when they have the contact map displayed. Creating a graphical compass display is beyond the scope of this book, so you will simply add a `TextView` to the `ContactMapActivity` toolbar to display the direction in text (E, W, N, and S).

The first step is to add the `TextView` to the toolbar. Open activity_contact_map.xml and add the `TextView` between the `Location` and `MapType` buttons using the code in Listing 8.3.

Listing 8.3   **Heading `TextView`**

```
<TextView
    android:id="@+id/textHeading"
    android:layout_width="wrap_content"
    android:layout_height="wrap_content"
    android:layout_centerHorizontal="true"
    android:layout_centerVertical="true"
    android:text="WNW"
    android:textAppearance="?android:attr/textAppearanceSmall" />
```

Be sure to place this widget within the toolbar `RelativeLayout`. Change the `layout_marginRight` and `layout_marginLeft` values of the button widgets from 20dp to 10dp. When complete, your toolbar should look like Figure 8.2.

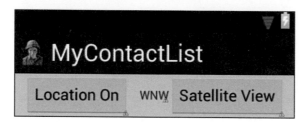

Figure 8.2   Toolbar with heading `TextView`.

To calculate the device heading, you need to capture information from two sensors: the accelerometer and the magnetometer. The accelerometer reports device acceleration in three dimensions. The magnetometer reports the geomagnetic field in three dimensions. The math behind the heading calculation using these measures is beyond the scope of this book. Fortunately, the Android SDK again does much of the work for you. However, implementing a compass using these sensors requires a bit more work than monitoring the battery.

Open ContactMapActivity.java and declare four variables where you declared the GoogleMap variable (just after the class declaration). Use the following code:

```
SensorManager sensorManager;
Sensor accelerometer;
Sensor magnetometer;
TextView textDirection;
```

To monitor sensors requires a `SensorManager` object and `Sensor` objects for each sensor used. Next, add the code in Listing 8.4 to the `onCreate` method of the activity.

Listing 8.4   **Registering Sensors for Monitoring**

```
                                                                    //1
sensorManager = (SensorManager) getSystemService(Context.SENSOR_SERVICE);
accelerometer = sensorManager.getDefaultSensor(Sensor.TYPE_ACCELEROMETER);
magnetometer = sensorManager.getDefaultSensor(Sensor.TYPE_MAGNETIC_FIELD);

                                                                    //2
if (accelerometer != null && magnetometer != null) {
    sensorManager.registerListener(mySensorEventListener, accelerometer,
                                ➥SensorManager.SENSOR_DELAY_FASTEST);
    sensorManager.registerListener(mySensorEventListener, magnetometer,
                                ➥SensorManager. SENSOR_DELAY_FASTEST);
```

```
} else {
    Toast.makeText(this, "Sensors not found", Toast.LENGTH_LONG).show();        //3
}
    textDirection = (TextView) findViewById(R.id.textHeading);
```

This code gets the references to the sensors and registers them to activate a
SensorEventListener object when they report changes. The SensorEventListener
has yet to be coded.

1. SensorManager is a system service so you get a reference to it rather than instantiate it. The SensorManager is used to get references to the two sensors used to measure heading.

2. As previously noted, not all devices have all sensors. Therefore, you test whether the sensor is available so that the lack of a sensor on a device does not cause the app to crash. If the sensors are present, the SensorManager associates each with the same event listener and passes a parameter indicating how frequently to process sensor events.

3. If sensors are not available, the user is informed with a Toast.

The next step is to implement the SensorEventListener, which is the class that handles the actual events from the sensors and takes action on them. Code this event just as you would a method. It should be within the class body but not within any other method. Refer to Listing 8.5 to implement the listener.

Listing 8.5 **SensorEventListener** Code

```
private SensorEventListener mySensorEventListener = new SensorEventListener() {

    public void onAccuracyChanged(Sensor sensor, int accuracy) {  }          //1

    float[] accelerometerValues;                                             //2
    float[] magneticValues;

    public void onSensorChanged(SensorEvent event) {                         //3
    if (event.sensor.getType() == Sensor.TYPE_ACCELEROMETER)
        accelerometerValues = event.values;
    if (event.sensor.getType() == Sensor.TYPE_MAGNETIC_FIELD)
        magneticValues = event.values;
    if (accelerometerValues!= null && magneticValues!= null) {               //4
        float R[] = new float[9];
        float I[] = new float[9];
        boolean success = SensorManager.getRotationMatrix(R, I,
                                      ➥accelerometerValues, magneticValues);
        if (success) {                                                       //5
            float orientation[] = new float[3];
            SensorManager.getOrientation(R, orientation);
```

```
    float azimut = (float) Math.toDegrees(orientation[0]);          //6
    if (azimut < 0.0f) { azimut+=360.0f;}                           //7
    String direction;
    if (azimut >= 315 || azimut < 45) { direction = "N"; }          //8
    else if (azimut >= 225 && azimut < 315) { direction = "W"; }
    else if (azimut >= 135 && azimut < 225) { direction = "S"; }
    else { direction = "E"; }
    textDirection.setText(direction);
      }
     }
    }
};
```

The sensor event listener code is relatively involved, even without needing to understand the math involved.

1. A SensorEventListener requires the implementation of two events, onAccuracyChanged and onSensorChanged. To calculate a heading, you don't need accuracy, so its method block is empty.

2. Sensor readings are returned as a float array. Two variables to hold the response from each sensor are declared.

3. The onSensorEvent first determines which sensor triggered the event and then captures the values it provided.

4. If there are values available for both sensors, the SensorManager is asked for two rotational matrices used for orientation calculation. Discussion of the rotational matrices is beyond the scope of this book.

5. If the matrices are successfully calculated, the SensorManager is asked to calculate the orientation of the device. Orientation is measured in three dimensions.

6. The first orientation measure is the value used to calculate the heading. It is reported in radians, so these are changed to degrees.

7. Convert the heading reported to eliminate negative numbers.

8. Use degree heading to get text description. These are done in 90-degree increments. You could add more code to get finer gradations of direction, such as NW or SE.

Test the app on a device. You'll need to move the device around to get different readings. This is not possible on the emulator.

Android Versus iOS: Creating a Compass

As you have seen in the preceding section, creating a compass in Android requires accessing two sensors and manipulating the data they provide. In contrast, the device's heading is included in the Core Location framework on iOS. Heading is reported as a function of the device's location, making creating a compass in iOS significantly easier than in Android.

Using the Phone

An Android device not only provides hardware devices that can be used in an app to collect information on the device's internal and external environment, but also includes hardware capabilities that can be accessed to provide certain functionality for an app. To access data from a sensor, the app listens for a broadcast from a sensor. However, other hardware on an Android device operates only when the user or an app wants to use it. In these cases, accessing the functionality provided by the hardware is accessed by calling the API associated with the hardware. One such piece of hardware provided by some devices is a telephone. In the MyContactList app, you will code the `ContactActivity` so that pressing and holding one of the contact's phone numbers will automatically call that number. This functionality requires accessing the phone's API and asking it to call the number provided.

Accessing phone functionality of an Android device requires user permission. Add the following line with the other permissions already in the AndroidManifest.xml file:

```
<uses-permission android:name="android.permission.CALL_PHONE" />
```

The next step is to add a listener to the phone number `EditText`s for the press-and-hold user action. This is done by adding a method to the ContactActivity.java file. Use the code in Listing 8.6.

Listing 8.6   **Initializing the `LongClickListener`**

```java
private void initCallFunction() {
    EditText editPhone = (EditText) findViewById(R.id.editHome);
    editPhone.setOnLongClickListener(new OnLongClickListener() {

        @Override
        public boolean onLongClick(View arg0) {
            callContact(currentContact.getPhoneNumber());
            return false;
        }
    });

    EditText editCell = (EditText) findViewById(R.id.editCell);
    editCell.setOnLongClickListener(new OnLongClickListener() {

        @Override
        public boolean onLongClick(View arg0) {
            callContact(currentContact.getCellNumber());
            return false;
        }
    });
}
```

The pattern in this method should be very familiar by now. A reference to the widget is created, and an event is added to the widget. Next, the widget's response to the event is coded. In this case, that is a call to another method that accepts the phone number in the `EditText` as a parameter. Add the `callContact` method using the code in Listing 8.7.

Listing 8.7   **`callContact` Method**

```java
private void callContact(String phoneNumber) {
    Intent intent = new Intent(Intent.ACTION_CALL);               //1
    intent.setData(Uri.parse("tel:" + phoneNumber));              //2
    startActivity(intent);
}
```

Using the phone requires starting the phone app. As you have seen before, all apps are made up of activities, and to start an activity you use an intent.

1. A new intent is instantiated with the parameter `Intent.ACTION_CALL`, which tells Android that you want to use the phone to make a call.

2. The telephone number to be called is passed to the intent as a Uniform Resource Identifier (URI). A URI is similar to a Uniform Resource Locator (URL) except that a URL identifies a location on the World Wide Web, whereas a URI can be used to identify a local resource.

That is all that is needed to make a phone call through an app! Remember to call the phone call initialization method in the `onCreate` method. If you run the app now, when editing is turned on, the call function works. However, when you are in viewing mode, it does not. This is because you disabled the `EditText`s in viewing mode because you didn't want any accidental changes to the user's information. To correct this, you need to modify the `setForEditing` method in ContactActivity.java.

An `EditText` has to be enabled to allow it to respond to a long click event. This means that you cannot ever disable them. Delete the `setEnabled` lines of code associated with the `editPhone` and `editCell` variables. The problem with doing this is that now the phone number will be editable even in viewing mode. To correct this problem, you need to set the `inputType` of the `EditText` to null when in viewing mode and set it back to accepting phone numbers when in editing mode. To do this, modify the `if (enabled)` block of code to include the following in the true block:

```java
editPhone.setInputType(InputType.TYPE_CLASS_PHONE);
editCell.setInputType(InputType.TYPE_CLASS_PHONE);
```

Add the following to the false block (the else block):

```java
editPhone.setInputType(InputType.TYPE_NULL);
editCell.setInputType(InputType.TYPE_NULL);
```

Your app can now call your contacts by pressing and holding on a phone number. Run the app. If you run the app in the emulator, the emulator will pretend to call a number, but running it on an Android Device will actually make the call.

Using the Camera

Many Android devices have a camera, which can be used independently by the user or integrated into an app. You can integrate it into an app by calling the camera API to start the camera so that the user can take a picture using the camera app provided by Android and then return the picture to the app. You can also do it in a more sophisticated manner in which the camera's API, and thus, functionality, is integrated right in the app. The former approach is similar to the way the phone functionality was used in the previous section. The latter is much more sophisticated and requires creating an activity and layout designed to provide the camera functionality desired in the app. This approach is beyond the scope of this book.

The camera will be used in the MyContactList app to capture a photo of the contact so that it can be displayed with the contact's data. To begin, there must be a place to show the image on the ContactActivity's layout. To do this, you add `ImageButton` to the layout. You use the button functionality of the `ImageButton` to access the camera. An `ImageButton` must have an image associated with it, so the first step is to import the photoicon.png file (available with the resources provided with this book) into the drawable-hdpi folder. To import, right-click the drawable-hdpi folder and select Import. Navigate to the location of the file and import it. Next, open activity_contact.xml and add an `ImageButton`. Configure the button using the code in Listing 8.8. Be sure to place the widget within the `ScrollView`—preferably after the `TextView` that displays the label Contact.

Listing 8.8   **`ImageButton`** Configuration

```
<ImageButton
    android:id="@+id/imageContact"
    android:layout_width="wrap_content"
    android:layout_height="wrap_content"
    android:layout_alignParentRight="true"
    android:layout_marginRight="10sp"
    android:layout_alignTop="@+id/textContact"
    android:src="@drawable/photoicon" />
```

Modify the attributes of the `editName` `EditText` so it does not overrun the `ImageButton` by adding the following attribute/value pair:

```
android:layout_toLeftOf="@+id/imageContact"
```

When complete, your layout should look like Figure 8.3.

Figure 8.3   Layout with `ImageButton`.

The camera is outside the app, so the app needs permission to use it. As always, this is granted by entering a permission in the app's manifest. Enter the following permission after the other permissions already in the manifest:

```
<uses-permission android:name="android.permission.CAMERA" />
```

Next, open ContactActivity.java to code the camera use. This requires initializing the `ImageButton` to listen for an `onClick` event, writing code to have the `onClick` method call a routine to start the camera, and writing code to listen to get the picture after it has been taken. Code the `ImageButton` initialization with the code in Listing 8.9. Again, remember to call the method in the activity's `onCreate` method.

Listing 8.9   **ImageButton** Initialization Method

```
private void initImageButton() {
    ImageButton ib = (ImageButton) findViewById(R.id.imageContact);
    ib.setOnClickListener(new View.OnClickListener() {
```

```
    public void onClick(View v) {
        takePhoto();
    }
  });
}
```

Next, add the code to access the camera and get the returned picture. The camera app is, of course, an activity, so it must be started with an `Intent`. Use the code in Listing 8.10 to create the `takePhoto` method and the method to capture the picture.

Listing 8.10   **Starting the Camera and Capturing the Result**

```
public void takePhoto(){
    Intent cameraIntent = new Intent(
                       ➥android.provider.MediaStore.ACTION_IMAGE_CAPTURE);    //1
    startActivityForResult(cameraIntent, CAMERA_REQUEST);                     //2
}


                                                                              //3
protected void onActivityResult(int requestCode, int resultCode, Intent data) {
    if (requestCode == CAMERA_REQUEST) {                                      //4
        if (resultCode == RESULT_OK) {                                        //5
            Bitmap photo = (Bitmap) data.getExtras().get("data");            //6
            Bitmap scaledPhoto = Bitmap.createScaledBitmap(photo, 72, 72, true);  //7
            ImageButton imageContact = (ImageButton)
                                   ➥findViewById(R.id.imageContact);
            imageContact.setImageBitmap(scaledPhoto);
            currentContact.setPicture(scaledPhoto);
        }
    }
}
```

Not much code is required to implement camera functionality! This is because the objects in the Android SDK do most of the work.

1. A new intent is instantiated with a parameter that tells the system to open the camera in image capture mode. You do not have to check whether the camera is present. The permission you added in the manifest would not let your app run on the device if it did not have a camera.

2. The `Activity` is started in a different way than you have seen before. In this case, you want the activity to return a value to the app after it has completed, so you use the `startActivityForResult` method. The parameters are the new `Intent` and a static variable called `CAMERA_REQUEST`. The variable `CAMERA_REQUEST` is identified as an error because it has not been defined. This variable is an integer that is used to identify the response from the cavmera when it finishes. The value is not fixed by the SDK but

should be given a large integer so it is not confused with other built-in responses. Add this line after the class declaration to fix the error:

```
private static final int CAMERA_REQUEST = 1888;
```

3. The onActivityResult method is declared. This method receives a request code that was sent to the camera, a result code, and an intent that includes the data (the picture in this case) from the intent you started. This method is executed when the camera finishes.

4. The returned request code is checked to see if it is the one sent to the camera.

5. Check if the camera returned with a picture.

6. The data from the Intent is assigned to a variable declared as a Bitmap. The method .get("data") doesn't specify a type of data to get from the extras, so it must be cast into a Bitmap. After the photo is captured, it is displayed in the ImageButton, and the contact object's picture attribute is set to hold the photo.

7. The picture is scaled so that a consistent-sized photo is displayed in the ImageButton. The parameters of this method are the picture to be scaled, the height and width to scale to in pixels, and whether a filter should be applied during the scaling operation. Generally when scaling down, this filter has no effect but can change the result when scaling up.

The setPicture method must be added, along with a Bitmap variable to the Contact object. Open Contact.java and add a variable to the class using the following code:

private Bitmap picture;

Next, add the setters and getters with the code in Listing 8.11. Save the file.

Listing 8.11   **Picture Variable Setter and Getter**

```
public void setPicture(Bitmap b) {
    picture = b;
}
public Bitmap getPicture() {
    return picture;
}
```

Almost done. But now that you have a picture to save, the method to display a contact must be modified to display the saved contact picture, the ContactDataSource methods to save and retrieve contacts must be modified to store and retrieve the picture, and the database must be modified to have a field in the table to hold the picture. First, open ContactDBHelper.java to add the field to the database. The first step is to tell the app that the database has changed. Locate the following line and increase the version number by 1.

private static final int DATABASE_VERSION = 2;

Next, add a picture field with a data type of blob to the contact table. The blob data type can hold any type of binary data and is typically used for picture, audio, and video objects. The data type, blob, is an acronym for Binary Large Object. Modify the last line in the CREATE_ TABLE_CONTACT string to the following:

```
+ "email text, birthday text, contactphoto blob);";
```

The last step is to modify the onUpgrade method. Technically, you would not have to modify this to get the change to the database. It is currently written to delete the current table and create a new one when the database is updated. However, there is one big drawback: all the user's contacts will be deleted! If you are in the development stage prior to release of the app, this is okay. If the app has been released, this is not an option. To handle a change to the database structure without losing all the user data, modify the onUpgrade method to match the code in Listing 8.12.

Listing 8.12   onUpgrade Modifications

```java
@Override
public void onUpgrade(SQLiteDatabase db, int oldVersion, int newVersion) {
    Log.w(ContactDBHelper.class.getName(),
        ➥"Upgrading database from version " + oldVersion + " to "
        + newVersion + ", which will destroy all old data");
//  db.execSQL("DROP TABLE IF EXISTS contact");
//  onCreate(db);
    try {
        db.execSQL("ALTER TABLE contact ADD COLUMN contactphoto blob");
    }
    catch (Exception e) {
        //do nothing
    }
}
```

The modifications comment out the deletion and re-creation of the table and add an SQL state to add the new field to the table. This line is surrounded by a try and catch statement so that if the field has already been added, it doesn't crash the app.

After the ContactDBHelper.java file has been modified, the ContactDataSource.java file needs to be modified to save and retrieve the picture. The code in Listing 8.13 must be added to both the insertContact and updateContact methods. The code must be placed prior to the call to update or insert the contact. Note that in the updateContact method, you need to use updateValues.put(contactphoto", photo) instead of initialValues. put("contactphoto", photo).

Listing 8.13   **Saving a Picture to the Database**

```
ByteArrayOutputStream baos = new ByteArrayOutputStream();
c.getPicture().compress(Bitmap.CompressFormat.PNG, 100, baos);
byte[] photo = baos.toByteArray();

initialValues.put("contactphoto", photo);
```

To store a bitmap to the database, it must first be converted to a byte array. This code uses standard objects in the Android SDK to do this conversion. After the photo is converted, it is placed into the values to be updated like any other value. Next, modify the getSpecificContact method to load the Contact object with the picture. This does not need to be done in the getContacts method because the picture is not used by any activity that uses the whole set of contacts. Returning the picture from the database is essentially the reverse process from saving to the database (Listing 8.14).

Listing 8.14   **Getting a Picture from the Database**

```
if (cursor.getBlob(10) != null) {
    byte[] photo = cursor.getBlob(10);
    if (photo != null) {
        ByteArrayInputStream imageStream = new ByteArrayInputStream(photo);
        Bitmap thePicture= BitmapFactory.decodeStream(imageStream);
        contact.setPicture(thePicture);
    }
}
```

Again, the objects supplied by Android do most of the work. The byte array is retrieved from the database and is then tested to determine if a picture has been stored. The 10 in the getBlob method is the index of the contactphoto field in the contact table. The conversion from byte array to Bitmap will cause a crash if no picture is stored. After the data has been converted, it is set in the Contact object.

The last step is to modify ContactActivity.java to display the retrieved picture along with the rest of the contact's data. This is done in the initContact method. Place the code in Listing 8.15 where appropriate in that method.

Listing 8.15   **Display the Photo**

```
ImageButton picture = (ImageButton) findViewById(R.id.imageContact);
if (currentContact.getPicture() != null) {
    picture.setImageBitmap(currentContact.getPicture());
}
else {
    picture.setImageResource(R.drawable.photoicon);
}
```

The code gets a reference to the `ImageButton` on the layout and checks if the contact has a picture. If there is a picture, it is set as the button's image. If not, the default image resource is displayed.

Test the app on an Android device. The camera display you see will depend on the device you are running the app on. After taking a picture, the `ContactActivity` should look similar to Figure 8.4.

Figure 8.4   Contact with a picture.

Summary

An Android device provides many hardware features that enable the creation of innovative apps or enhance the capabilities of more traditional apps. The approach used to access these features is dependent on the hardware device. However, regardless of the type of hardware to be accessed, the developer must always include a `permission` to use the item in the app's manifest file. Sensors that may be used to detect the environment that the device is currently in or how the device is moving are accessed by enabling methods in your code that listen for status changes of the sensor. The app can then use those status changes to do something useful for the user.

Hardware features provided by the Android system that may be used through an app (such as the phone) may also be accessed through other apps or integrated into apps. These features are accessed via calls to the device's API. Through API calls, the developer can ask the hardware feature to perform functions for the app.

Exercises

1. Modify the toolbar of the `ContactActivity` to display the proximity sensor readings. Add the proximity sensor service so that this works.

2. Modify the app so that when the user long-clicks the cell number of a contact, the text messaging service is opened instead of the phone service. You will have to have a permission in the manifest to send text (SMS) messages.

3. Modify the app to display an incoming text message as a `Toast`. You will have to register your app with a permission to read text (SMS) messages and set up a listener for text messages.

4. Modify the compass to report NW, NE, SE, and so on in addition to the N, W, S, and E headings.

Part III

Developing the iOS App

Using Xcode for iOS Development

This part of the book covers how to create iOS apps. You learn to use the powerful Xcode development environment. If you need to get this installed on your computer, refer to Appendix B, "Installing Xcode and Registering Physical Devices," before continuing. In this first chapter, you learn to build a simple but complete iOS app—a variation on the traditional "Hello World" app—and run it on the simulator.

Creating the Xcode Project

You're no doubt eager to get started creating your first iOS app, so jump right in and launch Xcode. You should find it in the Applications folder on your Mac. After Xcode starts, you should see the screen shown in Figure 9.1. Select the Create a New Xcode Project option.

Next, you're given a number of options for creating projects based on various templates, as shown in Figure 9.2. You'll notice in the left sidebar of the window that you can create projects for both iOS and OS X. Our focus here is on iOS applications, so choose that entry. You will see several templates that will make creating a new app simpler. For our first app, choose Single View Application, and click Next.

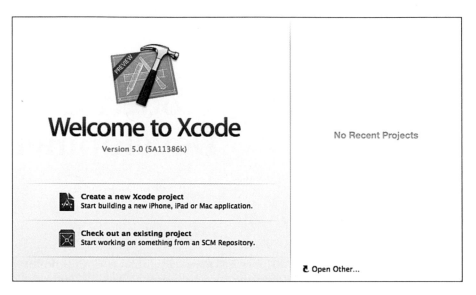

Figure 9.1   Xcode's Welcome screen.

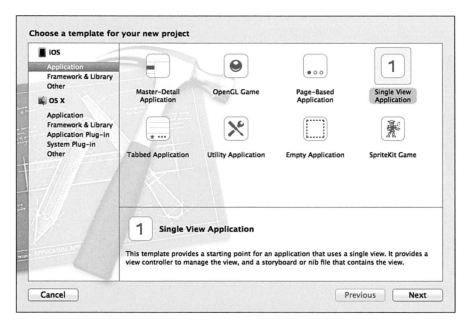

Figure 9.2   Choose the Single View template for the first project.

On the next screen (shown in Figure 9.3), you choose a name for your app. Type "Hello World!" The next fields are not all that important for sample projects like this, but for real projects, you should add your company's name, identifier (reverse web address), and class prefix. The class prefix is at least three capital letters that are prepended to any class you create to distinguish them from library classes. Apple has reserved two-letter prefixes for use with the frameworks that come with the platform, so you will see these in classes like NSArray, CLLocation, and UIButton. Although you don't have to use prefixes or stay with three-letter prefixes, it is a best practice that you should follow. I typically use my initials or initials of the organization. Throughout this book, we use the initials LMA (for Learning Mobile Apps). You can choose your own abbreviation, but it will be easier to follow the code examples if you use LMA. On this screen you can also choose which device to target (iPhone, iPad, or Universal). Universal creates a single app but with a different user interface for iPhone and iPad, enabling the same app to be installed on both devices.

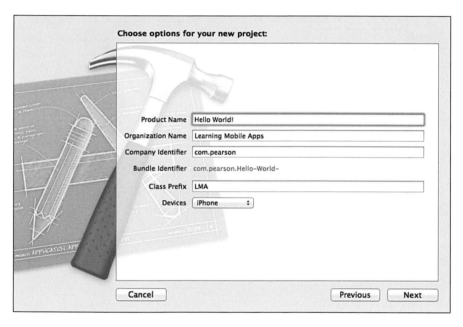

Figure 9.3   Choosing options for the iOS project.

Then click Next, and you will have to choose a location to save your project. You can navigate to an appropriate place on the disk to create the project files. Click Create.

Xcode Project Folder

The Xcode project is created in a folder and consists of a file with the extension .xcodeproj and a number of other files and folders. You can easily move the entire project between computers by copying the directory that contains the .xcodeproj file and any subfolders as well. We have found that when we work on our regular computers (office, home, and so on), using Google Drive or Dropbox works well to keep all the files of a project in sync. But we often find ourselves compressing the project folder and emailing or copying to a thumb drive to make sure we have a good copy of the project. To reopen a project that has been moved, you can double-click the .xcodeproj file. You also have the option of using version control systems by taking advantage of Xcode's built-in support of Git.

After creating the project, you're now looking at the main Xcode workspace window. Figure 9.4 shows an overview of the Xcode workspace.

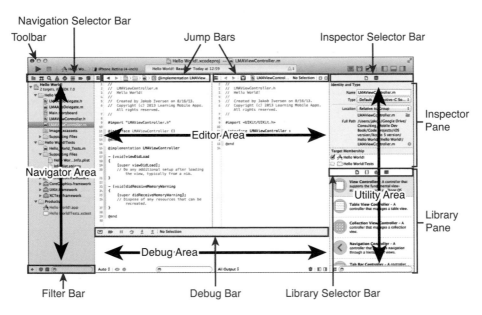

Figure 9.4   Overview of the Xcode workspace.

Xcode is a very powerful development environment with a lot of functionality. If you decide to do any serious development for iOS, you should take some time to figure out how everything works. You can find a detailed description of the Xcode workspace in the documentation (Help > Xcode Overview). We won't go into a lot of detail now, but you will discover some of the Xcode functionality as you need it. However, if you take some time to look through the documentation, you will likely save a lot of time later on.

Project Settings

After you've created the Hello World project, you should see the view of Xcode as shown in Figure 9.5. In the center of the workspace is a summary of the app and several appwide settings. The first section enables you to specify the version and build for the app. The version is used when the app is published to the App Store. Anytime an app with a higher version number is published, all your users will be prompted to download a new version. The build number is for internal use by the developer. You can choose which device types to target, as well as which version of iOS you want to target. As of this writing, the current version of iOS is 7.0. This setting determines the minimum version of iOS your users have to be running in order to run your app. This is just a signal within the app store. Apps are typically built using the latest available base SDK, so if you use features in a later SDK than your deployment target, you will need to insert checks in your code to make sure your app doesn't crash on devices with older versions of iOS.

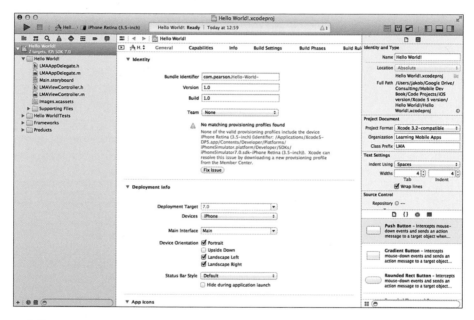

Figure 9.5   Overview of the Xcode workspace with our newly created Hello World app.

This is also where you can specify which device orientations are supported. By default, iPhone apps support Portrait and Landscape Left and Right but not Upside Down (iPad default is to support all four orientations).

On the left, in the navigation area, you can see the files that Xcode created for you. Figure 9.6 shows what it should look like. The exact number and types of files created depends on which choices you made when creating the project. Here's an overview of some of the files and folders created in this project:

- AppDelegate.h and AppDelegate.m—The App Delegate files manage issues related to the entire app and are primarily used to manage the life cycle of the app—how it is started, what happens when it goes to the background, and so on. This life cycle is covered in more detail in Chapter 2, "App Design Issues and Considerations," and in Chapter 11,

"Persistent Data in iOS." Objective-C programs follow the C-style and have both a header (.h) and method (.m) file. See Appendix C, "Introduction to Objective-C" for more detail.

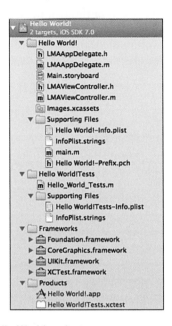

Figure 9.6   Contents of the Hello World project.

- Main.storyboard—The storyboard is used to design the interaction between multiple screens in your app as well as designing the layout of the individual screens.

- ViewController.h and ViewController.m—The view controller contains the code that controls the user interactions with the app. Most of the programming we do in this book will be in these files.

- Images.xcassets—This folder contains all the images, including icons, needed for your app.

- Supporting Files—This directory contains a number of files that the app may or may not use. Here's a description of a few of them:

    - Hello World!-Info.plist—This file contains a few app-specific settings. Most of these are controlled in other parts of Xcode.

    - main.m—The file that is responsible for launching the app.

- Hello World! Tests—Xcode comes with a built-in Unit Test framework, which you can use to create automated testing frameworks to ensure you deliver quality code. We recommend using Unit Tests on all production projects, but here the focus is on learning how to create iOS apps, so we don't have room to also cover unit testing. You can read more about this framework in *Test-Driven iOS Development* by Graham Lee.

- Frameworks—These are various libraries that you can include in your project to add functionality to your app, such as maps or audio capabilities. The default ones that are already included are *UIKit*, which is responsible for all the user interface controls, *Foundation*, which has a lot of the core functionality needed in any program, such as object-oriented data types, and *CoreGraphics*, which handles low-level graphical tasks and is used by UIKit.

- Products—This is your compiled app file.

Creating the User Interface

To open a file for editing in Xcode, you need to click it only once. Double-clicking will open it in a separate window. Click once on the Main.storyboard file. This opens the file in Interface Builder (see Figure 9.7), where you can easily create the user interface for your app. With the storyboard open, you can drag user interface elements from the utility pane on the bottom right and control a range of settings on the top of the utility pane.

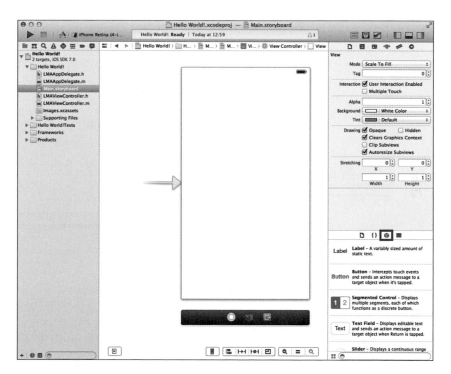

Figure 9.7   Interface Builder.

In the lower right of the utility area, you should see the Object Library, which contains all the user interface elements you can use in your app. If you don't see the Object Library, click the cube-shaped icon highlighted in Figure 9.7.

Start by dragging a label onto the user interface canvas (see Figure 9.8). You may have to scroll down the list of controls to find the label. You can also use the Search bar below the controls and type in **label**. Notice that you get blue dotted guidelines as you drag the label around. Drag it to the middle left of the screen and let go when both guidelines appear. Double-click the label to change the text of it to "Hello World!" and then press Enter. Expand the label by clicking the right side of it and dragging it to the right side until the blue dotted guidelines appear. Above the utility area on the right, you have a little menu bar of five items. The fourth one from the right should be selected. This is the Attributes Inspector, which enables you to set many properties for the currently selected user interface element. For the label, you can change its appearance quite a bit. Feel free to play around, but you just need to center the text of the label.

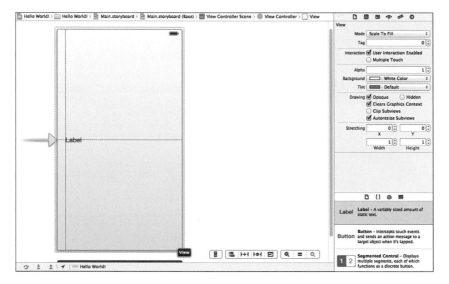

Figure 9.8   Dragging a label onto the canvas and using guidelines for placement.

Running the App in the Simulator

Launching the app in the built-in simulator that comes with Xcode is quite simple. In the top-right corner of Xcode, you will see a big Run button, and next to that, something called a Scheme, which enables choosing which device is targeted (see Figure 9.9). Click the right side of the scheme and choose the iPhone simulator. If you have a registered physical device connected to your computer, it will also show up in this list. See Appendix B for how to register physical devices to run your apps.

Figure 9.9   Choosing the iPhone simulator to run the app.

Click the Run button on the top left of the Xcode toolbar and wait a few seconds for the simulator to launch with your app (see Figure 9.10). You can control how the simulator looks and behaves in the Hardware menu. If you choose a device with a high-resolution screen, it may not fit on your computer screen comfortably. In that case, you can go to Window > Scale and choose a zoom level.

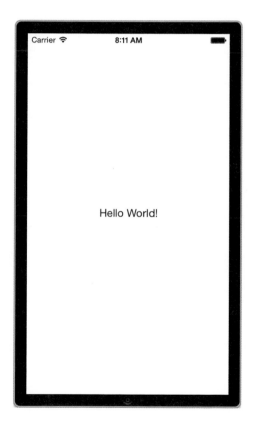

Figure 9.10   iOS simulator with the Hello World! App.

Adding App Behavior

Switch back to Xcode. Next, you'll see how to add some real functionality to your app. First, you'll need to set up the user interface, so make sure the storyboard is open. Then double-click the Hello World label and change it to **Please enter your name.** Drag a Text Field (scroll or search for it in the Object Library) onto the canvas and place it below the label. Then drag a button below the text field. Double-click the button and change its text to **Tap Here!** Finally, add a label below the button. Make the label as wide as the width of the screen, delete its text, and specify its content to be centered and blue.

Select the text field and look in the Attributes Inspector at some of the settings available. Change the Capitalization to Words, and then look at the Keyboards option. You can specify a keyboard that will show up on screen that is suited to the kind of data being input (for instance, if you need to have the user input only numbers, you can specify a Number Pad. This would be a good time to try out the different keyboards. You need to run the simulator to test the effect each time you choose a different one. Before moving on, make sure the keyboard is set to Default. Figure 9.11 shows the completed UI in both the Interface Designer and the iOS simulator with the default keyboard activated.

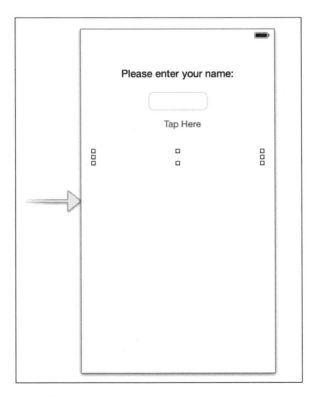

Figure 9.11   Completed UI in Interface Designer and the iOS simulator.

Having created the user interface, your next task is to add some action to the app. The action you want is to have the app take the name entered and say Hello to the user by name.

To do this, return to Xcode and click Stop to quit the simulator. Then make sure the storyboard is open. Next, click the Show Assistant Editor button in the top-right corner of the Xcode window (it's the second button from the left; see Figure 9.12).

Figure 9.12   Creating an outlet for a user interface element.

This opens an extra editor that by default contains the file that best matches what is displayed in the main window. For this user interface screen, this is the header file for the view controller (LMAViewController.h). We will need to create what's called outlets for those user interface elements we want to be able to access from the code. This includes the two text fields, where we need to be able to read the text the user entered and the bottom label that will be updated to contain our own text string based on the two text fields. To create the outlets, hold down the Control key, click the text field, and drag to the view controller between the @interface and @end entries. Then let go, and you should see the situation as shown in Figure 9.13.

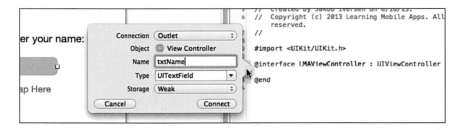

Figure 9.13   Creating an outlet for a user interface element.

Enter txtName in the Name field and click Connect. You should now have this line of code in LMAViewController:

```
@property (weak, nonatomic) IBOutlet UITextField *txtName;
```

For more detail on what this code means, you can look in Appendix C. For now, all you need to know is that this has provided a name for the text field that we can reference in our code by adding an underscore in front of the property name. Do the same for the bottom label, naming it lblOutput. Next, you'll add the code for the button. Switch back to the storyboard. The first step is the same: control-drag from the button to the view controller below the properties for the text fields and label. However, this time, in the top drop-down choose Action instead of Outlet (See Figure 9.14). Give it the name showOutput. For the Event, we will use the default Touch Up Inside, but take a moment and look through the list of all the possible events that this button will respond to. Touch Up Inside means that the button responds to events where users touched the button and then released their fingers while still inside the button. The convention in iOS is that to cancel a touch, you would drag your finger outside the target and then let go (try it on your own device to see how it works). Leave the Arguments as `Sender`.

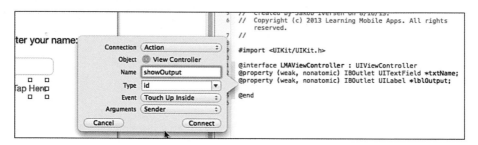

Figure 9.14   Creating the action for the button.

> ### Connecting Code to UI—iOS Versus Android
>
> In both Android and iOS, the user interface (UI) and the code that makes the UI work are stored in different files. This means that both types of app coding require that the code has to link to the UI in some way. In iOS, this is often referred to as "wiring up" the user interface. However, in Android, connecting the UI to the code is done entirely in the code itself.
>
> If you've ever created a program with a UI on a different platform, you're probably used to having to provide variable names for all UI elements. In iOS and Android, we just provide names to those UI elements we will need to access in code. So, the static label at the top of our UI isn't given a name. The same goes for the button, where we will need to intercept the event that happens when the user taps the button.
>
> In Android, whenever some code needs a reference to a control, we use a special command that will find it by its ID. This requires extra coding but provides great flexibility. Forgetting to connect the code to the UI widget needed in either operating system will result in a runtime error.

Switch the LMAViewController.m file, and notice that you now have a method at the bottom of the file called `showOutput:`. Between the curly braces of this method, enter the code shown in Listing 9.1.

Listing 9.1   **The `showOutput:` Method**

```
- (IBAction)showOutput:(UIButton *)sender {
    NSString *name = [_txtName text];
    NSString *output = [NSString stringWithFormat:
                                @"Hello %@!", name];
    [_lblOutput setText:output];
}
```

A brief explanation: The first line is the method declaration (Appendix C has more detail on how Objective-C methods are declared). The second line declares a string variable (NSString) and assigns the value in the text field (_txtName) by calling the text methods on the property. Notice the use of the underscore to refer to the property. The third line declares an NSString object that is initialized with a string that combines the string "Hello" with the name variable followed by an exclamation mark. The last line calls the setText method on the label, passing in the value of the output string. Run the app and test it by entering different names and touching the Tap Here! button.

UI Design—iOS Versus Android

UI design in iOS is done through absolute positioning, where each UI item is held to a fixed position on the screen. However, in Android, relative positioning is used. This enables creation of UI designs that are independent of the physical screen of the device. This means that app developers don't have to worry (too much) about screen sizes of different devices. However, relative positioning also means that the position of one control affects other controls. Often in Android, moving one control changes the whole design.

In iOS we need to provide a different UI layout for different screen sizes. If you want your app to run on both iPad and iPhone, you have to create two separate storyboard files and corresponding view controllers. These screens all run on the same code, so during design the developer must be sure to be perfectly consistent between the different screens needed.

Dismissing the Keyboard

As you may have noticed, the keyboard doesn't go away by itself when a text field loses focus. To get the keyboard to disappear, you have to add a little code to the program. What you need to do is change the View, which is the background of the app, so that it is able to respond to a tap. When the view intercepts a tap, it will then send a message to the text field to resign control. This makes the keyboard disappear. The first thing to do is set up the code to handle the event and then tie the event to the code.

In LMAViewController.h, add this line between the @interface line and the @end line to define a new action method:

```
- (IBAction)backgroundTap:(id)sender;
```

In LMAViewController.m, add the code in Listing 9.2 to implement the method.

Listing 9.2   **The backgroundTap: Method**

```
-(IBAction)backgroundTap:(id)sender
{
    [self.view endEditing:YES];
}
```

This code tells the View to end editing, which will cause the keyboard to disappear. Next, you will have to specify how this code gets called. Select the storyboard file. Make sure the Dock is in list mode. The Dock is the vertical bar between the left and center panes. To expand it to list view, click the triangle in a rounded rectangle (this is already done in Figure 9.15). After the Dock is in list mode, select the top-level View (see Figure 9.15). The View is the background canvas that all the other controls sit on. First, you will need to change this to a Control, so it can fire events. With the View selected, show the Identity Inspector in the far-right pane (you can also press Option-Cmd-3 to open the Identity Inspector—and the other options in that section can be accessed by just changing the number, so Option-Cmd-4 will open the Attributes Inspector). Change the Class field to `UIControl` by simply typing over `UIView` (see Figure 9.16). All controls that are capable of firing events are subclasses of `UIControl`, so by changing the underlying class from `UIView` to `UIControl` we make the View capable of firing events.

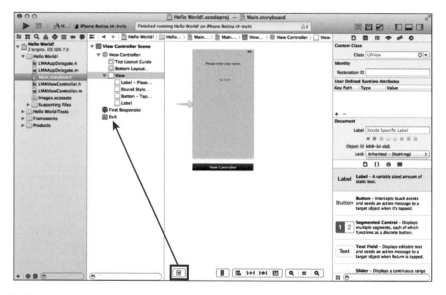

Figure 9.15   Xcode with the Dock in List View.

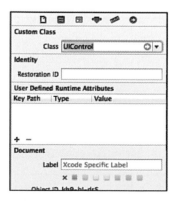

Figure 9.16   Changing the View class to `UIControl`.

Select the Connections Inspector in the right pane (Option-Cmd-6). This shows all the possible actions that can be taken for the current control and can be used to connect those actions to methods in the code. Drag the circle by Touch Down to the View Controller in the Dock (see Figure 9.17). When you release it, select `backgroundTap:`. This will then call the `background-Tap:` method every time the Touch Down event fires on the View.

> **Note**
>
> Touch Down means the event fires as soon as the user taps, in contrast to the Touch Up Inside event that we used earlier, which fires only if the user releases the finger inside the specified control.

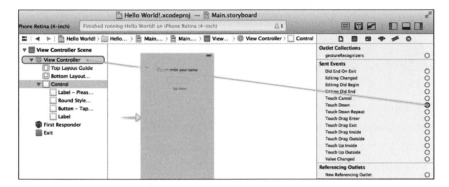

Figure 9.17   Connecting the Touch Down event for the View to File's Owner.

The View Controller object is the object that loads the current view controller (single screen in an iOS app)—typically the `UIViewController` class itself. Connecting to View Controller in this manner is the same as connecting to the methods in the code, so this is just a different technique for achieving the same result. Click some of the other controls to view them in the Connections Inspector and see how events are linked to methods (see Figure 9.18).

Run the app and see how the keyboard disappears when you tap outside the text field.

> **Note**
>
> If you are developing iPad apps, this is not an issue, because the iPad keyboard has a key to make it disappear, but this doesn't exist in the iPhone keyboard.

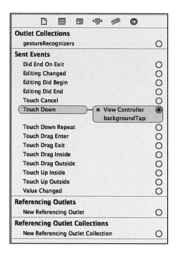

Figure 9.18   Connection Inspector after setting up the action to dismiss the keyboard.

Quick Reference: Dismiss the Keyboard

For future reference, here are the four steps needed to have the keyboard dismissed:

1. Make the View a control, by changing its class from `UIView` to `UIControl`.
2. Define the `backgroundTap:` action method in the .h file.
3. Implement `backgroundTap:` in the .m file to end editing (Listing 9.2).
4. Control-drag from Touch Down in Connections Inspector with Control (formerly View) selected to View Controller in the expanded Dock. Choose the `backgroundTap:` method.

App Icons and Launch Images

The images.xcassets folder is called the Asset Catalog and was introduced with Xcode 5 as a way to manage all the images needed for your app, including app icons and launch images.

App Icons are graphical images that are used to indicate your app on the home screen of the iOS device your app is running on. When you create the icon for your app, you should be prepared to create it in a number of resolutions so that it looks great on different devices, and for various uses within the app as well. The icon is used for three places:

- On the home screen, to give the user an easily recognizable image of your app.
- In Spotlight results when the user is searching on the device.
- In the Settings app where the user can change various settings for your app.

In each of these three places, the icon is supplied in different resolutions, and the resolutions also differ between iPad and iPhone as well as between whether the device is a regular display or a retina display. There can also be differences between whether your app is targeting iOS 7 or earlier versions of iOS. In all, a Universal app targeting both iPhone and iPad and made available for both iOS 6 and iOS 7 may have to have as many as 14 versions of the app icon.

Fortunately, the asset catalog makes it relatively simple to find out what you need. Click the images.xcassets folder and then AppIcon (Figure 9.19). On the right you see three spots for icons. For this app, the icons will be supplied only for iOS 7 and iPhone. To determine the resolution you need to supply, you look at the number in the last line under each spot (29pt, 40pt, and 60pt). This is how many logical points the image takes up. However, if you look just below each of these images, it says 2x, which means these images will be used on a retina display, so the resolution has to be doubled because a retina display has twice as many pixels in each direction as a regular display. This means that these three images have to be 58x58, 80x80, and 120x120 pixels, respectively.

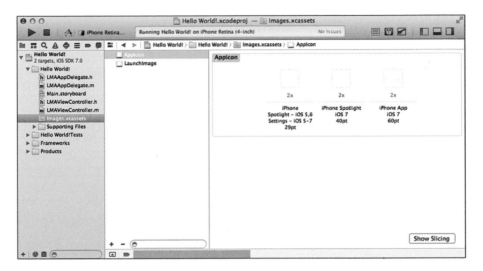

Figure 9.19   Asset catalog.

To supply icons for other situations, you can right-click anywhere with a white background in the asset catalog and select New App Icon. This will give you many more options, as shown in Figure 9.20. The same principle applies, though. Use the pt number and multiply by the 1x or 2x number to get the resolution of the image.

Test out the app icon resolutions by dragging the icons available into the appropriate spot. A very simple icon is available in various resolutions. You can test how the icon looks by running the app in the simulator and then clicking the Home button (Hardware > Home) to get to the home screen where the app icon will be shown along with the app name. You can see the Spotlight icon in the simulator if you click the home screen and drag down. This will pull down a search field. Type **Hello** into the resulting search field, and the icon will show up in the search results.

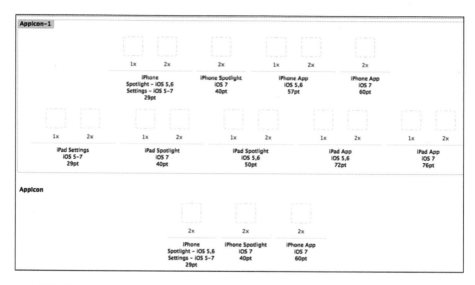

Figure 9.20   Possible app icon resolutions.

To have your app listed in the app store, you also need to supply icons in sizes of 512x512 and 1024x1024 pixels.

The other option that is available in the asset catalog is launch images. A launch image is shown as the app is launching. Apple recommends that your launch image is a blank version of the app's first screen. This way, the user will quickly see the app and what it looks like, before it is filled in with data. Launch images are also supplied in different resolutions depending on the device. Table 9.1 shows the possible resolutions for launch images.

Table 9.1   **Typical Launch Image Dimensions**

Device	Portrait	Landscape
iPhone and iPod touch	320 x 480 pixels	Not supported
	640 x 960 pixels (@2x)	
iPhone 5 and iPod touch (5th generation)	640 x 1136 pixels (@2x)	Not supported
iPad	768 x 1004 pixels	1024 x 748 pixels
	1536 x 2008 pixels (@2x)	2048 x 1496 pixels (@2x)

iPhone Screen Sizes and Resolutions

When the first iPhone was released, the resolution was set to 320x480 pixels. Programmers would use this coordinate grid to arrange their user interface. When the iPhone 4 was released, it sported a retina display with double the resolution (640x960). However, from the perspective of the programmer, the original 320x480 grid was still used to position everything on the screen, so apps didn't have to be updated to handle the higher resolution. But all the UIKit controls were rendered in higher resolution, and all images could now be supplied in retina versions with double the resolution. If you need an image in your app, you can create a regular file to be used on nonretina screens, as well as a version with double the resolution for retina screens. By dragging the file into the appropriate spot in the images.xcassets container, the system will automatically pick the right one for the device the app is running on.

With the iPhone 5 and iPod touch 5, Apple again changed the resolution, this time increasing the vertical size to 1136 pixels (giving a grid of 320x568). Images can now also be supplied in this higher resolution. The iPhone 5 increased the physical size of the screen from 3.5 to 4 inches, so when you see references to a 4-inch screen, this is the screen introduced with the iPhone 5 (and iPod touch 5).

Summary

Congratulations! You have built your first iOS app. You created an Xcode project, designed and coded a user interface, and finally made the app do something. Along the way you learned the process of iOS app development, the Xcode development environment, and the components of an iOS app.

Exercises

1. Split the name field into first and last name. Then make sure both first and last names show up when tapping the button.

2. Change the functionality of the `showOutput` method so that if no text has been entered, the output changes to Hello World!

3. Explore the properties for the text fields, buttons, and labels within Xcode. Change the label to green and bold text. Change the border style for the text field, and add a clear button.

4. Add a new button to the app, with a method that will change the `lblOutput` text to Hello World!

5. Rotate the simulator while running the app.

6. Run the app in the iPad simulator. Then change the Devices setting to Universal and run again in the iPad simulator.

7. Have the keyboard dismiss when the user taps the button.

8. Add a new field to enter a number, and set the keyboard to be numeric. Be sure that the keyboard dismisses appropriately from this new field.

iOS Navigation and Interface Design

Because the screens are small on mobile devices, as a developer, you have to pay careful attention to how you use that space and set up a logical navigation structure in your app. Many mobile apps use multiple screens with carefully arranged navigation between these screens. In iOS, several built-in controllers can help you create a logical flow in your app. It's very important to understand how these controllers work and how you can take advantage of them. In this chapter, you create the basic user interface for the MyContactList app and learn how to use two important ways to navigate around an iOS app: the Tab Bar Controller and the Navigation Controller. You also learn how to use many of the built-in user interface components available for iOS apps, as well as how to create the user interface for the app using the Storyboard feature in Xcode.

Views and Controllers

The user interface classes in iOS are contained in the UIKit framework. The UIKit framework contains a large number of classes that you can take advantage of in your apps. The classes are arranged in an inheritance hierarchy with the top class being UIView. This class describes a basic rectangle with width, height, background color, and so on. This class can contain subviews and may also have a parent view. One of the subclasses of UIView is UIWindow, which has been restricted to set its origin to the top left of the screen. Each iOS app has one UIWindow object that is created when the app launches. All other screens are subviews of UIWindow. Other subclasses of UIView include UILabel, UIScrollView, UINavigationBar, UITableCell, and UIControl (which is the parent class for most of the regular controls used for creating apps, such as UIButton, UITextField, and UISlider).

View Controller

When you create iOS apps, you often need to create multiple screens for each app. Each screen is managed by an instance of the UIViewController class, where other UIView objects for the various user interface elements are added. As you saw in the previous chapter, the screens can be designed using Interface Builder to add the various user interface elements needed for the app. In this situation, the View Controller is managed in three files: a .storyboard file that specifies the layout of user interface elements, a .h file that has information about any outlets and actions needed to control the user interface, and a .m file that contains the implementation of the user interface actions, as well as any setup needed for the user interface. In some situations there is no storyboard file for a view controller. Instead, the user interface is described entirely in code.

After the View Controller has been set up, it can be added to the application in different ways. It can be added as a root view, as you saw in the Hello World app in the previous chapter, as one of the tabs in a tabbed interface, as a page in a page layout, or as part of a navigation hierarchy.

Tab Bar Controller

The Tab Bar Controller shows up at the bottom of iPhone apps and allows the user to choose between different screens in the app. This user interface is used in many common apps, including the built-in GameCenter app (see Figure 10.1).

Figure 10.1   Tab Bar Controller shown at the bottom of the built-in GameCenter app.

Navigation Controller

The Navigation Controller is used to allow the user to drill down through multiple screens while keeping track of the path so the user can later go back the same way. This pattern is also used very frequently in iPhone apps, including the built-in Contacts app, as shown in Figure 10.2. When the user taps one of the contacts listed in the screen on the left, the app navigates to the screen on the right, but the button at the top left allows the user to navigate back to the list of all users.

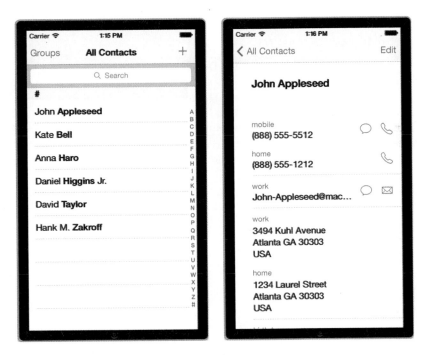

Figure 10.2   Navigation Controller in the built-in Contacts app.

Creating the Interface

In this section you see how to create the project and the user interface for the MyContactList app that will be the example for the next few chapters.

Creating the Project

Create a new project in Xcode (Shift-Command-N) using the following settings in the first two steps in the wizard:

- Template: Tabbed Application
- Product Name: MyContactList
- Organization Name: Learning Mobile Apps
- Company Identifier: com.pearson
- Class Prefix: LMA
- Devices: iPhone

Creating the Views

As described in more detail in Chapter 2, "App Design Issues and Considerations," MyContactList will have three basic screens: displaying and editing the contacts, a map view of one or more contacts, and a settings screen. The contacts screen will also have an associated screen to edit the birthdate of the contact. Your first task is to create views for each of these four screens. Because you chose the Tabbed template when creating the project, two of the view controllers and the tab bar have already been created for you in the storyboard. When you open the storyboard, you will see the Tab Bar Controller and two View Controllers (Figure 10.3)

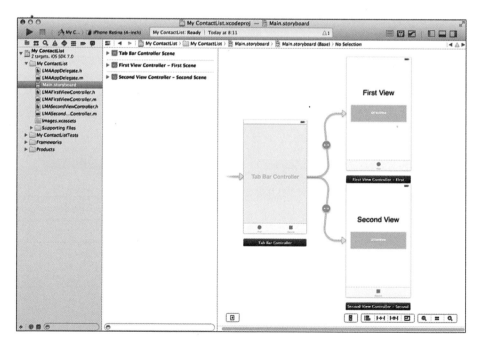

Figure 10.3 Tab Bar Controller and two View Controllers.

Because the tab bar needs three screens, start by adding a new View Controller for the third screen.

1. Drag a View Controller into the Storyboard.

2. Select the Tab Bar Controller.

3. Hold down the control key and then drag from the Tab Bar Controller to the new View Controller, then let go (this is called Control-dragging, and you will use this technique to accomplish a number of tasks when building user interfaces for iOS).

4. Choose View Controllers in the dialog that pops up (Figure 10.4). This will add an arrow from the Tab Bar Controller to the new View Controller and add a third element to the actual tab bar (Figure 10.5).

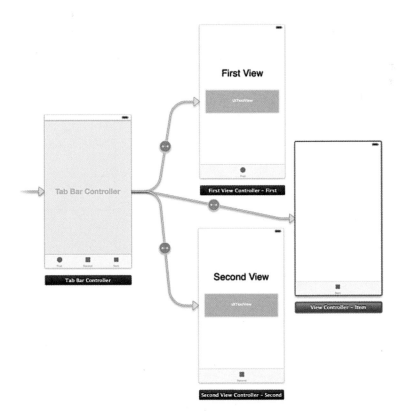

Figure 10.4   Adding a new View Controller.

5. To help distinguish among the three View Controllers, copy the label that says First View onto the new View Controller by selecting it and pressing Cmd-C; then select the new View Controller and press Cmd-V. You may have to zoom in a little to be able to select the label.

6. Double-click each of the three labels and change the text to **Contacts**, **Map**, and **Settings**, as shown in Figure 10.5.

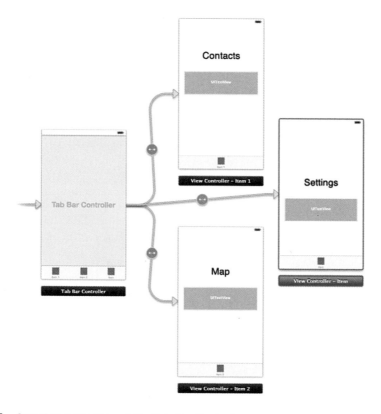

Figure 10.5   Completed interface of the Tab Bar Controller.

If you run the app now, you will see the Contacts screen come up, and then the three tabs at the bottom, named First, Second, and Item. Here's how to change the tabs to have the proper names:

1. Open the Storyboard and select the First View Controller in the Dock.

2. Make sure the Attributes Inspector is selected and then change the Title to Contacts (Figure 10.6).

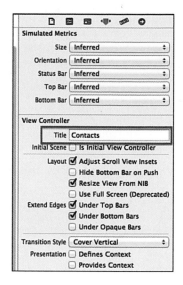

Figure 10.6   Changing the title of the Contacts View Controller.

3. Select the Tab Bar item at the bottom of the Contacts View Controller (see Figure 10.5) and change the Title in the Attributes Inspector to **Contacts** (Figure 10.7).

4. Repeat for the Map and Settings screen.

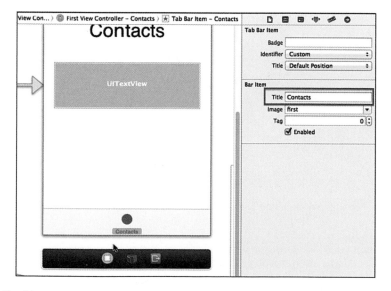

Figure 10.7   Changing the Title of the Tab Bar Item.

While you are renaming, you should also rename the code files that manage each View Controller. These were autogenerated with the Tab Bar template and are currently named LMAFirstViewController and LMASecondViewController. The name of a View Controller appears in many places in the project, so you have to be careful to rename in all those places. Fortunately, Xcode has good support for refactoring, which will find and rename everything for you:

1. With the Dock in List View, select the First View Controller and double check that this is the one that has the Contacts bar item. If it isn't, go back to the previous instructions and redo the renaming of the tab bar items.

2. Open LMAFirstViewController.h and right-click LMAFirstViewController in the `@interface` line.

3. Select Refactor > Rename.

4. Change the name to **LMAContactsController** and ensure that Rename Related Files is checked. Click Save.

5. You will see the screen in Figure 10.8. This shows all the files on the left that will be affected, and for each file you can see the current and potential changes if you carry out the rename operation. Click through each file and preview the changes. Note that in the Storyboard file, the code is shown as XML, as the Interface Builder generates XML code in the background.

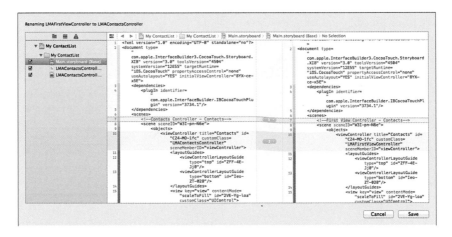

Figure 10.8   Renaming a file using the Refactor option in Xcode.

6. After you have reviewed the changes, click Save. You will see a message about taking snapshots (Figure 10.9). If you enable this, you will be able to roll back changes like this renaming operation. Click Enable, and the rename is carried out.

7. Repeat for the Second View Controller, renaming it **LMAMapController**.

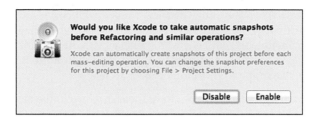

Figure 10.9   Enabling automatic snapshots.

The tab bar allows for having both a title and an image (icon). These images have to be around 20x20 pixels for regular screens and about 40x40 pixels for retina screens. iOS comes with a set of standard icon symbols you can use, but there are only 12 of them, so chances are they won't cover what you need. Instead, you can design your own using a graphics program or you can license a set of icons from someone who has already created them. One such source is Glyphish (www.glyphish.com), which provides several sets of icons, either free or at a low cost. The paid version provides both regular and retina sizes, whereas the free version has only a single size.

For the MyContactList app, we have included the free set from Glyphish with the download files for the book (www.informit.com/title/9780321947864). After you download it, open images.xcassets in Xcode and drag the following files to the right side of the asset catalog (where it says No Selection): 20-gear2.png, 103-map.png, and 111-user.png. The images are inserted in the 1x spot. If you had a retina version, you would simply drag that into the 2x spot. Because you won't need them anymore, you can delete the images named first and second (Figure 10.10).

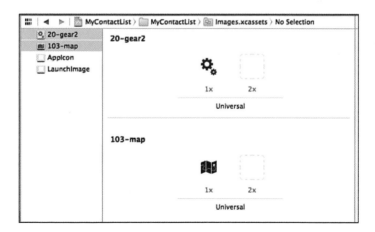

Figure 10.10   Adding images to the Asset Catalog.

The images are now available for use anywhere in your code. The icons are licensed under a Creative Commons attribution-only license, which means they can be used in any of your projects, as long as you put a note in your code with a reference to the Glyphish website. However, if you intend to create an app for use with real customers, you'll want to have the retina versions that are available in the paid version of the icon set.

With the images imported, you now need to have them show up in the tab bar. You probably noticed that no image was added for the Contacts tab. That's because there is a built-in image for Contacts that you will use instead. This does mean that the icons will end up not having the same look and feel, which is not something you should do for a real app. Here, it is done to show you both approaches.

1. Open the Storyboard and select the Tab Bar Item for the Contacts View Controller.

2. Make sure the Attributes Inspector is open, and then change the Identifier to Contacts. As you do that, you'll notice the other default options that you can use, such as Search, Bookmarks, History, and so on.

3. Select the Tab Bar Item for the Map View Controller.

4. In the Attributes Inspector, use the Image drop-down list to change the image to 103-map.

5. Use the same technique to change the Settings image to 20-gear2.

Run the app and you should see the three tabs with the text show up. Tap on each tab to make sure the proper View Controller shows up (see Figure 10.11).

Design the Contacts Screen

Now it's time to set up the user interface for the Contacts screen. Refer to Figure 10.12 as you create the screen.

1. Open the Storyboard and remove the Contacts label and the `UITextView` control by clicking each and pressing Delete.

2. Drag a Segmented Control to the canvas and place in the center of the screen toward the top. A Segmented Control can have multiple segments, only one of which can be activated at a time. This is the iOS equivalent to a radio button. Double-click the text First and change to **Edit**, then change Second to **View**. You can also change these in the Attributes Inspector by choosing the Segment and then changing the Title.

3. Drag a Label to the left side of the screen below the Segmented Control and change its text to **Contact:**.

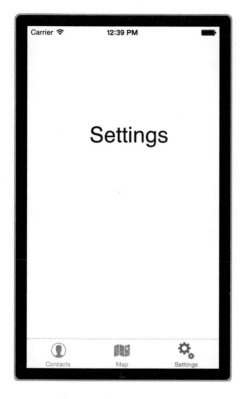

Figure 10.11   The completed Tab Bar with three view controllers.

Figure 10.12   Designing the Contacts screen.

4. Drag a Text Field below the label, and resize to the right until the blue guideline appears. Then continue with the remaining labels and text fields as shown in the screenshot. To make it a little easier to add all the fields, you can easily copy an existing control by holding down the Option key and dragging a control. If you select multiple controls, you can use the same technique to copy multiple controls. As you work, use the blue guidelines to place the controls.

5. The Birthday line has two Labels and a Button.

6. For the City, State, and Zip fields, select the Attributes Inspector and change the Placeholder property for each of them as shown in the screenshot.

7. Use the Attributes Inspector to change the Capitalization to Words for the Contact, Address, and City fields. Change Capitalization for the State field to All Characters.

8. Use the Attributes Inspector to change the Keyboard for the Zip field to Number Pad, and for the two phone fields to Phone Pad, and for the Email field to Email Address.

Run the app to see if things work as expected. You'll notice that you can't dismiss the keyboard, and that some of the controls are hidden behind the keyboard. Both of these problems can be fixed by using a scroll view control.

1. With the Dock in List View, select all the controls on the page except the Segmented Control. This may be easier to do using the Dock rather than on the screen (see Figure 10.13).

2. Select Editor > Embed In > Scroll View. This will embed all the controls in a Scroll View, and if you run the app again, you will see that you can indeed scroll the controls up from behind the keyboard.

3. Add an outlet named `scrollView` for the Scroll View by using the Assistant Editor and control-drag from the Control View (it's easiest to use the Dock for this) to LMAContactsController.h.

With the Scroll View in place, you will need to set its content size. This is the size of the container that will be scrolled, and is set in code. Listing 10.1 has the code you need to enter in LMAContactsController.m.

Listing 10.1   **Setting the Content Size for the Scroll View**

```
- (void)viewDidLoad
{
    [super viewDidLoad];
        // Do any additional setup after loading the view, typically from a nib.
    _scrollView.contentSize = CGSizeMake(320,500);
}
- (void)viewDidLayoutSubviews
{
    _scrollView.contentSize = CGSizeMake(320,500);
}
```

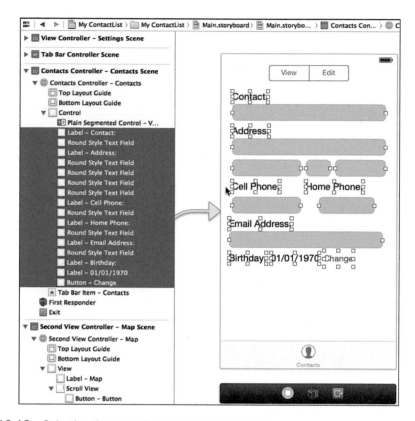

Figure 10.13   Selecting the controls to embed in Scroll View.

This code sets the content size to a rectangle that is 320 pixels wide and 500 pixels tall. This size means that the rectangle that will scroll will fill the screen horizontally (320 pixels wide), and is large enough to be scrolled far enough vertically for all the content to be visible (that's the second number). You can experiment with using different sizes for the vertical size and see the effect when scrolling.

The second method, `viewDidLayoutSubviews:`, needs to be added to the file because of an apparent bug in iOS 7 that sets the size of the scroll view to (0, 0) sometime after `viewDidLoad:`. This code was written on the iOS 7.0 SDK. You can try to remove this method to see if the bug has been fixed in new releases of the SDK.

Try running the app, and you should now be able to scroll the contents of the screen up and down, but the keyboard still can't be dismissed. However, this is easily fixed. Select the Scroll View in the Storyboard and Keyboard setting in Attributes Inspector (Figure 10.14). There are two ways to dismiss the keyboard. The first option, Dismiss on Drag, will dismiss the keyboard as soon as the user starts dragging the scroll view. Dismiss Interactively will dismiss the keyboard as the user scrolls down and starts to scroll into the space where the keyboard is; the keyboard will slide down with the scrolling, which is a very nice effect. You can try out both of them to see which you think works best. But since the primary purpose for having the scrolling is to bring controls up from underneath the keyboard, the best approach here is Dismiss Interactively.

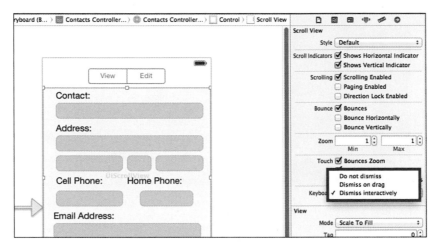

Figure 10.14   Selecting the controls to embed in Scroll View.

The scroll view is used extensively throughout iOS, and has been put to use even further in iOS 7. It would be worthwhile for you to spend some time understanding how it works to create very powerful user interfaces for your own apps. In addition to scrolling up and down as you have seen here, UIScrollView also allows for scrolling horizontally as well as zooming. So, for instance, if you want to display an image and allow the user to zoom in and then scroll around the image, you would use a UIScrollView to support both the zooming and scrolling.

You may notice that the scroll view overlaps the bottom edge of the Segment Control. This will cause an undesirable effect when the user starts scrolling where the Segmented Control gets clipped. To correct this problem, you can grab the top edge of the UIScrollView control and drag it down a little.

Add Navigation Controller for the Date Screen

The Birthday on the Contacts screen is changed by tapping the Change button, which will cause a new screen to appear where the date can be chosen. This illustrates several new elements, including the use of the DatePicker control and the use of the Navigation Controller to move between related screens in the app. It takes a little work to get this set up, so be careful as you go through these steps.

A Navigation Controller is a special control that allows users to drill down through several screens and then return the way they came by tapping a button in the top left of the screen to navigate back to the previous screen. In MyContactList, you implement this by adding a Navigation Controller to the Contacts Controller, so the Tab Bar will actually be connected to the Navigation Controller, which in turn is connected to the View Controller.

1. Select the Contacts Controller and then choose Editor > Embed In > Navigation Controller. This adds a Navigation Controller between the Tab Bar Controller and the Contacts Controller (Figure 10.15). It also adds a gray bar to the top of the Contacts screen covering the Segmented Control and part of the scroll view. This is the navigation bar, which will contain the title of the screen, the button for navigating back, and possibly some other controls. You'll need to move the Segmented Control and scroll view down to be visible under the navigation bar.

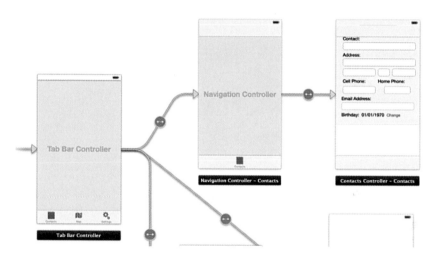

Figure 10.15   Adding a Navigation Controller.

2. Select the scroll view and drag down to free up some whitespace below the navigation bar.

3. The Segmented Control is hidden, so select it in the Dock, and then use the Size Inspector in the right sidebar to change the Y coordinate to 70 (Figure 10.16).

4. Set the title of the navigation bar by selecting the Contacts Controller's Navigation Item in the Dock and then use the Attributes Inspector to set the Title to **Contact** (Figure 10.17).

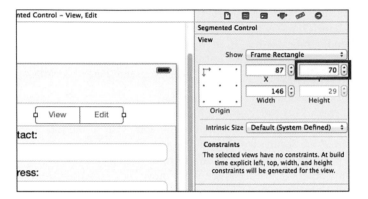

Figure 10.16   Setting the Y placement for the Segmented Control.

Figure 10.17   Setting the navigation bar Title.

If you run the app, you should see the navigation bar show up on the Contact screen, but otherwise, everything else should function as before. The next step is to add a View Controller for the Date screen and add that to the Navigation Controller as well.

1. Drag a new View Controller onto the Storyboard.

2. Use the Attributes Inspector to change the new View Controller's Title to **Birthdate**.

3. Control-drag from the Change button to the Birthdate View Controller, and pick Push in the action menu that comes up. This will push the new View Controller on to the Navigation Stack that the Contacts screen is already part of. You should see a navigation bar added to the new View Controller, and in the Dock you will see a Navigation Item appear for the Birthdate Controller.

4. Select the new Navigation Item and set its Title to **Pick Birthdate** (Figure 10.18).

The connections between the various view controllers are called segues, as they define how the various screens will transition back and forth.

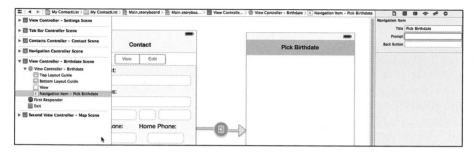

Figure 10.18   Setting the Navigation Bar Title for the Birthdate View Controller.

Run the app and tap the Change button, and you should see the Date screen as shown in Figure 10.19. The Contacts button will take the user back to the Contacts screen. The text for the Contacts button is the Title setting in the Navigation Item for the Contacts View Controller. You can set an alternative text for the button here by adding text to the Back Button setting for the Navigation Item.

Figure 10.19   The Date screen with the navigation controller and button to go back to Contacts.

The last step in setting up the user interface and navigation is to add the capability to choose a date on the Date screen. Open the Storyboard and drag in a Date Picker from the toolbox and place it at the top of the Date View Controller. The Date Picker can be configured to work with both time and date. However, you want to use only dates, so open the Attributes Inspector and change the Mode to Date. As you can see, you can also set the default date as well as constrain the picker between specific dates. You don't have to change these settings for this app. Run the app and make sure the Date Picker shows up as expected. Figure 10.20 shows the completed navigation control hierarchy for the Contacts and Date View Controllers. In the next chapter you will see how to bring the date chosen back to the Contacts screen.

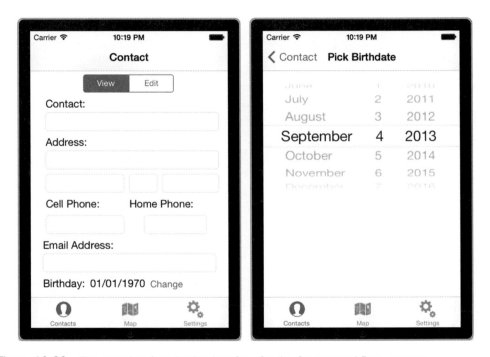

Figure 10.20   The completed navigation interface for the Contact and Date screens.

Activating the Interface

The next chapter is dedicated to implementing most of the functionality of saving data from the Contacts screen, but for now, we will implement the capability to switch between view and edit modes. The code for this is quite simple, but somewhat tedious.

The edit mode is controlled by the Segmented Control. When the user changes to View, all the controls will be disabled so they can't be edited. And when the user changes back again, they will be reactivated.

1. Open the storyboard in Assistant Editor mode and control-drag from the Segmented Control in the Contact View Controller to the @interface section of the LMAContactsController.h file.

2. Add an action named changeEditMode: (see Figure 10.21). Click Connect. The changeEditMode: method is called anytime the value of the Segmented Control is changed, but the method call doesn't indicate the current value of the control, so you need to add an outlet to be able to reference and read the value.

Figure 10.21   Adding an action to change the edit mode.

3. Control-drag again from the Segmented Control to the @interface section of LMAContactsConroller.h.

4. Add an outlet named sgmtEditMode. Click Connect.

5. You will also need to reference all the text fields and buttons in the interface. See Listing 10.2 for the names to give the text fields, the Birthdate label, and the Change button. If you make a mistake in connecting the fields and the outlets, you may have some strange results when running the app. It's always a good idea to check the connections if something doesn't work as expected. You can see all the connections made on a View Controller by selecting the Connections Inspector.

6. Implement the changeEditMode: method as shown in Listing 10.3.

7. Run the app and switch between view and edit modes.

Listing 10.2   **LMAContactsController.h**

```objc
#import <UIKit/UIKit.h>


@interface LMAContactsController : UIViewController
- (IBAction)backgroundTap:(id)sender;
- (IBAction)changeEditMode:(id)sender;
@property (weak, nonatomic) IBOutlet UISegmentedControl *sgmtEditMode;
@property (weak, nonatomic) IBOutlet UITextField *txtName;
@property (weak, nonatomic) IBOutlet UITextField *txtAddress;
@property (weak, nonatomic) IBOutlet UITextField *txtCity;
@property (weak, nonatomic) IBOutlet UITextField *txtState;
@property (weak, nonatomic) IBOutlet UITextField *txtZip;
@property (weak, nonatomic) IBOutlet UITextField *txtPhone;
@property (weak, nonatomic) IBOutlet UITextField *txtCell;
@property (weak, nonatomic) IBOutlet UITextField *txtEmail;
@property (weak, nonatomic) IBOutlet UIButton *btnChange;
@property (weak, nonatomic) IBOutlet UILabel *lblBirthdate;
@property (weak, nonatomic) IBOutlet UIButton *btnChange;

@end
```

Listing 10.3   **LMAContactsController.m**

```objc
#import "LMAContactsController.h"

@interface LMAContactsController ()
@end

@implementation LMAContactsController

 [ ... ]

- (IBAction)changeEditMode:(id)sender {
    NSArray *textFields = @[_txtName, _txtAddress, _txtCity, _txtState,    //1
                        _txtZip, _txtPhone, _txtCell, _txtEmail];

    if (_sgmtEditMode.selectedSegmentIndex == 0){                          //2
        for (UITextField *txtfield in textFields) {                        //3
            [txtfield setEnabled:NO];                                      //4
            [txtfield setBorderStyle:UITextBorderStyleNone];               //5
        }
        [_btnChange setHidden:YES];                                        //6
    }
    else if (_sgmtEditMode.selectedSegmentIndex == 1)                      //7
    {
```

```
        for (UITextField *txtfield in textFields) {
            [txtfield setEnabled:YES];
            [txtfield setBorderStyle:UITextBorderStyleRoundedRect];
        }
        [_btnChange setHidden:NO];
    }
}
@end
```

The code is relatively straightforward, but still deserves some description.

1. All the properties are changed in the same way for each of the text fields, so you set up a NSArray object containing all the text fields by separating the list of objects with commas and surrounding the entire list with square brackets.

2. Check the value of the Segmented Control. Viewing is 0 and Editing is 1.

3. Use a fast enumeration loop to go through all the text fields in the array.

4.-5. In view mode, the text fields are disabled, and the border is set to not be there (UITextBorderStyleNone).

6. The Change button should not be shown in view mode.

7. When switching to edit mode, the code is similar, but the values are opposite. The text fields are enabled and the border is set to the Rounded Rect mode (the default). The button is hidden.

Run the app and enter some data into the text fields, and then try switching back and forth between View and Edit.

Summary

Creating a user interface in iOS is relatively straightforward using the Interface Builder. However, as you saw, you still need to know how to write code to make some things work.

Navigation between screens can be tricky to get set up right, especially when both tab bars and navigation controllers are involved.

Exercises

1. Add a new tab to the tab bar with an associated view controller.

2. Change the Segmented Control to a Switch.

3. Split the Contact field into first and last name fields.

4. Set the Date Picker to start on your birthday, and limit the range to be from January 1, 1980 to January 1, 2000.

11

Persistent Data in iOS

Storing data that the user will need to run the app is an important part of developing for the mobile platform. In addition to the regular purposes for saving data, the mobile platform also presents unique challenges regarding the life cycle of an app that requires special consideration to saving data. Because the app can become inactive and be closed down at any point, it's important to save enough of the app's state on a regular basis to allow the user to continue working in a meaningful way when the app becomes active again.

In this chapter you will see several ways that you can save data on iOS. Most of the attention is going to be on a system called Core Data that provides strong support for a database-backed persistence solution for iOS apps, but you will also see how to save to files directly, as well as how to save app settings.

File Data Storage

Like most other operating systems, iOS enables saving data in files, either in regular text files or by archiving (what's known as *serialization* in Java and C#). The techniques for working with files are similar to many other programming languages, but it's worth noting that on iOS, apps are sandboxed, which means that each app is isolated from the other apps and from the operating system. One of the consequences is that each app has only a very simple file system that by default consists of a few standard directories: Documents, Library, and tmp. As a developer, you can store files in the Documents and tmp directories. The Documents folder is backed up when the device is backed up. The tmp folder is not. By storing data in files, you can quickly store user data and can even take advantage of Apple's iCloud to allow the user to sync documents between their devices. This is a powerful service, but it works only between devices for a single user. iCloud will not allow you to let your users exchange data. Although it is useful to store files, iCloud will not be covered further in this book.

User Defaults

When you need to save a little bit of data in your app, the NSUserDefaults object is a very simple and easy way to do so. NSUserDefaults is a front-end to a key-value file (often referred to as Plist files because of the .plist extension) that is stored in the app's Preferences directory. There's only one file, but in this file you can store as many values as you want. When storing values in the file, you have to supply a key string to identify the value when retrieving it later. You can store many data types in NSUserDefaults, including all scalar types as well as NSData, NSString, NSNumber, NSDate, NSDictionary, and NSArray. Other data types can be archived and stored as an NSData object.

Core Data

Core Data is a powerful data persistence solution developed by Apple to provide object-oriented storage. Core Data is an object-wrapper on top of a data store—typically a SQLite database. This allows the developer to work with objects that map to entities in the database without worrying too much about the underlying database design and queries. For apps that need business data stored, Core Data is a strong solution to meet this need.

Figure 11.1 shows an overview of the Core Data framework. The framework stores data in files. The default is SQLite database, but you can also choose to use XML or binary data. The Persistent Object Store wraps around the data file and presents a common interface to the rest of the stack. You will not need to interact with the Persistent Object Store except to choose which file format to store the data in. The Persistent Store Coordinator allows for having multiple data stores in the same app, and will then coordinate access to those stores. This is very rare for iOS apps, and you will never directly interact with the Persistent Store Coordinator.

The Managed Object Model is the description of the layout of the data. This is where you describe the structure of your data. The design of the data structure is similar to relational database design, in that data is organized into entities that are related through relationships.

When you need to access the data, you will not directly interact with the data store. Instead, you will work with the Managed Object Context, which allows you to access the objects that are stored in the data file. The Managed Object Context can keep track of multiple changes to the objects, and will periodically, or when instructed, save the changes to the persistent store.

Using SQLite Directly in iOS Apps

Just like Android, iOS apps can also work with SQLite databases directly. If you are developing an app to be available on both platforms, you might consider eschewing Core Data for shipping a regular SQLite database with your app. You can design and populate the database outside of the app and add it to the app bundle before shipping the app. The techniques used to work with SQLite on iOS are quite similar to those used on Android. However, one thing to be aware of is that the SQLite libraries used to interact with the database on iOS are written in C and not Objective-C, so the method calls are going to look different from what you have seen here.

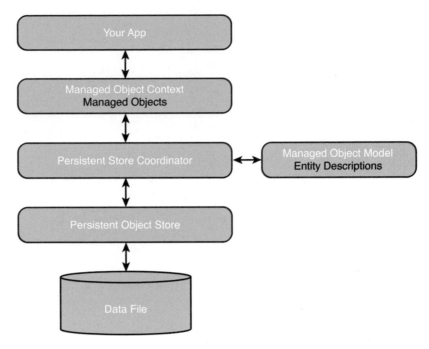

Figure 11.1   Overview of the Core Data framework.

Setting Up Core Data

There's a fair amount of setup required to add Core Data to an existing app, which is beyond the scope of this book. For more detail, you can reference *Core Data for iOS: Developing Data-Driven Applications for the iPad, iPhone, and iPod touch* by Tim Isted and Tom Harrington. Instead, you will start a new project and add Core Data using the project creation wizard. After creating the project, you have some work to copy the work you already did from the project created in the previous chapter.

Creating the Project

Start by creating a new project in Xcode (File > New > Project). Choose the Empty Application template and click Next. Fill in the settings on the next screen as shown in Figure 11.2. Make sure the Use Core Data check box is selected, then click Next and choose a place to save the new project.

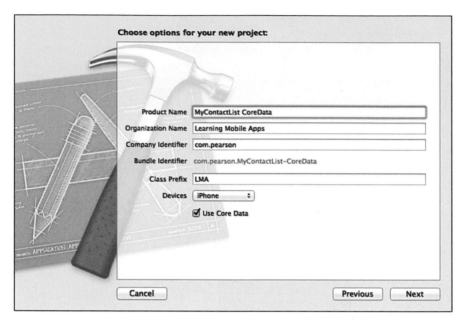

Figure 11.2   Setting up the project to support Core Data.

After you have created the project, you will need to add the functionality that you created in the previous chapter.

1. Open the new project and delete images.xcassets. Then click Move to Trash in the dialog that pops up.

2. Open both projects side by side and select all the files in the MyContactList folder of the original project *except* LMAAppDelegate.h and LMAAppDelegate.m, because these files contain important setup for Core Data (see the left side of Figure 11.3).

3. Drag all the selected files into the new project (see the right side of Figure 11.3 for the end result).

4. In the dialog that comes up, check Copy Items into Destination Group's Folder, as shown in Figure 11.4.

Next, you will need to modify the app delegate to have the correct View Controller show up when launching the app. First, open the Project Summary and change the Main Interface to Main.storyboard. After making the selection, the chosen text will change to Main, as shown in Figure 11.5.

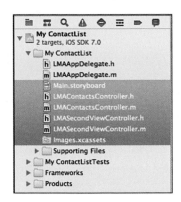

Figure 11.3   Selecting files to copy to the new project on the left. The result of the copy is shown on the right.

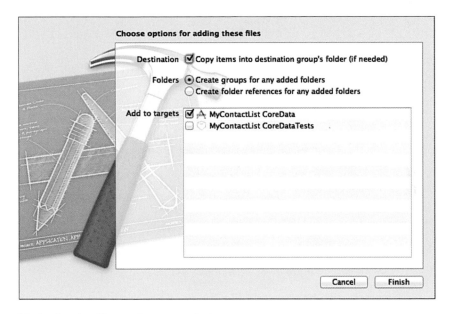

Figure 11.4   Copying files to the new project.

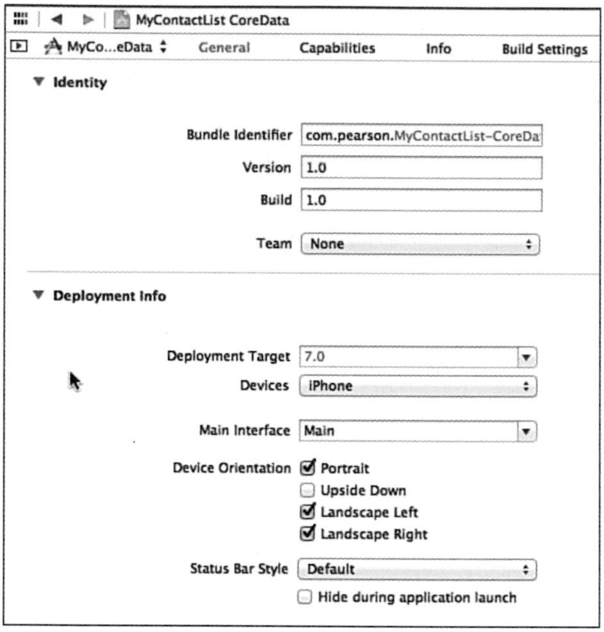

Figure 11.5 Setting the Main storyboard.

The Core Data template inserts code into LMAAppDelegate.m that launches the app with a blank window. You'll need to get rid of this, so open LMAAppDelegate.m and comment out all the code in application:didFinishLaunchingWithOptions: as shown in Listing 11.1.

Listing 11.1 **LMAAppDelegate.m**

```
- (BOOL)application:(UIApplication *)application
didFinishLaunchingWithOptions:(NSDictionary *)launchOptions
{
// self.window = [[UIWindow alloc] initWithFrame:[[UIScreen mainScreen] bounds]];
   // Override point for customization after application launch.
// self.window.backgroundColor = [UIColor whiteColor];
// [self.window makeKeyAndVisible];
    return YES;
}
```

If you look through LMAAppDelegate you will see a lot of code that manages the Core Data functionality. There are references to the Managed Object Context, the Managed Object Model, and the Persistent Store Coordinator. Further down in the file, you will see a method, saveContext, which can be called whenever changes to the managed objects need to be saved to disk. You don't really need to understand the functionality of all the Core Data methods. All you need to access is the `managedObjectContext` and `saveContext` methods. Later in the chapter you will see how to use these methods to work with Core Data.

Designing Data Structure

You may have noticed that a new file, MyContactList_CoreData.xcdatamodeld, has been added to the project. This is a representation of the Data Model and is where you can design the data structure for the MyContactList app. The data structure for the app is very simple with just a single entity. For the following steps, refer to Figure 11.6.

1. Open the data model file.

2. Click Add Entity and name the entity **Contact** (entity names must begin with as uppercase letter) by double-clicking the word Entity and typing **Contact**.

3. Click Add Attribute and name the first attribute **contactName** and give it the type **String**.

4. Add the remaining attributes as shown in Figure 11.7. Each of the attributes are of type **String** except birthday, which is **Date**.

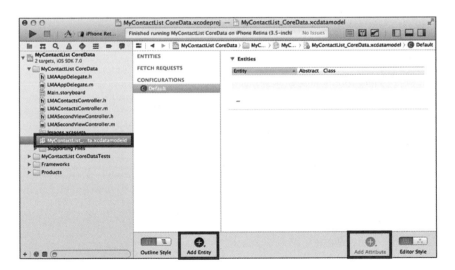

Figure 11.6   Using the Core Data Model editor.

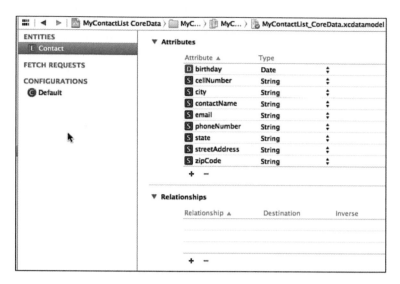

Figure 11.7   Attributes of the Contact entity.

After setting up the data design, you will need to create an Objective-C class that represents the data design.

1. Select the Contact entity and select Editor > Create NSManagedObject Subclass.

2. Choose the data model and click Next.

3. Select the Contact entity and click Next.

4. Make sure you have the MyContactList CoreData target selected and click Create.

This adds two files to your project, Contact.h and Contact.m. The content of the two files is very simple, with a property for each of the attributes in the data model. The Contact class is a subclass of NSManagedObject, which means it inherits the capability to be managed and stored by the Managed Object Context.

Modifying the Data Model

If you change the data model after the app has run the first time, your app is going to give an error message that the data model no longer matches the database created for the app. Core Data provides functionality for migrating your data model. There are several approaches to changing the data model design, but they are all based on providing different versions of the data model. Whenever you need to make a change, you add a new version by selecting Editor > Add Model Version. The new version starts out as a copy of the old version, and you can then make your changes in the new version. After you have created the new version, you create a mapping model that lets you specify how each entity and attribute in the old version maps to the new version.

The mapping model is then used in code when the app starts to check for changes and migrate the database to the new version of the model. If your changes are minor, such as adding or removing attributes and entities, the system may be able to infer the mapping model and you can simply ask it to do the conversion without setting up an explicit mapping model. This process is called Lightweight Migration.

This mapping process can be used both during development and after your app has been released. During development you also have the option of deleting the database file from the app's sandbox. Then Core Data will automatically create a new blank copy of the database the next time the app launches.

For more detail on how to migrate between data models, you should refer to *Core Data for iOS: Developing Data-Driven Applications for the iPad, iPhone, and iPod touch* by Tim Isted and Tom Harrington, as well as the Core Data documentation on Apple's Developer Portal.

Passing Data Between Controllers

The Birthday label on the Contacts screen is changed on the Date screen. When the user taps the Change button next to the birthday, the Date screen is opened with a Date Picker, where the user can choose the desired date. Tapping the Save button brings the user back to the Contact screen and changes the Birthday label to what was chosen in the Date Picker.

The standard way to pass data back from a View Controller is to use the *delegate pattern*. With this pattern, you will have a reference in the Date Controller back to whatever controller called it (allowing for the Date Controller to be used in many contexts), as well as one or more methods that the Date Controller knows exist in the calling controller. The delegate pattern is used widely in iOS, so you should spend some time to make sure you understand it well.

There are several steps to set up this pattern:

1. Define a delegate protocol in the .h file of the subview controller.

2. Set up a property called delegate in the .h file of the subview Controller to hold a reference to the main view controller.

3. Specify in the @interface declaration of the main controller that it should implement the delegate protocol.

4. Implement the methods specified in the protocol in the .m file of the main controller.

5. Set up the main view as a delegate of the subview.

6. Call the delegate methods from the subview.

In the next sections, you see how to do each of these steps in detail, but first, you need to add a View Controller for the Date screen.

1. Select the MyContactList Core Data folder. Then choose File > New > File, or press Command-N.

2. Select Objective-C Class and click Next.

3. Enter **LMADateController** for the Class name and **UIViewController** for the Subclass Of field. Ensure that none of the check boxes are selected (see Figure 11.8). Click Next.

4. Ensure that MyContactList CoreData is checked as a Target and click Create.

You now have two new files in your project: LMAController.h and LMAController.m.

Figure 11.8   Creating the View Controller for the Date screen.

Step 1: Set Up Delegate Protocol

Switch to LMADateController.h and add the lines between 1 and 2 in Listing 11.3.

This sets up the delegate protocol and specifies that any class implementing this method must also implement the `dateChanged:` method. What the class chooses to have the `dateChanged:` method do is up to the developer. This method is executed in the main view when called from the subview. In this case, the Date Controller calls this method on its delegate anytime the date changes. Use `@optional` to declare methods that aren't required to be implemented.

Step 2: Add Delegate Property

For the subview to call back to the main view, it needs a reference to the main view. You do this by setting up a property that will have a reference to the main view. Add item 3 in Listing 11.2. The delegate property can be any data type (id) as long as it implements the `LMADateControllerDelegate` protocol. This will allow any kind of controller (or other object) to take advantage of the Date Controller.

Listing 11.2   **Setting up the Delegate Pattern in LMADateController.h**

```
#import <UIKit/UIKit.h>

@protocol LMADateControllerDelegate <NSObject>                              //1

@required
-(void)dateChanged:(NSDate *) date;

@end                                                                        //2

@interface LMADateController : UIViewController
@property (strong, nonatomic) id<LMADateControllerDelegate> delegate;       //3
@end
```

Step 3: Specify That Main View Will Implement Delegate Protocol

Switch to LMAContactsController.m and specify that the class will import
LMADateController.h (item 1 in Listing 11.3) and implement LMADateControllerDelegate
(item 2 in Listing 11.3).

Listing 11.3   **Implementing Delegate in LMAContactsController.m**

```
#import "LMAContactsController.h"
#import "LMADateController.h"                                               //1

@interface LMAContactsController () <LMADateControllerDelegate>             //2

@end
[...]
```

Step 4: Implement the Methods of the Delegate Protocol

Having specified that the Contacts Controller implements the Date Controller delegate protocol, you now have to implement the required methods. In this case, just the dateChanged:
method, as shown in Listing 11.4.

Listing 11.4   **Implementing the dateChanged: Method in LMAContactsController.m**

```
-(void)dateChanged:(NSDate *) date {
    NSDateFormatter *dateFormatter = [[NSDateFormatter alloc]init];        //1
    [dateFormatter setDateStyle:NSDateFormatterShortStyle];                //2
    [dateFormatter setTimeStyle:NSDateFormatterNoStyle];                   //3
    [_lblBirthdate setText:[dateFormatter stringFromDate:date ]];          //4
}
```

This method formats the date using the short style (DD/MM/YY in the U.S. locale—this will format differently depending on the users' locale).

1. You can use NSDateFormatter to format dates in a variety of formats.

2. Set the date formatter to use the short style for the date. You can also choose Medium and Long, or even create a custom format.

3. To stop the time from showing up, you can specify NSDateFormatterNoStyle. This suppresses the time display.

4. Format the date and set the formatted date as the text of the birthday label.

Step 5: Set Up Main Controller as Delegate

The delegate property in the subview needs to be set up at the time the subview is called by the main view. In this case, the subview is called when the user taps the Change button. However, because the segue controls make the Date screen active, no code is being called directly. Instead, you can implement prepareForSegue:sender, which is called anytime a segue is executed in the app. Listing 11.5 shows how this method is implemented to set the delegate of the Date screen to be the Contact screen. You add the code to LMAContactsController.m.

Listing 11.5   Adding the Delegate Reference in LMAContactsController.m

```
- (void)prepareForSegue:(UIStoryboardSegue *)segue sender:(id)sender {
    if ([segue.identifier isEqualToString:@"segueContactDate"]) {       //1
        LMADateController *dateController = segue.destinationViewController;  //2
        dateController.delegate = self;                                 //3
    }
}
```

1. Check to see which segue initiated the call to the method. The string @"segueContactDate" is a unique identifier of the segue (Instructions for how to set this are right before Figure 11.9).

2. Get a reference to the destination View Controller, which is the Date controller in this case.

3. Set the delegate for the Date Controller to be the Contacts Controller (self). This allows the Date Controller to call the dateChanged: method in the Contacts Controller.

To set the identifier for the segue, open the Storyboard and select the Segue between the Contact and Date screens. Use the Attributes Inspector to set the Identifier to **segueContact-Date** (see Figure 11.9).

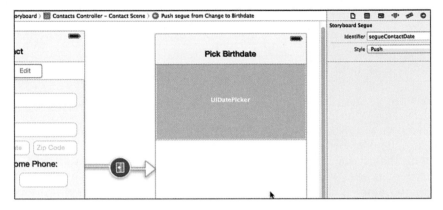

Figure 11.9   Setting the identifier for the segue.

Step 6: Call the Delegate Methods from the Subview

When the date is picked, the user taps the Save button on the toolbar to save the date and be brought back to the previous screen. The Contact button acts as a cancel, where the date will not be changed on the main controller.

To be able to reference the Date Picker on the Date screen, you need to add an outlet for it. Open the Storyboard with the Assistant Editor, and Control-drag from the Date Picker to LMADateController.h to create an outlet named `dtpDate`.

Switch to LMADateController.m and implement the `viewDidLoad:` and `saveDate:` methods, as shown in Listing 11.6.

Listing 11.6   **Calling the Delegate Methods in LMADateController.m**

```
- (void)viewDidLoad
{
    [super viewDidLoad];
        // Do any additional setup after loading the view.
    UIBarButtonItem *saveButton =
                [[UIBarButtonItem alloc]
                    initWithBarButtonSystemItem:UIBarButtonSystemItemSave      //1
                    target:self
                    action:@selector(saveDate:)];
    [self.navigationItem setRightBarButtonItem:saveButton];                    //2
    self.title = @"Pick Birthdate";                                            //3
}
```

```
-(IBAction)saveDate: (id)sender                                           //4
{
    [_delegate dateChanged:[_dtpDate date]];
    [self.navigationController popViewControllerAnimated:YES];
}
```

This code sets up the Save button and connects it to the method to save the date.

1. This sets up a `UIBarButtonItem` for the Save button. Many standard system buttons can be used. Here we used `UIBarButtonSystemItemSave`, but you should spend some time looking through the list of the options using code completion. The action parameter is important as well. This contains the method name for the method that will be called when the button is tapped. Unfortunately, the compiler doesn't check that the method exists by that name, so you have to be careful in spelling it correctly.

2. This line adds the Save button on the right in the navigation bar.

3. Although you already set the title of the View Controller in storyboard, this line demonstrates how to set the title of a View Controller in code. This can be useful to do when the title might have to be determined dynamically at runtime.

4. This method is the one that is called when the button is tapped. Remember to spell it exactly like it is in the `@selector` above. The method calls the `dateChanged:` method in the delegate, passing the chosen date from the date picker. Then it pops the View Controller off the stack, which returns the user to the previous view controller, which in this case is the contacts controller.

You can now run the app and change the date and have it show up on the main contacts screen.

iOS Versus Android: Delegates Versus Listeners

This pattern of using a delegate to pass data between controllers has a parallel in Android. In Chapter 4, "Android Navigation and Interface Design," you set up a custom dialog to capture the birthday of a contact. That custom dialog is implemented as a class, which declared a `SaveDateListener` interface (the delegate protocol in iOS) with the `didFinishDatePickerDialog` method (required delegate method). In the `ContactActivity`, you tell the class to implement the `SaveDateListener` (set up main controller as delegate) and implement the `didFinishDatePickerDialog` method (implement the methods of the delegate protocol). In that method you write code to handle the new birthday. After the user changes the date in the dialog and taps the OK button, the dialog calls the `didFinishDatePickerDialog` method, passing it the selected date (call the delegate methods in main controller).

Saving Data to Core Data

With the data model and the managed object set up, it's time to start saving the data from the user interface to Core Data.

But first, the user interface on the Contacts screen needs to be changed to add a Save button in the navigation bar. The code to do this is very similar to the Date controller. Open LMAContactsController.m and update the `viewDidLoad`: method to match Listing 11.7.

Listing 11.7   **Adding the Save Button in LMAContactsController.m**

```
- (void)viewDidLoad
{
    [super viewDidLoad];
        // Do any additional setup after loading the view, typically from a nib.
        _scrollView.contentSize = CGSizeMake(320,500);


    UIBarButtonItem *saveButton =
                    [[UIBarButtonItem alloc]
                            initWithBarButtonSystemItem:UIBarButtonSystemItemSave
                            target:self
                            action:@selector(saveContact:)];
    [self.navigationItem setRightBarButtonItem:saveButton];
    self.title = @"Contact";

}
```

Just like in the date controller, you'll need to implement the method specified in the `@selector`. This method is the one that will do the saving of data from the form (Listing 11.8). Before entering this code, add import statements for Contact.h and LMAAppDelegate.h.

You also need to handle the birthdate so it can be saved into the object. The birthdate is available only in the `dateChanged`: method, but if you set up an instance variable it can be stored there whenever it changes to make it available throughout the class. Add this line right after the `@implementation` line:

```
NSDate *birthdate;
```

Then in the `dateChanged`: method, add this line to the end of the method:

```
birthdate = date;
```

Listing 11.8   **The `saveContact`: Method in LMAContactsController.m**

```
-(IBAction)saveContact: (id)sender
{
    LMAAppDelegate *appDelegate =[[UIApplication sharedApplication] delegate];   //1
    NSManagedObjectContext *context = [appDelegate managedObjectContext];        //2
    Contact *contact = [NSEntityDescription                                      //3
                        insertNewObjectForEntityForName:@"Contact"
                        inManagedObjectContext:context];
```

```
NSError *error;                                                          //4
[contact setValue:_txtName.text forKey:@"contactName"];                  //5
[contact setValue:_txtAddress.text forKey:@"streetAddress"];
[contact setValue:_txtCity.text forKey:@"city"];
[contact setValue:_txtState.text forKey:@"state"];
[contact setValue:_txtZip.text forKey:@"zipCode"];
[contact setValue:_txtPhone.text forKey:@"phoneNumber"];
[contact setValue:_txtCell.text forKey:@"cellNumber"];
[contact setValue:_txtEmail.text forKey:@"email"];
[contact setValue:birthdate forKey:@"birthday"];

[context save:&error];                                                   //6
if(error !=nil) {                                                        //7
    NSLog(@"Error saving object: %@", error.description);
}
else {
    NSLog(@"Object saved successfully");
}
}
```

The saveContact: method creates the contact object, takes the values from the user interface to populate the object, and finally saves the object.

1. Get a reference to the application delegate, because that is where the Core Data methods are available.

2. Get a reference to the managed object context.

3. Create the contact object. You need to specify the name of the Core Data entity and the managed object context. After the object is created, it has a reference to the object context and knows which entity it is defined by. Note that the entity name is not checked by the compiler, so be sure to spell it correctly.

4. The error variable will contain any errors that occur during the saving of the object.

5. This set of statements populates the object with the values from the user interface by calling the setValue:forKey: method on the contact object passing in the text property from each of the text fields and the name of the Core Data attribute. Note that just like with the entity name, the compiler does not check the attribute. The birthday field is not included, because it requires special handling that will be shown a little later in this chapter.

6. This statement forces the context to save any changes, and will record any errors. If you don't call the save method, the data will be saved, but you will not know when, so your app may behave erratically.

7. Print out any errors to NSLog. These messages will not show up to the user but will appear in Xcode in the bottom-right part of the debug section.

Running the app right now will not provide any feedback as to what data was saved, but you can check that the database was created by opening up a Finder window and navigating to the location of the files for your app.

1. Open a Finder window and select Go > Go To Folder.

2. Enter ~/**Library/Application Support/iPhone Simulator**, and click Go.

3. You should see a directory with directories for each version of iOS you have developed apps for. Open the directory with the highest version number and drill into the Applications folder. You will see a folder for each app you have created. Unfortunately, they are only named with a long string of letters and numbers, so the only way to find the app you're looking for is to open each folder and look for the .app file, which will have the name of the app (Figure 11.10).

4. After you find the correct app, you can open up its Documents directory, and you should see a .sqlite file. Although you can't open it directly, you can convince yourself that it is being modified by looking at the file size and latest modified timestamp. However, there are many free tools available to examine SQLite files if you want to take a closer look. An easily accessible option is a Firefox extension called SQLite Manager.

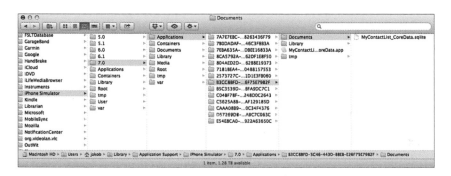

Figure 11.10   App file structure and SQLite database for MyContactList.

In the next chapter, you learn how to retrieve the data in the database and display it in the app.

Storing the Settings

In the settings part of the app, the user is able to change the sort order of the displayed contacts. The contacts can be sorted in either ascending or descending order by Name, City, or Birthday (Figure 11.11). Although the user interface for this screen might more logically be set up using Segmented Controls, you will get a chance to work with two new controls, the Picker View and the Switch. The user's preference for sorting will be stored in a NSUserDefaults object. The data will be stored in the Settings screen and read in the Contacts section of the app.

Figure 11.11   The completed Settings interface.

Creating the Settings Interface

In this section you will create the interface for the Settings screen. Use Figure 11.11 as a guide in completing the following steps.

1. Open the Storyboard and delete the Settings label.

2. Drag a new label to the top left of the screen and change its text to **Sort Order**.

3. Drag a Picker View and place it below the label and center it on the screen.

4. Drag a label below the Picker and change its text to **Ascending Sort:**

5. Drag a Switch and place it to the right of the label.

Next, you need to add a View Controller for the Settings screen.

1. Select the MyContactList CoreData folder. Then choose File > New > File, or press Command-N.

2. Select Objective-C Class and click Next.

3. Enter **LMASettingsController** for the Class name and **UIViewController** for the Subclass Of field. Ensure that none of the check boxes are selected. Click Next.

4. Ensure that MyContactList CoreData is checked as a Target and click Create.

5. Open the Settings screen in Storyboard, and change its Class to **LMASettingsController** in the Identity Inspector.

Now you need to set up outlets and actions for the Settings screen.

1. Open Storyboard and display the Settings screen on the left and LMASettingsController.h in the Assistant editor on the right.

2. Control-drag from the Picker View and Switch to the `@interface` section of `LMASettingsController.h` to create outlets named `pckSortField` and `swAscending` respectively.

3. Control-drag from the switch to add an action called `sortDirectionChanged`.

If you run the app now, you will get a blank Picker View, so you will need to initialize it with the field names to sort by. When working with a Picker View in a screen, you need to implement two protocols in the View Controller: `UIPickerViewDataSource` and `UIPickerViewDelegate`. The former has methods to specify the data source for the contents of the Picker View, whereas the latter has methods that allow you to find out which row the user has chosen in the Picker. Add the two protocols in LMASettingsController.h as shown in item 1 in Listing 11.9.

Listing 11.9 **Picker View Protocols in LMASettingsController.h**

```
#import <UIKit/UIKit.h>

@interface LMASettingsController : UIViewController
                          <UIPickerViewDataSource, UIPickerViewDelegate>        //1
@property (weak, nonatomic) IBOutlet UIPickerView *pckSortField;
@property (weak, nonatomic) IBOutlet UISwitch *swAscending;
- (IBAction)sortDirectionChanged:(id)sender;

@end
```

Now you can implement the methods to add the data to the Picker View, as shown in Listing 11.10.

Listing 11.10 **Implementing the Picker View Data in LMASettingsController.m**

```
#import "LMASettingsController.h"

@interface LMASettingsController ()

@end
```

```objc
@implementation LMASettingsController
//1
NSArray *sortOrderItems;                                                        //1

- (id)initWithNibName:(NSString *)nibNameOrNil bundle:(NSBundle *)nibBundleOrNil
{
    self = [super initWithNibName:nibNameOrNil bundle:nibBundleOrNil];
    if (self) {
        // Custom initialization
    }
    return self;
}


- (void)viewDidLoad
{
    [super viewDidLoad];
    // Do any additional setup after loading the view from its nib.
    sortOrderItems = @[@"Name", @"City", @"Birthday"];                          //2
    pckSortField.dataSource = self;                                             //3
    pckSortField.delegate = self;                                              //4
}


- (void)didReceiveMemoryWarning
{ [...] }


- (IBAction)sortDirectionChanged:(id)sender {
}


#pragma mark - UIPickerView DataSource                                          //5
// Returns the number of 'columns' to display.
- (NSInteger)numberOfComponentsInPickerView:(UIPickerView *)pickerView          //6
{
    return 1;
}


// Returns the # of rows in the picker
- (NSInteger)pickerView:(UIPickerView *)pickerView
➡numberOfRowsInComponent:(NSInteger)component                                    //7
{
    return [sortOrderItems count];
}


//Sets the value that is shown for each row in the picker
- (NSString *)pickerView:(UIPickerView *)pickerView titleForRow:(NSInteger)row
➡forComponent:(NSInteger)component                                              //8
{
    return [sortOrderItems objectAtIndex:row];
}
```

```
//If the user chooses from the pickerview, it calls this function;
- (void)pickerView:(UIPickerView *)pickerView didSelectRow:(NSInteger)row
➥inComponent:(NSInteger)component                                          //9
{
    NSLog(@"Chosen item: %@", [sortOrderItems objectAtIndex:row]);
}


@end
```

To have a fully functioning Picker View, you need to set up a data source, implement several methods that display the data, and respond to the user making a selection in the Picker.

1. Add an array to store the items that will show up in the Picker View. This needs to be declared at the class level because it needs to be accessed in several methods in the class.

2. Add the strings for the Picker View to the array.

3. Set up the View Controller (LMASettingsController) as the data source for the Picker View. This works, because the View Controller implements `UIPickerViewDataSource`.

4. Set the View Controller as the delegate for the Picker View, so whenever actions are taken on the Picker View, specific methods are called in the view controller. This works, because the View Controller implements `UIPickerViewDelegate`.

5. The `#pragma` notation is used for documentation. You can see this show up in Xcode if you click the right-most item in the selector bar above the LMASettingsController.m file (Figure 11.12). The dash right after pragma is what gives the horizontal line. Using the pragma mark notation can be a good way to easily navigate long source files.

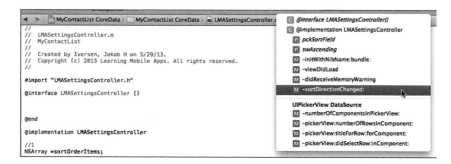

Figure 11.12   Drop-down menu on the right showing the result of #pragma mark in the code.

6. The Picker View can be configured to show multiple columns. This method returns the number of columns to display.

7. This method determines how many rows or elements to display in the Picker. By returning the number of elements in the array, we allow for just that many rows in the Picker.

8. This is the most crucial method for setting up the Picker View, because it is the one that makes the data show up in the Picker View. When the Picker is displayed on the screen, the system will make repeated calls to this method, passing in the row number and getting the corresponding text for the row back. In this case, the method uses the row number to return the corresponding item from the array.

9. This method is called whenever the user chooses a row in the Picker View. For now, the method simply prints a message to NSLog indicating which item was chosen. In the next section, you will use this method to update the stored data.

Run the app to make sure the Picker View shows up correctly, and the selected item is printed to NSLog every time a selection is made.

Working with **NSUserDefaults** Object

The NSUserDefaults object is used to store data values for an app in a key-value list on the disk. Working with NSUserDefaults is very simple. You start by getting a reference to the standard NSUserDefaults object with this line of code:

```
NSUserDefaults *settings = [NSUserDefaults standardUserDefaults];
```

To store a value in the settings object, you use code like this:

```
[settings setObject:@"City" forKey:@"sortField"];
```

This saves the value "City" with the key "sortField". Every value must have a unique key. In addition to the setObject:forKey: method, there are also methods that can be used to store scalar values such as BOOL and int. Here's an example:

```
[settings setBool:YES forKey:@"sortDirectionAscending"];
```

Retrieving the data is equally simple. Using the reference called settings to the NSUserDefaults object, you would retrieve an object using this call:

```
NSString *sortField = [settings objectForKey:@"sortField"];
```

The data is periodically saved, but to force saving, you can call the synchronize method:

```
[settings synchronize];
```

This will save any changes you've made to the Plist file.

> **iOS Versus Android: User Settings**
>
> The functionality provided by NSUserDefaults in iOS is provided by SharedPreferences in Android. In both cases, these objects are used to store single bits of information. However, whereas Android can store only simple data types in SharedPreferences, iOS has the capability to store more complex objects.

Activating the Settings Interface

Now that the Settings screen is set up with a Picker View and a switch, it's time to work on storing the data for the user preferences. For the settings to work consistently, they should be set to some default values when the app first launches. The place to do that is in the app delegate, so open LMAAppDelegate.m and add the code in Listing 11.11 to the `application:didFinishLaunchingWithOptions:` method.

Listing 11.11   **Saving Default Settings**

```
- (BOOL)application:(UIApplication *)application
➥didFinishLaunchingWithOptions:(NSDictionary *)launchOptions
{
    //Set default settings
    NSUserDefaults *settings = [NSUserDefaults standardUserDefaults];        //1
    if([settings objectForKey:@"sortField"] == nil) {                        //2
        [settings setObject:@"City" forKey:@"sortField"];                    //3
    }
    if([settings objectForKey:@"sortDirectionAscending"] == nil){            //4
        [settings setBool:YES forKey:@"sortDirectionAscending" ];
    }
    [settings synchronize];                                                  //5
    NSLog(@"Sort direction: %c", [settings                                   //6
                        boolForKey:@"sortDirectionAscending"]);
    NSLog(@"Sort field: %@", [settings objectForKey:@"sortField"]);
    return YES;
}
```

By putting this code in LMAAppDelegate.m, it will be executed anytime the app launches.

1. Get a reference to the standard NSUserDefaults object. In this case, it's named settings.

2. Check whether something is already stored by the sortField key.

3. If not, store City as the value in sortField. This is to ensure there is a value in the field, but also to avoid overwriting any existing value.

4. Repeat the same check for the sort direction. If no value is stored, it defaults to YES.

5. Save any changes back to the settings file.

6. Write the values of the two settings fields to NSLog. This shows how to retrieve a Boolean value using the boolForKey: method and retrieving a string by using objectForKey:

Next, we need to make sure the UI controls on the Settings screen get updated when the view is loaded. Implement viewWillAppear: in LMASettingsController.m, as shown in Listing 11.12.

Listing 11.12 **Setting the User Controls Based on the Stored Values**

```
- (void)viewVillAppear
{
    //set the UI based on values in NSUserDefaults
    NSUserDefaults *settings = [NSUserDefaults standardUserDefaults];         //1
    [_swAscending setOn:[settings boolForKey:@"sortDirectionAscending"]];     //2
    NSString *sortField = [settings objectForKey:@"sortField"];               //3
    int i = 0;
    for (NSString *field in sortOrderItems) {                                 //4
        if([field isEqualToString:sortField]) {
            [_pckSortField selectRow:i inComponent:0 animated:NO];            //5
        }
        i++;
    }
    [_pckSortField reloadComponent:0];                                        //6
}
```

This code reads the values from the standard NSUserDefaults object and updates the UI with those values.

1. Just like in the previous listing, start by getting a reference to the settings object.

2. The Switch can be changed by calling the setOn: method and passing in a Boolean. In this case, the value is read from the settings object using the boolForKey: method.

3. The Picker View is a little more complex to set. First, read the sortField value into a NSString variable.

4. The Picker View is updated by telling it which number row to select, so this loop goes through the sortOrderItems array, which is where you stored the items that are displayed in the Picker View.

5. If a match is found, the Picker View is told to select that row. There's only one component, or column, so that is set to 0. The selection can be animated so the Picker View spins to the selection, but this is not appropriate here because the selection is already made before the user opens the Selection screen, so we set animated to NO.

6. To have the Picker View change, you call reloadComponent: (you could also have called reloadAllComponents: and not needed to specify which component to reload).

To store the values chosen by the user, implement sortDirectionChanged: as shown in Listing 11.13 to store the value of the switch, and update the implementation of PickerView: didSelectRow:inComponent: as shown in Listing 11.14.

Listing 11.13 **Storing the Value of the Switch**

```
- (IBAction)sortDirectionChanged:(id)sender {
    NSUserDefaults *defaults = [NSUserDefaults standardUserDefaults];
    [defaults setBool:_swAscending.isOn forKey:@"sortDirectionAscending"];
}
```

Listing 11.14 **Setting the User Controls Based on the Stored Values**

```
- (void)pickerView:(UIPickerView *)pickerView didSelectRow:(NSInteger)row
➥inComponent:(NSInteger)component
{
    NSString *sortField = [sortOrderItems objectAtIndex:row];
    NSUserDefaults *defaults = [NSUserDefaults standardUserDefaults];
    [defaults setObject:sortField forKey:@"sortField"];
    [defaults synchronize];
}
```

If you run the app, you should be able to make a selection in the Settings screen and have those settings stored for later. If you try stopping the execution of the app in Xcode and relaunching the app, you should see that the settings persist.

Global Constants

The code you wrote previously uses literal string values to identify the key fields used in NSUserDefaults. This can be a problem, because if they aren't spelled the same everywhere you use them, you will get some very strange error messages. One solution to this problem is to create an object to hold global constants, and then define the string keys in that object. Here's how to update the code to be more robust.

1. Select File > New > File, and select Objective-C class in the Cocoa Touch category. Click Next.

2. Name the class **Constants** and enter **NSObject** for Subclass Of. Click Next and make sure to save the file inside the project folder, and that the Target for MyContactList CoreData is checked.

3. Open the Constants.h file and add lines 1 and 2 as shown in Listing 11.15. This declares the two keys as constant strings that are globally available to any class that imports the Constants.h file.

4. Add lines 1 and 2 as shown in Listing 11.16 to Constants.m. This assigns the values to the two strings. Make sure they are the same as you used for the keys for the settings.

5. Open LMAAppDelegate.m and add #import Constants.h below the other import statements.

6. Replace all occurrences of the literal strings with the keys to the constant variables in `application:didFinishLaunchingWithOptions:` The relevant lines of code are shown in Listing 11.17 and marked by 1–5.

7. Repeat steps 5 and 6 for LMASettingsController.m by importing `Constants.h` and updating `viewDidLoad:`, `sortDirectionChanged:` and `pickerView:didSelectRow:inComponent:` to use the constant string variables instead of the literal string values. The two updated methods are shown in Listing 11.18. The relevant lines are marked 1–4.

Run the app and make sure the saving and retrieving of the settings still work as expected.

Listing 11.15   **Constants.h**

```
#import <Foundation/Foundation.h>

extern NSString *const kSortField;                              //1
extern NSString *const kSortDirectionAscending;                //2

@interface Constants : NSObject
@end
```

Listing 11.16   **Constants.m**

```
#import "Constants.h"

NSString *const kSortField = @"sortField";                           //1
NSString *const kSortDirectionAscending = @"sortDirectionAscending"; //2

@implementation Constants
@end
```

Listing 11.17   **Using the Constant Variables as Keys in the LMAAppDelegate.m**

```
- (BOOL)application:(UIApplication *)application
➥didFinishLaunchingWithOptions:(NSDictionary *)launchOptions
{
    //Set default settings
    NSUserDefaults *settings = [NSUserDefaults standardUserDefaults];
    if([settings objectForKey:kSortField] == nil) {                    //1
        [settings setObject:@"City" forKey:kSortField];                //2
    }
    if([settings objectForKey:kSortDirectionAscending] == nil){        //3
        [settings setBool:YES forKey:kSortDirectionAscending];         //4
    }
    [settings synchronize];
    NSLog(@"Sort direction: %c", [settings
```

```
                                    boolForKey:kSortDirectionAscending]);        //5
    NSLog(@"Sort field: %@", [settings objectForKey:kSortField]);         //6
    return YES;
}
```

Listing 11.18 Using the Constant Variables as Keys in LMASettingsController.m

```
- (void)viewDidLoad
{
    [super viewDidLoad];
    // Do any additional setup after loading the view.
    sortOrderItems = @[@"Name", @"City", @"Birthday"];
    _pckSortField.dataSource = self;
    _pckSortField.delegate = self;
    //set the UI based on values in NSUserDefaults
    NSUserDefaults *settings = [NSUserDefaults standardUserDefaults];

    BOOL sortAscending =[settings boolForKey:kSortDirectionAscending];        //1
    [_swAscending setOn:sortAscending];
    NSString *sortField = [settings objectForKey:kSortField];         //2
    int i = 0;
    for (NSString *field in sortOrderItems) {
        if([field isEqualToString:sortField]) {
            [_pckSortField selectRow:i inComponent:0 animated:NO];
        }
        i++;
    }
    [_pckSortField reloadComponent:0];
}


- (IBAction)sortDirectionChanged:(id)sender {
    NSUserDefaults *defaults = [NSUserDefaults standardUserDefaults];
    [defaults setBool:_swAscending.isOn forKey:kSortDirectionAscending];        //3
}

//If the user chooses from the pickerview, it calls this function;
- (void)pickerView:(UIPickerView *)pickerView didSelectRow:(NSInteger)row
➥inComponent:(NSInteger)component
{
    NSString *sortField = [sortOrderItems objectAtIndex:row];

    NSUserDefaults *defaults = [NSUserDefaults standardUserDefaults];
    [defaults setObject:sortField forKey:kSortField];         //4
    [defaults synchronize];
}
```

Summary

Being able to store data in an app is very important to almost all apps. You have seen two important ways to do this in this chapter. Core Data is a very powerful object-oriented wrapper around a persistent data store (SQLite by default), which allows you to store any kind of data in a relatively simple way. In the next chapter, you will see how to retrieve the data and display multiple contact records. You also saw how to store simple pieces of data like that used for the settings in the app. It is common for both these approaches to coexist in the same app.

Along the way you gained some experience with additional user interface controls, allowing you to learn how to use a Picker View and a Switch. Finally, you saw how to set up a class with global constants to reduce possible errors from using literal strings to access keys in the `NSUserDefaults` object.

Exercises

1. Add a few more items to the Picker View for sort fields.

2. Store the array with the values for the Picker View in `NSUserDefaults`.

3. Experiment with adding `#pragma mark` notations to a few more of the source code files and observe the effects.

4. Change the Picker View and the Switch on the Settings screen to segmented controls.

5. Add an additional attribute to the Core Data model to store a home email address.

12

Tables in iOS: Navigation and Information Display

One of the big innovations on the small screen is the introduction of structured content that can be scrolled up and down and that allows for drilling down for more detailed content. On Android, this pattern of navigation is called Lists, as described in Chapter 6, "Lists in Android: Navigation and Information Display." On iOS, it is called Tables and has a number of built-in but very customizable layouts and controls. The Tables layout is used in many apps you use every day and in many of the built-in apps that come with iOS devices.

Anytime you see data presented in a single-column format, whether it's in the Settings app, the list of Music in the iTunes app, or the list of emails in the Mail app, those are examples of using a TableView configured in different ways.

There are project templates in Xcode that have table views included, but because the data for MyContactsApp is from a database, it is just as easy to generate the table and associated view programmatically. MyContactList doesn't have a way to show all the contacts in the database. It can only save contacts right now. In this chapter you will see how to set up a table and populate it with data from MyContactList. You will also learn how to use the table features to modify the data directly from the table, such as deleting records.

Overview of Tables

A table in iOS is a single-column table where each cell contains data to be displayed to the user. The user can scroll-flick through the content by flicking a finger up and down the screen. The individual cell objects are reused when they scroll off the screen, and then they show up at the other end of the screen. This saves tremendous amounts of memory on the device by not having to create an object for every entry in potentially very long tables.

Tables are often used as navigation controllers to allow users to select content in a cell in the table and get more detailed information and/or take action on the data on a separate view controller. You will see the important role that navigation controllers play when you are working with tables.

The cells in a table can be set up with several standard style options. UITableViewCellStyleDefault has a single title and an optional image, whereas UITableViewCellStyleSubtitle adds the option of a subtitle below the title (Figure 12.1 uses the subtitle style). UITableViewCellStyleValue1 does not permit images and right-aligns the subtitle in blue, and UITableViewCellStyleValue2 puts the title in blue and aligns the title and subtitle against each other down the middle.

Table cells can also be adorned with various accessories on the right edge of the cell to indicate what functionality is available when the user taps the cell. You can choose from three standard accessories, as shown in Figure 12.1, in addition to supplying your own image as an accessory. In this chapter, you work with standard layout options for the cells, but you can also provide a complete customized experience.

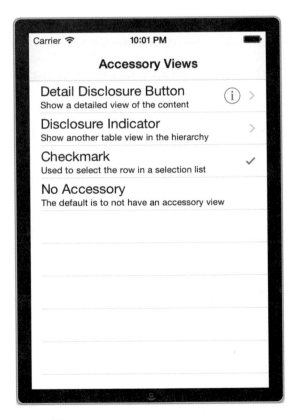

Figure 12.1   Cell Accessory Views.

Setting Up Tables

Open your project from Chapter 11, "Persistent Data in iOS," or open this chapter's project. The first step is to create a new View Controller to hold the table. For the table to show up, you need to insert it in the tab controller. It replaces the controller that allows for editing and viewing a single Contact, which is then called from the Table Controller instead of directly from the Tab Controller.

1. Open the Storyboard and drag a Table View Controller onto the canvas.

2. Select the Navigation Controller and control-drag from the yellow Navigation Controller icon in the bar below the Navigation Controller screen to the new Table View Controller. Select Rootview Controller in the menu that pops up when you release the mouse. This makes the new Table View Controller the first controller in the Navigation Controller, and it shows the Table View instead of the Contact editing screen. Later in the chapter, you will connect the Contact screen to the Table View.

3. To create the code file used to control the Table View Controller, right-click the yellow MyContactList CoreData folder in the left navigator area in Xcode and select New File. Choose Objective-C class in the Cocoa Touch category, and click Next.

4. Change the Subclass Of field to **UITableViewController**, and change the Class to **LMAContactsTableController**. Make sure both check boxes are unchecked, and click Next. On the next screen, verify that the file is being saved in the top-level folder of the project and that the Target for MyContactList Core Data is checked. Click Create.

5. Switch back to Storyboard and select the Table View Controller. Use the Identity Inspector to change the Class to **LMAContactsTableController**. This ties the code file to the screen.

Try running the app. You should see a lined screen above the tab bar, as shown in Figure 12.2. If you click and drag on the screen in the simulator, you will notice that you can drag the lines up and down, as you would with a regular table.

Populate the Table with Data

A table without data isn't very exciting, so the next task is to have some data show up in the table. Switch to LMAContactsTableController.m and scroll down until you see several premade methods related to the table. These are all methods that are declared in UITableViewDelegate and UITableViewDataSource. The Table Controller is a subclass of UITableViewController, which conforms to these two protocols, so the template added all the required methods from those protocols.

The system will make calls to the delegate methods as it needs to work with the table, so most of your work in setting up a table is to implement the methods in the two protocols. Throughout the rest of this chapter, you see how to use several of the delegate methods. To see the rest of them, you can look up the documentation on the two protocols by opening the Documentation (Help > Documentation and API reference), and searching for UITableViewDelegate and UITableViewDataSource.

Figure 12.2 App with empty table.

Before you can get started using these methods, you need to create some data. Initially, the data is stored in a simple array, so you can easily see what's going on.

Declare an array to hold the data by adding this line in LMAContactsTAbleController.m between @end and @implementation:

```
NSArray *contacts;
```

As a quick demonstration of how the table works, you can add some static data to the contacts array and display it in the table. Later, you can switch to working with the full Contact objects. At that point, the contact data will be editable as well.

To populate the array with data, add these lines to the end of the viewDidLoad:

```
contacts = @[@"Jim", @"John", @"Dana", @"Rosie", @"Justin", @"Jeremy",
             @"Sarah", @"Matt", @"Joe", @"Donald", @"Jeff"];
```

To have the data actually show up in the table, you modify some of the autogenerated methods. Locate the numberOfSectionsInTableView: method. This method returns the number of sections (or groupings) in a table. For this table, there's a single section. (See the built-in Settings app for an example of multiple sections in a table.) Change the method to return a value of 1 and remove the line that begins with #warning.

Just below is the tableView:numberOfRowsInSection: method. This returns the number of data rows a particular section has. In this case, the number of rows will equal how many names are in the array above (later, it will return how many Contact objects are in the database). Replace the return line with this line:

```
return [contacts count];
```

This returns the number of elements in the contacts array. Then remove the #warning line.

The tableView:cellForRowAtIndexPath: method is the workhorse method when it comes to tables. This method is called by the system to generate the data for a particular cell, so it is passed the section and row as the indexPath parameter. You use this to configure the actual cell. Listing 12.1 shows the content for this method.

Listing 12.1   Populating the Table with Data

```
- (UITableViewCell *)tableView:(UITableView *)tableView
➥cellForRowAtIndexPath:(NSIndexPath *)indexPath
{
    static NSString *CellIdentifier = @"ContactsCell";            //1
    UITableViewCell *cell = [tableView
➥dequeueReusableCellWithIdentifier:CellIdentifier forIndexPath:indexPath];

    // Configure the cell...

//  if(cell==nil){                                               //2
//      cell = [[UITableViewCell alloc]
//              initWithStyle:UITableViewCellStyleDefault
//              reuseIdentifier:CellIdentifier];
//  }
    cell.textLabel.text = [contacts objectAtIndex:[indexPath row]];   //3
    return cell;
}
```

This code is fairly standard when working with tables, so it's important to understand what's going on.

1. The CellIdentifier is a unique identifier for all cells in the table that are set up in the same way so the objects can be reused when the cell scrolls off the screen. If you created an app where some rows need to look different, you would also use different reuse identifiers for the different types of cells. In all, only about a dozen cell objects will end up being created in the system. Change the existing string, Cell, to ContactsCell. This string also needs to be entered in Storyboard (see below).

2. These lines need to be commented out because we use Storyboard, where the method call in the line above (dequeueReusableCellWithIdentifier:forIndexPath:) is always guaranteed to not return a nil.

3. You use the textLabel property of the cell to set the text that will show up. The data is pulled from the contacts array using the requested row number as the index.

As mentioned in item 1, the table cell needs to be identified in Storyboard as well. Open Storyboard and select the Table View Controller, and then use the Attributes Inspector to change the Identifier to ContactsCell (see Figure 12.3).

Figure 12.3   Setting the reuse Identifier.

Now you can run the app and see the names from the Contacts array show up in the table. You can scroll up and down and see the cells scroll off the screen. One thing missing, though, is the title of the screen. It should say Contacts in the navigation bar at the top. This is an easy fix. You select the Navigation Item under the Table View Controller and change the Title to **Contacts**. Figure 12.4 shows the app with the title set.

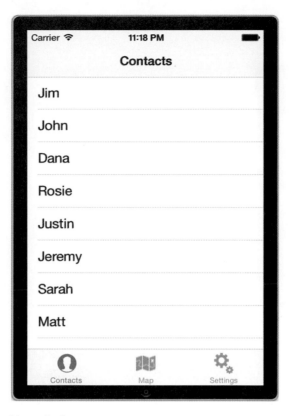

Figure 12.4   Table with static data.

Now that you've seen how to work with the table using the delegate methods to configure the table and populate the table cells, it's time to retrieve the data from the database and display real Contacts objects.

Retrieve Data from Core Data

In the previous chapter, you saw how to save data to Core Data by inserting a Contact object into the managed object context. Retrieving data is similar, but instead of inserting objects, you will fetch them, and then specify some action to take on the retrieved objects. Listing 12.2 shows the changes you need to make in LMAContactsTableController.m to have the data show up from the database.

Listing 12.2   **Retrieving Data from Core Data in LMAContactsTableController.m**

```objective-c
#import "LMAContactsTableController.h"

#import "LMAAppDelegate.h"                                                    //1
#import "Contact.h"

@interface LMAContactsTableController ()
@end

NSArray *contacts;
LMAAppDelegate *appDelegate;                                                  //2
NSManagedObjectContext *context;

@implementation LMAContactsTableController

- (void)viewDidLoad
{
    [super viewDidLoad];

    // Uncomment the following line to preserve selection between presentations.
    // self.clearsSelectionOnViewWillAppear = NO;

    // Uncomment the following line to display an Edit button in the navigation bar
    // for this view controller.
    // self.navigationItem.rightBarButtonItem = self.editButtonItem;
//    contacts = @[@"Jim", @"John", @"Dana", @"Rosie", @"Justin", @"Jeremy",
//                 @"Sarah", @"Matt", @"Joe", @"Donald", @"Jeff"];
    [self loadDataFromDatabase];                                             //3
}
[...]

#pragma mark - Core Data methods
- (void) loadDataFromDatabase
{
    appDelegate = [[UIApplication sharedApplication] delegate];              //4
    context = [appDelegate managedObjectContext];
    NSEntityDescription *entityDescription = [NSEntityDescription            //5
                                       entityForName:@"Contact"
                                       inManagedObjectContext:context];
    NSFetchRequest *request = [[NSFetchRequest alloc] init];                 //6
    [request setEntity:entityDescription];                                   //7
    NSError *error;

    contacts = [[NSArray alloc]                                              //8
              initWithArray:[context executeFetchRequest:request
                                                   error:&error]];
}
```

```
#pragma mark - Table view data source
[...]
- (UITableViewCell *)tableView:(UITableView *)tableView
➥cellForRowAtIndexPath:(NSIndexPath *)indexPath
{
    static NSString *CellIdentifier = @"ContactsCell";
    UITableViewCell *cell = [tableView
➥dequeueReusableCellWithIdentifier:CellIdentifier forIndexPath:indexPath];

    // Configure the cell...

Contact *contact = [contacts objectAtIndex:[indexPath row]];                //9
    cell.textLabel.text = [contact contactName];
    return cell;
}

[...]
```

The code is relatively simple, but spread out over several places in the file.

1. Import the Contact and App Delegate classes.

2. Eventually, it will be necessary to access the context from multiple places in the code, so these two lines set up class variables for the app delegate and context.

3. When the view controller is first loaded into memory, the contacts array is populated with data by calling the `loadDataFromDatabase:` method.

4. The `loadDataFromDatabase:` method starts by setting up the app delegate and context variables.

5. This line specifies that objects from the Contacts entity will be retrieved.

6. Create a `NSFetchRequest` object, which describes the search criteria used to retrieve objects from the store.

7. Relate the fetch request and the entity.

8. Execute the fetch request and return the results as an array, which is stored in the contacts array.

9. To have the data show up in the table, you still get the correct object from the array, but instead of having just a string to show, you can now work with the entire object. In this case, the cell's text label is set to the Contact Name for the contact.

If you run the app, you should see whatever data you entered and saved when testing the app in the previous chapter. If the table shows up blank, the most likely explanation is that you didn't save any data in the previous chapter. You will enable the app to save data again a little later in this chapter.

Adding Contact Data

To be able to add a new Contact, you need to add the Contact editing screen back in to the Storyboard. You will add a special Add button with a plus sign that will display the Contact editing screen.

1. Open Storyboard and select the Table View Controller.

2. Drag a Bar Button item from the Object Library to the navigation bar and drop it to the right of the text Contacts. Before dropping it, you should see a blue rectangle appear on the navigation bar. Drop it into this rectangle.

3. Use the Attributes Inspector to change the Identifier to Add. This changes the button to a plus sign.

4. Control-drag from the Bar Button item to the Contact editing screen and select Push. This sets up a segue between the Table View Controller and the Contact editing screen and pushes the Contact editing screen onto the navigation stack, so the proper buttons for navigating back to the table view will be set up in the navigation bar (see Figure 12.5).

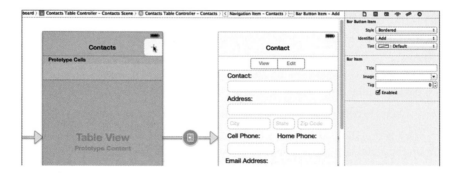

Figure 12.5   Setting up the navigation from the table view to the Contact screen.

You can run the app now and click the plus button on the table to have the Contact editing screen show up with the proper navigation buttons on it.

You'll notice that the Contact editing screen shows up with View selected in the segmented control, but all the text fields are active. To set the controls to a consistent state, add this line of code to the end of viewDidLoad: in LMAContactsController.m:

```
[self changeEditMode:self];
```

This calls the method that checks the value of the segmented control and hides/shows fields accordingly.

Display Detailed Data

The next step is to allow the user to select an entry in the table and have the full Contact object displayed on the Contact screen.

For the Contact screen to receive a Contact object to display, you need to set up a property to hold the Contact object. Add this line to LMAContactsController.h, along with the other @ property declarations:

```
@property (strong, nonatomic) Contact *contact;
```

Next, you'll need to set up a segue from the Prototype cell to the Contact screen.

1. Control-drag from the Prototype cell to the Contact screen and select Selection Segue > Push (see Figure 12.6). This creates a second segue between the two screens.

2. Select the new segue and use the Attributes Inspector to change the Identifier to **EditContact** (see Figure 12.7). This identifier will be used to uniquely identify the segue.

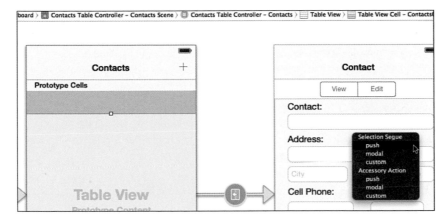

Figure 12.6   Setting up the navigation from the table view to the Contact screen.

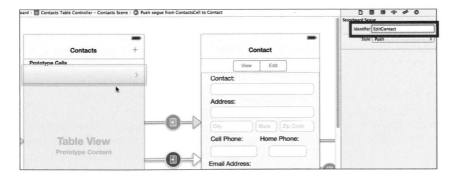

Figure 12.7   Setting up the navigation from the table view to the Contact screen.

To pass data from the table view to the Contact screen, you need to set up a property in the Contact screen to hold the current Contact object being edited. To do this, open LMAContactsController.h and add an import statement to import `Contact.h`, and then add this property line:

```
@property (strong, nonatomic) Contact* contact;
```

Switch to LMAContactsController.m and remove the import statement for `Contact.h`.

To pass the selected Contact from the table, you implement the `prepareForSegue:sender:` method in LMAContactsTableController.m, as shown in Listing 12.4.

The first step is to implement the action to take when a row is selected in the table. The table controller has a delegate method, `tableView:didSelectRowAtIndexPath:` that is already stubbed out toward the bottom of LMAContactsTableController.m. This method is called whenever the user selects a row in the table. All you have to do is provide the implementation that will create an instance of the detail view controller and open it, passing in the `Contact` object from the selected row. Listing 12.3 shows the code you have to enter.

Listing 12.3   Retrieving Data from Core Data in LMAContactsTableController.m

```
- (void)prepareForSegue:(UIStoryboardSegue *)segue sender:(id)sender
{
    if ([segue.identifier isEqualToString:@"EditContact"]) {                //1
        LMAContactsController *contactController =
➥segue.destinationViewController;                                           //2
        NSIndexPath *selectedPath = [self.tableView indexPathForSelectedRow];   //3
        Contact *selectedContact = [contacts objectAtIndex:[selectedPath row]]; //4
        contactController.contact = selectedContact;                        //5
    }
}
```

This is similar to the code you saw previously for passing data from the Contact editing screen to the Date screen.

1. Check to see if the segue matches the identifier we set up in Storyboard.

2. Get a reference to the Contact editing screen view controller, because that is the destination for the segue.

3. Find out which row was selected in the table.

4. Get a reference to the corresponding `Contact` object.

5. Pass the selected `Contact` object to a property in the Contacts Controller.

If you run the app now, you will be able to select a row in the table and have the detailed view controller show up. But the data from the Contact object doesn't show up. Listing 12.4 shows the code you need to add to the `viewDidLoad:` method in LMAContactsController.m to populate the fields in the user interface.

Listing 12.4   **Populating the User Interface**

```
- (void) viewDidLoad
{
    [super viewDidLoad];
    // Do any additional setup after loading the view, typically from a nib.
    _scrollView.contentSize = CGSizeMake(320,500);

    UIBarButtonItem *saveButton =
                [[UIBarButtonItem alloc]
                        initWithBarButtonSystemItem:UIBarButtonSystemItemSave
                        target:self
                        action:@selector(saveContact:)];
    [self.navigationItem setRightBarButtonItem:saveButton];
    self.title = @"Contact";
    [self changeEditMode:self];

    if (_contact) {                                              //1
        _txtName.text = _contact.contactName;
        _txtAddress.text = _contact.streetAddress;
        _txtCity.text = _contact.city;
        _txtState.text = _contact.state;
        _txtZip.text = _contact.zipCode;
        _txtPhone.text = _contact.phoneNumber;
        _txtCell.text = _contact.cellNumber;
        _txtEmail.text = _contact.email;
        [self dateChanged:_contact.birthday];                   //2
        [_sgmtEditMode setSelectedSegmentIndex:0]; //set to view mode  //3
        [self changeEditMode:self];
    }
}
```

This code should be fairly self-explanatory, but a few notes are necessary.

1. The if statement checks to make sure the contact object is instantiated. In Objective-C, if the contact object is nil, it will return NO where a Boolean is expected. The following statements populate all the text fields.

2. This statement calls the dateChanged: method in order to format the birthdate label consistently.

3. The last two statements ensure that the controller is in view mode, initially by first setting the selected segment index to 0, which corresponds to View, and then calling changeEditMode:, which makes the actual changes to the user interface.

With these changes, if you run the app, the Contact controller interface will populate when the user selects a row.

Save Changes to Records

There are some significant issues with the app at this point when it comes to saving data. If you have been running the app, you may have noticed a few things. First, when saving a Contact on the detail editing screen and going back to the table screen, the contact isn't updated. Second, when the app is launched again, the changed Contact shows up as a new row in the table. There are two issues that cause these problems. The first is in the table view controller where we load the database data in the `viewDidLoad:` method. This method is executed once when the controller is first instantiated. Moving to the detail screen to make changes and back again to the table doesn't execute the `viewDidLoad:` method again. However, `viewWillAppear:` is executed just before the view is displayed (see Chapter 2, "App Design Issues and Considerations," for more detailed description of the app life cycle and the order these methods are called in).

For the data to be loaded reliably every time the view becomes active again, we will use `viewWillAppear:` to load the data from the database. Listing 12.5 shows the method, which you will need to type in after the `viewDidLoad:` method in LMAContactsTableController.m. As you start typing, you may notice that code completion in Xcode is smart enough to also help you write an entire method header.

Listing 12.5   **Reloading the Data for the Table**

```
-(void)viewWillAppear:(BOOL)animated{
    [super viewWillAppear:animated];
    [self loadDataFromDatabase];
    [self.tableView reloadData];
}
```

The code should be obvious, except for the last line. This method call reloads the data in the table itself. It basically redraws all the visible cells for the table, so that the data from the database is also displayed in the table after being refreshed. After adding this method, you can comment out the call to `loadDataFromDatabase:` in `viewDidLoad:`.

If you test the app, you will see that every time you tap Save on the detail editing screen, a new record is added to the database. This isn't exactly desirable, but the fix is very simple.

Open LMAContactsController.m and find the `saveContact:` method. This method creates a new `Contact` object, inserts it into the managed object context, populates the object with values from the user interface, and then saves the object context, causing the new object to be inserted into the database. The problem is that when the user picks a row in the table view, the `Contact` object is already populated and exists in the database. To avoid creating a new object every time, you switch to using the contact property instead of a locally created `Contact` object by commenting out lines 1–3 in Listing 12.6, and then add an underscore to change from using the local `contact` variable to the `_contact` property. Line 4 shows how you check to see whether the contact object is nil. If it is, you create a new object in the managed object context. Otherwise, you change the existing object.

Listing 12.6   Avoid Inserting New Objects When Editing

```
-(IBAction)saveContact: (id)sender
{
    LMAAppDelegate *appDelegate = [[UIApplication sharedApplication] delegate];
    NSManagedObjectContext *context = [appDelegate managedObjectContext];
//    Contact *contact = [NSEntityDescription                                 //1
//                        insertNewObjectForEntityForName:@"Contact"          //2
//                        inManagedObjectContext:context];                    //3
    if(!_contact){                                                            //4
        _contact = [NSEntityDescription
                    insertNewObjectForEntityForName:@"Contact"
                    inManagedObjectContext:context];
    }
    NSError *error;
    [_contact setValue:_txtName.text forKey:@"contactName"];
    [_contact setValue:_txtAddress.text forKey:@"streetAddress"];
    [_contact setValue:_txtCity.text forKey:@"city"];
    [_contact setValue:_txtState.text forKey:@"state"];
    [_contact setValue:_txtZip.text forKey:@"zipCode"];
    [_contact setValue:_txtPhone.text forKey:@"phoneNumber"];
    [_contact setValue:_txtCell.text forKey:@"cellNumber"];
    [_contact setValue:_txtEmail.text forKey:@"email"];
    [_contact setValue:birthdate forKey:@"birthday"];

    [context save:&error];
    if(error !=nil) {
        NSLog(@"Error saving object: %@", error.description);
    }
    else {
        NSLog(@"Object saved successfully");
    }
}
```

Deleting Records

If you've been running the app to test it along the way, you probably have a long list of contacts that cannot be deleted. This is not an ideal situation, so now it's time to add the capability to delete records from both the table and the database.

The pattern here is slightly different from what you did to be able to add records. You still need to create a button for the navigation bar that will put the table in edit mode. In edit mode, the user can tap a row to delete it from both the table and data source. This requires implementing a UITableViewDataSource delegate method that is called when the user selects a row for deletion.

Start by adding this line to the end of `viewDidLoad:` in LMAContactsTableController.m:

```
self.navigationItem.leftBarButtonItem = self.editButtonItem;
```

This will put a button with the word Edit in the left part of the navigation bar. If you run the app now, and tap the Edit button, each row will get a Delete icon in front of it. If you tap that, a red Delete button will show up on the right side of the row. Tapping this button would delete the row without further warning, which isn't necessary because the user has already confirmed the intent by tapping three distinctly different areas of the screen (see Figure 12.8). You might be tempted to use Storyboard to add the Edit button, but doing so doesn't set up the three-step process of deleting the row.

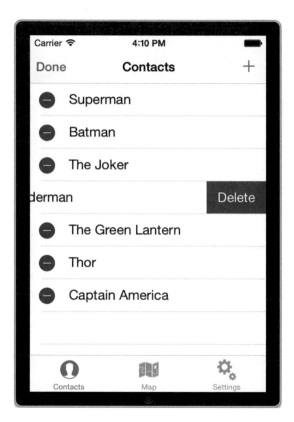

Figure 12.8   Deleting records.

If you run the app now, nothing happens when the Edit button is tapped. For this, you need to implement `tableView:commitEditingStyle:forRowAtIndexPath:`, which is already included in LMAContactsTableController.m. You just need to add the lines of code shown in Listing 12.7

Listing 12.7   **Deleting Rows from the Table**

```
- (void)tableView:(UITableView *)tableView
➥commitEditingStyle:(UITableViewCellEditingStyle)editingStyle
➥forRowAtIndexPath:(NSIndexPath *)indexPath
{
    if (editingStyle == UITableViewCellEditingStyleDelete) {          //1
        // Delete the row from the data source
        Contact *contactToDelete = [contacts objectAtIndex:[indexPath row]];   //2
        [context deleteObject:contactToDelete];                        //3
        NSError *error;
        [context save:&error];                                         //4
        [self loadDataFromDatabase];                                   //5
        [tableView deleteRowsAtIndexPaths:@[indexPath]                 //6
➥withRowAnimation:UITableViewRowAnimationFade];
    }
    else if (editingStyle == UITableViewCellEditingStyleInsert) {
        // Create a new instance of the appropriate class, insert it
        // into the array, and add a new row to the table view
    }
}
```

The code in this method is similar to code you have seen already.

1. This method is called for both insert and delete operations; however, in this app you use only the delete operation here, because the insert was already coded in a different way.

2. Retrieve the object for the row that the user tapped on.

3. Delete the object from the context.

4. Force the context to save changes, forcing the object to be deleted from the data store immediately.

5. Reload the data from the database into the contacts array. You could also redefine the contacts variable to be of type NSMutableArray, in which case you would be able to delete the individual object directly from the array.

6. Remove the row from the table. In this case, it is done with an animation. You can Option-click the method name to see more options for fading the row out.

You can now run the app and delete records by tapping the Edit button. However, after you have implemented tableView:commitEditingStyle:forRowAtIndexPath: you get an additional way to delete rows by swiping across the row. To try this in the simulator, use the mouse and click one end of a row and drag toward the other, and you will get a Delete button for that row. This way, you don't even need the Edit button set up.

Accessory Buttons

When you added the segue to the Prototype cell to allow for navigation to the detail screen, a gray arrow was added to the right side of the cell. This is a Disclosure Indicator, which tells the user that more detail will show up when the row is tapped. You can choose from several Accessory buttons to add to the row, and you have the option of taking different actions whether the Accessory buttons or the row itself is tapped.

To illustrate how this works, you show the user an Alert View when the row itself is tapped, and the detailed editing screen when a Detail Disclosure Accessory Button is tapped.

1. Change the Accessory button in the Attributes Inspector for the Prototype Cell to a Detail Disclosure. The typical functionality of iOS apps for the Detail Disclosure button is to show the detailed controller.

2. Delete the segue between the table view and the Contacts screen.

3. Control-drag from the Prototype Cell to the Contact screen and select Accessory Action > Push in the pop-up menu. This will ensure that when the user taps the Disclosure Indicator, the Contacts screen is pushed onto the navigation stack.

4. Change the Identifier for the new segue to EditContact.

5. Add the following line of code between @end and @implementation in LMAContactsController.m:

   ```
   LMAContactsController *contactController;
   ```

   This sets up a reference to a view controller that you will use a little later.

6. Implement the tableView:accessoryButtonTappedForRowWithIndexPath: method shown in Listing 12.8. This method is called whenever an accessory button is tapped, and allows you to know which row was selected.

Listing 12.8   **Determining the Selected Row**

```
-(void) tableView:(UITableView *)tableView accessoryButtonTappedForRowWithIndexPath:
➥(NSIndexPath *)indexPath
{
    Contact *selectedContact = [contacts objectAtIndex:[indexPath row]];
    contactController.contact = selectedContact;
}
```

7. Change the `prepareForSegue:sender:` method as shown in Listing 12.9. This method now provides a reference to the destination view controller. Be sure that the reference gets assigned to the variable declared in step 5.

The code changes in steps 5–7 above are necessary because we need to know both which view controller will be shown and the row that the selected Disclosure Indicator is in, but neither method will provide both.

Listing 12.9   Setting Up the Segue with a Reference to the Destination Controller

```
- (void)prepareForSegue:(UIStoryboardSegue *)segue sender:(id)sender
{
    if ([segue.identifier isEqualToString:@"EditContact"]) {
        contactController = segue.destinationViewController;
    }
}

-(void) tableView:(UITableView *)tableView
accessoryButtonTappedForRowWithIndexPath:(NSIndexPath *)indexPath
{
    Contact *selectedContact = [contacts objectAtIndex:[indexPath row]];
    contactController.contact = selectedContact;

}
```

Alert View

An Alert View is used as a common way to provide feedback to a user of an iOS device. An Alert View (`UIAlertView`) pops up a message on the screen with one or more buttons for the user to click. It's quite simple to set up. In this example, the message displays the row number the user selected and the name of the contact for that row. In this case, an OK button dismisses the alert, and the Show Details button takes the user to the Contacts Controller to see all the data for the contact (Figure 12.9).

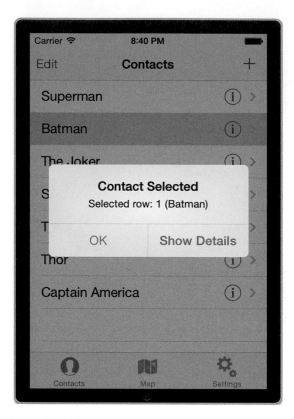

Figure 12.9   Displaying an Alert View.

Implement `tableView:didSelectRowAtIndexPath:` as shown in Listing 12.10 to show the
Alert View when a row is tapped.

Listing 12.10   **Showing an Alert View When User Selects a Row**

```
- (void)tableView:(UITableView *)tableView didSelectRowAtIndexPath:(NSIndexPath
➥*)indexPath
{
    int selectedRow = [indexPath row];
    selectedContact = [contacts objectAtIndex:selectedRow];
    UIAlertView *alert = [[UIAlertView alloc]                          //1
                    initWithTitle:@"Contact Selected"                  //2
                    message:[NSString                                  //3
                            stringWithFormat:@"Selected row: %d (%@)",
                            selectedRow, selectedContact.contactName]
                    delegate:self                                      //4
                    cancelButtonTitle:@"OK"                            //5
```

```
                          otherButtonTitles:@"Show Details", nil];        //6
    [alert show];                                                          //7
}
```

The method starts by getting the selected row and the contact object associated with that row. Then it sets up the Alert View.

1. Create the Alert View object.

2. Pass in a title for the Alert View.

3. The message is shown below the title. This uses the `stringWithFormat:` method to concatenate a string based on the selected row and the name of the selected contact.

4. Set the Alert View's delegate to the table view controller. This enables the table view controller to take action when a button is pressed in the alert view, as you will see a little later.

5. The default button is called the Cancel button. This statement sets the title for that button to OK.

6. Additional buttons can be set up by giving them a title. In this case, there's just one other button. If you needed more buttons, you can list their titles separated by commas before the nil.

7. Show the alert view on the screen.

To distinguish between the buttons and take appropriate action, implement the `UIAlertViewDelegate` protocol by adding `<UIAlertViewDelegate>` to the `@interface` line in LMAContactsTableController.h, like this:

```
@interface LMAContactsTableController : UITableViewController <UIAlertViewDelegate>
```

Then you can implement the delegate method `alertView:clickedButtonAtIndex:` in LMAContactsTableController.m, as shown in Listing 12.11.

Listing 12.11   Taking Action When User Selects a Button in Alert View

```
-(void) alertView:(UIAlertView *)alertView
➥clickedButtonAtIndex:(NSInteger)buttonIndex{
    if(buttonIndex == 1){                                                  //1
      LMAContactsController *controller = [self.storyboard              //2
➥instantiateViewControllerWithIdentifier:@"contactController"];
      NSIndexPath *selectedPath = [self.tableView indexPathForSelectedRow];
      Contact *selectedContact = [contacts objectAtIndex:[selectedPath row]];
      controller.contact = selectedContact;
      [self.navigationController pushViewController:controller animated:YES];  //3
    }
}
```

This method is executed whenever the user taps a button in the Alert View. It will then create the View Controller object, determine the object that was selected, and then push the View Controller onto the navigation stack.

1. Check the `buttonIndex`, which is passed to the delegate method from the Alert View. The `buttonIndex` indicates which button was pressed. The `cancelButton` is index 0 (in this case, the OK button is the cancel button), and the rest of the buttons are numbered as they are listed in `otherButtonTitles`. That means that the Show Details button has index 1. When this button is tapped, the method sets up the Contacts Controller and populates with the currently selected contact object.

2. This line creates an instance of `LMAContactsController` based on an identifier entered in Storyboard. You will see in the following section how to set the identifier in Storyboard.

3. Push the view controller onto the navigation stack in an animated fashion.

To set the identifier for the Contact Controller, open Storyboard and select the Contact screen's view. In the Identity Inspector, set the Storyboard ID to **contactController** and check Use Storyboard ID (see Figure 12.10).

Now you can run the app, and the alert view should work as expected.

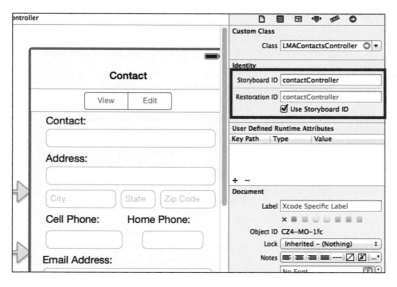

Figure 12.10   Setting the Storyboard ID for the view controller.

Show Subtitles in the Table

With the full object available in the table, you can now add a subtitle to the table display. To do this, you need to change the cell style and specify what text to show as the subtitle.

1. Select the Prototype Cell in Storyboard and change the Style in Attributes Inspector to Subtitle.

2. Add line 1 in `tableView:cellForRowAtIndexPath:` in LMATableContactsController, as shown in Listing 12.12.

Listing 12.12   **Setting the Subtitle for the Table**

```
- (UITableViewCell *)tableView:(UITableView *)tableView
➥cellForRowAtIndexPath:(NSIndexPath *)indexPath
{
    static NSString *CellIdentifier = @"ContactsCell";
    UITableViewCell *cell = [tableView
➥dequeueReusableCellWithIdentifier:CellIdentifier forIndexPath:indexPath];

    // Configure the cell...
    Contact *contact = [contacts objectAtIndex:[indexPath row] ];
    cell.textLabel.text = [contact contactName];
    cell.detailTextLabel.text = [contact city];                            //1
    return cell;
}
```

Running the app will now show the city as well as the name of the contact.

> **iOS Versus Android: Creating Tables**
>
> Creating a table like the one shown in this chapter takes quite a bit more work on Android, because much more of the design and coding has to be done manually. On Android, there isn't a ready-made table with editing capability as you have seen here. Instead, the Android developer needs to design and create similar functionality from scratch.
>
> Although the iOS controls provide a lot of functionality, and can be customized, you do have less freedom than what is available in Android.

Sort the Table

One of the features of MyContactList is to be able to sort the table by different criteria as specified on the Settings screen. The code changes to enable sorting are relatively minor because the Core Data framework handles the heavy lifting. You need to import `Constants.h` and then make changes to `loadDataFromDatabase:` in LMAContactsTableController.m, as shown in Listing 12.13.

Listing 12.13   **Enable Sorting of the Table**

```
- (void) loadDataFromDatabase
{
    //read settings to enable sorting
    NSUserDefaults *settings = [NSUserDefaults standardUserDefaults];          //1
    NSString *sortField = [settings stringForKey:kSortField];                  //2
    bool sortAscending = [settings boolForKey:kSortDirectionAscending];        //3


    //Set up App delegate and Core Data Context
    appDelegate = [[UIApplication sharedApplication] delegate];
    context = [appDelegate managedObjectContext];
    //Set up Request
    NSEntityDescription *entityDescription = [NSEntityDescription
                                            entityForName:@"Contact"
                                            inManagedObjectContext:context];
    NSFetchRequest *request = [[NSFetchRequest alloc] init];
    [request setEntity:entityDescription];
    //Specify sorting
    NSSortDescriptor *sortDescriptor = [[NSSortDescriptor alloc]               //4
                                        initWithKey:sortField
                                        ascending:sortAscending];
    NSArray *sortDescriptors = [[NSArray alloc]                                //5
                                initWithObjects: sortDescriptor, nil] ;
    request.sortDescriptors = sortDescriptors];                               //6
    NSError *error;
    //Execute request
    contacts = [[NSArray alloc]
                initWithArray:[context executeFetchRequest:request
                                                error:&error]];
}
```

Before making these changes, you also need to import `Constants.h`.

1. Get a reference to the default settings file.

2. Retrieve the sort field from the settings file using the key defined in the Constants file.

3. Retrieve the sort direction field from the settings file using the key defined in the Constants file.

4. `NSSortDescriptor` is a class that contains instructions on how to order objects. By passing in the sort field and whether to sort in ascending or descending order, the fetch request will use these instructions to do the actual sorting.

5. You can create multiple sort descriptors, which will then be applied in the order listed in this array. This would allow for sorting by one field first and then another field (for example, sort by name within city). In this case, there's only one sort field, so the array contains only one object.

6. Add the sort descriptors to the array.

7. Execute the fetch request as before to populate the contacts array.

This is all the code we need to be able to sort the data based on the user selections on the Settings screen. However, if you run the app now, it will promptly crash with a message like this:

```
*** Terminating app due to uncaught exception 'NSInvalidArgumentException', reason:
'keypath City not found in entity <NSSQLEntity Contact id=1>'
```

The reason for this is that when we stored the sort fields in the previous chapter, they were stored with uppercase initial letters (hence 'City' in the error message). However, attributes in Core Data are always stored with lowercase. To fix this, you need to make sure that everywhere there's code to store the sort fields that they are stored in lowercase. There are two places to make the fix: First, in `viewDidLoad:` in LMASettingsController.m the sort fields are added to the `sortOrderItem` array. Change these to lowercase, like this:

```
sortOrderItems = @[@"contactName", @"city", @"birthday"];
```

Second, in `application:didFinishLaunchingWithOptions:` in LMAAppDelegate.m, there's a check for whether the sort field is nil, and if not, the sort field is stored as `City`. Change this to lowercase:

```
if([settings objectForKey:kSortField] == nil) {
     [settings setObject:@"city" forKey:kSortField];
  }
```

These are all the code changes needed. However, the app still crashes with the same error message, because the value in the Plist file wasn't changed.

There are a couple of ways to fix it:

1. Delete the Plist file from the app's directory in the simulator (~/Library/Application Support/iPhone Simulator/...). This causes it to be re-created with default values on the next launch.

2. Edit the Plist file and change the value of the sort field. The file is in the app's /Library/ Preferences folder and can be edited by right-clicking in Finder and selecting Open With > Xcode. Then you can click the `sortField` entry and change its value.

3. Comment out the line of code in `loadDataFromDatabase:` that applies the sort descriptor to the fetch request (item 6 in Listing 12.12). Then run the app and change the settings so the proper value is stored in the file. Then uncomment the sorting again in code and launch the app again.

You can choose whichever approach you prefer. Run the app and check that the sorting works as intended.

Summary

Congratulations! You have mastered one of the most important parts of developing apps for the iPhone: Navigation using tables. In addition, you saw how to integrate tables with data stored in Core Data. Like so many other aspects of iOS development, it is crucial to know which methods to override to make the built-in functionality work to do what you want it to do.

Exercises

1. Change the cell layout to use the other two styles.

2. Expand the settings screen to allow for specifying two sort fields. Then have the sorting be done by first one and then the other field.

3. Choose different fields from the Contact class to display in the table.

4. Change the display in the table to be on this form:

   Main label: Superman from Metropolis. Detail Label: Born on: April 18, 1938.

5. Find a way to have the picker for the sort field display the fields with uppercase words and the name as Contact Name, rather than contactName.

13

Maps and Location in iOS

To truly realize the benefits of mobile computing, you will often want to take advantage of the device's capability to know where it is located and display maps of information to the user. Knowing the location of the device can be useful to many types of apps, but the precision needed for the location will be very different for various types of apps. For instance, an app used to let users track the route of their exercise run will need much more detailed location data than an app showing a user the nearest movie theater.

This chapter examines some of the powerful tools that the iOS platform provides to help you work with location and map data. The chapter covers how to expand My Contact List to find the current location of the user, do both forward and reverse geocoding (translate between coordinates and addresses), and plot multiple locations on a map.

Overview of Location and Mapping

iOS has very strong and integrated support for location and mapping. This support includes several hardware sensors, such as GPS, Wi-Fi and cellular radios, as well as software frameworks that make it easy for you as a programmer to access the information from the hardware.

Hardware and Sensors

Different devices running iOS will have different hardware sensors to provide location data. The most accurate sensor for outdoor use is the GPS, which can provide accuracy down to a few meters, but it isn't available on iPod touch or the Wi-Fi iPad versions. The iPhone and 3G iPad can also take advantage of cell tower triangulation, and all devices can use the location of Wi-Fi access points to provide location data. Some devices also have a GPS and altimeter built in to provide data on where the device is headed and how high it is above or below sea level. Whenever a location or heading is reported, it also reports an accuracy that you can use to understand the quality of the data received.

As a developer, you don't decide which sensors to use, but you should understand that different devices may not provide the same level of accuracy, which may impact the way your app works. Further, the user also has the option of turning off location services entirely. And, because this is a device setting that can be controlled by Parental Controls, some users may not be able to turn on location services. You should design your app to take all these things into account and provide a good experience to the user.

Core Location

Apple provides two frameworks for working with location: Core Location and MapKit. Core Location allows for finding and working with current location and heading information. In addition, Core Location also lets you set up geographic regions (called *geo fences*) to help you take action when the device enters or leaves a region. The framework uses the available hardware sensors to provide location data as close as possible to the accuracy you have requested. In addition, Core Location also handles geocoding, which allows for translation between a geographic point and an address, or vice versa. Geocoding requires an active Internet connection because the lookup between address and coordinate is done by Apple's servers. All Core location classes are prefixed with CL.

MapKit

For displaying a map, Apple provides the MapKit framework, which uses Apple's mapping service and lets you very easily display a map, detect the user's location, add overlays, and plot any location on the map using different kinds of pins and callouts. The map can also perform reverse geocoding. All the MapKit classes are prefixed with MK.

iOS Versus Android: Setting Up to Use Maps

There's quite a bit more work in setting up to work with maps on Android. Whereas iOS comes bundled with all the necessary frameworks and libraries, on Android, the developer needs to download the Google Play SDK and register for a Google Maps API key.

By registering for an API key, any hits to the Google Maps API can be associated with a particular app. With its integrated set of offerings, Apple has made it simpler for developers to get started with development. However, in the end, the result is the same, because all iOS apps have to be digitally signed, and thus Apple can associate any hits to its map API to a particular app.

To take advantage of this ease of use, you have to use the Apple Maps data, which was often criticized after its initial launch, but has improved significantly since then. If you would rather use Google Maps as the engine for mapping in your apps, you can download the Google Maps SDK for iOS and sign up for an API key in the same way as described in Chapter 7, "Maps and Location in Android."

Adding Location Information to the App

Working with location data and maps on iOS is relatively simple. By tapping into the provided frameworks, you can build powerful apps very quickly that take location data into account. You expand the MyContactList app with a map that shows all your contacts as well as the user's location on a map.

To better understand the capabilities available when working with location, the first step is to build a temporary screen to explore the location functions before building the final app. The Map Screen controller is used to provide the location information until it is replaced later in the chapter with an actual map.

Finding Location

When working with maps, you need to use coordinates, expressed in latitude and longitude degrees. You can find the device's location from the sensors (GPS, cell towers, and Wi-Fi), which give you coordinates directly. However, the coordinates are not very people-friendly, so it's important to be able to convert an address into coordinates. This process is called *geocoding*, and it lets you take a human-readable address and convert it to a coordinate.

Forward Geocoding

To demonstrate how geocoding works, you add a screen to show location data in the MyContactList app you worked on in the previous screen. Open the project from the previous chapter or the project for this chapter that comes with the book. Then open the Storyboard and drag a new View Controller into the Storyboard. Change the UI to match that shown in Figure 13.1. The text fields enable the user to type in a street, city, and state. When the user taps the Address to Coordinates button, the address information will be converted to a coordinate and the latitude and longitude will be output to the corresponding labels. Tapping the Device Coordinates button will get the location of the device and output the information to all the labels. The output labels have been given a gray background so they are visible without content. To set up this user interface, first set up one control the way it should be, then hold down the Option key on the keyboard and drag the control to a new location. This copies the location with all its properties intact. You can use this to quickly create the output labels after one is set up with the correct length and background.

After building the UI in Interface builder, you need to add a code file for the view controller.

1. Right-click the yellow MyContactList folder and select New File.

2. Choose the Cocoa Touch Category and then select Objective-C Class. Click Next.

3. For Class, enter **LMALocationDemoController**, and for Subclass Of enter **UIViewController**. Make sure none of the check boxes are checked, and click Next.

4. Make sure the Target for MyContactList is selected. Click Create.

5. In Storyboard, select the new location view controller, and change the Class in the Identity Inspector from UIViewController to **LMALocationDemoController**. Be careful to select the top-level view controller, and not the View inside that. You should see the entire screen has a blue frame.

6. To add the new view controller into the Tab Bar, control-drag from the Tab Bar Controller to the new Location View Controller and select Relationship Segue > View Controllers in the pop-up dialog.

7. Find the Glyphish icons you used in Chapter 10, "iOS Navigation and Interface Design," and drag 71-compass.png into the images.xcassets folder.

8. Select the Tab Bar item underneath the new Location View Controller and use the Attributes Inspector to change the title to **Location** and the image to 71-compass.

Figure 13.1   User interface for exploring Core Location.

Now you can wire up the screen. Use the Assistant Editor to control-drag from the controls on the screen to LMALocationDemoController.h to add outlets for the three text fields with these names: txtStreet, txtCity, and txtState. Then add outlets for the labels with these names (from top to bottom): `lblLatitude`, `lblLongitude`, `lblLocationAccuracy`, `lblHeading`, `lblHeadingAccuracy`, `lblAltitude`, and `lblAltitudeAccuracy`.

Next, add actions for the two buttons named `addressToCoordinates` and `deviceCoordinates`. Before you leave Interface Builder, you'll need to prepare for being able to dismiss the keyboard, so change the `UIView` to a `UIControl` and declare the `dismissKeyboard:` method marked by 1 in Listing 13.1.

Listing 13.1   **Outlets and Actions in LMALocationDemoController.h**

```
#import <UIKit/UIKit.h>

@interface LMALocationDemoController  : UIViewController
@property (weak, nonatomic) IBOutlet UITextField *txtStreetAddress;
@property (weak, nonatomic) IBOutlet UITextField *txtCity;
@property (weak, nonatomic) IBOutlet UITextField *txtState;
@property (weak, nonatomic) IBOutlet UILabel *lblLatitude;
@property (weak, nonatomic) IBOutlet UILabel *lblLongitude;
@property (weak, nonatomic) IBOutlet UILabel *lblLocationAccuracy;
@property (weak, nonatomic) IBOutlet UILabel *lblHeading;
@property (weak, nonatomic) IBOutlet UILabel *lblHeadingAccuracy;
@property (weak, nonatomic) IBOutlet UILabel *lblAltitude;
@property (weak, nonatomic) IBOutlet UILabel *lblAltitudeAccuracy;

- (IBAction)addressToCoordinates:(id)sender;
- (IBAction)deviceCoordinates:(id)sender;
- (IBAction)dismissKeyboard:(id)sender;                                //1
@end
```

Select the Control for the Map screen in the Dock, and use the Connections Inspector to drag from Touch Down to the icon with a white square inside a yellow circle beneath the Map screen. Select `dismissKeyboard:` from the menu that pops up.

Next, switch to LMALocationDemoController.m and implement the `dismissKeyboard:` method by adding this line:

```
[self.view endEditing:YES];
```

Now the user interface is set up and it's time to start work on geocoding the address. The Core Location framework first needs to be added to your project. There are two elements to this. First, you need to import the framework in the .m file where you will use it, by adding this line:

```
#import <CoreLocation/CoreLocation.h>
```

Notice how the frameworks are imported using angle brackets, whereas your own files are imported using quotation marks. The next step is to add the actual library files to the project. This is done in the General settings for the project. Click the blue icon with the project name in the navigation pane, and then click the General tab and scroll all the way to the bottom, where you will see a list of Linked Frameworks and Libraries. Click the + to bring up a window where you can find the Framework you need to add. You can start typing in the search box to narrow the list. Figure 13.2 shows the process for adding a framework.

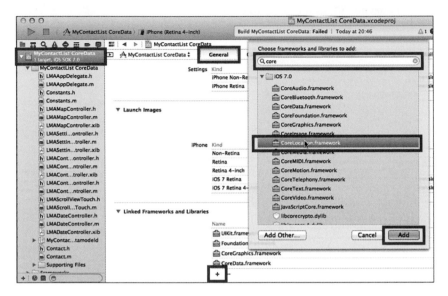

Figure 13.2   Adding the Core Location framework to the project.

> **Note**
>
> One of the common mistakes the beginner iOS developer makes is to add an import statement for a framework in the code, but then forget to also add the framework file to the project. If you do forget, your app will compile and run just fine until the user tries to access some of the objects that use the framework. At that point, it is likely that an exception will be thrown. The error messages can be less than helpful.
>
> The best recommendation, therefore, is to remember to add the framework to the project as soon as you import the framework in the code, and test your app extensively.

With the framework imported and added, open LMALocationDemoController.m again and implement `addressToCoordinates:` as shown in Listing 13.2.

Listing 13.2 **Forward Geocoding**

```
- (IBAction)addressToCoordinates:(id)sender {
    NSString *address = [NSString stringWithFormat:@"%@, %@ %@",        //1
                        _txtStreetAddress.text, _txtCity.text, _txtState.text];
```

```
    CLGeocoder *geoCoder = [[CLGeocoder alloc] init];                //2
    [geoCoder geocodeAddressString:address completionHandler:^(NSArray    //3
➥*placemarks, NSError *error) {
        CLPlacemark *bestMatch = [placemarks objectAtIndex:0];       //4
        CLLocationCoordinate2D coordinate = bestMatch.location.coordinate;  //5
        _lblLatitude.text = [NSString stringWithFormat:@"%g\u00B0",   //6
                             coordinate.latitude];
        _lblLongitude.text = [NSString stringWithFormat:@"%g\u00B0",
                             coordinate.longitude];
    }];
}
```

This code shows several interesting things, not only about location data, but also about multi-threaded programming in iOS.

1. This line constructs a single string containing the address information from the three text fields. The geocoding can handle strings similar to what you would type into an online mapping website like Google Maps. It is also possible to create a more structured entry, called a Dictionary, to use for the lookup, but for many situations, a simple string will do just fine.

2. CLGeocoder is a class that is used to do both forward and reverse geocoding. This line instantiates it.

3. Call the method geoCodeAddressString:completionHandler: to do the actual geocoding. This method sends the string to an Apple service across the Internet. The results come back in an NSArray containing CLPlacemark objects. Since this method can take a while to complete depending on Internet speeds, a *completion handler* will finish the work of dealing with the results while the rest of the program continues. This ensures that the app remains responsive during the call to the geocoding service.

4. The result from the geocoding call is returned in an NSArray. Sometimes results can be ambiguous and multiple results are returned. You could set up a loop to go through all the results, but here we keep it simple and assume that the first result is good enough.

5. The CLPlacemark object contains a large amount of information, such as state, city, and points of interest for the location, but the actual coordinates are also stored in there. Here, they are pulled out and stored in a CLLocationCoordinate2D, which is a simple struct containing latitude and longitude.

6. The last two statements put the coordinate values in the corresponding labels. The code \u00B0 is the Unicode for a degree symbol that is added to the end of the numerical value.

If you run the app now, you can type in an address, tap the Address To Coordinates button and get a set of coordinates. You can check the accuracy by typing the coordinates into Google Maps to get a map of the point.

> **Note**
>
> If your primary programming experience is from a modern object-oriented language like Java and C#, the notion of a `struct` may be unfamiliar to you. The `struct` is in a way a precursor to objects, because it is a data structure that you can define and that acts as a data type. However, unlike objects, `structs` don't have methods and are much lighter weight than objects. They are, therefore, used in many places throughout the Cocoa framework, especially in areas where performance is important. As an example of a `struct`, here is the definition of CLLocationCoordinate2D:
>
> ```
> typedef struct {
>     CLLocationDegrees latitude;
>     CLLocationDegrees longitude;
> } CLLocationCoordinate2D;
> ```
>
> This defines the `struct` to have two data members, latitude and longitude, which are essentially doubles that have been given another type name.

Finding the Device Location

It can be very useful in many apps to find the location of the device. The location is available through a CLLocationManager object, which acts as an interface to the sensors that measure both location and heading (compass) information.

1. Open LMALocationDemoController.h and use the assistant editor to move the import statement for CoreLocation from the .m file to the .h file.

2. Change the `@interface` line in LMALocationDemoController.h by specifying it should implement `CLLocationManagerDelegate`:

   ```
       @interface LMALocationDemoController  : UIViewController
   <CLLocationManagerDelegate>
   ```

3. Switch to the .m file and add a class variable between `@end` and `@implementation` to hold a reference to a CLLocationManager object:

   ```
   CLLocationManager *locationManager;
   ```

4. To start and stop the location manager, implement the deviceCoordinates: and viewDidDisappear: methods as shown in Listing 13.3.

Listing 13.3   **Starting the Location Manager**

```
- (IBAction)deviceCoordinates:(id)sender {
    if(locationManager == nil)                                           //1
        locationManager = [[CLLocationManager alloc]init];
    locationManager.delegate = self;                                     //2
    locationManager.desiredAccuracy = kCLLocationAccuracyHundredMeters;  //3
    locationManager.distanceFilter = 100;                               //4
```

```
    [locationManager startUpdatingLocation];                                    //5
    [locationManager startUpdatingHeading];                                     //6
}


-(void)viewDidDisappear:(BOOL)animated{                                         //7
    [locationManager stopUpdatingLocation];
    [locationManager stopUpdatingHeading];
}
```

The Location Manager is started when the user presses the Device Coordinates button and is stopped anytime the view disappears, to conserve battery.

1. If the location manager object has already been created, no need to create a new object.

2. Set the location manager's delegate to the view controller. Later, you will see several of the delegate methods implemented.

3. Set the desired accuracy. Table 13.1 lists the possible values to choose from. It's always best to choose the least accurate option your app can use and still do what it needs to do. This lets the system conserve battery power as much as possible.

4. Another battery saving feature is to set up a distance filter. This indicates the distance in meters the device has to move before an update location event is generated. Here, the device has to move 100 meters before an update happens.

5. This starts the location manager running and updating the location.

6. This last statement tells the location manager to also report on changes to heading (compass) information.

7. The viewDidDisappear: method is called when another view moves to the foreground. There's no need to keep the Location Manager running when the view is no longer visible.

Table 13.1   Overview of Accuracy Options for Location Services. All Indicators Are Prefaced with 'kCLLocationAccuracy'.

Distance Indicator	Precision
BestForNavigation	Use for navigation apps. Combines the highest level of accuracy with additional sensor data. Intended for use only when the device is plugged in.
Best	Highest level of accuracy.
NearestTenMeters	10 meters.
HundredMeters	100 meters.
Kilometer	1 kilometer.
ThreeKilometer	3 kilometers.

To take advantage of the Location Manager, you need to implement some of its delegate methods. The first will be called whenever the device location is updated and is shown in Listing 13.4.

---

iOS Versus Android: Access to Hardware Location Sensors

Android developers can choose which specific location sensor to use (GPS or network sensor), giving some additional flexibility. In iOS, by contrast, you have seen how you can specify an accuracy and a distance filter, but you can't request that location data has to come from the GPS. Instead, the operating system decides how to best achieve the desired accuracy while balancing performance and battery usage.

In both systems you have to be mindful of how much you use the location sensors and remember to turn off location services when not needed anymore, because they do use extra battery.

Listing 13.4   Getting Location Updates

```
-(void) locationManager:(CLLocationManager *)manager didUpdateLocations:(NSArray
➡*)locations{
    CLLocation *location = [locations lastObject];                              //1
    NSDate* eventDate = location.timestamp;                                     //2
    NSTimeInterval howRecent = [eventDate timeIntervalSinceNow];                //3
    if (abs(howRecent) < 15.0) {                                                //4
        CLLocationCoordinate2D coordinate= location.coordinate;
        _lblLongitude.text = [NSString stringWithFormat:@"%g\u00B0",
                               ➡coordinate.longitude];                         //5
        _lblLatitude.text = [NSString stringWithFormat:@"%g\u00B0",
                               ➡coordinate.latitude];
        _lblLocationAccuracy.text = [NSString stringWithFormat:@"%gm",
                                      ➡location.horizontalAccuracy];           //6
        _lblAltitude.text = [NSString stringWithFormat:@"%gm",
                               ➡location.altitude];                            //7
        _lblAltitudeAccuracy.text = [NSString stringWithFormat:@"%gm",
                                      ➡location.verticalAccuracy];
    }
}
```

Whenever the Location Manager updates the location of the device, it calls the `locationManager:didUpdateLocations:` method. Because some time may have passed since the last call to the method, several locations may be available in the locations array. The most recent location is in the last position in the array.

1. Get the most recent location from the array.

2. Get the timestamp for the most recent location.

3. Find out how old the location is in seconds.

4. Take action only if the location is less than 15 seconds old. This ensures that old data isn't used to update the UI. How old of data you can live with, of course, depends on the purpose of the app.

5. Update the labels in the UI with the coordinates.

6. Accuracy is reported in much the same way as the coordinates. It gives you the radius in meters of the circle within which the device may be found. The coordinates indicate the center of the circle.

7. The Location Manager also reports altitude in meters above or below sea level, as well as vertical accuracy in meters to this number.

To get the heading (compass) information for the device, you implement the `locationManager:didUpdateHeading:` method, as shown in Listing 13.5.

Listing 13.5   **Getting Heading Updates**

```
-(void)locationManager:(CLLocationManager *)manager
➥didUpdateHeading:(CLHeading *)newHeading
{
    if(newHeading.headingAccuracy > 0){                                     //1
        CLLocationDirection theHeading = newHeading.trueHeading;           //2
        _lblHeading.text = [NSString stringWithFormat:@"%g\u00B0", theHeading];  //3
        _lblHeadingAccuracy.text = [NSString stringWithFormat:@"%g\u00B0",
                                   ➥newHeading.headingAccuracy];
    }
}
```

This method works in the same way as the location updates and is called whenever the heading information for the device is updated.

1. In this case, the accuracy is checked to see if it's valid. The heading information can be invalid if the device isn't calibrated or if there is strong interference from local magnetic fields.

2. The `CLHeading` object contains information about both the magnetic heading and the true heading. In this case, we use the true heading.

3. The last two lines update the labels with the heading and accuracy. The accuracy is reported as the number of degrees the heading may be off in either direction (for example, if the heading is reported as 300 degrees and accuracy as 10 degrees, the actual heading may be anywhere from 290 to 310 degrees).

The last delegate method to implement deals with error conditions and is shown in Listing 13.6.

Listing 13.6   **Handling Errors from the Location Manager**

```
-(void) locationManager:(CLLocationManager *)manager didFailWithError:(NSError
➥*)error{
    NSString *errorType = (error.code == kCLErrorDenied) ? @"Access Denied" :      //1
➥@"Unknown Error";
    UIAlertView *alert = [[UIAlertView alloc]                                       //2
                        initWithTitle:@"Error Getting Location"
                        message:errorType
                        delegate:nil
                        cancelButtonTitle:@"OK"
                        otherButtonTitles:nil];
    [alert show];                                                                   //3
}
```

The `locationManager:didFailWithError:` method is called if the location manager encounters an error situation. In this case, the app shows an Alert View, but in a more realistic app, you would want to deal with this in a more intelligent way.

1. The most common error situation is that the user has turned off Location Services. You can check for this by looking at `error.code`. If this is set to `kCLErrorDenied`, then Location Services is turned off for the app or the entire device. This statement uses a conditional assignment statement to assign one of two literal strings to the `errorType` variable.

2. Create the alert view with the error type as the message.

3. Show the Alert View.

Now you can run the app and test that it can find the location of the device. The location information can be tested in the simulator by selecting Debug > Location and choosing one of the options for locations. The default is Apple, which is the location of Apple's headquarters in Cupertino, CA. Custom Location lets you enter a set of coordinates yourself. The remaining options simulate a moving device at various speeds. Try them out and see what they do. Unfortunately, none of the options provide heading or altitude information. These need to be tested on an actual device.

This section showed the standard Location Services, but you can also use the significant-change location service, which relies only on cell tower placement to provide location updates when the user has moved a significant distance. This option uses much less battery and also allows the app to monitor locations in the background.

Adding a Map

Next, you see how to add a map and get location information directly from the map, as well as how to display the location of the contacts in the database on the map.

1. Select the Map View Controller in Storyboard and delete the `Label` and `UITextView`.

2. Add a new view controller to hold the map by dragging a View Controller from the Object Library to the Storyboard.

3. Drag a Map View from the Object Library to the Map View Controller. It should expand to fill the entire space available. Use the blue guidelines to center the Map View inside the View Controller.

4. Open LMASecondViewController.h and right-click LMASecondViewController in the `@interface` line. Select Refactor > Rename.

5. Change the name to **LMAMapController**, and make sure Rename Related Files is checked. Click Preview. If you're asked, click OK to Enable Snapshots.

6. The next screen shows all the files that will be changed (see Figure 13.3). Click Save.

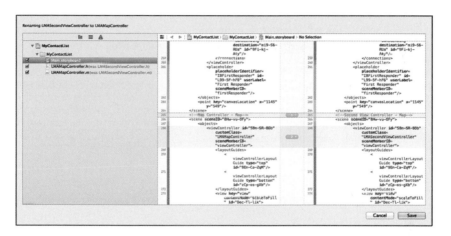

Figure 13.3   Renaming the map controller.

Next, add the `MapKit` framework to the project following the instructions earlier in the chapter for adding the `CoreLocation` framework (Figure 13.2). You can now run the app, and the map shows up in the map screen, but it is zoomed out very far. However, you can interact with the map just like the regular Maps app by zooming, scrolling, and the like.

If you want to show the user's location on the map, you can go back into the Attributes Inspector for the map and check the box to Show User Location. If you run the app again, you will see a blue dot where the user is located (by default at Apple in California). Try zooming in close enough to see city streets and then select Debug > Location > Freeway Drive. You will now see the blue dot moving as the device movements are simulated. To zoom in, using the Simulator, hold down the Option key while clicking on the map, and you will get two gray dots that simulate a user with two fingers on the screen.

Although it is very easy to show the user's location on the map like this, it is also very limited, because you won't be able to do anything with it beyond showing the location. For instance, later in the chapter you learn how to add a description of the user's location to the map. To do this, and other more sophisticated operations with the map, you need to add an outlet for the map. Just control-drag as usual to the .h file and add an outlet named mvMap. You also need to import the MapKit framework in the .h file.

There are a few ways to display the user's location on the map. The simplest is to enable user tracking. This is one line of code that will show the user's location and keep the map centered and zoomed in on that location:

```
[_mvMap setUserTrackingMode:YES];
```

This could go in viewWillAppear: and then as soon as the map is displayed, it will zoom in on the user's location.

For more sophisticated operations, you need to implement the MKMapViewDelegate protocol, which allows you to be notified of updates to the map, including the user's location. To display a map that's zoomed in on the user's current location, follow these steps:

1. Specify that LMAMapController should implement MKMapViewDelegate protocol by adding <MKMapViewDelegate> to the end of the @interface line in LMAMapController.h.

2. In viewDidLoad:, set the map to show the user's location and set the delegate of the map view to be the map view controller:

   ```
   _mvMap.showsUserLocation = YES;
   _mvMap.delegate = self;
   ```

3. In LMAMapController.m, implement mapView:didUpdateUserLocation: as shown in Listing 13.7.

When running the app, you can see that it shows the user's location and zooms in to where you can see the city level. If it doesn't seem to be working, go to Debug > Location in the Simulator and make sure it isn't set to **None**.

Listing 13.7   **Display the User's Location on the Map**

```
-(void)mapView:(MKMapView *)mapView didUpdateUserLocation:(MKUserLocation *)
➥userLocation
{
    CLLocationCoordinate2D location;                                         //1
    location = userLocation.coordinate;
    MKCoordinateSpan span;                                                   //2
    span.latitudeDelta = .5;
    span.longitudeDelta = .5;
    MKCoordinateRegion viewRegion = MKCoordinateRegionMake(location, span);  //3
    [_mvMap setRegion:viewRegion animated:YES];                             //4
}
```

1. The first few lines convert the location data in the `MKUserLocation` object that the map passes in to a `CLLocationCoordinate2D` that is needed to provide the center point for the visible region of the map.

2. The span is used to indicate how many degrees are visible on the map. This is used to specify the zoom level. The lower the span numbers, the farther the map is zoomed in. You may very well need small fractional numbers to see a city-street level map. There are several other ways you can use to set the zoom level of the map. One common approach is to use a statement like this to define the visible region:

```
viewRegion = MKCoordinateRegionMakeWithDistance(location, 10000, 10000);
```

This sets the view region to 10,000 meters on either side of the user's location. You can read Apple's Location Awareness Programming Guide for more detail on how to work with location data.

3. The region is the rectangle that indicates the visible area on the map. This line creates the region based on the center location and the span.

4. Finally, the region is applied to the map.

Adding Annotations to the Map

One of the nice features of Map Kit is the capability to show an exact location on the map with a pin. These pins are called annotations, and you can add as many as you need to the map. Annotations are created in a class that implements the `MKAnnotation` protocol, so start by adding a new Objective-C class called `LMAMapPoint` as a subclass of `NSObject`. Open the new .h file and change it as shown in Listing 13.8.

Listing 13.8 **LMAMapPoint.h**

```
#import <Foundation/Foundation.h>
#import <MapKit/MapKit.h>

@interface LMAMapPoint : NSObject<MKAnnotation>                           //1
@property (nonatomic, readonly) CLLocationCoordinate2D coordinate;        //2
@property (nonatomic, readonly, copy) NSString *title;
@property (nonatomic, readonly, copy) NSString *subtitle;
-(id) initWithCoordinate:(CLLocationCoordinate2D) location               //3
                   title:(NSString *) contactName
                subtitle:(NSString *) address;
@end
```

This sets up the interface for the `MapPoint` class, which will be used to store the annotation for a single point on the map.

1. The last item in this line specifies that the class implements the `MKAnnotation` protocol. This protocol specifies three properties used to describe the annotation.

2. The three properties are `coordinate`, `title`, and `subtitle`. It's important to spell the names of the properties correctly, as they are defined in the protocol. The only required property is coordinate, so this is the only one the compiler will complain about if you misspell it. If either of the other two are misspelled, the annotation just won't show up.

3. This method will be used to initialize the `MapPoint` with data for the three properties. Because the properties are read-only, they cannot be changed after they have been set.

Next, implement the .m file as shown in Listing 13.9.

Listing 13.9 **LMAMapPoint.m**

```
#import "LMAMapPoint.h"

@implementation LMAMapPoint

- (id) init
{
    self = [super init];
    if(self){
        //Initialization code
    }
    return self;
}

-(id) initWithCoordinate:(CLLocationCoordinate2D)location title:(NSString
*)contactName subtitle:(NSString *)address
{
    self = [self init];
    if(self)
    {
        _coordinate = location;
        _title = contactName;
        _subtitle = address;
    }
    return self;
}

@end
```

Most of the code in this file is very straightforward and shouldn't require any explanation. There are two simple methods for initializing the object.

Now, to have the annotation for the user's location show up on the map, you need to add an import statement for LMAMapPoint.h to LMAMapController.m and add a few lines of code to `mapView:didUpdateUserLocation:` as shown in Listing 13.10.

Listing 13.10   **Adding an Annotation for the User's Location to the Map**

```
-(void)mapView:(MKMapView *)mapView didUpdateUserLocation:(MKUserLocation
➡*)userLocation
{
    CLLocationCoordinate2D location;
    location = userLocation.coordinate;
    MKCoordinateSpan span;
    span.latitudeDelta = .5;
    span.longitudeDelta = .5;
    MKCoordinateRegion viewRegion = MKCoordinateRegionMake(location, span);
    [_mvMap setRegion:viewRegion animated:YES];
    LMAMapPoint *mp = [[LMAMapPoint alloc] initWithCoordinate:location          //1
                                               title:@"You"
                                           subtitle:@"Are here"];
    [_mvMap addAnnotation:mp];                                                  //2
}
```

You need to add the last two lines in the method.

1. Create the `LMAMapPoint` object with the user's location and two literal string values for title and subtitle.

2. Add the annotation to the map.

You can run the app, and you should see the result in Figure 13.4 (with the simulated location set to Apple, and after clicking the pin).

Display Contacts on the Map

The last piece of functionality to add to the app is the capability to plot the contacts on the map. To do this, you will need to add a property to the map controller to hold the array of all the contacts in the database, populate the array from the database, and then use a loop to look up the location of each contact and annotate locations for them on the map. This section goes through each of those steps.

First, open LMAMapController.h and add the following line after the other `@property` statement:

```
@property (nonatomic) NSArray *contacts;
```

This creates the property to hold an `NSArray` of all the contacts to be displayed. To populate the array, add import statements to import `LMAAppDelegate.h` and `Contact.h` in LMAMapController.m, then add the `viewWillAppear:` method as shown in Listing 13.11.

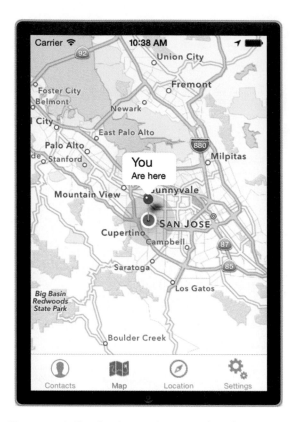

Figure 13.4   Map with an annotation for the user's current location.

Listing 13.11   **Adding Annotations for All Contacts**

```
-(void)viewWillAppear:(BOOL)animated{

    LMAAppDelegate *appDelegate = [[UIApplication sharedApplication] delegate];    //1
    NSManagedObjectContext *context = [appDelegate managedObjectContext];
    //Set up request
    NSEntityDescription *entityDescription = [NSEntityDescription
                                              ➥entityForName:@"Contact"
                                              ➥inManagedObjectContext:context];
    NSFetchRequest *request = [[NSFetchRequest alloc] init];
    [request setEntity:entityDescription];
    NSError *error;

    _contacts = [[NSArray alloc]
                    initWithArray:[context executeFetchRequest:request
                                                 ➥error:&error]];
```

```
    //find location for all contacts
    for (Contact *contact in _contacts) {                          //2
        NSString *address = [NSString stringWithFormat:@"%@, %@ %@",
                        ➥contact.streetAddress, contact.city, contact.state];
        //geocoding
        CLGeocoder *geoCoder = [[CLGeocoder alloc] init];          //3
        [geoCoder geocodeAddressString:address completionHandler:^(NSArray
➥*placemarks, NSError *error) {
            CLPlacemark *bestMatch = [placemarks objectAtIndex:0];
            //set up annotation
            CLLocationCoordinate2D coordinate = bestMatch.location.coordinate;
            LMAMapPoint *mp = [[LMAMapPoint alloc]                 //4
                            initWithCoordinate:coordinate
                                    title:contact.contactName
                                subtitle:contact.streetAddress];
            [_mvMap addAnnotation:mp];
        }];
    }
}
```

There's no new code here. You've seen all of it in previous listings, so just a high level description of what's going on here follows.

1. This section pulls in all the contacts from the database.

2. Set up a loop to go through all the contacts in the array, and set up an address string for each of them.

3. Use CLGeocoder to look up the location of each address.

4. Create a map point for each contact, and send it the location of the contact, the name, and the street address to use for the annotation, and then display the annotation on the map.

If you run the app, be sure to have a few contacts in the database with address, city, and state included. You should then see a pin for each contact on the map, and tapping the pin should bring up the contact's name and street address.

Switch Between Map Types

You can display the map as standard, satellite, or hybrid. To demonstrate how to set the map type, you add a segmented control to the top of the display to allow the user to choose which map type to display.

1. Open Storyboard and add a segmented control to the top of the map screen. You can add it right on top of the map, which would allow you to programmatically hide it at some point and then have the map take up more of the screen. You should make sure it is added below the status bar. Stretch the control to go across the entire screen and then

rename the segments, Standard, Hybrid, and Satellite, as shown in Figure 13.5. To add
a third segment, select the segmented control in Interface Builder, then go to Attributes
Inspector and set the Segments attribute to 3.

Figure 13.5   Segmented control to choose map type.

2. Add an outlet for the segmented control, named `sgmtMapType`.

3. Add an action for the segmented control named `mapTypeChanged`.

4. Implement the `mapTypeChanged:` method in LMAMapController.m as shown in
   Listing 13.12.

Listing 13.12   **Changing the Map Type**

```
- (IBAction)mapTypeChanged:(id)sender {
    switch (_sgmtMapType.selectedSegmentIndex) {
        case 0:
            mvMap.mapType = MKMapTypeStandard;
```

```
        break;
    case 1:
        mvMap.mapType = MKMapTypeHybrid;
        break;
    case 2:
        mvMap.mapType = MKMapTypeSatellite;
        break;
    default:
        break;
    }
}
```

Summary

Maps and location are very important for many mobile applications, so having a solid understanding of how to integrate these features into your apps is crucial to becoming a professional mobile developer. In this chapter you saw many of the techniques and learned the skills necessary to create location-aware apps. However, there's much more to learn in this area, so you should keep studying Apple's documentation on maps and location programming.

Exercises

1. Add a control to allow the user to change the accuracy setting for the sensor and notice how the output changes when moving about using different settings.

2. The app now has database access code in several view controllers. To support a cleaner design, add a database access class that controls all access to Core Data and provides useful methods and properties to the rest of the app.

3. Turn off the user's permission to access location for the App (in the Simulator, go to Settings > Privacy > Location). Run the app again and observe what happens. Is this appropriate behavior? How could it be improved?

4. What would happen if the code in Listing 13.10 was placed in `viewDidLoad:` instead of `viewWillAppear:?`

5. Change the text displayed on the pin to include the City for the contact.

14

Access to Hardware and Sensors in iOS

A big part of the promise of mobile computing is that the mobile devices today offer features that aren't available in any other general-purpose computing devices. Besides mobility, the availability of hardware sensors on the device is what makes it possible to create truly innovative solutions that would not be possible otherwise.

This chapter demonstrates several approaches to interacting with the hardware on the device.

- *You can use UIDevice to get basic information about the device, including OS Version and its current orientation (Landscape, Portrait, and so on).*

- *The Notification Center can be used to get regular updates on the state of the battery, including charge level and whether the device is plugged in.*

- *A simple approach to taking a picture is to use a ready-made view controller that allows for taking still pictures or videos.*

- *The phone and messaging (SMS) system can be opened using a URL that will send data to a default app for a variety of functions on the phone (including the browser and email).*

- *Finally, you can use the powerful Core Motion framework to detect and work with a range of sensors on the device, including accelerometer, magnetometer, and gyroscope.*

Knowing how to interact with the hardware on the device is an important step toward being able to create apps that take advantage of the full promise of mobile computing. This will allow you to create systems that could not have been possible without a capable mobile device.

Getting Device Information

One of the basic ways to interact with the hardware on the device is to retrieve data about the device itself. In iOS, the device is represented by the UIDevice class, which contains information about the device itself, such as its assigned name, operating system version, and device model (iPad, iPhone, iPod touch). The class also can tell you the orientation of the device (portrait and landscape) and provide status on the battery and the proximity sensor (whether the phone is close to the face of the user).

Listing 14.1 shows some of the ways you can use the UIDevice class. Later sections in this chapter contain other examples of interacting with this data.

Listing 14.1   **Getting Information About the Current Device**

```
- (void)viewWillAppear:(BOOL)animated
{
    UIDevice *device = [UIDevice currentDevice];                        //1
    NSLog(@"Device Info:");
    NSLog(@"Name: %@", device.name);                                   //2
    NSLog(@"Model: %@", device.model);                                 //3
    NSLog(@"System Name: %@", device.systemName);                      //4
    NSLog(@"System Version: %@", device.systemVersion);               //5
    NSLog(@"Identifier: %@", device.identifierForVendor);             //6
    NSString *orientation;
    switch (device.orientation) {                                      //7
        case UIDeviceOrientationFaceDown:
            orientation = @"Face Down";
            break;
        case UIDeviceOrientationLandscapeLeft:
            orientation = @"Landscape Left";
            break;
        case UIDeviceOrientationPortrait:
            orientation = @"Portrait";
            break;
        case UIDeviceOrientationFaceUp:
            orientation = @"Face Up";
            break;
        case UIDeviceOrientationLandscapeRight:
            orientation = @"Landscape Right";
            break;
        case UIDeviceOrientationPortraitUpsideDown:
            orientation = @"Portrait Upside Down";
            break;
        case UIDeviceOrientationUnknown:
            orientation = @"Unknown";
            break;
        default:
            break;
    }
    NSLog(@"Orientation: %@", orientation);
}
```

You can add this code to `viewDidAppear:` in LMASettingsController.m, so it runs every time the Settings screen is selected. The code gets several pieces of information about the device and prints it to the console to demonstrate what you can find out about the user's device.

1. Get a reference to the device object. Notice that you can't instantiate the object; you just get a reference to it.

2. This is the name the user has given to the device. You could use this if your app might run on several of the user's devices and you need to provide an easy way for the user to distinguish among them.

3. The model of the device, such as iPhone and iPad.

4. The name of the OS, such as iPhone OS.

5. OS Version number.

6. Unique identifier of the app for the vendor. All apps from the same vendor running on one device will have the same value. But the same app on different devices owned by the same user will have different values. You can use this identifier to uniquely identify the devices your app is running on. If a user deletes all your apps and then installs one again, the value will change.

7. The orientation of the device. A switch statement is used to identify all the ways the device can be oriented. Note that the value of this property is of the physical device, regardless of whether your app supports a given orientation.

If you run the app with the code in one of the view controllers, you will likely get output like this for running on the Simulator (time stamps removed for better readability):

```
Device Info:
Name: iPhone Simulator
Model: iPhone Simulator
System Name: iPhone OS
System Version: 7.0
Identifier: <__NSConcreteUUID 0x9a91cd0> 18F70308-D3DF-478F-9584-DF4CE5E96157
Orientation: Unknown
```

The simulator doesn't have a physical orientation, so the orientation is reported as Unknown

And here's an example from running it on one of the authors' iPhone:

```
Device Info:
Name: Jakob's iPhone
Model: iPhone
System Name: iPhone OS
System Version: 7.0
Identifier: <__NSConcreteUUID 0x2089cec0> 01FB524E-AFDC-4E6E-935A-452578FFF9C4
Orientation: Face Up
```

Monitoring Battery Status

One of the hardware devices available through UIDevice is the battery. Although the user always has a battery meter in the status bar of the device, you can use access to the battery information in various ways in your app, such as not starting certain operations if the battery is really low or requiring the device to be plugged in to execute something that is likely to drain the battery significantly.

The pattern for checking the battery is instructive and is used in other situations when developing for iOS. To access the battery information, you set up an NSNotificationCenter object, which provides a mechanism for broadcasting information within a program. In this case, you will set up a view controller to be an observer to changes in either the charge level of the battery or its charging state (full, plugged in, or unplugged). When either of these events occur, a method is called in the view controller and you can take appropriate action.

It isn't particularly relevant to MyContactList to monitor the battery status, but to demonstrate how it works you will add a simple battery indicator to the Settings screen, showing the battery charge level and state (see Figure 14.1). You will need a physical device to test this code, because the simulator doesn't simulate a battery. When you run the app, the battery percentage doesn't always match the one listed in the status bar. This is because of limitations in the API available to developers limiting updates to every few minutes and to increments of 5%.

Figure 14.1   Battery monitor.

Start by setting up the user interface. Open Storyboard and add a label to the top-right corner of the Settings screen. Use the Attributes Inspector to right-align the text in the label, and the Size Inspector to set the width to **100** pixels. Add an outlet for the label called lblBattery. To start monitoring the battery and update the label with the battery information, add the code in Listing 14.2 to the end of viewDidLoad: in LMASettingsController.m.

Listing 14.2   **Start Monitoring the Battery Status**

```
UIDevice *device = [UIDevice currentDevice];                          //1
device.batteryMonitoringEnabled = YES;                               //2
[[NSNotificationCenter defaultCenter]                                 //3
                      addObserver:self
                      selector:@selector(batteryChanged:)
                      name:@"UIDeviceBatteryLevelDidChangeNotification"
                      object:device];
[[NSNotificationCenter defaultCenter]                                 //4
                      addObserver:self
                      selector:@selector(batteryChanged:)
                      name:@"UIDeviceBatteryStateDidChangeNotification"
                      object:device];
_lblBattery.text = [self batteryStatus];                             //5
```

This is the core piece of code in keeping track of the battery.

1. Get a reference to the device.

2. Start monitoring the battery. You have to do this to get the battery data.

3. To be notified on an ongoing basis, you set up a notification as shown here. Each of the four parameters is important to understand.

   - addObserver: This adds the view controller (the current object is referred to as 'self' in Objective-C) as an observer to the notification center.

   - selector: This has the name of the method that will be called when the event occurs. The method is shown in Listing 14.3.

   - name: The name of the event being observed. In this case it is the notification that the battery level changed.

   - object: This indicates the object where the notification is coming from.

   Taken together, this method sets up a notification that when the level of the battery changes in the device, an event is generated that calls the batteryChanged method in the current class.

4. Monitoring for changes in the battery charging status (full, plugged in, or unplugged) is set up in the same way. Notice that the method to be called is the same, but the name of the notification object is different.

5. Set the text on the label by calling the method `batteryStatus` (Listing 14.3). Notifications about changes in battery level occur about every minute, so rather than relying only on the notification to update the status, this call updates it immediately.

After you have entered the code in Listing 14.2, you will see several warnings and errors in Xcode, because you still need to code the two methods referenced that actually handle the changes to the status. These are both shown in Listing 14.3.

Listing 14.3 Handling Changes to the Battery Status

```
- (void)batteryChanged:(NSNotification *)notification            //1
{
    _lblBattery.text = [self batteryStatus];
}


-(NSString *) batteryStatus
{
    UIDevice *device = [UIDevice currentDevice];                 //2

    NSString *batteryState;
    switch (device.batteryState) {                              //3
        case UIDeviceBatteryStateCharging:
            batteryState = @"+";
            break;
        case UIDeviceBatteryStateFull:
            batteryState = @"!";
            break;
        case UIDeviceBatteryStateUnplugged:
            batteryState = @"-";
            break;
        default:
            batteryState = @"?";
            break;
    }
    float batteryLevelPercent = device.batteryLevel * 100;       //4
    NSString *batteryLevel = [NSString stringWithFormat:@"%.0f%%", //5
                                            batteryLevelPercent];
    NSString *batteryStatus = [NSString stringWithFormat:@"%@ (%@)", //6
                          batteryLevel, batteryState];
    return batteryStatus;
}
```

The `batteryChanged:` method is called whenever notification is sent for either a change in battery level or battery state. The `batteryStatus:` method is called by both `viewDidLoad:` and `batteryChanged:` to actually get the values from the battery and create a formatted display for the label.

1. The `batteryChanged:` method is very simple. Whenever a notification occurs, it calls `batteryStatus:` and updates `lblBattery` with the result. The method can be called with two notifications, but in this case, the label is updated with the results, regardless of which notification occurs. If you need to distinguish between notifications, you can use the name attribute of the notification object.

2. In the `batteryStatus:` method, the first step is to get a reference to the device that we can use to get the battery information.

3. The battery state is reported as an integer, so to turn it into a string symbol, you can use a switch statement. The switch statement shows all the possible values for the battery state.

4. The battery level is reported as a float between 0 and 1, so it is multiplied with 100 to turn it into a percentage value.

5. Format the numerical float value as a string with no decimal places followed by a percent sign (use two percent symbols to get a percent sign included in the string).

6. Concatenate the level and state strings into the final string to be returned.

If you run the app, you should see the battery information on the Settings screen. If you have turned on the option in your device to show the battery percentage in the status bar (Settings > General Usage > Battery Percentage), you'll notice that the number doesn't necessarily match what the battery indicator in the status bar shows. This is because the notification is sent, at most, once a minute and is reported in 5% increments, whereas the system supplied percentage in the status bar is far more accurate. If you ran the app in the Simulator, the display would show -100% (?), because the Simulator doesn't include battery simulation.

If you want to just check the battery status to see if an operation can proceed rather than monitor the status, you don't need to set up the notifications, but you do need to enable battery monitoring as shown by item 2 in Listing 14.2. When you are done checking the battery, you should turn off the monitoring.

Controlling the Camera

There are a couple different ways to capture images within an iOS app. The simplest method involves using a built-in navigation controller that contains all the necessary controls to take a picture and return it to your app.

To expand the MyContactList app to allow for taking a picture, you have to carry out the following steps:

1. Make room in the UI for the image and a button to take/choose an image.

2. Implement code to bring up camera control.

3. Change Core Data design to make room for the picture (and control migration of existing data).

4. Save the image to Core Data.

5. Make sure the image is brought back to UI when view control is loaded.

The first step is to change the UI layout in the Contacts editing screen. If you make the Contact field a little shorter, you can then drag a UIImage view and place in the top-right corner of the screen. Then drag a button and place it to the left of the image toward the top. To make the button easier to interpret and smaller, you can add an image icon to the button.

1. Use the same Glyphish icons you used previously, but this time drag 86-camera.png to the images.xcassets folder in the project.

2. Select the button and in the Attributes Inspector in the right pane in Xcode, delete the Title text and use the drop-down by Image to choose 86-camera.

3. Drag the button to reposition, as shown in Figure 14.2.

Figure 14.2   User interface for adding an image to a Contact.

Set up an outlet for the image named imgContactPicture and wire the button to an action called changePicture. Specify that the controller should implement UIImagePickerControllerDelegate and UINavigationControllerDelegate by adding the two delegates to the end of the @interface line in LMAContactsController.h:

```
@interface LMAContactsController : UIViewController
➥<UIImagePickerControllerDelegate, UINavigationControllerDelegate>
```

Next, switch to LMAContactsController.m and add this line inside the `@implementation` section at the top, right next to the definition of birthdate:

```
BOOL atLeastIOS6;
```

Add this line to the end of `viewDidLoad:` to give the variable a value:

```
atLeastIOS6 = [[[UIDevice currentDevice] systemVersion] floatValue] >= 6.0;
```

This uses the information about the device the app is running on to check the version of the operating system. You will see a little further down how this information is used to avoid the app crashing on devices running older versions of the operating system.

Next, you implement the button's action method, as shown in Listing 14.4.

Listing 14.4 **Launching the Image Picker**

```
- (IBAction)changePicture:(id)sender {
    if([UIImagePickerController isSourceTypeAvailable:            //1
➥UIImagePickerControllerSourceTypeCamera]){
        UIImagePickerController *cameraController =[[UIImagePickerController   //2
➥alloc] init];
        cameraController.sourceType = UIImagePickerControllerSourceTypeCamera;  //3
        cameraController.delegate = self;                         //4
        cameraController.allowsEditing = YES;                     //5
        if(atLeastIOS6){                                          //6
            [self presentViewController:cameraController
                              animated:YES
                            completion:nil];
        }
        else{ //deprecated from iOS 6                             //7
            [self presentModalViewController:cameraController
                                    animated:YES];
        }
    }
}
```

This code is executed when the user taps the camera button to bring up the camera controller.

  1. Not all iOS devices have a camera, so to avoid the app crashing if the camera isn't present, you should always check for the presence of hardware sensors. It doesn't seem very logical to ask `UIImagePickerController` whether a camera is available, but that is the recommended pattern.

  2. This statement creates the controller for the camera.

3. The controller can be used to capture video as well as stills. The `sourceType` property can be used to restrict to only one of them, as it is done here because only the still camera option will work for this app. If this is not set, the camera control will include a toggle to allow the user to choose.

4. Set the camera delegate to the view controller, so any method calls from the camera controller can be handled (Listing 14.5 is a delegate method).

5. If you set the `allowsEditing` property to `YES`, the user will be allowed to move and scale the image after it has been taken.

6. With iOS 6, the approach to presenting a view controller changed, and the old method was deprecated. This statement illustrates how to handle this situation by checking the OS version number. The actual presenting of the view controller is completely standard, as you've seen before.

7. This line is used for older devices and shows the old way of presenting a view controller. You will see a warning in this line, because the code has been deprecated, but this is expected and intentional; the line was added to support older devices that can't use the approach in the previous line.

With `changePicture:` implemented, the camera control now comes up when the camera button is tapped, and the user can take a picture. Figure 14.3 shows the camera user interface for taking the picture and editing after it has been taken. However, nothing happens with the image when the user returns to the app. The picture was supposed to show up in the image view.

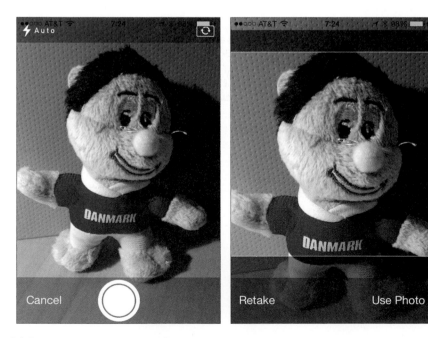

Figure 14.3   Camera controller interface.

To actually do something with the image, you need to implement a delegate method, `imagePickerController:didFinishPickingMediaWithInfo:` that the camera controller will call when it's done with its work (see Listing 14.5).

Listing 14.5 Handling the Image Picker Returned

```
-(void) imagePickerController:(UIImagePickerController *)picker
➥didFinishPickingMediaWithInfo:(NSDictionary *)info
{
    UIImage *image = [info objectForKey:UIImagePickerControllerEditedImage];    //1
    _imgContactPicture.image = image;                                           //2
    if(atLeastIOS6){                                                            //3
        [self dismissViewControllerAnimated:YES completion:nil];
    }
    else{
        [self dismissModalViewControllerAnimated:YES];
    }
}
```

The camera controller is a `UIImagePickerController` that returns its data in an `NSDictionary` called `info`.

1. Get the image that was taken after the user edited it and store it in a `UIImage` variable. Even if the user didn't move or scale the image, the image is still available in this variable. If you want to disregard any edits made by the user, you can retrieve `UIImagePickerControllerOriginalImage` instead.

2. In either case, the image that was returned is assigned to the image control's image property so it shows up in the user interface.

3. Using the proper method for the OS version, dismiss the camera controller so the regular app becomes visible again. If you forget this step, the camera control won't disappear when the user taps Use, so this is very important.

Now you can run the app, take a picture, and see how it shows up in the user interface in the proper place, as shown in Figure 14.4.

To save the image to the database, you first have to make a few changes to the Core Data Model to include the image in the Contact entity.

1. Open MyContactList_CoreData.xcdatamodeld in the project, and click the + under the list of attributes.

2. Add a property named image with a type of **Binary Data**. Be careful if you use the mouse to add the data type in, because the list of attributes is automatically sorted as soon as you enter the name, so you may end up changing the type of the birthday attribute and leaving the image type as undefined. If this happens, you will get compiler errors when you try to run or build it, but they can be fixed by making the birthday a Date type and the image a Binary Data type.

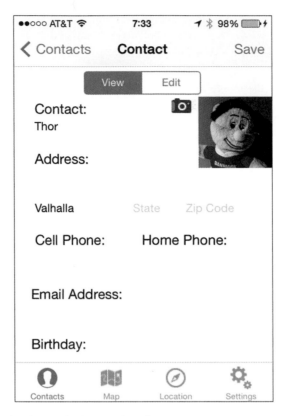

Figure 14.4   Image showing up in the user interface.

3. Go to Editor > Create NSManagedObject Subclass to re-create the Contact class. Go through the wizard. Be sure to check the box next to the data model, and then next to the Contact entity. On the last screen, be sure to check the box next to the Targets for MyContactList to add the file to the project. Accept the option to replace the existing Contact.h and Contact.m. Open Contact.h and check that image was added. You'll note that the data type for image is NSData. This is the Objective-C data type corresponding to binary data.

4. You have now changed the data model design, and if you try to launch the app now, it will crash with an error message about an incompatible version of the data model. This can be fixed by deleting the database files or, for simple changes like this, by requesting that the Persistent Store Coordinator make a lightweight migration of the data model. To do that, start by opening LMAppDelegate.m.

5. Locate the persistentStoreCoordinator: method toward the bottom of the file. Add the code in Listing 14.6 after the long block comment, and just before the NSLog statement. The details of the code are beyond the scope of this book, but it is the code

that runs if there is a problem setting up Core Data. This code requests that an attempt be made to do a lightweight migration from the old data model to the new one. This may succeed in certain situations where the changes are not too significant.

6. Make sure that the image is saved and retrieved from the database. To save the image, you add these two lines to saveContact: in LMAContactsController.m:

```
NSData *imageData = UIImagePNGRepresentation(_imgContactPicture.image);
[contact setValue:imageData forKey:@"image"];
```

Add after all the other fields are added to the contact. The first line converts the image to NSData, and the second line adds it to the contact object.

7. To retrieve the image from the database, add this line along with the other lines for populating the user interface with data from the contact object in viewDidLoad::

```
_imgContactPicture.image = [UIImage imageWithData:_contact.image];
```

This takes an image that's stored as NSData and turns it into a UIImage that can be displayed, and assigns it to the image property of the Image View control.

Try running the app on a device with a camera. If the app crashes with an error message that includes this line:

```
reason = "Can't find model for source store";
```

something went wrong with the lightweight migration. This is prone to happen in development environments. One simple solution is to uninstall the app and launch it again. This will, of course, remove the entire database of contacts, so it isn't a good solution in production environments. However, in production, you should be sure to migrate your users' data using the lightweight migration shown in Listing 14.6 or another approach. You can find more detail about migrating Core Data models in Apple's Core Data Model Versioning and Data Migration Programming Guide.

Listing 14.6   Requesting Lightweight Migration of Core Data

```
NSDictionary *options = [NSDictionary dictionaryWithObjectsAndKeys:
    [NSNumber numberWithBool:YES], NSMigratePersistentStoresAutomaticallyOption,
    [NSNumber numberWithBool:YES], NSInferMappingModelAutomaticallyOption, nil];
BOOL success = [_persistentStoreCoordinator
                        addPersistentStoreWithType:NSSQLiteStoreType
                                     configuration:nil
                                               URL:storeURL
                                           options:options
                                             error:&error];
if (success)
    {
        NSLog(@"Core Data Model converted successfully");
        return _persistentStoreCoordinator;
```

```
    }
    else
    {
        NSLog(@"Error Converting Core Data: %@, %@", error, [error userInfo]);
        abort();
    }
```

You should now be able to add a picture to a contact and have it be saved to the database and show up again in the user interface.

As you have seen, taking a picture is quite easy (Listing 14.4 and 14.5), but handling the image takes a little more work. The controller used to take pictures here is easy to use but not very flexible; it uses a lot of memory and is rather slow. But if you don't need a lot of sophistication, it works well. If you do require more power, you can look at the AVFoundation framework, which allows for very customizable and powerful image solutions.

Calling a Phone Number

One of the most important hardware features of most mobile devices is the phone. You can also integrate the phone functionality into your app by letting the user call relevant numbers from within the app. Calling a phone number launches the Phone app on the phone, but control is returned to your app when the call is done.

Calling a phone number from within your app is very simple and requires only a single line of code:

```
[[UIApplication sharedApplication]openURL:
                        [NSURL URLWithString:@"telprompt://1234567894"]];
```

This tells the phone to launch the URL. Any URL starting with telprompt:// will be treated like a phone number. Other URL schemes open other apps. For instance, http:// opens Safari, and sms:// opens the Message app.

Long Press Gesture

In MyContactList, calling a phone number is a very useful feature. It will be implemented to allow the user to long press on the phone number on the Contact screen to call the number. A *long press* means that the user holds a little longer than a regular tap—about one second. To set this up, you need to add these two lines to viewDidLoad: in LMAContactsController.m:

```
UILongPressGestureRecognizer *longPress = [[UILongPressGestureRecognizer alloc]
                                initWithTarget:self
                                        action:@selector(callPhone:)];

[_txtPhone addGestureRecognizer:longPress];
```

The first line sets up a gesture recognizer, which is a special object that is designed to recognize a long press. The gesture recognizer is given the view controller as a target meaning that any long presses will be sent to the view controller, and the action to take when that happens is specified in the action selector. In this case, the `callPhone:` method is called. The second line adds the gesture recognizer to the `txtPhone` field so that long presses on this field are recognized. It would be convenient to also add the gesture recognizer to the cell phone field; however, only one view can be associated with a gesture recognizer at a time. If you want to have multiple controls recognize a long press, you would have to create a gesture recognizer for each of them.

Next, you need to implement `callPhone:`, which is shown in Listing 14.7.

Listing 14.7   **Method to Call Phone Number on Long Press**

```
- (void)callPhone:(UILongPressGestureRecognizer*)gesture {
    if (gesture.state == UIGestureRecognizerStateBegan) {            //1
        NSLog(@"Long Press");                                       //2
        NSString *phoneURL = [NSString                              //3
                        stringWithFormat:@"telprompt://%@", _txtPhone.text];
        [[UIApplication sharedApplication]openURL:[NSURL URLWithString:phoneURL]]; //4
    }
}
```

This method illustrates several important features.

1. The long press gesture is recognized many times by the system as long as the user keeps holding the finger, so to avoid handling all those events, you should always use an if statement to check the state of the gesture. `UIGestureRecognizerStateBegan` is only called once for an entire gesture press, and this statement will be true only the first time through this method.

2. The simulator doesn't show the phone call, so the `NSLog` statement is included to give some feedback that the long press gesture was recognized.

3. This line of code sets up the string that holds the phone number to call by concatenating the protocol prefix (telprompt://) with the phone number from the `txtPhone` field.

4. The final statement opens the phone number URL using the `sharedApplication` object, which launches the Phone app, which calls the number.

Now you can run the app. If you have an iPhone to run this on, it will prompt you with an Alert View asking you to call the number (see Figure 14.5). If you run the app on the simulator, you need to watch the console for the Long Press message when you click and hold the phone number. One thing to note is that the long press currently works only when the Contacts screen is in edit mode, because the Text Field is disabled in view mode.

Fixing this requires a few careful changes to make sure the app still works as intended.

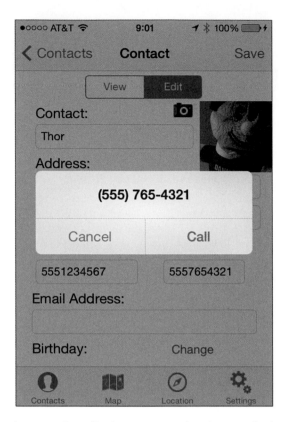

Figure 14.5   Calling phone number after long press gesture is recognized.

Adding Long Press to Enabled Text Field

The UIResponder class is responsible for all the events that happen in the user interface of iOS apps. It is the superclass of UIApplication and UIView, and thus, all
of their subclasses, including UITextField. One of the methods in UIResponder
is canPerformAction:withSender:, which is implemented in the subclasses of
UIResponder to allow them to specify whether they can perform a particular action. In
UITextField, the action that is relevant to be carried out is to begin editing the text
field. Normally, canPerformAction:withSender: will return YES for UITextField.
However, if the txtPhone field would return NO when it is in view mode, it could be kept
enabled but still not allow editing. By creating a subclass of UITextField that overrides
canPerformAction:withSender:, you can control more precisely whether the field can be
edited or not. This subclass can then have a Boolean variable that specifies whether the text
field is in edit mode, which is then what canPerformAction:withSender: will return.

Here's how to set it up:

1. Add a new Objective-C class named `LMAPhoneTextField` that is a subclass of `UITextField`.

2. Add a property to the .h file with this definition:

   ```
   @property (nonatomic) BOOL editMode;
   ```

   This sets up a Boolean to specify whether the text field can be edited.

3. Implement `canPerformAction:withSender:` in LMAPhoneTextField.m with this code, to return the value of the `editMode` property that you just set up:

   ```
   -(BOOL)canPerformAction:(SEL)action withSender:(id)sender
   {
       return _editMode;
   }
   ```

4. The next steps then change the implementation of the `txtPhone` field to use the new subclass. Open Storyboard and select the `txtPhone` field on the Contact screen.

5. Go to the Identity Inspector in the right pane in Xcode and change Class to `LMAPhoneTextField`.

6. Add an import statement for LMAPhoneTextField.h to LMAContactsController.h and then change the data type of the `txtPhone` outlet in LMAContactsController.h, like this:

   ```
   @property (weak, nonatomic) IBOutlet LMAPhoneTextField *txtPhone;
   ```

7. The last step is to make a few changes to `changeEditMode:` in LMAContactsController.m as shown in Listing 14.8.

Listing 14.8 **Setting the Editing Mode for the `txtPhone` Field**

```
- (IBAction)changeEditMode:(id)sender {
    NSArray *textFields = @[_txtName, _txtAddress, _txtCity, _txtState,
                            _txtZip, _txtPhone, _txtCell, _txtEmail];
    if (_sgmtEditMode.selectedSegmentIndex == 0){
        for (UITextField *txtfield in textFields) {
            [txtfield setEnabled:NO];
            [txtfield setBorderStyle:UITextBorderStyleNone];
        }
        [_btnChange setHidden:YES];
        [_txtPhone setEnabled:YES];                                    //1
        _txtPhone.editMode = NO;                                       //2
    }
    else if (_sgmtEditMode.selectedSegmentIndex == 1)
    {
        for (UITextField *txtfield in textFields) {
            [txtfield setEnabled:YES];
```

```
            [txtfield setBorderStyle:UITextBorderStyleRoundedRect];
        }
        [_btnChange setHidden:NO];
        _txtPhone.editMode = YES;                                    //3
    }
}
```

The three numbered lines are what you need to add to the method to properly set the edit mode on the txtPhone field.

1. When View mode is selected, the edit mode is set to NO. The loop above has disabled the field along with all the other text fields. However, the txtPhone field needs to be kept enabled.

2. But the editMode property is set to NO to avoid the user editing the field.

3. When Edit mode is selected, all the text fields are enabled in the loop, and now the editMode property is also set to YES, so editing is allowed.

Run the app again and make sure the phone field behaves as it's supposed to while still recognizing the long-press gesture.

Using Core Motion for Accelerometer Data

Included in iOS is a framework called Core Motion, which provides access to several sensors, including gyroscope, magnetometer, and accelerometer. In this section, you learn how to access the data from the accelerometer to move an object around the screen of the device by tilting the device.

The accelerometer provides data about the velocity that the device is moving in in three dimensions. If the device is held vertically in front of you, the X-axis measures movement left and right, the Y-axis measures movement away from and toward you, and the Z-axis measures movement up and down. When working with the accelerometer, you create an object of the class CMMotionManager. It's important to create only a single instance of this class in your app to avoid performance issues. After the CMMotionManager is created, you set up a block of code to execute asynchronously anytime motion data is updated. You can set an update interval to make sure the app receives all the data it needs without causing too much performance drain. To keep battery drain to a minimum, it's important to also remember to stop the accelerometer updates when they are no longer needed.

Device movement is not relevant to MyContactList, so you will do something a little silly and have the battery display you added previously move around the Settings screen when the user tilts the device.

To make sure that only a single instance of CMMotionManager is created, the instantiation is handled in the application delegate, and any other class that needs accelerometer data will then get a reference to the single object. Here's how to set up the app delegate:

1. Add the `CoreMotion` framework to the project by clicking the blue project icon in the left navigation pane and scrolling down in the General tab to the Linked Frameworks and Libraries and clicking the plus button.

2. Add an import statement for `<CoreMotion/CoreMotion.h>` to LMAAppDelegate.h.

3. Add this property:

   ```
   @property (readonly) CMMotionManager *motionManager;
   ```

4. Synthesize the property in LMAAppDelegate.m by adding this line of code:

   ```
   @synthesize motionManager;
   ```

   Then implement the method in Listing 14.9 for any clients to call when they need the motion manager object.

Listing 14.9   **Creating the `CMMotionManager` Object**

```
- (CMMotionManager *)motionManager
{
    if(!motionManager) motionManager = [[CMMotionManager alloc]init];
    return motionManager;
}
```

The method is very simple. It checks whether the `motionManager` property is nil, and if so, it creates a new `CMMotionManager` object. Otherwise, it just returns the existing object.

Next, open LMASettingsController.m and add an `import` statement for `<CoreMotion/CoreMotion.h>` and the method in Listing 14.10 to retrieve the motion manager from the app delegate as needed.

Listing 14.10   **Retrieving the Motion Manager from the App Delegate**

```
-(CMMotionManager *)motionManager
{
    CMMotionManager *motionMManager = nil;                                    //1
    id appDelegate = [[UIApplication sharedApplication] delegate];            //2
    if([appDelegate respondsToSelector:@selector(motionManager)]) {          //3
        motionMManager = [appDelegate motionManager];
    }
    return motionMManager;
}
```

This method shows an alternative approach to getting a reference to the app delegate that doesn't require importing the delegate code.

1. Set up a variable to hold the CMMotionManager reference.

2. Get a reference to the app delegate. By using id as the data type, there is no need to add an import statement for LMAAppDelegate.h.

3. Instead, this line asks whether the app delegate retrieved contains the method motionManager:. If it does, the method is called to get a reference to the motion manager object.

Next, add the method in Listing 14.11 to start the detection of motion.

Listing 14.11 **Start Motion Detection**

```
-(void) startMotionDetection
{
    CMMotionManager *mManager = [self motionManager];                      //1
    [mManager setAccelerometerUpdateInterval:0.05];                        //2
    [mManager startAccelerometerUpdatesToQueue:[[NSOperationQueue alloc]init]  //3
                    withHandler:^(CMAccelerometerData *data, NSError *error)
    {
        dispatch_async(dispatch_get_main_queue(),^{                        //4
            [self updateLabel:data];                                      //5
        });
    }
    ];
}
```

Several of the elements in this method are beyond the scope of this book, so the explanations are not intended to be a full exploration.

1. Call the motionManager method in Listing 14.10 to get the motion manager object from the app delegate.

2. Set the update interval for the accelerometer in seconds. This interval corresponds to updates 20 times per second. The interval of updates can be set for updates as frequently as 100 times per second.

3. Start the updates to the accelerometer with a completion handler that will be executed each time the accelerometer's update interval occurs. The accelerometer provides its results in the data parameter as a CMAcceleromterData object, which contains the x, y, and z velocities.

4. To avoid blocking the main thread in the program, this statement sends the updates of the UI to be executed asynchronously.

5. Call the updateLabel method (Listing 14.12) to update the label's movements around the screen.

Next, add the `updateLabel:` method as shown in Listing 14.12.

Listing 14.12   **Update Label to Be Moved Around the Screen**

```
-(void) updateLabel: (CMAccelerometerData *) data
{
    float moveFactor = 15;                                              //1
    CGRect rect = _lblBattery.frame;                                   //2
    float moveToX = rect.origin.x + (data.acceleration.x * moveFactor); //3
    float moveToY = (rect.origin.y + rect.size.height) - (data.acceleration.y *
➥moveFactor);                                                          //4
    float maxX = self.view.frame.size.width - rect.size.width;         //5
    float maxY = self.view.frame.size.height;                          //6
    if(moveToX > 0 && moveToX < maxX){                                 //7
        rect.origin.x += (data.acceleration.x * moveFactor);
    }
    if(moveToY > rect.size.height && moveToY < maxY){                  //8
        rect.origin.y -= (data.acceleration.y * moveFactor);
    }
    [UIView animateWithDuration:0 delay:0                              //9
                        options:UIViewAnimationOptionCurveEaseInOut
                     animations:^{ _lblBattery.frame = rect; }
                     completion:nil];
}
```

This method is called 20 times per second with new accelerometer data and moves the label to its new position based on data in the accelerometer. In this case, only movement along the x and y axes are used, and not the z-axis.

1. The `moveFactor` is a multiplier that decides how far the label is moved with each update.

2. Get a rectangle based on the frame around the label. The rectangle is used in the calculations of where to move the label.

3. Calculate the next position along the x-axis by multiplying the `moveFactor` with the acceleration along the x-axis and adding it to the original x-axis location of the label. The accelerometer data is reported between -1 and 1, with 0 being at rest.

4. Repeat for the y-axis.

5-6. To keep the label from moving off the screen, the dimensions of the screen are calculated, taking the width of the label into account.

7. Check to see if the new position will move the label off the screen along the x-axis, and if not, update the x value for the position of the label.

8. Repeat for the y-axis. This time you have to take the height of the label into account.

9. Update the display by animating the movement from the old to the new location. By setting `duration` and `delay` to 0, the animation is carried out immediately (and thus not really animated), but if you had an object you wanted to animate from one location to another, you could set the duration to some value in seconds and it will then be animated from one place to another on the screen. The `options` parameter is a way to specify how the animation is done. In this case, the label is moved a small distance each time, so no transition is needed. The `animations` parameter is where you specify the code that will run to update the display. In this case, it is the animation of moving the label from its original location to the newly calculated one. If you wanted to run code after the animation was done, you could add a similar block in the `completion` parameter.

The only thing left is to start the collection of accelerometer data and then stop it again. In this case, the animation should keep going as long as the user is viewing the Settings screen, but stop as soon as the user leaves it. The ideal place to achieve this is to start in `viewDidAppear:` and stop in `viewDidDisappear:` Add the following line to the end of `viewDidAppear:` to start the motion detection:

```
[self startMotionDetection];
```

Then add the `viewDidDisappear:` method, as shown in Listing 14.13, to stop the motion detection when the user leaves the Settings screen.

Listing 14.13 Stop Motion Detection

```
-(void)viewDidDisappear:(BOOL)animated
{
    [[self motionManager] stopAccelerometerUpdates];
}
```

The method is very simple; it gets the motion manager and stops the updates of accelerometer data.

If you run the app, you should now be able to tilt the device and have the label move around the screen. You may notice that the app doesn't handle rotation particularly well, sending the label offscreen. To keep your app in portrait mode, you can open the General tab on the project information screen in Xcode and uncheck all but Portrait for the supported Device Orientations. Being able to support both landscape and portrait modes is important, but it is beyond the scope of this book to discuss the details of how to make sure the user interface works in both modes.

Summary

With the skills you have learned in this chapter, you have the foundation to start taking advantage of using the hardware features of the user's device in your own apps. When you do so, be careful to check for the availability of sensors on the device and turn off sensors when not needed to avoid draining the battery. For most of the examples in this chapter, it is necessary to have a physical device for testing, because the Simulator doesn't simulate most of the hardware sensors.

Exercises

1. Make sure the camera button shows up only on devices that support a camera.

2. Make sure the camera button is shown and hidden appropriately when the user changes between edit and view modes.

3. Implement a long-press recognizer for the cell phone field, but instead of calling the number, send a message.

4. Create a new Single-View project and use the accelerometer data to create a simple game where the player gets points by tapping a button that can be moved around the screen by tilting the device.

5. Add three sliders and use them to display the accelerometer data in all three dimensions in real-time.

Part IV

Business Issues

Monetizing Apps

The market for apps is big and getting bigger. Vision Mobile has estimated the mobile app economy to be worth $53 billion in 2012 and growing to $143 billion in 2013. How do you get a piece of that pie? You've created and tested a great app. Now you want your efforts to pay off. What is the best way to do this? What options do you have to make money from apps? What do you have to do to start? In this chapter you explore the various avenues for monetizing apps.

App Monetization Strategies

Making money from apps is possible but difficult. There are hundreds of thousands of apps available. The revenue generated from an individual app is typically very small, and the app stores take a 30% cut of all the revenue that your app generates. How do you get people to pay you to use yours? What are the different ways you can collect money for the use of your apps? More importantly, how can you get a lot of people to pay you to use the app so that the revenue generated is enough to fund further development or expansion? These are some of the questions that many developers are asking. Some questions have concrete answers. Others are still very much open for debate.

Paid Apps

The simplest approach to monetizing an app is to charge for the download. The price is advertised in the app store and the user decides, based on your description of the app, whether to buy it. If the user buys the app, you get the money. No need to worry about getting clicks or designing features to be purchased. The problem is getting enough customers to generate significant income. One approach to solving this problem is to raise the price of the app. However, as the price of the app goes up, the number of downloads goes down. As mentioned before, the market is very price sensitive. You will need a very enticing description of your app to get downloads. Additionally, after users have purchased the app, future updates are free. You would need to add a new app to charge again.

A significant problem for all strategies, which is exacerbated with paid apps, is getting the potential customer to find your app among the thousands of apps in the app stores. If the user searches the app store using keywords, and your app is displayed along with a number of free apps, the user will often not even read your app's description, focusing only on the free ones. To attempt to remedy this, you need to advertise. Advertising is a double-edged sword. It costs money! Even a limited Google ad campaign where you pay Google to display an ad whenever someone searches on a set of keywords costs hundreds of dollars. It takes a lot of $.99 app sales to cover this cost.

An up-and-coming approach to the paid app approach is to build apps for business use. An app such as Bossy (described in Chapter 1, "Why Mobile Apps?") is designed to solve a business problem. A Bossy download costs $24.99. However, if your app solves a business problem, a business will be happy to pay the cost. This approach does require marketing. It is unlikely that businesses will search the Play Store for a solution to their business problems. This approach requires a much larger commitment than is typical for many app developers. It requires a business plan, establishing a target market, and directly contacting the market with information about your product. It also requires a potentially significant monetary investment.

Ad Supported Apps

The app market is very price sensitive. Free apps get downloaded at a much greater rate than any paid app. However, a totally free app is hard to make money with. That is why although many apps appear to be free, they often have a way to make money built within the app. The most common approach to making money from a free app is to embed ads within the app screens. Ads take up screen real-estate, so you will have to plan and code the user interface with this in mind.

Because setting up for supporting ads in your app mostly involves registering for the ads with either Google or Apple, as well as submitting bank account information (so you can be paid) and a W-9 tax form (so you can pay taxes on your ad revenue), it isn't feasible to have a tutorial in this chapter on setting up ads. Instead, here are the basic steps you need to follow to embed ads in an Android app, after you have properly registered for AdMob with Google:

1. Download the Google AdMob Ads SDK using the SDK manager. You will find it under the `extras` folder in the SDK manager.

2. Copy the downloaded `GoogleAdMobAds` file to the `libs` folder of your application. If the folder is not present, create it.

3. Right-click the `GoogleAdMobAds` jar file in the `libs` folder and select Build Path > Add to build the path.

4. Open a layout file and add the xml in Listing 15.1 to place the ad widget to the layout.

Listing 15.1 Ad Widget XML

```
<com.google.ads.AdView
     xmlns:ads="http://schemas.android.com/apk/lib/com.google.ads"
     android:id="@+id/adView"
     android:layout_width="wrap_content"
     android:layout_height="wrap_content"
     android:textStyle="normal"
     ads:adSize="BANNER"
     ads:adUnitId="your ad mob id" />
```

5. Add the code in Listing 15.2 to the onCreate or onResume method of the activity that uses the layout. This code can be added to any method you want. It retrieves a new ad each time it is executed. The line that is commented out is for testing. To test, uncomment the line, find your testing device ID, and enter it. Unfortunately, finding your ID is not simple. It must be accessed by downloading an app (search for device ID), or you can look at the logcat in Eclipse when your device is attached. There is no way to get it directly from the device.

Listing 15.2 Code to Retrieve an Ad

```
AdView adview = (AdView)findViewById(R.id.adView);
AdRequest re = new AdRequest();
// re.addTestDevice("test device id");
adview.loadAd(re);
```

6. The final step is to add the ad activity to the manifest file. Add the code in Listing 15.3 after all other activity declarations in the manifest file.

Listing 15.3 Add Ad Activity to Manifest

```
<activity
    android:name="com.google.ads.AdActivity"
    android:configChanges="keyboard|keyboardHidden|orientation|
        ➥screenLayout|uiMode|screenSize|smallestScreenSize">
</activity>
```

You can also use AdMob in an iOS app. Download the SDK from https://developers.google.com/mobile-ads-sdk/download#downloadios. The process to add an ad to an iOS project is a bit lengthy to discuss here, but in essence you add the Objective-C files and the AdSupport Framework from the unzipped download file to your project and then add the ad view where needed to your xib files. A complete description of the process is located at https://developers.google.com/mobile-ads-sdk/docs/.

To use AdMob to make money from ads on your app, as well as test the ads, you need to sign up with AdMob (www.google.com/ads/admob/). Ads generate money for you only when they are clicked. Each click generates only a few cents, so you need a lot of clicks to make any real income. For example, we have a free card game on Android that is ad supported. It has been downloaded by almost a thousand people. The money it generates is measured in dollars per month. In contrast, we have an app that costs $1.99. It gets only a couple of downloads per month but generates as much money as the more frequently downloaded and used ad-supported app.

Apple also offers its own ad network, called iAd, which provides the same features as AdMob, and is built in to the iOS platform. To enable iAd support in your app, you need to sign up for the iAd Network on iTunes Connect and explicitly enable it for each app that will have iAd support. Then you can import the iAd framework and add an `ADBannerView` control to the view controller. Unlike Google's ad service, iAd pays both for clicks on the ad and per impression (displays of ad in your app). However, the rate per impression is very small.

In-App Purchases

Making enough money from ad-supported apps to support a business is difficult. You need a very popular app to generate a significant amount of money. Another approach for monetization is to release a free app that is supported by in-app purchases. The basic theory for an in-app purchase monetization strategy is that you generate downloads with the free app, get the users hooked, and then allow them to add features by advertising the feature in the app. The sale is made during use of the app. This is a very popular approach among app developers. In fact, more than 75% of the revenue going to iPhone developers in February 2013 came from in-app purchases. Another advantage over the basic paid app is that in-app purchasing opens up the possibility of a regular revenue stream from the same user, instead of relying on a single purchase up front.

In-app purchasing is one way to establish a *freemium* business model, where most of your users use the free version, but a small percentage becomes heavily invested in your app and service and convert to paying for the service, thus underwriting the free experience for everyone else.

You can use several approaches to create products for in-app purchase. Most are dependent on the type of app and its designed use. Game apps often limit the user to only a few game levels and then provide an in-app purchase option for moving to the next level. Other games have consumables that can be purchased during game use. For example, a number of lives are purchased and used up. If users want to continue playing, they have to buy more. Other apps include features that can be unlocked with an in-app purchase. For example, an app may have a mapping feature, such as in the MyContactList app. The button opens the map screen but rather than display the contact, it presents the user with a message that the feature needs to be purchased before the contacts will be displayed. Another approach is to limit the amount of data that can be saved or the number of times the app can be used before the user needs to pay for it. Finally, if your app includes access to content, that content could be purchased on a subscription basis. For example, services that provide weather information cost the developer money, depending on the number of times the weather service is accessed. If the user wants that information in the app, the developer could charge a subscription fee to cover the cost and generate revenue for themselves. Often an in-app purchase strategy is combined with an ad-supported strategy. The free version includes ads that are eliminated as a bonus for an in-app purchase.

To implement in-app purchases in Android, you have to get the Google Play Billing Library from the Android SDK Manager. It is found in the extras folder in the SDK manager. Import the `IInAppBillingService.aidl` file into the `src` folder of your project. Also import the files in the `util` folder of the example app included in the library. Complete information on implementing in-app purchases in Android is available here: http://developer.android.com/google/play/billing/index.html.

Implementing in-app purchases in iOS is easier because all you have to do to get the code is add the `StoreKit` framework to your project. The complete process is too detailed for coverage here, but complete information is available at http://developer.apple.com/library/ios/#documentation/NetworkingInternet/Conceptual/StoreKitGuide/Introduction/Introduction.html.

Understanding the Economics of App Stores

Often developers are surprised that they have to pay Google and Apple 30% of any sales made in the app stores (whether from paid apps or in-app purchases). We have often heard from clients that paying 30% to Google and Apple makes it impossible to do business, because they don't have 30% margins in the rest of their business to give away. To the extent that a mobile app sale replaces a regular sale of the same product, this argument makes sense. However, if the sales of the mobile apps are often incremental to the rest of the business, the additional revenue could be lower.

You have to remember that you pay Apple and Google to set up an entirely new sales channel. They run and operate the stores, so you don't have to worry about setting up a new infrastructure to handle sales of mobile apps.

If you wanted to avoid giving 30% of your sales to Google and Apple, you can carry out the sales outside of the app stores. For instance, you could set up your own website where users register for an account and then any sales made on your website could be made accessible to the app with a login in the app. This is the model that Amazon uses with the Kindle app. If you want to read a Kindle book on a mobile device, you buy the book on Amazon's website, and then you log in to the Kindle app and your content from Amazon is available to you.

Apple is particularly strict about restrictions on the purchasing of content outside the app store, so Amazon isn't even allowed to have a link in its app that takes users to their store where they can buy the books.

If you wanted to avoid the need to register users, you could also create a system where you email an unlock code to users who have made a purchase. The app could then unlock specific functionality based on the unlock code. However, you have to be careful in designing the system for the unlock codes, both technically and because of the workload involved. You might find that the work involved makes in-app purchasing more appealing.

Owning Your Own Business

If you are going to sell apps, you should have a business. This is not an absolute requirement. The Play and App Stores will let you sell apps as an individual. However, it is good practice because you can cleanly separate your individual life, income, and assets from your business income and assets. This is important for both tax and liability purposes. The vehicle for setting up your own business is in most cases a Limited Liability Corporation, or LLC.

Create an LLC

An LLC is a legal entity that is organized by registering the business with a state. The process should take no more than an hour or so and cost under $200. The basic process is as follows:

1. Establish the business name. Some form of Limited Liability Corporation, or LLC, should be in the name. Check your proposed name against the database of names maintained by your state to make sure it has not been used.

2. Download the Articles of Organization form from your state and fill it out.

3. Identify a registered agent. This is the individual who will receive legal documents for the business. It can be you.

4. Create an Operating Agreement that details the financial and management responsibilities of the members of the LLC (owners are called members). This is not required by every state but is good practice.

5. File the forms with your state and pay the registration fee.

That's it. You now own a business! The LLC shields your personal assets in the event your app causes a problem that you get sued for. If you are found liable, they can take your business assets but not touch your personal assets. An LLC is also useful for tax purposes. The expenses you have incurred during app development, distribution, and marketing can be subtracted from the revenue you receive. The final number, whether it is positive or negative, is then transferred to your personal income taxes. If the number is positive, you will pay taxes through your personal income. If the number is negative, it reduces the amount of personal income taxes you pay.

Plan Your Business

If you plan to sell your app, you should get an LLC. However, you do not necessarily have to plan your business. If the app is a passion for you and you don't necessarily want to run a business, don't worry about it. Just put it on the market and keep it up to date. However, if you want to try to make real money in the app development business, you should develop a business plan.

The details of developing a business plan are not covered here. There are many resources available on the Web to help you do this. The Small Business Administration (www.sba.gov) is an excellent resource. The purpose here is to encourage you to do so. There are many benefits to the act of developing a business plan. Developing the plan will help you think about what the mission of your organization is, who the market is, who the competitors are, and how you want to run your business. Making a significant amount of money from apps requires money for marketing and development. A good business plan is a necessary condition for attracting enough capital to develop and test the app and begin establishing demand for your products.

Other Income Possibilities

Making money from selling apps or advertising in apps is possible. However, your income is very dependent on how successful your app is in terms of number of downloads. In fact, only a limited number of app development organizations get the lion's share of the billion dollar market place described earlier in this chapter. The rest of the market is divided up by thousands of developers. Even so, you should create, publish, and attempt to monetize an app in at least one of the markets. This will give the knowledge and "street cred" to make money in other ways from app development. Although the authors of this book have several apps available in both markets, we make far more money doing training and consulting than we do from the monetization of our apps.

One of the surest ways to make money from app development is to get paid to do it for someone else. This way, you get paid whether the app sells or not. App developers are a very hot commodity in the business world. The average salary for an app developer employed by an organization is around $100K/year. You have to sell a lot of $.99 apps each year to make this kind of money. If you establish your ability by publishing apps for both iOS and Android, you can greatly increase your marketability. This is true if you are willing to work for a corporation or if you want to work for yourself as an independent developer.

You can approach independent development as a consultant or a contract developer. Developing a consulting business requires business planning. You need to identify your potential market, get your business name out to potential customers, and develop marketing materials to sell your ability to perform the job they need done. Another approach is to become a freelancer. There are sites that post small jobs that businesses need done (for example, www. elance.com). You find a job that you are interested in and place a bid. If the organization accepts your bid, you develop the app for them and get paid when you're done. The advantage to this approach is that you can do it as a sideline business to pick up extra income. The disadvantage is that most projects have fairly small price tags, so it is much more difficult to make a significant income as your only business.

Choosing a Platform

Should you develop for Android or iOS? Both? There are advantages and disadvantages to all three options. You will have to consider your app audience, market size, how committed you are to making a successful app, and what your goals are in publishing an app. Each of the three options will be considered in this section.

What About Windows Phone and Blackberry?

You may have seen the ads for some great handsets from Nokia running Windows Phone 8 and you're a whiz at ASP.NET development, or you really enjoy the experience of a great physical keyboard available on a Blackberry. Why not develop for these platforms as well? Although it may be easy to start developing apps for Windows Phone if you're very comfortable with Visual Studio, C#, and .NET, the market share of the Windows Phone operating system means that you will not have very many potential customers for your apps. Blackberry and Windows Phone are both below 5% market share, so your efforts are likely better spent making sure you have developed great iOS and Android apps.

Android has the biggest market share in terms of devices sold. Therefore, it also has the biggest potential for app sales. However, much of the market growth is outside the United States. Your app would have to have universal appeal to take advantage of the growth. A second problem with the Android smartphone market is that although the market is big, many of the owners of these phones primarily use them as dumb phones. They are not a likely market for your app. Finally, Android app users are much less willing to pay for an app than their iPhone compatriots are. Studies have shown that each iOS user spends about three times as much on apps as an Android user. On the other hand, some industry segments you might target may have a tendency to use Android devices at a much greater rate than iOS devices. In particular, small businesses, such as the fence builder industry discussed in Chapter 1, are primarily Android users, and the potential to develop apps for these industries is very big.

Android has an advantage in that the barrier to entry is lower for the casual developer than it is for iOS. The fee to be a developer is a one-time fee, and all the tools are free. You can develop Android apps on either Windows or Mac computers. Finally, publishing an app is relatively easy. If you want to publish apps for fun, bragging rights, or to demonstrate your credentials as a developer, Android is a good choice.

Although the iOS market is smaller than the Android market, people get iPhones because they want to use the apps. They are much more likely to look for apps to use, and iPhone users are also much more willing to pay for an app. This makes selling an app using the simple paid approach as well as in-app purchase discussed earlier much more feasible. On the other hand, Apple charges a higher annual fee to be a developer, the publishing process is more complicated, and is in no way guaranteed. Finally, you must have a Mac to use Xcode to create your app. You cannot create an iOS app on a Windows machine.

Why not publish on both? If you are trying to make money from apps, this is probably the way to go. You get access to a larger market and thus more potential revenue generation. Additionally, after you've gone through the effort of designing a user experience, user interface, and logic to create an app for one market, you can leverage that effort by creating an app for the other environment. You will have to completely recode the app, but coding is much easier if you already know what you want the app to do. Additionally, many of the control structures are almost identical on the two platforms (for example, a `for` loop) so much of the code structure can be copied directly between the code files. You will have to learn both development environments in-depth, but you've got a good start from what you have learned by completing this book. The primary problem with targeting both markets is that you will have to keep your app current on both platforms. This means more work just to keep the lights on.

Summary

You can make money from mobile apps in several ways. Revenue can be generated through monetization of the app itself using ads, in-app purchase, or charging for the download. If you choose to generate revenue from your apps, you should create a Limited Liability Corporation for both tax and liability purposes. You can also make money by coding apps for other people or organizations as a consultant or freelancer. Finally, money can be made by getting hired as an app developer in a larger company. This is a much more reliable source of income than any of the other approaches.

Exercises

1. Add an ad to the ContactListActivity in the Android version of MyContactList. Be sure to set the test device ID if you want to test it. Try this in the iOS version as well.

2. Write a brief business plan for MyContactList. How would you monetize the app? Who is the market?

3. What kind of app do you want to make? Who is the target audience? How will you monetize it? Why would somebody want your app? How difficult would it be to make?

16

Publishing Apps

Creating an app can be a fun and challenging exercise, but for most developers this is not enough. The finished app has to be available for someone to use to complete the process. Apps are made available to their audience by publishing them. The manner of publication is dependent on the target audience and the platform. The two primary audiences are typically the employees of an organization for which the app was developed or the public. Many aspects of publishing are the same for both audiences. However, some important differences exist that the developer needs to be aware of. Likewise, publishing Android and iOS apps have many similarities and some significant differences. One of the most important differences from publishing traditional desktop software is that the ways to publish mobile apps are much more restricted. For consumer apps, there are gatekeepers in the form of app stores that you will have to interact with to distribute your app. In this chapter you learn the basics of publishing apps for both consumer and enterprise audiences and both platforms.

App Distribution Through the App/Play Stores

Both Apple and Google provide a marketplace where developers can sell their apps. To publish an app in either of these stores, a developer must configure the app and conform to the requirements established by their sponsors. A significant amount of the work required to publish the app should be done during development. Both Google and Apple have requirements and guidelines for apps that should be incorporated during development. You should read through these guidelines prior to development so that you are not doing a lot of rework just to get the app published. Apple is especially meticulous about these rules. Every app is reviewed before it is published, and if your app does not conform, it will be rejected. Google will publish an application that does not meet its store requirements, but will remove the app from the store later if it finds that the app violates its rules.

When you are confident your app meets publication requirements of the market you are targeting, the process of publishing requires several steps in either market and is greatly facilitated by preparing prior to beginning the process. The preparation is similar for both stores. You will need to prepare an icon for your app. Android requires an app icon sized to 512 x 512, whereas iOS requires the icon to be 1024 x 1024 pixels. Both platforms require at least one screenshot of your app for each targeted screen size. If you are targeting Android phones, the required size of the screen shot is 320 x 480. If you are targeting iPhone, you must provide a screenshot for the regular size phone (640 x 960) and the 4-inch display phone (640 x 1136). If you are targeting tablets, you also will need to provide screenshots. You can provide up to eight screenshots for each targeted Android device and up to four screenshots for each targeted iOS device. For iOS apps, you also have to supply a launch image that matches the resolution for the devices that the app will run on (for example, 640 x 1136 for 4-inch phone and 1536 x 2008 for high-resolution iPad). The launch image is displayed while the app is loading and is typically a blank image of what the first screen looks like or a splash screen.

In addition to preparing screenshots, you should also prepare a description of your app. This narrative is presented to potential customers, so you should be as clear as possible in describing exactly what the app is designed to do and why it is advantageous for the customer to buy the app. For iOS apps, you will also have to provide a description of any specific conditions or requirements that the tester will need to know to adequately review your app.

Other considerations prior to beginning the publication process include determining what price you want to charge for the app. In Android, you enter this price. In iOS you will be prompted to select from a set of pricing tiers. You should also determine what general category best describes the app (for example, game, sports, tool, and so on) because you will have to indicate this during the publishing process. Finally, you will need to determine in which countries your app should be made available.

After you have completed the previous steps, you are ready to publish. Although there are many similarities, each store has its own process and requirements. You may want to look at the specific description of the procedure online. To get access to these resources for iOS, go to http://developer.apple.com. You will need to have a developer ID to access these resources. To access Android resources go to http://developer.android.com/distribute/index.html. You do not have to sign in to access this information.

Android Play Store Distribution

The Google Play Store does not provide any copy protection for your app. Instead, Google provides a Licensing Library, which allows developers to add copy protection to their apps. The Licensing Library needs to be added to the workspace just like the Google Play Services library was added (Chapter 7, "Maps and Location in Android"). After the library is added, search the developer site for detailed instructions for adding licensing to your app. When you add licensing to an app, each time the user opens the app, the Play Store is queried to determine whether the user bought the app. If the user did not buy the app, the developer can have the app close or take whatever action is deemed appropriate. If you do not use licensing, your app can be copied to other devices quite easily.

After you have added licensing (if you want to), the app needs to be compiled into a signed Android application package (APK) file. Prior to compiling the app, you need to go through the code and remove any logging operations, all debug breakpoints, and address as many of the warnings identified by Eclipse as you think necessary. To create a signed APK (which is required by the Play Store) you need to set a private key. Fortunately, you can do this using the Export Wizard at the same time you are creating the APK.

1. Right-click the app name in the Package Explorer and select Android Tools > Export Signed Application Package from the pop-up menu. If the export fails because of errors or warnings, you should fix those errors or turn off Lint Error Checking. For an app that you want to put on the market, you should focus on correcting errors before turning off the error checking. If you try this with MyContactList, it will fail because the strings.xml file was not translated into other languages. If you are targeting only English-speaking countries, you can turn off this specific warning by changing your Android preferences (Window > Preferences > Android > Lint Error Checking). Enter **Correctness:Messages** in the Issues: text box and click Missing Translation. Click the Severity: button at the bottom right and select Ignore. Click OK.

2. In the window that opens, make sure that your project name is displayed. If it is, click Next. Otherwise, use the Browse button to select it and then click Next.

3. In the next window, click the Create New Keystore option button, choose a name and location for the keystore, and enter a password (see Figure 16.1). Click Next. Be sure to note the location of the keystore and back it up because after the app is published you will need it for many years.

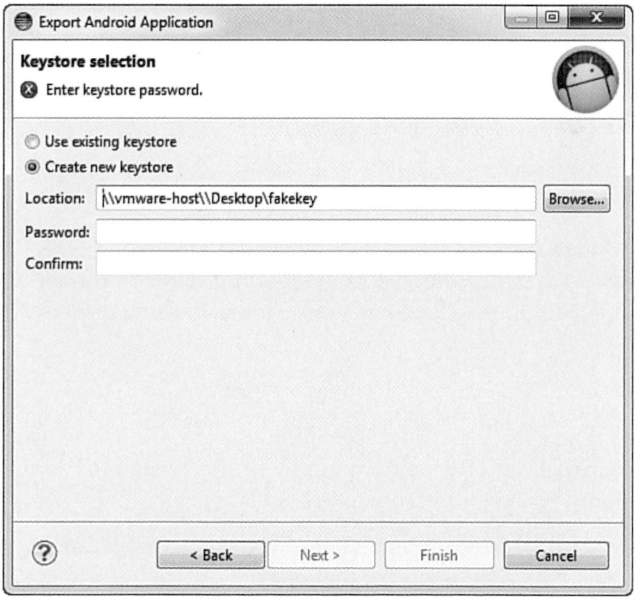

Figure 16.1   Creating a new keystore.

4. On the next window, for alias use the keystore name you entered concatenated with alias. For example, the alias for the keystore named mykeystore would be mykeystorealias. Enter another password for the alias. Enter the number of years you want this key to be valid. Google requires that it be valid past October 22, 2033. Finally, fill in any company information you want and click Next (see Figure 16.2).

Figure 16.2   Key configuration.

5. In the next window, you select where you want the APK to be created. Select a location and click Finish. The signed APK will be created and stored in the specified location. This APK will be uploaded to the Play Store during the publishing process.

An app is published through the Developer Console (https://play.google.com/apps/publish/). To publish apps, you need to sign up as a Google developer. The cost is a one-time fee of $25, which must be paid from a Google Wallet account. If you are going to sell your apps, you will need this account for payments. The account can be set up through the console. After you have set up all your accounts, you are ready to publish!

After setup, the Developer Console displays all the apps you have published. To start, click the + Add New Application button at the top of the screen. You will be prompted to choose the default language and title of your app. Then you can choose to either Upload APK or Prepare Store Listing. It doesn't matter which one you do first. You have to do both eventually.

The left side of the console has a menu with five choices: APK, Store Listing, Pricing and Distribution, In-app Products, and Services & APIs. You have to complete the first three to publish your app. The steps in each are fairly self-explanatory but very detailed, so we will not explain them line by line. The APK menu item is where you upload your app APK. You can upload it for production, or for alpha or beta testing. Alpha testing is usually done by your developers, and beta testing is performed after alpha test by real users. To use either of these features you have to set up a Google Group or Google+ Community. If you upload for testing, it will not be available to the public, but you, your developers, or selected users can test its performance as a user would experience it. The Store Listing menu item is where you provide product details, such as its description and screenshots. You must also categorize the app and provide contact details for you or your company. Finally, in the Pricing and Distribution area, you provide the price for the app and specify the countries where you want to sell it.

When you've completed all three of these items, a green check mark will appear next to each one. You can publish it using the button at the top right of the console. The publishing process takes a few hours before your app appears in the Play Store. Congratulations! You are now in the Android business.

iOS App Store Distribution

The Apple App Store provides strong controls over illegal copying of your app. As a developer, unlike in Android, you don't have to worry about setting up any licensing. However, the built-in copy protection requires other additional work to get your app published. The first step is to set up your Distribution Certificate and Distribution Provisioning Profile (explained in Appendix B, "Installing Xcode and Registering Physical Devices"). The next step is to set up an entry for your app in iTunes Connect (https://itunesconnect.apple.com). You will have to use your developer ID to sign in. iTunes Connect is the website that is used to manage many aspects of your app, including seeing reports on how the app is performing.

In iTunes Connect you provide information about the app, pricing, and screenshots prior to being able to upload the app. To start, click Manage Your Apps in the console. In this section you can add iOS or Mac OS X apps, depending on your developer license. Click Add New App. If you have a Mac Developer account, you will be asked to select either iOS App or Mac OS X app. Select iOS app.

The App Information screen requires selecting the default language of the app, entering the app name, entering a SKU number, and selecting the Bundle ID. The SKU number is a unique number used to identify your app. A standard approach is to concatenate the year of publication, the number of the app in your stock, and the version number. For example your first app could be 201300010001. For Bundle ID, it is best to select Xcode iOS Wildcard AppID and then enter the app name in Bundle ID Suffix. The Bundle ID Suffix must match the name that's entered as the last part of the Bundle Identifier in the Project Summary in Xcode. For the MyContactList app, the Bundle ID you used was com.pearson.MyContactList. The Bundle ID Suffix is MyContactList for this app. When it's complete, click the Continue button.

The next section is too detailed to go through in depth here. In this section you provide an app description, screenshots, icon, rating and categorization, and specific review information, much like you did for your Android app. Once it is complete and you click the Save button, you will get a summary screen for the app. The app status should be listed as Prepare for Upload. Click View Details below the app icon, and then click Ready to Upload Binary at the top right of the next screen. You will be asked to verify that your app is compliant with export laws if it contains any cryptography. Choose the answer that fits your app and click Save, and then Continue. Your app status is now Waiting for Upload. Open your app in Xcode to complete the process.

When your app is open in Xcode, do the following to upload the app to iTunes Connect.

1. Change the active scheme from the simulator to iOS Device in the upper-left corner of Xcode (see Figure 16.3).

Figure 16.3   Changed scheme to iOS Device.

2. Select Product > Archive from the menu. An archive file will be compiled and the Organizer opens (see Figure 16.4).

3. In the Organizer, make sure the latest archive file is selected and click the Validate button. If you have not set up the app correctly in iTunes Connect, you will get an error and will have to go back to the website to correct any problems. Otherwise, it asks you to log in with your developer ID, and validation will begin. This may take a while. If you get a message that there are no issues, you are ready to submit to the App Store.

4. Click the Distribute button. Click the Submit to App Store option button. Click Next.

5. Enter your developer login information (it may already be there). Select an identity. The identity is your Distribution Profile you created earlier (Appendix B). The identity may already be filled in. If so, check to make sure that it is your Distribution Profile. Click the Next button. You will get a message "Your application is being uploaded." This may take a while. When it is complete, you will get a success message. Your app is now waiting to be reviewed by Apple.

The app review process is very thorough and may take several weeks to complete. After the app is accepted, it will be available for purchase. If it is rejected, Apple will inform you of the reason and give you a chance to correct the problems. Generally, your first app takes the longest to get reviewed. Future apps typically get a less-thorough review because you have demonstrated that you can conform to the App Store requirements. Congratulations! You are now in the iOS app business.

Figure 16.4   Xcode Archive Organizer.

App Distribution for the Enterprise

App distribution within an organization differs between iOS and Android. Generally, distribution is easier because you are not required to conform to the specifications of the Play or App stores.

Android Enterprise Distribution

Distributing Android apps within an organization is very easy. You prepare an APK just like you did for the Play Store, and then you give it to your users. The easiest way to do this is by sending users an email with the APK attached. If users open the email on an Android device, the device automatically asks if they want to install it. However, for this to occur, users must have set their device to accept apps from unknown sources. To do this, go to the Settings app on the Android device and check the box next to Unknown Sources. Unfortunately, this item is not located in exactly the same spot in Settings on every Android device. Some common locations are under Applications or Security.

Another approach would be to set up an internal website to distribute the app. Again, accepting apps from unknown sources must be checked. Although these are the two most common approaches, because Android is open, you can choose whatever method works for your organization.

Many organizations also implement Mobile Device Management (MDM) solutions to manage their mobile devices and app distribution. These systems can help organizations implement security controls on both devices owned by employees as well as devices owned by the enterprise. In addition, they can also be used to distribute both in-house and purchased apps to users. A detailed discussion of MDM is well beyond the scope of this book.

iOS Enterprise Distribution

Distribution of iOS apps within the organization is a bit more complicated in iOS than it is in Android. The first step is to get an iOS Enterprise Developer license. The cost of the license is $299 per year but allows unlimited distribution of apps within the organization. You cannot sell apps in the App Store with this license. Organizations that want to do both internal and public development need both an Enterprise Developer license and an iOS Developer license.

Distributing within the organization requires setting up both an enterprise distribution certificate and an enterprise distribution provisioning profile. These are then packaged with the app using Xcode. There is no need to use iTunes Connect with in-house apps. However, the provisioning profile expires after a year. Prior to that time, a new profile must be created, packaged with the app, and redistributed, or the app will stop working.

After an app is compiled with the appropriate certificate and profile, it can be distributed through iTunes, using the iPhone Configuration Utility, or wirelessly from a secure server.

Testing and Fragmentation

Testing is a critical component of app development. This is especially true for Android because of the wide array of devices that the operating system is installed on. However, it is critical that apps developed on either platform be tested on real devices prior to release. However, testing an app is very much like testing any other piece of software in that a comprehensive test plan must be established and followed. Testing should also be performed by individuals outside the development team.

A comprehensive test plan should include thorough black box unit testing, including equivalence partitioning, boundary value analysis, and cause-effect graphing. Fortunately, the innate organization of apps into individual screens makes it easy to test each screen as a unit. To use equivalence partitioning in a screen, identify all the possible outcomes of the user interaction with the screen and identify the input or other data that would lead to that outcome. For example, in the ContactActivity screen in the MyContactList app, there would be nine possible outcomes (refer back to Figure 2.5). Each navigation button opens the corresponding screen, the toggle button enables and disables editing, the Save button saves the contact, the Picture button opens the camera and returns a photo, the Phone buttons open the phone app and dial the correct number, the Change Birth Date button changes the birthday. Each of these outcomes should be tested in every iteration of the app.

In boundary value analysis, the limits for each input should be identified, and each side of the limit should be tested. Again, using the ContactActivity screen as an example, one limit might be that the app shouldn't store birthdays that are a future date. A test for this limit would enter a date equal to the date the app is being tested and the next day. The today's date test should be displayed; the next day's date should result in an error message. Other boundary values for this screen might include entering too many and too few digits for a telephone number.

Finally, in cause-effect graphing, each outcome identified in equivalence partitioning is examined to identify the possible paths that could lead to the expected outcome. For example, the Save button on the ContactActivity screen should either save the contact or alert the user to any errors that may have caused the save to fail. Should the contact be saved only if all the inputs on the screen have data, or is some subset acceptable? Will the app save only a name? If a street address is entered, are the city and state required? All possible combinations that lead to either a saved contact or an error message should be tested.

The testing just described may initially be performed on the Android Emulator or the iOS Simulator, but it should also be performed on an actual device. This is especially true for apps that access the hardware features of the device. Apps that use location or other sensors cannot be adequately tested in either Eclipse's Android emulator or Xcode's iOS simulator.

After all the unit tests have been passed successfully, the app should be tested for usability. The ability to provide help and/or training in the use of your app is extremely limited. Users should be able to figure out how to use it with relative ease. This requires testing by someone unfamiliar with the app. Developers have a relatively difficult time testing this themselves because they are too familiar with the way the app should work.

The final set of tests requires access to a variety of devices. Because of the large number of manufacturers that provide Android devices this is a much more difficult problem in Android than in iOS. For Android, you should have at least one device that runs the minimum SDK and one that runs the target SDK. You also should have one device for each screen size supported by your app. (You can limit screen size in the manifest like you did for minimum and target SDK.) This set of devices should be considered the minimum number required. If possible, you should also test devices from different manufacturers. There are differences, and these can cause interesting problems.

Why Did that Happen?

One of our Android apps uses a standard list similar to what you have seen in Chapter 6, "Lists in Android: Navigation and Information Display." The app worked fine. Then we started getting complaints from users who had a new phone from a specific manufacturer. The manufacturer had made some changes that required a specific attribute value in the `ListItem` to display properly. Although this change couldn't have been foreseen by us, it does illustrate the need to test on multiple devices.

The iOS world has a much more limited set of devices, and the platform is more standardized between devices. However, each device class (iPod touch, iPad, and iPhone) should still be used in testing your app.

Keeping Up with the Platform

Both Apple and Google make changes to their respective operating systems on a regular basis. This can be challenging for developers with apps "in the wild." Updates to the operating system can, and although infrequently, do disrupt apps that previously ran fine. To avoid problems with users of your app or to prevent getting bad reviews in the app stores, it pays to keep on top of platform changes.

Keeping up with changes to the OS is not rocket science, but it does require diligence. At a minimum, as soon as the new OS is released, you should recompile your app to include the new version as a target. Correct any errors that occur when you do this until you get a new version that can be tested on an actual device. Next, get a device with the updated OS installed and run through your complete test plan to ensure that it works on that device. Finally, test the new version of your app on a device running an older version of the OS. When you are satisfied that your app works, release an upgrade to the app through the appropriate app store.

Beyond the bare minimum previously outlined, as a registered developer you also have access to prerelease software so you can test your app in advance of the general release to the public. For instance, Apple typically releases the first beta version of a new version of iOS and Xcode at its WWDC conference in June, several months before the public release in September. Because most iOS users update their devices very quickly after the public release, it's very important that you have tested your app thoroughly before the release.

> ### Why Did That Happen?—Continued
>
> One of our Android apps uses GPS coordinates from the device to record information. After a new release to the OS, any app that was running on an updated device would "Force Close" almost immediately after the app opened. A "Force Close" is a cardinal sin in the Android world, and users will quickly come to hate your app if it happens even infrequently. This was a difficult problem because the app ran on the emulator and on many devices, but not those with the updated OS! The only way we could figure it out was to run debug with Eclipse connected to a phone with the updated OS and step through the code line by line. It turned out that the new OS was reporting the GPS coordinates in a slightly different manner than older versions did. We had to modify the code to handle both situations to get the app to run on both the new and older OS. This problem was not detectable by just recompiling the app to use the new SDK.

Summary

Publishing apps has both similarities and differences in Android and iOS. They both require the same type of information to be entered for the app that is to be sold. However, the exact procedure is different. Prior to publication of an app, thorough testing is required. An app that crashes frequently or does not do what it says it does will not pass the Apple review process. An Android app that has the same problems may be allowed to be published, but it will get bad reviews and may be eventually removed by Google. After you have published apps it is impera-tive that you keep up with platform changes. New versions of the OS can create problems for apps that currently run perfectly.

Exercises

1. Compile the Android version of MyContactList for release. Send an email to yourself or a friend with the APK attached. Install it on the Android device.

2. Write a test plan for the ContactList screen for both the Android and iOS platforms. How are they similar? Different?

3. Look up the app publication policies for Android and iOS. Describe any similarities and differences between them. (Note: you will have to log in as a developer to get the iOS guidelines).

Part V

Appendixes

Installing Eclipse and Setup for Android Development

The Integrated Development Environment (IDE) used most often for Android development is Eclipse. Eclipse is open source software available for free download for both the Windows and Mac operating systems. Setting up Eclipse for Android development is relatively easy but does require some time. Eclipse, like most IDEs, makes the basic assumption of one developer, one machine, which is not an issue for individuals developing on their own machine but can pose problems for the classroom environment. This appendix covers installing Eclipse and Android on a Windows machine and setting up the classroom environment to work effectively when you can't assume that the same person will be using the same machine all the time.

Android development requires installing several individual pieces of software, including Java SE SDK, the Eclipse IDE, and the Android SDK. The following sections show you where to download the relevant pieces of software and how to set them up. The instructions can be used for both Mac and PC environments.

Setting up Java and Eclipse

Eclipse is available for download at www.eclipse.org/downloads/. The version of Eclipse used in this book is Keplar (Eclipse 4.3). Android development uses the Java programming language, which means the Java Development Kit (JDK) must also be installed on the development machine.

Download and Install Java SE SDK

The first step is to download and install the JDK from Oracle. You can use Java from other sources if you want. However, be sure to select the most recent release that matches your machine. To install Java, follow these steps:

1. Open a web browser and navigate to the site www.oracle.com/technetwork/java/javase/downloads/index.html. Find the area titled Java SE Downloads. You may have to click the download tab. Select the Java Platform (JDK) button.

2. On the page that opens, locate the section titled Java SE Development Kit and accept the license agreement. Select the version that best matches the machine you will be installing on.

3. Choose to save the file. The download will take a couple of minutes depending on your Internet connection.

4. After the file has downloaded, double-click it to begin installation (see Figure A.1).

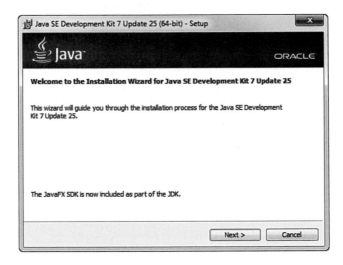

Figure A.1   Begin the installation process.

5. The installation will go through several steps. If you are using Windows, you need to make a note of the destination path that Java is installed in, because you will need that during the Eclipse installation. This is available on the Select Destination screen. Be sure to note the destination path, because you will need this later. Accept all the defaults on each screen by selecting the Next button until you complete the installation (see Figure A.2). Click Close. If you are installing on a Mac, open the DMG file and double-click the package inside. Then follow the installation wizard. There is no destination path to record on the Mac.

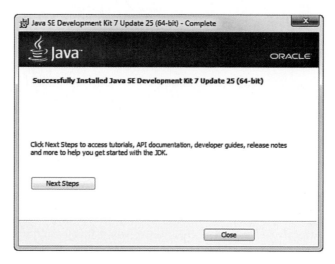

Figure A.2   Java installation complete.

Downloading Eclipse

Now that Java is installed you can install Eclipse. Follow the next steps to download the proper package:

1. Navigate your browser to www.eclipse.org/downloads/. Find Eclipse Standard and select the version that matches your machine on the right. The website will detect the basic type of OS you are using, so you should be able to click the proper version on the right.

2. After you select a version of Eclipse, a new page asks you to select a mirror site to download from. You can select the default at the top of the page or navigate down the page to a mirror site closer to where you are located. The download is large (around 190MB) and can take a long time, so selecting a site closer to your location is advantageous.

3. After you choose a download site, a new page asks for a donation to the Eclipse project and you will be asked to open or save the file. Choose Save and click OK.

Installing Eclipse on Windows

1. Eclipse downloads as a zip file. It does not need to be installed like Java. However, you do have to extract the files to a new folder. Double-click the downloaded file.

2. A Windows Explorer window opens. Click the Extract All Files button located just above the Eclipse folder (see Figure A.3). Choose a location to extract to. By default, the file extracts to the Downloads folder. It is better to install to a folder on the C: drive. If you don't have administrative privileges on the machine, use the Desktop. Click Next.

The files will be extracted to the folder. This operation will also take some time. When completed, the folder with the extracted files will be displayed.

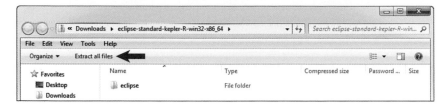

Figure A.3   Extract Eclipse files.

3. Double-click the Eclipse folder in the newly opened window. Find eclipse.exe and right-click it. Select Create Shortcut. Place the shortcut where it is useful to you.

4. Double-click the shortcut. If you were successful, Eclipse will ask you for a location for the workspace. The workspace is where all code projects are stored. You can accept the default location. If this doesn't work for your setup, enter a new location.

A successful install will conclude with the screen in Figure A.4.

Figure A.4   Eclipse Welcome after successful install.

If you were not successful, it is probably due to an error in the finding Java Virtual Machine (VM). To correct the error "Can't find a Java virtual machine," do the following:

Right-click the shortcut and select Properties. In the Properties window locate the target input box (see Figure A.5). The target shows the eclipse executable. You need to append the Java virtual machine command to the end of this line so that Eclipse knows where Java is located. The completed entry for target should look something like this:

```
"C:\Users\<User Name>\EclipseKeplar\eclipse\eclipse.exe" eclipse -vm "c:\Program
Files\Java\jre7\bin\javaw"
```

Figure A.5   Modifying the shortcut target.

The `eclipse -vm` command tells eclipse to use the Java virtual machine at the location where you installed it (this is the path you recorded in step 5 during the Java installation). Your path will be different depending on where you installed Java. However, the line should end with `\jre7\bin\javaw` regardless of the location of Java.

Click Apply and then OK. You are now ready to run Eclipse.

Installing Eclipse on Mac

The Mac version of Eclipse is downloaded as a .tar.gz archive.

1. Double-click the file to extract it. This gives you an Eclipse folder that you can drag to the Applications folder. If you need to run or keep multiple versions of Eclipse, you can rename them by version number, as needed.

2. You launch Eclipse by double-clicking the Eclipse.app file inside the Eclipse folder. If your Mac doesn't have a Java runtime installed, you may get the message in Figure A.6 about needing to install it. This is fairly common because Apple tries to avoid Java due to some security concerns.

Figure A.6   Installing Java runtime on Mac.

3. If needed, click Install to install the Java runtime.

4. After installation completes, Eclipse will launch. You may see the message in Figure A.7 about not being able to launch Eclipse because it comes from an unidentified developer. To get around this restriction, you can open the app by right-clicking the Eclipse.app file and selecting Open. When you have done this once, the setting will be remembered, and the app will always open.

Figure A.7   Unable to open Eclipse.

5. Similar to Windows, Eclipse asks for the location of a workspace. You can select the default or specify another location.

Successful installation of Eclipse on the Mac will complete with a screen similar to Figure A.5.

Installing Android

After you have successfully installed Eclipse, you have to set it up to have the capability to create Android apps. This requires downloading the Android Software Development Kit (SDK) and installing the Android Development Tools (ADT) plug-in. Both the ADT plug-in and Android SDK are downloaded and installed through Eclipse.

Follow these steps to install the plug-in:

1. Open Eclipse and select Help > Install New Software.

2. The Install New Software window opens (Figure A.8). Click the Add button.

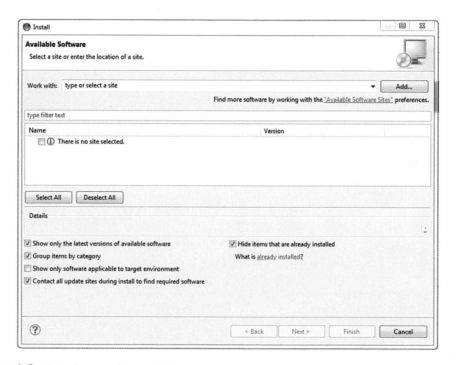

Figure A.8   Install new software window.

3. The Add Repository window opens (see Figure A.9). Enter the following information:

   a. Name: Android Plugin

   b. Location: https://dl-ssl.google.com/android/eclipse/

   Click OK.

4. The window closes and the original window will display Pending in the Name section that says There Is No Site Selected in Figure A.8 while information on the plug-in is downloaded. When the information is downloaded, you should see two items listed (see Figure A.10). Select Developer Tools and click the Next button.

Figure A.9   Add Repository window.

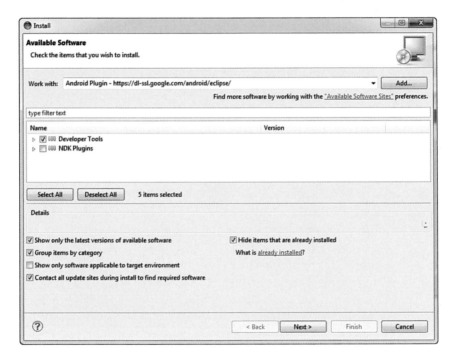

Figure A.10   Available Software.

5. The Install window will open, listing the software to be installed. Click Next.

6. The Review License window opens. Click the Accept License agreements option button and click Finish. The ADT plug-in will begin downloading and installing. You may get a security warning that the software to be installed contains unsigned content. If you do, accept the installation. The download and installation will take a few minutes. When it is complete, you will have to restart Eclipse.

> **Note**
>
> The ADT installation is known to have problems. In most cases it works without a hitch. However, if you do experience problems, the first step is to repeat the preceding steps but change the location of the plug-in from https to http. If that doesn't work, review the Troubleshooting ADT Installation tips at http://developer.android.com/sdk/installing/installing-adt.html.

When Eclipse restarts, it will open to the Welcome to Android Development window. That window will likely display an error message stating that the location of the Android SDK has not been set up in preferences. Fortunately, you can set it up from the Welcome window.

1. Close the Error window and click the Install New SDK (may be already clicked).

2. Mark the check box before both Install the Latest Available and Install Android 2.2. If you want, you can change the location where the SDK is installed. Otherwise, click the Next button.

3. The next page asks if you want to send usage statistics to Google. It's up to you what you choose. Click Finish.

4. The next screen displays the license agreement. Click Accept License and then click Next. The Android SDK will begin downloading. This will take quite a bit of time to complete, so plan to do something else while you are waiting.

After the SDK finishes downloading and installing, you are done! You can now begin developing Android apps with Eclipse.

Setting Up the Classroom

The classroom violates the one developer, one machine paradigm most IDEs assume. This provides some challenges for the students and instructor. When Eclipse opens, it asks for the folder where the projects are located. The default location for Eclipse projects is a folder called workspace. Eclipse creates this folder in the folder that is the root folder of the Eclipse installation. This is not likely to work in the classroom because students can move between machines and they will want their work to move with them. Many classroom and lab settings also freeze the machines so any changes made are deleted when the machine reboots. Nothing will frustrate a student more than logging off before they store their work and subsequently losing it.

There are several potential solutions:

1. Instruct students to create a folder called Workspace on a flash drive. When they run Eclipse they can tell it to use that folder; all their work will be automatically saved to the folder, and they can take it to a different machine or take it home to work on it. The drawback is that the student has the responsibility to back up the work, keep track of the flash drive, and remember to bring the drive to class.

2. Another option is to instruct students to use a service such as Google Drive or Dropbox. Students can create a folder called Workspace on either of these and then instruct Eclipse to use that location when it starts. The advantage is that students can't forget the work, and it is automatically backed up. However, they must have an Internet connection, and in most lab situations, it isn't feasible to have the desktop sync clients of Google Drive and Dropbox installed.

3. Ask students to save their work to a network drive. This ensures that data is backed up according to your organization's backup scheme, and students will have easy access to their workspace from any computer within the lab. However, shared drives are often not available outside the campus, making it difficult for students to work remotely. If the drive is available, it will likely be very slow to work outside. There is work in progress to enable Eclipse workspaces to reside on FTP and WebDAV servers.

4. Use version control software to allow students to upload their work to a version control server, and then download when they get to a new computer. Eclipse supports several version control systems, including CVS and git out of the box. Subversion can also be added through an Eclipse plug-in. To use version control, you would need to set up a version control server, which is beyond the scope of this book. Within Eclipse you can share your project to version control by right-clicking the project in Project Explorer and selecting Team > Share Project, and then selecting the appropriate version control solution for your scenario.

Getting Eclipse to work in a classroom setting is similar to setting up many other types of software in that kind of restricted environment, so you will have to rely on your IT administrators to help you determine the best option for your situation. You will also have to provide detailed instructions for students to follow to be successful in the classroom.

B

Installing Xcode and Registering Physical Devices

When developing for iOS, Xcode is the primary tool. This is a very capable Integrated Development Environment (IDE) that is available for free through the Mac App Store. The free version lets you develop apps and test them on the iOS Simulator. However, if you want to load your software on an actual device, or submit an app to the App Store, you need to have a developer account.

This appendix shows you how to set up Xcode, get a Developer Account, and set up for testing your apps on real devices.

Download and Install Xcode

Getting Xcode installed is simple. You just launch the Mac App Store on your Mac and search for Xcode (see Figure B.1). Then you click Free, which turns the button green and changes to Install App. Click again to install Xcode. This takes a while because Xcode is several gigabytes large.

After it is downloaded, Xcode will be automatically installed. You launch Xcode from the Applications folder, like any other program on the Mac. When updates are released, they will show up as updates in the Mac App Store. One of the requirements for running Xcode 5 is that you need a Mac running OS.X version 10.8 (Mountain Lion). If you have Macs that cannot be upgraded, you can download older versions of Xcode from the Apple Developer Site. For instance, Xcode 4.6 can run on OS X 10.7 and later. Most of the material in this book can be easily adapted to work with Xcode 4.6.

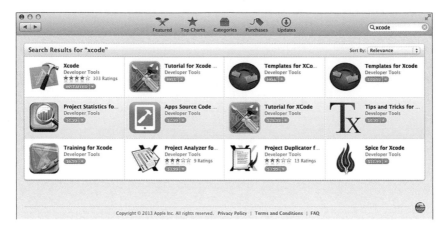

Figure B.1   Finding Xcode in the Mac App Store.

Apple Developer Programs

As mentioned earlier, Xcode is free to download and use, but you can only test your apps on the iOS Simulator. To test on a device or submit to the App Store, you need a developer account. Apple offers four developer programs for iOS development: iOS Developer Program (individual), iOS Developer Program (Company), iOS Developer Enterprise Program, and iOS Developer University Program.

Table B.1 outlines some of the significant differences among the programs. In short, the biggest differences are that the iOS Developer program lets you distribute apps through the App Store, Enterprise program lets you distribute apps to users within your company without having to go through Apple, and the University program allows for up to 200 instructors, professors, and students to develop and test apps on real devices.

Table B.1   **Comparison of Apple Developer Programs**

Feature	iOS Developer	iOS Developer Enterprise	iOS Developer University
iOS SDK	Yes	Yes	Yes
Beta versions of SDK and Xcode	Yes	Yes	No
Test apps on iOS devices	Yes	Yes	Yes
Number of test devices per year	100	N/A	200
App Store distribution	Yes	No	No
iAd Network	Yes	No	No
In-house Distribution	No	Yes	No
Cost	$99 / year	$299 / year	Free

The process for registering for each program can be a bit cumbersome. The University and Enterprise programs require several levels of approval within your organization, and you also have to submit documentation to Apple. The whole process can take a few weeks to complete.

Setting Up the Classroom

Developing apps on iOS in the classroom is relatively simple. You do need Macs in your lab with Xcode installed. Project files are stored in a directory that can easily be moved to other places, such as a thumb drive or a network location. See Appendix A, "Installing Eclipse and Setup for Android Development," for a fuller discussion of options for storing files in different locations. Xcode supports both git and Subversion for source control.

Deploying Apps to Real Devices

The iOS Simulator is very powerful and allows for doing most of the testing you need for most business apps. In a classroom situation you can do a lot of interesting and worthwhile things without using real devices. However, students get excited about seeing their creations running on a real device, and there are certain features where it is necessary to test on a device. Following are some limitations of the simulator where you need to test on a real device:

- No phone or messaging. The Simulator can toggle the in-call status bar, but doesn't make or receive calls.
- Access to camera.
- Realistic access to network (perhaps to test for network coverage in a specific location).
- Access to gyroscope and altimeter (perhaps for developing game controls).
- Realistic user touch interactions.

Because of the nature of the iOS ecosystem, it is a challenge to configure for deployment to real devices. Apple requires that every app be digitally signed to enhance the end users' confidence that apps are reliable and developers are held accountable. This means that every developer must have a digital certificate that can be used for signing apps before they can be submitted to the App Store. There are two different kinds of certificates: one for debugging and one for releasing apps.

To ensure that all apps are distributed either through the App Store or through controlled enterprise means, Apple also requires every device used for testing to be registered with Apple and have a provisioning profile installed. The provisioning profile is a digital file that links the developers that are allowed to deploy to the devices listed in the profile. As you saw in Table B.1, each developer program has a maximum number of devices that can be used for testing.

To simplify the explanation, the following assumes that an instructor is responsible for inviting students in his/her class to join the developer program and will use a set of classroom devices for testing apps. Here is a brief overview of the steps involved:

To set up students as developers:

1. Instructor must be set up with the Admin role in the iOS Developer University Program.

2. Instructor sends invitations by email to each of the students who will get the Member role in the program.

3. Students accept the invitation and register as developers.

4. Students add their account to Xcode, which generates a request for a developer certificate.

5. Instructor logs in to the Apple Developer Site and approves each request.

6. Students refresh their account in Xcode to get the certificate (which will be listed under Signing Identities).

To set up devices:

1. Instructor registers devices for development.

2. Student connects device to Mac and opens the Organizer and clicks Use for Development.

3. Student checks to make sure that provisioning profile is valid on the device. If not, the student downloads the provisioning profile from the Apple Developer Site.

Important Terms

Registering developers and setting up devices involves a large number of terms that can be difficult to keep track of. Here's a brief definition of some of the major concepts to understand.

- Team Agent—The person who originally signed up for the iOS Developer Program and is responsible for agreeing to the legal terms of the contract. The team agent has all the same rights as a Team Admin.

- Team Admin—A person who can register devices and manage members in the iOS Developer Program.

- Team Member—A registered developer who has accepted an invitation to join the team (note that registered developers can be members of multiple teams).

- Developer Certificate—A digital certificate issued to a developer that he/she can use to sign apps before submitting to the app store or deploying to a test device.

- Provisioning Profile—A digital file that specifies which developers can deploy specific apps to a specified device. The same provisioning profile can contain information about multiple apps, developers, and devices. Provisioning profiles are stored on devices that are used for testing apps.

- Team Provisioning Profile—A provisioning profile is one that includes all developers and devices on a team. Apps are specified by a wildcard App ID.

- App ID—A unique identification of a particular app. Used in provisioning profiles to specify which apps the profile is valid for. You can generate a wildcard App ID that covers multiple apps.

- UDID—A unique identifier for each device. Used when registering devices to be used for development.

Creating Developer Accounts

The iOS Developer University program allows for up to 200 people to be added as developers to your account. This allows you to add both students and faculty as developers who are able to run apps on a device and get access to the support resources in the iOS Development Center. Note that it isn't necessary to be registered to develop apps that are going to be tested only on the simulator.

To register developers, the administrator for the program needs to log in to the Member Center on the Apple Developer Site (developer.apple.com); along the top of the screen, choose the People tab (see Figure B.2). Developers can be invited individually or in bulk. Each person invited will receive an email with a link to register as a developer or sign in with an existing developer account. The same developer account can be associated with multiple development programs (that is, you may be in both the iOS University Program and an Enterprise Development program).

Figure B.2   Click People to add developers to an iOS University Developer Program.

When registering as a developer, students and faculty may choose to use an existing Apple ID (any iTunes account has an Apple ID), which would be the simplest way to get started. However, they can also create a new one if they choose. Getting registered and accepting the invitation to join the team can take a bit of time—and can be a confusing process. If you have the option, you may choose to use some time in the classroom for students to set up accounts and register. An administrator of the program can monitor the status of the invitations sent to see when they move to the accepted state.

After the developer account has been created, it can be added to Xcode by selecting Xcode > Preferences > Accounts. Then click the + sign at the bottom and choose Add Apple ID (see Figure B.3). The developer will then have to log in, and if successful, the developer's Apple ID should be shown in the Accounts pane.

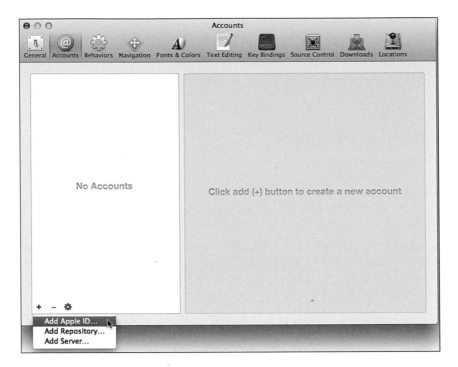

Figure B.3   Adding Apple ID to Xcode.

After students have added the account to Xcode, they should click View Details, click the + under Signing Identity, and choose iOS Development. This generates a request for a certificate to be generated. The certificate has to be approved by a Team Agent (class instructor) on the Apple Developer Site. After approval, students can click the Refresh button on the View Details screen under their account in Xcode to fetch the certificate to the Mac.

Backing Up the Development Certificate

When you start development, Xcode will generate a public/private key pair that is installed in the Keychain Access app on the Mac you develop on. When moving to a different Mac, you will need to bring this public/private key pair along. So, as soon as the development certificate is set up, be sure to take a backup to use on other Macs. This is especially important for students working in labs. If you don't have your students do this, they will have to revoke their existing certificate and request a new one, because the private key would be only on the machine where it was generated.

To back up the certificate, in Xcode, choose Xcode > Settings > Accounts, click the gear icon in the lower left, and then select Export Accounts (see Figure B.4). You will then have to supply a name for the exported file and a password (see Figure B.5). The exported file will contain all your credentials, including certificates and provisioning profiles. To set the profile up on a different Mac, you go back to Accounts, choose Import Accounts, and pick the file you exported.

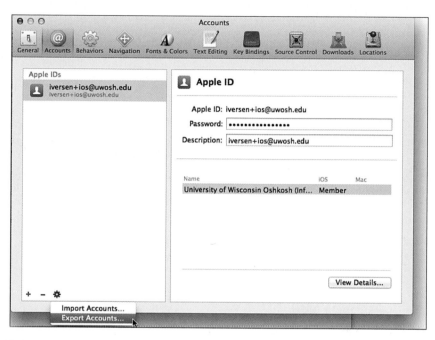

Figure B.4   Export Accounts from Xcode for backup.

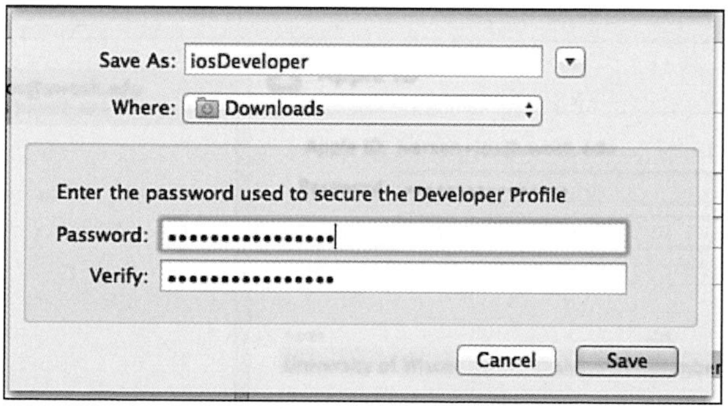

Figure B.5   Saving the Developer Profile.

Registering Devices

Each device that is used for testing must be registered with Apple. This can be done in several ways.

If you have a classroom set of devices to be used for development, the simplest option is to use the iOS Developer Center website and choose Certificates, Identifiers & Profiles. Then choose Devices, which will give you an option to add new devices. You can add devices individually or as a batch of up to 100 devices at a time. You need to supply the UDID for each device. These are very long strings of letters and numbers that uniquely identify each iOS device. To find the UDID of a device, you can connect the device to iTunes and then open the Summary tab for the device. This is where you will see the serial number. If you click this, it will change to show the UDID. At this point you can right-click the UDID to copy it to the clipboard. The UDID will look something like this: 5e28157c1c7c49ae61549bee50d5dfc85aed7f4d (this is not an actual UDID). You can also find the UDID in the Organizer in Xcode (see Figure B.6). If your devices are managed by Apple Configurator, you can also export all the UDIDs from there. Some mobile device management systems put the devices in a Supervised mode (which also installs a profile on the device). These devices cannot be used for development, and you have to reset such devices. To do this, on the device go to Settings > General > Reset > Erase All Content and Settings. Note that this will delete all apps, data, and settings on the device.

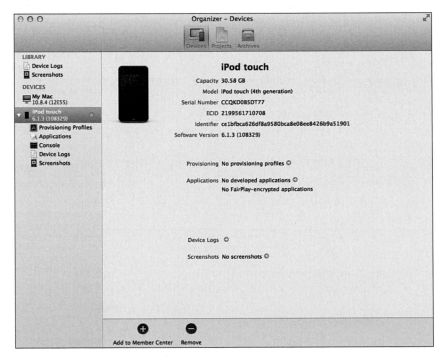

Figure B.6   Register a device for development using the Organizer.

Another way to register devices is to connect them to Xcode one by one; then, using the Device Organizer, click Use for Development (see Figure B.6), and then choose the development team to register the device with (see Figure B.7). This does require being signed in with an account with the Admin role.

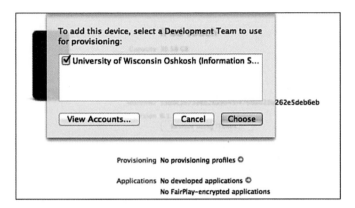

Figure B.7   Choose a Development Team to use for provisioning of a device.

If a device has already been used for development under a different developer account, the Use for Development option will not be present. Instead, you can click Add to Member Center, which will register the device and download the provisioning profiles.

Checking the Development Environment

To ensure that the environment is set up properly, you can open Organizer and check that the device has a valid provisioning profile (see Figure B.8). You also need to ensure that the developer's account is added to Xcode (Xcode > Preferences > Accounts > View Details) and has a valid certificate (see Figure B.9).

The most frequent problem that occurs in deploying to a device is that the device doesn't have a valid provisioning profile. If this happens, you can download the provisioning profile from the Developer Site under Certificates, Identifiers & Profiles, click the provisioning profile, and then click Download (see Figure B.10). The downloaded file can then be dragged into the Organizer.

If you find that you have problems with the Team Provisioning Profiles and get a Valid Signing Identify Not Found error, you can also create a new provisioning profile manually on the developer site and add all the devices and developers that are allowed to use that profile. Developers will then be able to download this profile and add to the Organizer on their machine.

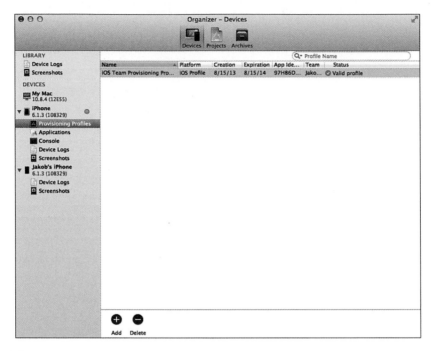

Figure B.8   Checking that the device has a valid provisioning profile.

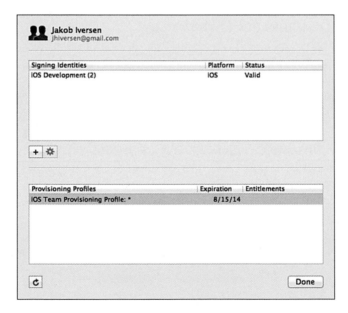

Figure B.9   Checking that the developer has a valid signing identity and provisioning profile.

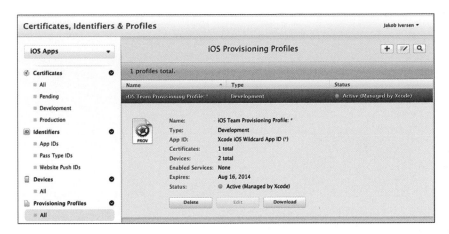

Figure B.10   Downloading a provisioning profile from the Apple Developer Site.

After a device is registered, the provisioning profile is properly installed, and the device is connected to the Mac, you can then run an app on the device by switching the scheme in Xcode to the device (Figure B.11).

Figure B.11   Changing the scheme to an actual device.

If a developer wants to use his/her own personal device for development, it has to be registered by a Team Admin. The developer will need to send the UDID to the admin who can then register the device. If you need to register many devices for a class, you may want to set up a survey for students to submit their device UDIDs.

C

Introduction to Objective-C

One of the biggest obstacles in learning to develop mobile apps for iOS is the need to use Objective-C as the language for native development. This language is not taught in many schools and is used only for Mac and iOS development, so you likely don't know how to develop in Objective-C. On top of that, at first glance, Objective-C code can look very intimidating to developers used to more common languages like Java and C#. However, it's not as bad as you might think. Although the syntax includes many elements that are unfamiliar, the basic object-oriented model is very similar to Java and C#. So, if you know either of those languages, you should be able to pick up the syntax of Objective-C pretty easily. For those who are familiar with Java, this appendix contains numerous references and comparisons to that language. Most of those comparisons are also valid for C#.

A Brief History of Objective-C

It might seem odd to you that Apple chose such an obscure language as the basis for its smartphone platform. Why didn't they pick a language that more developers knew about so as to have more developers able to develop apps for the platform? The answer to that question goes back to the initial creation of the language. Objective-C was created in 1986 by Tom Love and Brad Cox as a way to add object-oriented principles to the C language. At the time, C was one of the most popular computer programming languages, so this was an important development. The object-oriented principles they chose were based on the Smalltalk language, which was one of the first truly object-oriented languages. By combining the two, C-programmers could add object-oriented extensions to their programs. In fact, to this day, Objective-C is a strict superset of C, which means that any properly written C program can be compiled and run within an Objective-C program.

When Steve Jobs was forced out of Apple in 1988, he went on to found a small company called NeXT, which licensed the Objective-C language from Cox and Love as the basis for the operating system, NeXTStep, which would power their NeXT computer workstations. Later, when Steve Jobs returned to Apple, he brought back NeXTStep, which became the basis for OS X, and along came Objective-C as the primary language used to develop OS X programs.

Objective-C has been very influential among programming languages, in part due to a partnership between NeXT and SUN that resulted in the development of an open source version of NeXTStep called OpenStep. The engineers at SUN who worked on this project later went on to create the Java programming language and brought along many of the best features from Objective-C. In particular, this means that the object-oriented model of classes, objects, single inheritance, interfaces (called protocols in Objective-C), and polymorphism is largely the same in Java and Objective-C, as well as C#.

Two Languages in One

Objective-C was designed as a strict superset of C, which means that any C program is also a valid Objective-C program. The Objective-C designers decided to keep the C language intact and add special syntax for object-oriented features to make it easy to distinguish between the two. Also retained from C is division of the code for each class into two files: a header file with a .h extension that defines publicly available interface of methods and properties for the class and a method file with a .m extension that defines the implementation of the methods. If you have read any of the iOS chapters, you have already seen these files in your project.

The following is a brief overview of some of the coding constructs that the C language is used for when you are programming in Objective-C. Most of these should be familiar to you if you are comfortable with Java or C#.

- Primitive data types, such as integers, real numbers, and characters.

- Variable declarations, which are similar to Java. You specify the data type followed by the variable name and an optional initialization, like this:

```
int age;
char initial = 'a';
BOOL editMode = YES;
```

- All the usual mathematical operators, such as plus and minus.

- Conditional operators, such as if-then-else and switch statements.

- Loops, including for, do-while, and while.

- Functions can be declared in C-style, which is similar to Java, listing first a return type, then the method name, and finally an optional list of parameters in parentheses, like this:

```
float average(float num1, double num2, BOOL round) { ... }
```

This method, named average, takes a float, a double, and a boolean, and returns a float. As this shows, function bodies are in curly braces in C.

- Pointer operators. In C, variables can be declared to be either a value stored directly in the memory location referenced by the variable, or they can be declared in a memory location referenced by the variable. In Java, primitive values always work in the former way, whereas objects always are referenced. In C, an asterisk is used to denote referenced variables, like this:

```
int *b = 20;
```

This notation becomes especially important when working with objects, because they are always referenced in Objective-C. If you are used to writing Java programs, it will likely take some time to get used to adding the asterisk to most of the variables you declare.

The Objective-C functionality is added to the previously mentioned C features and is used for anything that is object-oriented, including instantiating objects and calling methods on objects. The rest of this chapter will focus on the object-oriented features of Objective-C.

Objects and Classes

Just like in Java, Objective-C uses a concept of classes that describe a real-world phenomenon, such as a Customer, a Book, or an Account. Classes are written in code and form the blueprint for instantiation of multiple objects from the same class. Each object is then a representation of a single real-world instance from the class. For instance, if you were to write an application to keep track of all the books you own, you would likely instantiate an object for every one of those books.

For the examples in the rest of this chapter, create a project in Xcode (File > New > Project). Use the Single View Application template under iOS Application. Name the product Objective-C Examples, and limit Devices to just target iPhone.

You will begin exploring the structure of Objective-C by creating a class.

1. Create a new class by right-clicking the yellow top-level folder in the project and selecting New File.

2. Choose the Cocoa Touch category under iOS and select Objective-C Class.

3. Click Next and name the new class LMABook. Make sure the Subclass Of is set to NSObject, and then click Next.

4. On the next screen you have to be sure to choose a Target for your new class. This should at least be the project (Objective-C Examples, in this case), but if you're using unit testing, you should also choose that target. Click Create, and two new files are added to your project, LMABook.h and LMABook.m. You can use the Assistant Editor to see them side by side.

Listings C.1 and C.2 show the two files that together define the Book class.

Listing C.1   **LMABook.h**

```
#import <Foundation/Foundation.h>                                    //1

@interface LMABook : NSObject                                        //2

@end                                                                 //3
```

The .h file is often called the interface file because it defines the public interface for the class.

1. Import statements are used to add additional functionality to a class and make it aware of features in other classes. Here, the Foundation framework, which includes a lot of the basic data structures such as strings, is imported. Frameworks are always in angle brackets in import statements.

2. The class starts with the `@interface` keyword followed by the class name. After the colon is the name of the super class for the class. In this case, LMABook inherits from NSObject. This is similar to Java, which inherits from Object, except the inheritance is explicit in Objective-C.

3. The class interface ends with the `@end` keyword.

Listing C.2   **LMABook.m**

```
#import "LMABook.h"                                                  //1

@implementation LMABook                                             //2

@end                                                                 //3
```

The interface is implemented in an implementation file with a .m extension.

1. For the implementation file to know about the interface, you have to import it. Notice that classes in your project are imported using double quotes around the filename.

2. The `@implementation` directive tells the compiler that this is the implementation for the class.

3. The class implementation is concluded with the `@end` directive.

Now that the class is added, you will add a few relevant properties and methods to the class. Start by modifying LMABook.h as shown in Listing C.3.

Listing C.3   **Completed LMABook.h**

```
#import <Foundation/Foundation.h>

@interface LMABook : NSObject

@property (nonatomic, strong) NSString *title;                          //1
@property (nonatomic, weak) NSString *author;
@property (nonatomic, readonly, strong) NSString *lender;
@property (getter = isOut, readonly) BOOL out;                          //2
@property int pages;

- (id) initWithTitle: (NSString *)aTitle;                               //3
+ (id) bookWithTitle: (NSString *)aTitle andAuthor:(NSString *)anAuthor; //4
- (void) lendOut: (NSString *)lenderName;                               //5
- (void) returnBook;                                                    //6
@end
```

This shows several important elements of how to define a class.v

1. The properties are the class variables that contain the data and are declared with the `@property` directive. To access the properties, an `accessor` method is also needed. In Java, these are the set and get methods that you have to declare for every class variable. In Objective-C, this is streamlined, so you can declare how you want the accessors to be generated, and then the compiler will automatically generate them for you.

   Properties are declared with a data type and name as regular variables. Note the asterisk used for `NSString` properties, because these are objects, but not for `BOOL` and `int`, because these are primitives. The parentheses contain various attributes for the property. These are described in more detail later in this appendix.

2. You have an option to specify the name of the getter (and setter) method by using getter = method name. The default is that the getter is given the same name as the property, and the setter is named `setPropertyName`. For booleans in particular, the convention is to prepend the property name with 'is' as shown here.

3.-6. Four methods are declared. The method syntax is one of the most difficult aspects of Objective-C to wrap your head around when coming from Java, so these are explained in more detail later in this appendix.

   One thing to note is that several of the methods have a return type of id. This is kind of a wildcard type that can be used in place of any kind of return type. This allows for implementing something akin to dynamic types where at runtime, any object can be returned from the method. The id type can be very useful, but it also means that the compiler can't typecheck your code, so you should use it sparingly.

Before delving into some of the deeper explanations of methods and properties, go ahead and implement the class methods by adding the code in Listing C.4 to LMABook.m.

Listing C.4 **Completed LMABook.m**

```objectivec
#import "LMABook.h"

@implementation LMABook

- (id) init                                                          //1
{
    self = [super init];
    if (self) {
        // Initialization code here.
    }
    return self;
}

-(id) initWithTitle:(NSString *)aTitle                                //2
{
    self = [super init];
    if(self) {
        _title = [aTitle copy];
    }
    return self;
}

+(id) bookWithTitle:(NSString *)aTitle                                //3
{
    LMABook *book = [[self alloc] initWithTitle:aTitle];
    return book;
}

+(id) bookWithTitle:(NSString *)aTitle andAuthor:(NSString *)anAuthor //4
{
    LMABook *book = [[self alloc] initWithTitle:aTitle];
    book.author = anAuthor;
        //or: [book setAuthor:anAuthor];
    return book;
}

-(void) lendOut:(NSString *)lenderName                                //5
{
    _lender = lenderName;
    _out = YES;
}
```

```
-(void) returnBook                                                    //6
{
    _lender = nil;
    _out = NO;
}

@end
```

There are quite a few things going on in this file, which has all the implementation of the methods that you declared in the .h file.

1. This is a standard method used to create an object. Every class has an init method that initializes variables. The init method is similar to a constructor in Java. However, the init method explicitly calls the super class version of init (in Java, this call is implicit). After the call to the super class init completes, the init method checks to see if an object actually was created, in which case, any initialization can be done. Creating an object using this method would look like this:

   ```
   LMABook *book = [[LMABook alloc] init];
   ```

   This pattern is very common when creating objects. It calls the alloc method on the LMABook class, which allocates memory space for the object. The init method then initializes the variables. This two-stage process is functionally equivalent to a Java constructor call, like this:

   ```
   Book book = new Book();
   ```

2. Instead of overloading constructors as you would in Java, Objective-C classes contain multiple methods whose names starts with init and then use the rest of the name to specify which parameters are being passed in. This method takes a title, which is passed into the property title. Notice the use of _title to refer to the property here (see the section, "Properties in Detail" for explanation).

3. An alternative to creating an object with an init method is to use a class factory method as shown here. A class factory method is a method that creates and returns a new object from a class by both doing allocation and initialization, so a client doesn't have to worry about that. These methods are very common in the various standard frameworks you will use to create your iOS apps and are declared as static methods (indicated by the plus in front). The method here gets a title for the book and then a local variable is set up and initialized with an object created using alloc and the initWithTitle: method. Finally, the completed object is returned to the caller.

4. This method is similar to the one in item 3, except it also takes an author as a parameter. Because there is no init method that takes both an author and a title, the object is first created with the title only, and then the author property is set. Note that the property value can be set using either dot notation or by calling setAuthor.

5-6. These two methods manage lending out and returning books. Because the `lender` and `out` properties are set to `readonly` (refer to Listing C.3), they can be set using only these two methods.

With the `LMABook` class declared, the next step is to look at how to create and work with objects of the class. To keep things simple, all the work on this will be done in a single method, and all output will be done to the console.

Open LMAAppDelegate.m and add this import statement after the other import statement:

`#import "LMABook.h"`

This makes the `LMABook` class available to use within LMAAppDelegate.m. Objective-C doesn't have a concept of namespace, like in C#, or packages, as in Java, that allow for resolving names within a single app, so you have to explicitly import the classes you want to reference—even within your own app. You can add the import to either the .h or .m file, but unless you need to reference it in the .h file, the recommended approach is to import in the .m file. This is because the imported file is essentially copied into the target file by the compiler, and thus any declared properties and methods in the imported file become available from the target file as well.

Change `application:didFinishLaunchingWithOptions:` as shown in Listing C.5.

Listing C.5 **Declaring and Manipulating Objects**

```
- (BOOL)application:(UIApplication *)application
➥didFinishLaunchingWithOptions:(NSDictionary *)launchOptions
{
    // Override point for customization after application launch.

    LMABook *book1 = [[LMABook alloc] init];                          //1
    book1.title = @"Moby Dick";
    book1.author = @"Herman Melville";
    book1.pages = 899;

    LMABook *book2 = [LMABook bookWithTitle:@"To Kill A Mockingbird"  //2
                                  andAuthor:@"Harper Lee"];
    [book2 setPages:359];                                             //3

    [book1 lendOut:@"Jim Smith"];                                    //4
    [book2 lendOut:@"Mary Jane"];
    [book2 returnBook];

    if([book1 isOut]){                                               //5
        NSLog(@"%@ is lent out to %@", book1.title, book1.lender);    //6
    }
    else {
        NSLog(@"%@ is not lent out", book1.title);
    }
```

```
    NSArray *books = @[book1, book2];                                    //7
    for (LMABook *book in books) {                                       //8
        NSLog(@"%@, %d pages.", book.title, book.pages);
    }

    return YES;
}
```

This code demonstrates several ways to interact with objects in Objective-C.

1. This is the standard way of creating an object using `alloc` and `init`. Because no properties are initialized, the following lines use dot notation to set each of the three properties to specific values. The @ sign in front of the string values is used to signify that it is a literal string value and is an instance of `NSString`. If you omitted the @ sign, the string would be a C string literal, which would not be able to be used anywhere an `NSString` is expected. So, in practice, anytime you need a string literal, you need to include the @ sign in front of it.

2. The second book object is created using `bookWithTitle:andAuthor:` to populate two of the parameters.

3. This illustrates the alternative way to set a property by calling the accessor method using square bracket notation.

4. These three lines illustrate calling methods on the two book objects. First, `book1` is lent out to Jim Smith, then `book2` is lent out to Mary Jane, and finally `book2` is returned.

5. This `if` statement checks whether `book1` is lent out by calling the `isOut` accessor method. It then uses the `NSLog` method to print to the console.

6. `NSLog` prints any strings passed to it, to the console, and is frequently used for debugging purposes. The console is not available to users running your app on an iOS device, so you cannot use this for messages to the user. The string here is a concatenation where the two instances of `%@` inside the string are placeholders to be replaced by the two values following the string—in this case, the title and lender of `book1`.

7. This line creates an array with `book1` and `book2` as entries. An alternative approach to declaring and initializing an array is this:

   ```
   NSArray *books = [NSArray arrayWithObjects:book1, book2, nil];
   ```

   This is more verbose, but perhaps a little clearer about what is going on in the code. `NSArray` has a number of methods to create arrays based on different starting points (another array, contents of a file, and contents of a URL). Note that `NSArray` cannot be modified after it has been created. If you wanted to add or remove entries, you would need to declare an `NSMutableArray`, which is a subclass of `NSArray`, so it has all the same features of `NSArray`, in addition to capabilities to insert and delete objects.

8. This is the fast enumeration loop to go through all the elements in a collection. It works in the same way as the `foreach` loop in C# and the enhanced `for` loop in Java

by declaring a local variable of the class that is in the collection and then iterating over all the elements in the collection, assigning them to the local variable one by one, and executing the body of the loop on each element. In this case, it is used to print the title and number of pages for all the books.

Try running the app now, and you should see the following output in the console in Xcode (time stamps removed for readability):

```
Objective-C Examples[5447:a0b] Moby Dick is lent out to Jim Smith
Objective-C Examples[5447:a0b] Moby Dick, 899 pages.
Objective-C Examples[5447:a0b] To Kill A Mockingbird, 359 pages.
```

To Dot or Not to Dot?

There is some debate in the Objective-C community as to whether dot notation is the best way to write code, but it largely comes down to personal choice. Dot notation leads to more concise code that is easier to read, especially for new Objective-C programmers. However, it may also be confusing to try to remember when dot notation is okay and when it isn't. Apple uses dot notation in all its examples, and in this book we generally follow that approach. The dot-notation is newer (available from Objective-C version 2.0, released in 2006). You can use the dot notation to call an accessor method, but not to call a regular method, in which case you have to use square bracket notation.

For easy comparison to Java, Listing C.6 has the Book class as it would be implemented in Java, and Listing C.7 is a main method with the same functionality as Listing C.5.

Listing C.6   **The Book Class Implemented Using Java**

```java
class Book {
    private String title;
    private String author;
    private int pages;
    private String lender;
    private boolean out;

    public Book() {
    }

    public Book(String title) {
        this.title = title;
        this.author = author;
    }

    public static Book createBook(String title) {
        Book book = new Book(title);
        return book;
    }
}
```

```java
    public static Book createBook(String title, String author) {
        Book book = new Book(title);
        book.author = author;
        return book;
    }

    public String getTitle() {
        return title;
    }
    public void setTitle(String title) {
        this.title = title;
    }

    public String getAuthor() {
        return author;
    }
    public void setAuthor(String author) {
        this.author = author;
    }
    public int getPages () {
        return pages;
    }
    public void setPages(int pages) {
        this.pages = pages;
    }

    public String getLender() {
        return lender;
    }

    public boolean isOut() {
        return out;
    }

    public void lendout(String lenderName) {
        this.lender = lenderName;
        out = true;
    }

    public void returnBook() {
        lender = null;
        out = false;
    }

}
```

Listing C.7   **Main Method in Java**

```java
public static void main(String[] args) {
        Book book1 = new Book();
        book1.setTitle("Moby Dick");
        book1.setAuthor("Herman Melville");
        book1.setPages(899);

        Book book2 = Book.createBook("To Kill a Mockingbird", "Harper Lee");
        book2.setPages(359);

        book1.lendout("Jim Smith");
        book2.lendout("Mary Jane");
        book1.returnBook();

        if(book1.isOut()) {
            System.out.println(book1.getTitle() + " is lent out to " +
➥book1.getLender());
        }
        else {
            System.out.println(book1.getTitle() + " is not lent out");
        }

        ArrayList<Book> books = new ArrayList<>();
        books.add(book1);
        books.add(book2);
        for(Book book : books) {
            System.out.println(book.getTitle() + ", " + book1.getPages() + "
➥pages.");
        }

    }
```

Properties in Detail

When getting into Objective-C programming, the declaration of properties is sometimes confusing. In Java, you declare some private variables in the class, and then create getters and setters as needed. Things seem much more involved in Objective-C, so a more detailed look at the properties is warranted. The properties in Objective-C are very similar to the automatic properties available in C#.

When you declare a property like this in Objective-C:

```
@property (nonatomic, strong) NSString *title;
```

you actually tell the compiler to do several things in a single line:

- Declare a class variable called `title` of type `NSString`.

- Create an accessor method called `title` that will return `NSString`.

- Create an accessor method called `setTitle` that will take an `NSString` and assign it to the title variable.

- Do not ensure thread-safe access to the title variable by specifying `nonatomic` (this is less safe in multiuser and multithreaded environments, but is faster).

This makes the code much more streamlined and faster to write. The biggest problem in understanding the properties is how you can customize the implementation of the accessor methods by using various keywords in the parentheses. Table C.1 gives an overview of the options available for property attributes.

Table C.1   **Property Attributes**

Attribute	Purpose
`getter=<name>`, `setter=<name>`	Specifies name of the accessor methods that will be used for this property.
`readwrite` or `readonly`	Which accessor methods are created. Default: readwrite.
`strong, weak, assign, retain,` or `copy`	How will data be assigned to the attribute? *Strong:* Keep ownership of object after assignment. Use with ARC and objects. *Weak:* Keep the object until it is otherwise discarded. Use with ARC and objects. *Assign:* Regular assign. Similar to weak. Use for nonobjects.
	Copy: Makes a copy of the data and assigns. Any changes to original object will not be reflected in assigned object, and vice versa. *Retain:* Retains argument. Similar to strong. Use for objects.
	Default: assign.
`nonatomic`	If specified nonatomic, the attribute is not threadsafe. Default: atomic. Note: nonatomic is faster, but use only in single-threaded situations.

Most of these shouldn't require more explanation, but the difference between strong and weak can be quite confusing. A strong reference is the most common and is how most object assignments are made in Java and C#. A reference is made to the object, and even if all other references to the object are discarded, the object will not be discarded. However, with a weak reference, if the only reference left is the weak reference assigned through the property, the object will be discarded. Weak references are most often used for delegate properties and for subviews of a main view, because there is already a strong reference from the main view.

After the properties are declared, to use them in the .m file, you can use an underscore followed by the name of the property. For instance, the `title` property could be referenced like this in LMABook.m:

```
_title = aTitle;
```

When the properties are referenced outside the class, you can use either dot notation or bracket notation to call the accessor methods as discussed earlier.

Declaring and Calling Methods

As you have already seen, method declarations are very different from what you're used to seeing in Java and C#. Objective-C instead uses `SmallTalk` method syntax. Figure C.1 shows a breakdown of the declaration of a static method that takes two parameters and returns an object of type `id`.

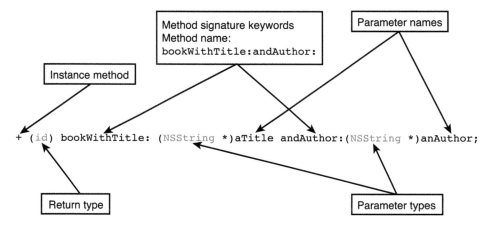

Figure C.1   Method signature.

There are two types of methods in Objective-C: instance and class methods. Instance methods work on specific objects, whereas class methods are similar to static methods in Java and can be invoked using the class name. Class methods do not have access to any data stored in the class properties.

The return type in this example is `id`, which is a wildcard type that allows for any type to be returned from the method. This is similar to declaring a method to return Object in Java.

Rather than list parameters in parentheses, Objective-C lists parameters following a colon with the type of the parameter in parentheses before the parameter name. If there are multiple parameters, a word is added to describe subsequent parameters. These method keywords are part of the method name and are also listed when calling the method, making it easier to understand what role a particular parameter plays. The method in Figure C.1 is thus called bookWithTitle:andAuthor: (notice the colons separating each keyword). In contrast, the method signature in Java would look like this (although the method name would typically not be so long in Java):

```
public static Object bookWithTitleAndAuthor(String title, String author);
```

You may be wondering how to specify which properties and methods are private and public in Objective-C. There is no designation of public and private as there is in Java and C#. However, only those properties and methods listed in the .h file are part of the public interface. You can declare private variables, properties, and methods in the .m file, and they will not be visible outside the file which, in essence, makes them private.

Inheritance and Protocols

One of the important concepts of object-oriented programming is inheritance, which allows for creating simpler and more efficient code by allowing one class to inherit all the properties of another class. This gives the benefit of polymorphism, where a variable can be declared to hold a particular type in the code, but at runtime, any object declared of that class or any of its subclasses can be assigned to the variable.

Inheritance in Objective-C works exactly like it does in Java and C#. Only the syntax is slightly different. To specify inheritance, you add a colon and the super class name to the @interface line in the .h file. For instance, the Book class you created earlier could form the basis for a PhotoBook class, which would then be declared like this:

```
@interface LMAPhotoBook : LMABook
```

You do have to remember to import the super class.

Objective-C allows only for single inheritance and has a class, NSObject, which plays the same role as Object in Java of being the top-most class in the inheritance hierarchy.

To allow for a class to have multiple identities, object-oriented programmers turn to interfaces in Java and C#. The same concept is called a *protocol* in Objective-C, and rather than implement an interface, Objective-C classes are said to *conform* to a protocol. But the concepts are the same: A protocol defines a set of methods and properties, and when a class conforms to the protocol, any variable declared to hold a type of the protocol will be able to hold an object of any class that conforms to the protocol. Specifying that a class conforms to a protocol is also done in the @interface line by putting the protocols in angle brackets like this:

```
@interface MyClass : NSObject <MyProtocol, AnotherProtocol, YetAnotherProtocol>
```

As you can see, classes can conform to multiple protocols. A protocol can declare that some methods are optional, but otherwise, the class will need to implement all methods declared in all the protocols.

When declaring variables that conform to delegates, you have to specify a regular data type as well as the protocol, so you will often see code like this to specify that a variable must conform to a particular protocol:

```
id <protocolName> variable;
```

This specifies that the object assigned to `variable` can be of any type (`id`) as long as it conforms to `protocolName`.

Memory Management

It used to be that memory management was one of the most challenging aspects of learning Objective-C. Fortunately, that is no longer the case because Apple has introduced a system called Automatic Reference Counting (ARC) that hides most of the complexity of memory management. However, although you don't need to know all the intricacies of managing memory in your apps, it's still important to understand what's going on and how it works.

In object-oriented programming, it's always a problem to reclaim the memory left behind when all references to an object are removed. For instance, imagine you create two objects and assign them to variables a and b, respectively. But then later, you assign variable a to point to variable b. Now both variables point to the same object. But what happens with the second object? With no references pointing to it, there is no way to retrieve that object from anywhere in your program, so the memory it occupies should be reclaimed, but how?

Many object-oriented languages implement a garbage collection process that periodically scans the objects in the system and removes any that aren't referenced anymore. This is a simple solution for us programmers because we don't have to think about it—it just happens in the background. However, a garbage collection process uses processing power, which reduces battery life, so Apple decided to not implement a garbage collector for iOS. Instead, they used a system of reference counting where each object has an internal counter of the number of references to the object. Anytime a new reference is added, this counter is incremented. Anytime a reference is removed (for instance, if a variable goes out of scope), the counter is decremented. When the counter reaches zero, the object is deallocated and the memory reclaimed.

It used to be that programmers would have to add statements in their code to explicitly manage these counters, calling retain if they wanted to increment the counter when making a reference to an object, and release when dereferencing.

Fortunately, as of iOS 5, Apple introduced a system called ARC, which alleviates the need to manually retain and release objects. Instead, the compiler analyzes the code and inserts those method calls as needed. You will, therefore, rarely need to worry about the memory management aspects of Objective-C. However, if you intend to do professional programming in Objective-C, you still need to learn in detail what's going on, because there are times when ARC needs a little help. However, it is beyond this appendix to examine those situations. Instead, you should study this issue by reading *Programming in Objective-C* by Stephen G. Kochan.

Index

H

I

W

FREE
Online Edition

Your purchase of *Learning Mobile App Development* includes access to a free online edition for 45 days through the **Safari Books Online** subscription service. Nearly every Addison-Wesley Professional book is available online through **Safari Books Online**, along with over thousands of books and videos from publishers such as Cisco Press, Exam Cram, IBM Press, O'Reilly Media, Prentice Hall, Que, Sams, and VMware Press.

Safari Books Online is a digital library providing searchable, on-demand access to thousands of technology, digital media, and professional development books and videos from leading publishers. With one monthly or yearly subscription price, you get unlimited access to learning tools and information on topics including mobile app and software development, tips and tricks on using your favorite gadgets, networking, project management, graphic design, and much more.

Activate your FREE Online Edition at
informit.com/safarifree

STEP 1: Enter the coupon code: YZAWHFH.

STEP 2: New Safari users, complete the brief registration form.
Safari subscribers, just log in.

If you have difficulty registering on Safari or accessing the online edition,
please e-mail customer-service@safaribooksonline.com